RESEARCH TO PRACTICE
IN
MENTAL RETARDATION

U.S. Capitol Building, Washington, D.C.

RESEARCH TO PRACTICE IN MENTAL RETARDATION

Fourth Congress
of the International Association
for the Scientific Study of Mental Deficiency (IASSMD)

Volume II

EDUCATION and TRAINING

Edited by

Peter Mittler, Ph.D.

Technical Editor

Jean M. de Jong

University Park Press
Baltimore • London • Tokyo

UNIVERSITY PARK PRESS
International Publishers in Science and Medicine
233 East Redwood Street
Baltimore, Maryland 21202

Typeset by The Composing Room of Michigan, Inc.
Manufactured in the United States of America by Universal Lithographers, Inc.,
and The Optic Bindery Incorporated.

Library of Congress Cataloging in Publication Data
International Association for the Scientific Study of
Mental Deficiency.
Research to practice in mental retardation.

Includes bibliographies and indexes.
CONTENTS: v. 1. Care and intervention.—v. 2. Education and training.—v. 3. Biomedical aspects.
1. Mental deficiency—Congresses. 2. Mentally
handicapped—Care and treatment—Congresses. 3. Mentally
handicapped—Education—Congresses. I. Mittler, Peter J.
II. Title. [DNLM: 1. Mental retardation—Congresses.
2. Education of mentally retarded—Congresses. W3 IN12U
1976r/ WS107 I61r 1976]
RC569.9.I57   1977   616.8'588   77-5455
ISBN 0-8391-1122-3 (v. 1)
ISBN 0-8391-1123-1 (v. 2)
ISBN 0-8391-1124-x (v. 3)

Contents

ASSESSMENT

COGNITION AND LEARNING

EDUCATIONAL AND BEHAVIORAL INTERVENTION

PROCEEDINGS OF THE FOURTH CONGRESS
OF THE INTERNATIONAL ASSOCIATION
FOR THE SCIENTIFIC STUDY
OF MENTAL DEFICIENCY

Washington, D.C., U.S.A.   22–27 August, 1976
The American University

Research to Practice
in
Mental Retardation

Published in three volumes:
Volume   I: Care and Intervention
Volume   II: Education and Training
Volume III: Biomedical Aspects

Edited by
Peter Mittler, Ph.D.
Director,
Hester Adrian Research Centre
for the Study of Learning Processes
in the Mentally Handicapped
University of Manchester,
Manchester M13 9PL, England

Editorial Board:
M. J. Begab, Ph.D. (United States)
J. M. Berg, M.B., B.Ch., M.Sc., M.R.C. Psych. (Canada)
P. Berry, M.Ed., Ph.D. (Australia)
J. Dobbing, M.B., B.S., B.Sc., F.R.C. Path., M.R.C.P. (England)
A. Dupont, M.D. (Denmark)
D. A. Primrose, M.D., B.L., C.A., F.R.C. Psych., M.R.C.G.P., M.R.C.P.
(Scotland)

Contents of Volume I

Contents of Volume III

Preface

The Fourth Congress of the International Association for the Scientific Study of Mental Deficiency was held in Washington, D.C., in August, 1976, in a year celebrating not only the bicentennial of the United States but also the hundredth anniversary of the American Association on Mental Deficiency, who acted as hosts to the conference. The event was attended by 1,152 registered participants with spouses and associates representing 63 different countries; there were about 500 speakers.

The conference theme "Research to Practice" reflects the expressed needs both of research workers and of practitioners to come to a closer understanding of each others' work and skills, and to take steps to reduce what has in the past been too large a gap between them. Because the conference was attended both by full-time research workers and by practitioners working daily with mentally retarded people, ample opportunities were available both during and between sessions for them to discuss mutual problems and to realise how much they had in common.

We look forward to renewal of acquaintance and meeting newcomers in the field at the Fifth Congress of IASSMD to be held in Israel in 1979.

In bringing together the principal papers presented at the conference, we have tried to identify the main themes of the presentations and to group these under separate headings. In doing so, we have on occasion regrouped papers under one heading that were presented in different sections or symposia. Our aim in arranging the material into themes was to provide more coherence and unity to the volumes as a whole, particularly for readers who were not themselves present at the congress.

The material is presented in three volumes: *Care and Intervention, Education and Training,* and *Biomedical Aspects.* The first volume focuses on developments in service provision, and reflects a particularly strong emphasis on the theme of early intervention and multidisciplinary treatment, on the provision of community and residential services, and on questions concerned with the evaluation of such services to ensure that the needs of mentally handicapped people are met. The second volume is devoted to the theme of education and training, and is largely concerned with questions of what and how to teach, with methods of assessing the individual's abilities and needs, and with methods of determining outcome. The third volume encompasses a wide range of biomedical studies, including prevention, detection, and early treatment, as well as a consideration of the many environmental factors related to intervention, particularly those that lend themselves to treatment. The number of pages devoted to questions concerned with the effects of malnutrition was a marked feature of this congress.

Despite a generous allocation of space, we have been able to find room for only a selection of the many papers presented at the congress. We have been guided in the selection of papers by members of our editorial board, to whom the editor owes a profound debt for their immediate response to his many requests for assistance, particularly in areas outside his own competence. We also gratefully acknowledge similar valuable help from other referees, namely Professor Schneiden and Drs. G. Claridge, T. Ingram, B. H. Kirman, B. W. Richards, N. de M. Rudolph, and J. Stern.

This is the first time that the proceedings of an IASSMD congress have been printed and published commercially. We are therefore grateful for an opportunity to express our appreciation to University Park Press, whose cooperation and efficiency have been exemplary.

But the chief credit for the prompt appearance of these volumes goes to our technical editor, Mrs. Jean de Jong, who has worked tirelessly and enthusiastically to bring order out of chaos and who has brought to the task of editing these volumes her wisdom and experience gained from assisting with the proceedings of previous congresses. Readers will be in her debt to a greater extent than they can possibly realise.

P. M.

Officers of the
International Association
for the Scientific Study
of Mental Deficiency:
1973—1976

President: **Alan D. B. Clarke,** Department of Psychology, The University, Hull, Yorkshire, England.

President-Elect: **Michael J. Begab,** NIH/NICHD/MRP, Landow Building, Room C-708, 7910 Woodmont Avenue, Bethesda, Maryland 20014, United States.

Honorary Vice-President: **Harvey A. Stevens,** Waisman Center on Mental Retardation and Human Development, University of Wisconsin, 2605 Marsh Lane, Madison, Wisconsin 53706, United States.

Vice-Presidents: **Bernard E. Cohen,** Department of Pediatrics 'B', The Chaim Sheba Medical Center, Tel Hashomer, Israel.
Annalise Dupont, Demographic-Genetic Research Department, Aarhus Psychiatric Hospital, DK-8240, Risskov, Denmark.

Past Presidents: **Harvey A. Stevens, Alexander Shapiro, Stanislau Krynski.**

Secretary: **David A. A. Primrose,** The Royal Scottish National Hospital, Larbert, Stirlingshire, Scotland FK5 4EJ.

Treasurer: **Jan B. Meiresonne,** N.O.Z., Postbus 415, Utrecht, The Netherlands.

Officers of the
International Association
for the Scientific
Study of Mental Deficiency:
1976—1979

President: **Michael J. Begab,** NIH/NICHD/MRP, Landow Building, Room C-708, 7910 Woodmont Avenue, Bethesda, Maryland 20014, United States.

President-Elect: **H. O. Åkesson,** Psychiatric Department III, Lillhagen's Hospital, S-422 03 Hisings Backa 3, Sweden.

Honorary Vice-Presidents: **Harvey A. Stevens,** Waisman Center on Mental Retardation and Human Development, University of Wisconsin, 2605 Marsh Lane, Madison, Wisconsin 53706, United States.
Alan D. B. Clarke, Department of Psychology, The University, Hull, Yorkshire, England.

Vice-Presidents: **Bernard E. Cohen,** Department of Pediatrics 'B', The Chaim Sheba Medical Center, Tel Hashomer, Israel.
Ignacy Wald, Instytut Psychoneurologiczny, Al. Sobieskiego 1/9, 02-957 Warsaw, Poland.

Honorary Officers: **Stanislau Krynski, Alexander Shapiro.**

Secretary: **David A. A. Primrose,** The Royal Scottish National Hospital, Larbert, Stirlingshire, Scotland, FK5 4EJ.

Treasurer: **Jan B. Meiresonne,** N.O.Z., Postbus 415, Utrecht, The Netherlands.

Congress Organized by the
International Association
for the Scientific Study
of Mental Deficiency
in Association with the
Local Organizing Committee

Host Organization: **American Association on Mental Deficiency**

President: **Burton Blatt** (1976–1977)
Executive
Secretariat: **George Soloyanis**
Ellen Horn
Carolyn A. Bardwell
Susan J. Annis
John E. Loth, Jr.
Valerie Ducker

Local Organizing Committee

James D. Clements
David Rosen
George Soloyanis
Robert Erdman
Mortimer Garrison

Local Arrangements Committee

Chairperson: George 'Bud' deHaven
Ruth Adams   William McCahill
Emily Baker   James Melton
Pat Nuse Carlson   Mitzi Parks
Joseph Fenton   Stan Phillips
Hilda Fishback   Muriel Rose
Iris Gordon   Stella Gore Lansing
Darryl Hagy   Raymond Terry
Elaine Hollander   Bathrus Williams
Roma Kaplan   Janice Williams
      Dennis Wyant

Scientific Program Committee

Chairperson: Michael J. Begab
Members: H. Olof Åkesson
Joseph M. Berg
Alan D. B. Clarke
H. A. A. Gresnigt
Stanislau Krynski
Jan B. Meiresonne
David A. Primrose
Harvey A. Stevens
Ignacy Wald

Proceedings Editor:
Peter Mittler

Film Review Committee

Co-Chairpersons:
Molly Gorelick
David A. Primrose

Members:
Neil Goldstein
James Magary

Acknowledgments

The International Association for the Scientific Study of Mental Deficiency gratefully acknowledges support for this publication from the President's Committee on Mental Retardation, the National Institute of Child Health and Human Development, the Bureau for the Education of the Handicapped, the Office for Handicapped Individuals, and the Rehabilitation Services Administration.

IASSMD Congress Publications

Editor and *Distributor* of the Proceedings of the *First* Congress:
Barry W. Richards, St. Lawrence's Hospital, Caterham, Surrey, CR3 5YA, England
Publication date: October, 1968
Price: $23.00 or £8.00 (inclusive)
Pages: xliv + 982; 175 figures, 155 tables
(supplies still available)

Editor of the Proceedings of the *Second* Congress:
David A. A. Primrose, The Royal Scottish National Hospital, Larbert, Stirlingshire FK5 4EJ, Scotland.
Publication date: December, 1971
Price: 115 guilders
Pages: xxiii + 774; 136 figures, 155 tables
Distributed by: Swets & Zeitlinger, B.V., Heereweg 347B, Lisse, The Netherlands.

Editor and *Distributor* of the Proceedings of the *Third* Congress:
David A. A. Primrose, The Royal Scottish National Hospital, Larbert, Stirlingshire FK5 4EJ, Scotland.
Publication date: April, 1975
Price: $34.00 or £12.00 (inclusive) for two volumes
Pages: Volume 1 xxv + 775; 151 figures, 208 tables
      Volume 2 x + 100; 22 figures, 25 tables

Editor of the Proceedings of the *Fourth* Congress:
Peter Mittler, Hester Adrian Research Centre, The University, Manchester M13 9PL, England.
Publication date: July—September, 1977
Prices: $24.50 per volume
Pages: Three volumes; 1718 pages
Published by: University Park Press, 233 East Redwood Street, Baltimore, Maryland 21202, U.S.A.

ASSESSMENT

RESEARCH TO PRACTICE IN MENTAL RETARDATION
Education and Training, Volume II
Edited by Peter Mittler
Copyright 1977 I.A.S.S.M.D.

USING TESTS TO ASSESS INTELLECTUAL FUNCTIONING

S. A. Warren
Department of Special Education,
Boston University,
Boston, Massachusetts 02215, United States

Debate on the use and misuse of intelligence tests has reached epidemic proportions in recent years. To illustrate, Block and Dworkin (1976), in *The I.Q. Controversy,* called for a moratorium on certain types of research using intelligence tests:

> . . . at this time, in this country, in this political climate, individual scientists should voluntarily refrain from the investigation of genotypic racial differences in performance on I.Q. tests. (p. 520)

Reluctant as one may be to tell other scientists what to investigate, one must grant Block and Dworkin the point. There seems little to gain and perhaps much to lose by continued study of racial differences in IQ. However, should one discard instruments useful for other purposes because they have been grossly misused to support prejudice or to downgrade other humans? One relevant comment on this matter comes from the review of the Wechsler Intelligence Scale for Children by Freides (1972) in Buros' *Seventh Mental Measurements Yearbook:*

> Our methods are quite primitive. We are working with an accumulated lore consisting of procedures that enable us to compare people but not to measure innate qualities or specific skills. The Wechsler tests represent the acme of such pragmatic accumulation. (p. 43)

Another reviewer, Osborne (1972), adds:

> For the WISC just to have survived the last six years in an atmosphere of test burnings, congressional investigations, restrictive legislation, and claims that the I.Q. test is an instrument of subtle torture is no small accomplishment. For the WISC to have survived and grown in professional respect lends support to Burstein's characterization of the WISC . . . as a well standardized, stable instrument, correlating well with other tests of intelligence. (p. 432)

Intelligence tests have been subjected to massive research. As of 1971, the latest year for which data are readily available, the numbers of studies of some of the well-known intelligence tests were:

Bayley Scales of Infant Development (1969)	31
Cattell Infant Intelligence Scale (1940)	49
Columbia Mental Maturity Scale (1954)	78
Detroit Tests of Learning Aptitude (1935)	14
Full Range Picture Vocabulary (1948)	73
Leiter International Performance Scale (1936)	70
Peabody Picture Vocabulary Test (1959)	71
Porteus Mazes (1913)	241
Stanford-Binet (1916)	1,414
WAIS (1939)	940
Wechsler-Bellevue (1939—47)	991
WISC (1949)	1,037

Over 5,000 efforts to test the tests! Were those efforts to develop viable tools for assessment of intellectual functioning wasted? I think not.

David Wechsler did not invent the idea of assessing intelligence. (He did, however, work with Yerkes, Stoddard, and Woodworth in developing and using the Army Alpha and Beta with 1,700,000 army recruits in World War I to aid in selection of leadership.) Alfred Binet did not start the idea when he developed a scale to identify retarded children in Paris schools at the turn of this century. The idea was not the brainchild of J. McKeen Cattell, who worked in the 1890s with the then infant American Psychological Association on the development of scales of intelligence. Samuel G. Howe did not originate the idea when he devised a simple scale to determine whether or not there were sufficient retarded persons in his state to warrant establishing a program for them. Even the ancient unknowns who, centuries ago, devised the Chinese Civil Service tests did not invent the idea of assessing intelligence (Warren, 1968).

What Wechsler, Terman, and Binet did was devise ways of making quantifiable and consistent the kinds of observations that men have always made of each other. For ages, human beings have looked at and listened to each other and drawn conclusions about intellectual functioning. People still do it every day. At work, personnel workers, teachers, preachers, and politicians do it. At home, parents and siblings do it. Retarded persons draw conclusions about the intellectual functioning of others. (If you doubt that, listen to conversations of a few retarded groups and you will soon hear another person described as "really retarded" or "bright kid" or "low grade.")

The problem with informal everyday assessments is that different observers use different criteria and arrive at different conclusions about the same individual. The frame of reference provided by past experience (personal norms) differs across observers. So, one child is called retarded by Teacher A, and not retarded by Teacher B. Both teachers are probably using the "rubber tape measures" of personal judgments. One can reduce problems introduced by such personal predilections by the use of a standardized format, prescribed administration of items, specific criteria for scoring, and norms as bases for comparisons. Thus, use of standardized tests of intelligence can *protect* children against the vagaries of informal individual observations.

It would seem unreasonable, however, to rely solely on standardized measures of intellectual functioning in determining whether or not an individual is retarded. The American Association on Mental Deficiency (AAMD) noted this point in 1959 (Heber, 1959) and in the more recent revision of the *Manual on Terminology and Classification* (Grossman et al., 1973), by giving the definition of retardation as:

> Mental retardation refers to significantly subnormal general intellectual functioning existing concurrently with deficits in adaptive behavior, and manifested during the developmental period.

This definition indicates that *one* important criterion for determining retardation is general intellectual functioning, as measured by an individually administered, standardized test. Other criteria include those behaviors that have been grouped as "adaptive behaviors" and that include developmental delays, difficulties in academic work, and problems in occupational achievement. Whereas assessment of intellectual functioning can be made in a few hours or less by competent professionals, it is rather difficult to gather quickly and accurately the information required for assessment of adaptation to "the real world out there." Furthermore, changes in adaptive behavior with environmental changes appear to be more common than changes in intellectual functioning. Thus, a person may be "deficient" when he exists in a sterile, limiting environment, but not "deficient" when he is in an enriched one that permits full opportunity for him to develop and to use all his coping skills.

There is difference in opinion about whether an individual must first display deficits in adaptive behavior before being considered as possibly retarded, or whether he be so considered only if he has first demonstrated retardation in measured intelligence. Although both deficiencies should exist, according to AAMD definition, before final determination is made, some individuals have suggested that retardation should not even be considered until the person has been found to have adaptive problems in everyday social life. However, many individuals with average or above intellectual functioning are maladaptive socially; for example, criminals, delinquents, some overprotected children, and some persons with sensory handicaps may have adaptive behavior deficits. Others with limited intellectual functioning may cope adequately in society, especially if that society places few demands on individual members. Neither group would be considered retarded by AAMD definition, but one must decide on approaches to assessment and consideration of retardation in differential diagnosis.

There seems to be some merit in first giving consideration to measured intelligence to rule out retardation during assessment procedures, before studying adaptive behavior. Perhaps, because of their greater reliability and demonstrated validity, the measures of intellectual functioning should even be given greater weight than the information about adaptive behaviors. Some professionals would argue against this pragmatic approach. Adams (1973), for example, appeared to be highly critical of psychologists when he reported that psychologists were using only intelligence tests to determine level of retardation. One must not overgeneralize from the data of Adams, since the psychologists on whom he reported were a small sample under the supervision of one chief psychologist, all making those particular determinations of level of retardation for statistical, administrative purposes rather than for individual program planning. The AAMD scheme provides no procedures for combining measured intelligence and adaptive behavior into a single index of level of retardation, and psychologists must either use clinical judgment, with its inherent fallibility, or decide on whether or not to ensure that both measured intellectual functioning and adaptive behavior functioning are within the retarded range before determining the level of retardation. Some may be using the procedure that Adams apparently considered inappropriate, but there is rather limited evidence on the policies of psychologists in general. It might be argued that the high correlations between adaptive behavior and measured intelligence would lead to similar decisions on levels of retardation, but, in planning for individuals, the kinds of data reported for administrative purposes would probably not loom large for most professionals.

Psychologists have been widely criticized for "labeling" individuals as retarded on the basis of intelligence tests. Intelligence tests have been called unfair, discriminatory, and useless. This issue is discussed in detail by Bialer and Sternlicht (1977). Criticisms have often come from groups concerned with civil rights and other groups, who are convinced both that "labels" are inherently bad, and that psychologists, especially school psychologists, have been determined to label children from specific groups as retarded because the psychologists are prejudiced. In fact, few school psychologists do intellectual assessments for individual planning except on referral from another source: This means, then, that the children are already having difficulty of the kind considered under "adaptive behavior deficits" before the intellectual functioning is assessed. School psychologists are usually overworked and few are likely to be engaged in case-finding or retardation hunts. It seems obvious to all but the most dense critic that testing of intellectual functioning has been done by school psychologists only after the child has demonstrated to others (usually teachers) that there might be deficits in adaptive behavior. Ordinarily psychologists also determine certain aspects of adaptive behavior in routine evaluations. It may be that some children have been recommended for placement in special classes for the retarded even though the psychologist was aware that the child did not fit classic descriptions of retardation, or even though the child's adaptive behavior problems were primarily in academic learning. It should also be recognized that until recently there was little program choice available for children who were functioning poorly in regular classrooms, but perhaps not "really retarded." In some cases, the decision may have been to provide special help even when it meant a classification (negatively called "labeling") of retardation, at least for the time needed to provide the special services. In a number of states in this country, laws or regulations permitted administrators to assign a few children who were not retarded to special classes, perhaps in recognition of the problem described here. Laws that mandate special educational provisions of wide variety for retarded and other handicapped children (e.g., laws in Massachusetts, Arkansas, Illinois, and the federal Public Law 94-142) may decrease complaints that psychologists rely on intelligence tests only. There may be additional reduction in criticism when more professionals accept the emphasis on current level of functioning, as opposed to a layman's opinion that intelligence tests indicate what can be expected in the long-term future, that is, that intellectual level does not vary across time.

It seems highly probable that competent psychologists are quite aware of the limitations of intelligence tests, as well as of their uses. It is difficult to believe that anyone who understands test construction, test manuals, cognitive development, and such simple constructs as error of measurement would place sole reliance on a single measurement device, or a single bit of information (e.g., IQ) from that device, at least not in planning for an individual's training and treatment. Stethoscopes do not give all the information needed by physicians for diagnosis and treatment planning; menus do not give all information needed to plan for adequate nutrition. Yet no critic has suggested abolishing stethoscopes or menu cards because they might be misused by those not able to understand their contributions.

Intelligence tests can provide objective, current information for service providers, research workers, and those concerned with administration or epidemiology. Any tool that aids in establishing a viable classification system and improves communication, and that aids in preventing individuals from being misclassified by unreliable observations, is valuable. The AAMD classification system, which requires the determination of current intellectual functioning as one criterion for determination of retardation, is imperfect. "Users of the system will realize that no system of classification is going to provide a precise blueprint for treatment of individuals needing service" (Warren, 1973, p. 2). But a reasonably good classification system, even using less than perfect criteria, can help determine need for services, facilitate research, improve communications, and aid in dissemination of research findings, as well as aid administrative decisions. There is little merit in discarding a tool that is useful, imperfect though the tool may be, before a more useful tool is available.

Some persons strongly disagree with the idea of continued use of intelligence tests and would return to clinical observations. This may be illustrated by a poster that seems to be popular now. The poster depicts two buildings, both crumbling and falling down; one building is shaped as the letter "I" and the other as the letter "Q." What does it mean? Like a Rorschach card, it might be interpreted several ways. Are the IQs of our population falling and all of us becoming less intelligent? Is the term "IQ" crumbling and falling into disrepute? Dorothea McCarthy has already "felled it" by using the initials "GCI" for General Cognitive Index, and the original meaning of "Intelligence Quotient" is no longer accurate for the majority of tests, since they use deviation or standard scores. Does the poster mean the demise of intelligence tests, which are represented on the poster by the initials "IQ?"

Apparently, the poster is intended to mean that the fall of intelligence tests is imminent, and presumably desirable. If so, it could be an ill-advised effort. Perhaps a more effective effort would be to attempt to ensure better ways of gaining understanding of those now identified as retarded, with tests aiding in that identification. A more constructive effort might be to restrict the use of currently available tests to professionals who have demonstrated competence in test use, as suggested by the delivery of psychological services guidelines published by the American Psychological Association. A more helpful effort might be to aid in training professionals in effective use of all kinds of assessment procedures. A more humane effort might be to investigate relationships between intellectual functioning and such variables as specific environmental manipulations (such as those used in the Milwaukee study), educational strategies, or age of intervention. But efforts of this kind are difficult, time consuming, and expensive. Many reputable professionals are not yet convinced that measures of intellectual functioning per se are either harmful or useless. Nor are they convinced that the use of tests to determine classification or labels is necessarily bad. As an avid reader of studies on labeling, I have yet to find good evidence that classifying on the basis of tests is any more harmful than classifications made on the basis of clinical observations, or even ordinary everyday observations. Is the label "mental retardation" any more painful to a child than the label "stupid," "dummy," "dumbell," or "766-kid?" (The last is a term sometimes employed in Massachusetts, where the term retardation is discouraged and all handicapped children have "special needs" under the new law, Chapter 766).

Perhaps one problem may be that too many individuals expected too much of intelligence tests. Tests only provide some needed information, not all. By the same token, a physician's classification of an individual's medical problem into the category of severe malnutrition aids him in planning treatment; he can then consider those treatments that relate to malnutrition rather than having to consider all possible medical treatments in all medical textbooks. He does not require a therapeutic fishing expedition.

There is an accumulation of information about retarded individuals, and there are indications of ways in which services may be made increasingly effective by use of some techniques that are not ordinarily required for nonretarded persons. There are tax funds available to provide services to individuals for whom retardation has been determined on the basis of the most reliable and valid measuring instruments now available. There are professionals who are trained to treat the mentally retarded and who have expertise in working with those individuals. It appears unwise at this time to abandon measurement tools that aid in selecting those persons for whom specific educational or other treatment procedures, funds, and trained personnel are needed, and to revert to imprecise ways of determining retardation, thus making it likely that some individuals needing services may not get them, and that others not in fact eligible for them receive the limited services available. At least, it appears unwise to me, as I make decisions with my own current level of intellectual functioning.

REFERENCES

Adams, J. (1973) Adaptive behavior and measured intelligence in the classification of mental retardation. Amer. J. Ment. Defic. 78:77.

Bialer, I., and Sternlicht, M., (eds.) (1977) The Psychology of Mental Retardation: Issues and Approaches. New York: Psychological Dimensions.

Freides, D. (1972) Wechsler intelligence scale for children. *In* Seventh Mental Measurements Yearbook (Ed. Buros, O.) Highland Park, New Jersey: Gryphon Press.

Grossman, H. J., Warren, S. A., Begab, M. J., Eyman, R., Nihira, K., and O'Connor, G. (1973) Manual on Terminology and Classification in Mental Retardation. Washington, D.C.: AAMD.

Heber, R. (ed.) (1959) Manual on Terminology and Classification in Mental Retardation. Washington, D. C.: AAMD.

Osborne, R. T. (1972) Wechsler intelligence scale for children. *In* Seventh Mental Measurements Yearbook (Ed. Buros, O. Highland Park, New Jersey: Gryphon Press.

Warren, S. A. (1968) Psychological evaluation of the mentally retarded. *In* Mental Retardation (Ed. Grossman, H. J.), Pediatr. Clin. North Amer., Vol. 15.

Warren, S. A. (1973) Classification systems and AAMD. Ment. Retard. 11:2.

RESEARCH TO PRACTICE IN MENTAL RETARDATION
Education and Training, Volume II
Edited by Peter Mittler
Copyright 1977   I.A.S.S.M.D.

ALTERNATIVES TO NORMATIVE ASSESSMENT

H. C. Haywood
Box 40, George Peabody College for Teachers,
Nashville, Tennessee 37203, United States

I am concentrating herein on a set of beliefs, instead of offering new data on some problems of scientific interest, because I believe the matter is urgent. It is necessary for us to develop, construct, and use methods of clinical assessment that depart radically from the normative model. Such a development is necessary because the purposes of diagnostic assessment of persons who are thought to be mentally retarded have changed greatly in the last few years. Our view of the possibility of enhancing the development of mentally retarded persons through carefully constructed intervention programs has become much more optimistic. We are no longer concerned primarily with classification. Along with our more optimistic view of the chances to enhance development, we have developed a great need for methods of identifying specific deficiencies in development in such a way as to enable us to construct development-enhancing programs of education and social-behavioral treatment.

I shall discuss the nature of normative assessment and what is wrong with it, the nature of mental retardation, and the nature of the diagnostic process. Finally, I shall discuss clinical assessment and give four examples of it that can be used today.

The essence of normative assessment is the belief that all important human characteristics are roughly normally distributed, and that one can define pathology as some agreed-upon deviation from the average value, i.e., the relative standing of the individual in some larger group, rather than against any absolute standard. A corollary implication is that the further one deviates from average, the more pathological one is in that particular characteristic.

Normative tests are constructed by assembling a large pool of possible items, giving those items to children of different ages, and establishing the distribution of scores of those children. If all the children in a particular age group complete an item successfully, it is too easy and is eliminated, or may be retained only as an "encouragement" item that is not scored. One winds up with a picture of the performances of statistical abstractions, i.e., the "person" whose performance is reflected in the norms of the test does not exist, but has been constructed wholly from the scores of other individuals treated statistically. There may be no single individual who performs on the test exactly at the 50th percentile across the various parts of the test.

The most defensible use of normative assessment is for policy makers. It is useful to know how large groups of individuals behave with respect to certain measurable criteria in order to make certain public policy decisions. Normative assessment is also invaluable in research, since one needs to be able to apply the same criteria across individuals, and to relate their performances to standards that are clearly quantifiable and that have statistical meaning. When one attempts to use the products of normative assessment for educational or other behavioral/social intervention, the results are less than satisfactory, and may be quite amusing. I recall with horror one school superintendent who excoriated his teachers because fully 50% of the students in the school had been found to fall below average on both intelligence and achievement tests.

No evils are *inherent* in tests or in particular approaches to psychological and social measurement. The greatest evil comes from the misuse of such techniques. The point of most frequent breakdown of normative techniques is in their use in the individual case, specifically in inappropriate comparison of individuals with the normative sample. That is to say, individuals who are not like those in the normative sample are compared with the statistical abstractions derived from the normative process, and thus are assigned some characteristics that may or may not be true on the basis of the deviation of their scores from the scores of those unlike normative individuals. The most blatant example, familiar to all of us, is the comparison of black American school children with the norms of tests that have been standardized on middle class white populations. There are equally bad examples closer to our own experience as mental retardation specialists. Only recently have mentally retarded persons been included systematically in the stratified samples used to standardize psychological tests. In the older practice, one simply did not test many mentally retarded persons, but relied instead on statistical extrapolation of the norms. When one compares an individual with norms derived from a standardization process, the fundamental assumption is that he is somehow like the individuals in the normative sample. If that assumption is not tenable, any further use of the normative process is inappropriate for that individual.

Mental retardation has come to be defined as a set of behavioral/social deficits, rather than as an entity that necessarily inheres in the individual. To be sure, in many cases of mental retardation there are structural deficits in the nervous system that can certainly be said to inhere in the individual, but we have come to emphasize for definition the behavioral/social deficits, rather than any pathological process. For our present discussion, it will be most profitable to remain entirely at the psychosocial level of discourse.

The behavioral/social deficits that characterize mental retardation have at least the following four categories of associated sources: 1) deficiencies in "intelligence", which may mean specific failures to develop significant cognitive skills; 2) deficiencies in "adaptive behavior," which may be related to the expectations of other individuals; 3) deficiencies in personality/motivational development, which in interaction with the intellectual deficits may lead to significant inefficiency at learning; and 4) deficiencies in the quality of person-setting interactions, e.g., failure to discriminate the different qualities of behavior that are appropriate in different settings.

Because of these different sources of the behavioral/social deficits that characterize mental retardation, it is reasonable to attempt to examine an individual's performance in these different areas. There is no single normative technique, or yet any combination of them, that is capable of covering this range of areas of functioning in a normative way. We can do a reasonably good job of examining intelligence and adaptive behavior, and we are beginning to develop some capability in the normative assessment of personality and motivational development; but there is not even a bare beginning in the area of person-setting interactions, and no standard battery that I know of for assessing all of these areas in a standardized way and then comparing them, not only within each dimension, but also across dimensions. Thus, as our understanding of the nature of mental retardation has grown increasingly complex, we have become less and less able, rather than more and more so, to apply the normative model to our developing models of mental retardation.

In addition to its multi-dimensional nature, the behavioral/social deficit associated with mental retardation is a dynamic developmental phenomenon, rather than a static state. This dynamic developmental view of the areas of behavioral/social deficit associated with mental retardation creates a different set of needs with respect to assessment. First of all, we need methods to assess behavioral/social processes, rather than simply to catalog the products (or more frequently the lack of products) of past opportunities. We have begun to make some progress in the measurement of the processes of learning and of thought, but this progress has not come in the normative realm. In addition, in the application of assessment procedures, we need to look for outcomes that affect programming for development, rather than outcomes that have the goal of permanent classification. This model is neither one of static classification nor one of the treatment of illness. Since there is hope, permanent classification is no longer appropriate. Since the goal is development, treatment in the sense of the treatment of disease is inappropriate. The goal of intervention in mental retardation is to enhance development, i.e., to bring about a level of development that the particular individual has never experienced before. This is a goal quite different, for example, than that in the treatment of psychiatric illness, in which one seeks to restore the individual to a previously enjoyed state of health.

For these reasons, we need, especially in the field of mental retardation, assessment techniques that lead directly to development-enhancing procedures, rather than to static classification.

NATURE OF DIAGNOSIS

Let us now examine briefly the nature of diagnosis. There are three general approaches to diagnosis that will be useful for us to consider: the disease model, widely followed with considerable benefit in medicine, although many physicians have begun to deny its use; the deviation model; and the habilitation model.

Disease Model

According to the disease model, one determines that there either is or is not a pathological condition present, although pathological conditions may be more or less severe, more or less extensive, may be developing with greater or lesser speed, and may be chronic or acute. One employs various tests, and if the critical signs are present, one concludes that the disease process is present. This model has the virtue of leading rather directly to treatment, whose goal in turn is to rid the system of that disease process, i.e., to restore the individual to a formerly enjoyed state of health. Such a model is inappropriate for mental retardation because (a) we do not assume that disease is present, and (b) the goal of intervention is not that of restoring the person to a formerly enjoyed state of health.

Deviation Model

I have already described the deviation model, which simply assumes that there is a known distribution of whatever characteristics we are concerned with and that one can establish specified degrees of deviation from the average in that distribution as pathological. We have had our difficulty with that model in mental retardation. Most recently, we have the example of several million mentally retarded persons having been cured instantly, with one stroke of the pen as it were, when a committee of the American Association on Mental Deficiency decided that it is necessary to be at least two standard deviations below the mean in measured intelligence in order to be considered mentally retarded. In the previous edition of the AAMD diagnostic manual, it was possible to be diagnosed as borderline if one were at least one standard deviation below the mean in measured intelligence. Thus, a change of opinion about the degree of deviation that constituted abnormality resulted in a vast change in the number of persons who are considered to be mentally retarded (and who are entitled to special services). The whole process seems rather arbitrary.

If one defines mental retardation in terms of the behavioral/social deficits, and especially with respect to the four or more sources of those deficits described earlier, it becomes exceedingly difficult to relate the definition to the deviation model. The condition of mental retardation may constitute a highly idiosyncratic combination of behavioral/social deficits associated with each of the four sources of these deficits.

Habilitation Model

The habilitation model of diagnosis is one in which the goal is intervention, and therefore part of its nature must be to identify ways of helping the individual, not just areas that need help. Under this model, the processes of assessment and of intervention are intertwined deliberately, so that some intervention takes place during assessment, and assessment continues throughout the process of intervention. The habilitation model is not used to determine who will and who will not get services, but is used instead to determine which services are most appropriate for which individuals, for how long a period, and what the most appropriate immediate objectives of those services ought to be. In other words, part of the goal of the habilitation model is to determine the desired person-environment fit, and then to help supply the processes for accomplishing that fit. In applying the habilitation model, one should resist the human impulse to convert everything to numbers. That results altogether too often in static classification. Test constructors should be extraordinarily clever in devising ways to make it impossible to derive numbers from habilitation assessment procedures.

According to the habilitation model, one does not compare the individual with the average performance of some normative sample, nor is one trying to find disease process. Instead, one still uses comparison, but that may be a comparison of the individual with himself over time. One may also compare the individual with himself across situations, finding efficient performance in one set of circumstances and inefficient performance, by comparison with the former, in another set of circumstances. Instead of determining how many items on a test the individual cannot complete, one goal might be to determine how much help each individual requires in order to complete all the items. One might also determine what kinds of help might be needed across which areas of deficient functioning within the individual.

There are some methods that are legitimately characterized as clinical assessment by the habilitation model. I should like to describe briefly just four of them.

The first example is one that I believe bridges the gap between normative assessment and clinical assessment by the habilitation model. That example is *neuropsychological assessment* (see, for example, Haywood, 1968; Haywood and Gordon, 1970; L'Abate, 1968; Reed, 1968). Neuropsychological assessment is a set of behavioral techniques for assessing the relative integrity of the central nervous system, but it has a much broader set of applications. In the hands of a skilled neuropsychologist, these procedures enable one to compare the individual with himself in the strictest sense (for example, to compare the two sides of the body simultaneously) and to compare the individual with himself over time. Further, it is possible to relate performances in different areas to each other, for example, to relate verbal and performance efficiency, or to compare expressive vocabulary with receptive vocabulary, or to compare the efficiency of motor-expressive functions and sensory functions. While it is quite possible, and indeed desirable, to establish norms on all of these individual instruments, and especially to establish age norms for children, it is the skilled use and interpretation of these procedures that makes neuropsychological assessment a procedure for bridging the gap between normative assessment and the habilitation model. Especially in use with children, the principal goal of neuropsychological assessment is not to find brain tumors, but to discover educational methods by which the behavioral/social deficits that may be associated with central nervous system dysfunction can be overcome and the development of the individual enhanced.

Another example is *operant assessment,* or direct behavioral assessment, as some of its adherents prefer to call it. In this set of procedures one actually gives performance tasks to the subject and attempts to discover the environmental manipulations that will result in increases in the rate of desired behavior, or in decreases in the rate of undesired behavior. The assumption is that there is some optimal combination of environmental circumstances, principally schedules of reinforcement, that can be applied in each individual instance of deficient behavior. Operant assessment is a particularly good example of the nature of ongoing assessment, i.e., assessment that continues throughout the process of intervention. Operant assessment techniques have been described in a number of places (e.g., Haywood, Filler, Shifman, and Chatelanat, 1975).

In the realm of *classroom behavior and academic learning,* one of the best examples of clinical assessment is a commercially available set of teaching methods known as DISTAR (Engelmann and Bruner, 1969; Englemann and Carnine, 1970; Engelmann, Osborn and Engelmann, 1969). This is a study-test procedure in which the level of achievement of children in areas of academic content is determined first, then teaching methods are applied, then testing is done again, teaching is applied, testing is done still again, and so on. There is daily assessment of progress, and the assessment leads directly to the next step in the teaching and learning process. DISTAR constitutes, in essence, a branching program whose branches are determined by the results of the periodic assessment. It may be that the fact that the children do a good share of the assessment themselves, and of the charting, is reinforcing in itself, and leads to considerable enthusiasm for learning. There are many such techniques available now. They all have the virtue of allowing children to compare their contemporary performance with their own previous performance, rather than to establish relative standing in a group. Further, they all have the desirable characteristic of combining educational intervention with continuing assessment.

The last example is one that is identified primarily with Feuerstein in Israel (Haywood, Filler, Shifman, and Chatelanat, 1975; Feuerstein, 1972; Feuerstein, Shalom, Narrol, Hoffman, Kiram, Katz, Schachter, and Rand, 1972). This is the *Learning Potential Assessment Device* (LPAD), a technique for assessing the process of learning across a large number of the cognitive operations that are necessary for relatively complex learning, and for relating performance in these areas to specified educational intervention techniques. One essential characteristic of learning potential assessment is that the children always succeed; i.e., the goal is to establish how much help and of what kind might be required to bring about successful performance in the various areas of cognitive function that are examined. Another characteristic of LPAD is that its goal is enhancing development rather than either classifying or treating disease. It has the advantage of being followed by a set of educational techniques, known as Instrumental Enrichment (IE), designed to enhance development in the very areas of cognitive deficiency that have been identified by the LPAD. It has the further advantage of combining assessment of intellectual functions, adaptive behavior, and personality/motivational development in a single instrument. To be sure, use of this technique requires a highly skilled clinician, and its interpretation is not done by referring to a table of norms. Even so, the LPAD comes closer than any set of instruments that I have yet seen to the ideal of conforming to the habilitation model while providing assessment of the multiple sources of the behavioral/ social deficits associated with mental retardation, assessing processes of learning rather than the products of prior learning, and specifying outcomes that affect programming for development. (See also this volume, p. 112.)

All of these techniques of habilitative assessment are "unscientific" in the sense that they rely upon the intelligence, the skill, and the subjective interpretation of a clinician. I do not apologize for that. It is time to return the intelligent observer to psychology, and to stop trying to reduce the psychologist to a mere recorder of data that can then be referred to a computerized set of comparison norms. Those who do behavioral assessment are usually intelligent human beings. We should take advantage of that fact, rather than deny it. If we are willing to do that, it is possible that we shall be able to move beyond the assessment of static states and the classification of individuals into clinical assessment under the habilitation model, and to do so without apology.

REFERENCES

Engelmann, S., and Bruner, E. C. (1969) DISTAR Reading: An Instructional System. Chicago: Science Research Associates.

Engelmann, S., and Carnine, D. (1970) DISTAR Arithmetic: An Instructional System. Chicago: Science Research Associates

Engelmann, S., Osborn, J., and Engelmann, T. (1969) DISTAR Language I: An Instructional System. Chicago: Science Research Associates.

Feuerstein, R. (1972) Cognitive assessment of the socioculturally deprived child and adolescent. *In* Mental Tests and Cultural Adaptation (Eds. Cronbach, L. J. and Drenth, P.) The Hague: Mouton.

Feuerstein, R., Shalom, H., Narrol, H., Hoffman, M., Kiram, L., Katz, D., Schachter, B., and Rand, Y. (1972) Studies in Cognitive Modifiability: The Dynamic Assessment of Retarded Performers, Vol. 1, Clinical LPAD Battery. Jerusalem: Hadassah-Wizo-Canada Research Institute.

Haywood, H. C. (1968) Introduction to clinical neuropsychology. *In* Brain Damage in School Age Children (Ed. Haywood, H. C.) Washington, D.C.: Council for Exceptional Children.

Haywood, H. C., Filler, J. W., Shifman, M. A., and Chatelanat, G. (1975) Behavioral assessment in mental retardation. *In* Advances in Psychological Assessment (Vol. 3) (Ed. McReynolds, P.) San Francisco: Jossey-Bass.

Haywood, H. C., and Gordon, J. (1970) Neuropsychology and learning disorders. Pediatr. Clin. North Amer. 17:337.

L'Abate, L. (1968) Screening children with cerebral dysfunctions through the laboratory method. *In* Brain Damage in School Age Children. (Ed. Haywood, H. C.) Washington, D.C: Council for Exceptional Children.

Reed, H. B. C. (1968) The use of psychological tests in diagnosing brain damage in school children. *In* Brain Damage in School Age Children (Ed. Haywood, H. C.) Washington, D.C: Council for Exceptional Children.

RESEARCH TO PRACTICE IN MENTAL RETARDATION
Education and Training, Volume II
Edited by Peter Mittler
Copyright 1977 I.A.S.S.M.D.

ASSESSMENT OF AUTISTIC BEHAVIORS IN THE SEVERELY RETARDED
Case for Stereopathy

E. E. Balthazar
Central Wisconsin Colony and Training School,
317 Knutson Drive,
Madison, Wisconsin 53704, United States

The study of stereotyped acts and their relationship to "autistic-like" behavior in a more severely retarded population is an extremely interesting and complex task. An investigation of these matters is difficult, however, because the etiology of the behavior is obscure. For this reason, causality becomes a problem. We are also limited in our investigation because we cannot perform experiments and are confined to description. It is on this basis, then, that we shall refer to the literature of stereotyped acts, to the various theories and causes of them, then to references to autism in the psychiatric literature, and, finally, to our own efforts.

STEREOTYPED ACTS

In summing up the literature on stereotyped acts, one must begin by stating that they are learned (Baumeister and Forehand, 1973) and that their pathological nature lies in their frequency and persistence over time. Nevertheless, according to Schroeder (1970), stereotyped acts, when persistent, have clinical meaning; they provide little basis for specific reinforcement and they are noncontingent. A number of individual investigators have concluded that stereotyped acts are an expression of "tension, discomfort, or unsatisfied needs" (Brody, 1960; Gerard, 1957; Ilg and Ames, 1955; Kaufman and Levitt, 1965; Lourie, 1959; and Mahler, 1945). Kubie (1941) concluded that repetitious acts can be attributed to the occurrence of ungratified demands. Klaber and Butterfield (1968) share a similar view. Berkson and Mason (1964) have proposed *arousal* as a construct in their studies of chimpanzees reared in isolation.

Baumeister and Forehand (1973) and Forehand and Baumeister (1971) have associated systematic *frustration* with stereotyped acts. They perceive stereotypy as a learned instrumental behavior. On the other hand, Hutt and Hutt (1965) hold that these behavioral acts in *autistic* children are displacement activities in response to high-drive states that block subsequent sensory input associated with the arousing function. Thus, stereotyped acts serve to monitor incoming stimuli. Stone (1964) attributed stereotypy to sensory stimulation that produces changes in the state of consciousness leading to sleep. Stereotypy, then, decreases arousal. Keiper (1969), in studying several types of animals, demonstrated that cage size is directly associated with stereotypy, a view that is similar to the self-stimulation concept. Similarly, Levy (1944) had concluded that stereotyped acts occurred when normal children were confined to cribs because of illness.

The self-stimulation theory is also formulated by Berkson and Mason (1964), who hold that stereotyped acts provide self-stimulation through kinesthetic and vestibular channels. Cleland and Clark (1966) proposed that stereotyped movements are related to neural mechanisms that impair the quantity and quality of sensory input. Baumeister and Forehand (1973), in their thorough review of the literature, contend, and rightfully so, that most theoretical positions regarding stereotyped acts are impressionistic and are not rigorously formulated; they all make "sense" and none of the hypotheses can be supported without excluding the others.

It is the self-stimulation view that I hold, with some qualifications. It is also my view that stereotyped behaviors over-generalize and replace normal adjustment. It is the *generalization principle,* which is based upon developmental arrest and restricted environmental conditions, that ultimately connects the self-stimulating, arousal, and frustration theories in stereotyped acts. This point of view will be discussed in a later section of this paper.

THE PSYCHIATRIC LITERATURE

In discussing the psychiatric literature, however, we must proceed cautiously because autistic features encountered in the psychiatric literature often rest on the basis of categorical judgments (Balthazar and Stevens, 1975). Eisenberg and Kanner (1956), for example, subsequent to Kanner's (1943) celebrated paper on infantile autism, reduced considerably the number of characteristics that they felt were associated with early infantile autism. They described these as: 1) the lack of object relations, and 2) the maintenance of sameness via stereotyped behavior. Subsequently, Kanner had provided the view that autism could be extended to other types of childhood psychopathology. According to Bender (1959), Kanner himself stipulated later that some autistic children may be brain-damaged and that *all* may be schizophrenic.

Benda (1952) took the position that children suffering from anoxia or infection due to encephalitis may also be autistic. In addition to other autistic features, such as delay in speech, all investigators seemed to agree that stereotyped behavior had a profound effect upon the personality of the child.

In an interesting digression, the Viennese pediatrician Asperger had independently classified a number of patients whom he diagnosed as having autistic psychopathy (Asperger, 1944; Van Krevelen, 1971). Unlike Kanner's view of autism, autistic psychopathy represents certain personality traits rather than a psychotic process. Stereotypy does not play a critical role. Van Krevelen (1971) believes that individuals with early infantile autism of a persistent nature (Kanner's group) were brain-damaged. If it were not for the organicity, he thinks, autistic psychopathy would be the result.

To summarize, the psychiatric literature we have cited does not emphasize the role of mental retardation per se, particularly severe mental retardation as it relates to stereotyped mannerisms *and* unsocial acts. It is to this point that I turn.

STUDIES OF STEREOTYPING
WITH A PROFOUNDLY AND SEVERELY RETARDED GROUP

In an investigation of stereotyping *and* social isolation, Balthazar observed a wide range of stereotyped acts in a group of more severely mentally retarded residents, some of whom were described categorically as demonstrating "autistic-like" or schizoid behavior (Balthazar, 1973; Balthazar and English, 1969). These were studied in conjunction with physical withdrawal or avoidance from others, unresponsiveness to communication, and unresponsiveness to persons. On the basis of these investigations, there appeared to be a number of cases where stereotyped behavior was associated with external awareness when the arousal factor appeared to be of significance. On the other hand, our studies of severely and profoundly mentally retarded residents indicated that stereotyping was associated with inappropriate responsiveness and lack of orientation to external cues in some cases. It is likely that both self-stimulation (reinforcement) and frustration were contributing variables. In extreme cases, stereotyping was associated with random, aimless trial-and-error activities that were dissociated from group activities. Stereotyping was associated with indefinite periods of inactivity as well.

It was presumed from our observations that there were various stages associated with stereotypy. In each stage, unresponsiveness to external events was seen in an ascending order. This order included those who stereotyped and appeared to be reasonably alert (arousal); those who did not generally respond to external events but did withdraw from other persons while performing stereotyped acts; and those who performed stereotyped acts, did *not* withdraw from others, appeared to be oblivious to them, and did not usually respond to others. On the basis of these preliminary observations, stereopathy was inferred when stereotyped acts were persistent and when there seemed to be a negative reaction or no response to interpersonal cues. On the basis of these initial observations, then, it was decided to provide more formal observations of this behavior.

Subjects

Seventy-seven ambulant severely and profoundly mentally retarded residents constituted the sample. The event sampling method was used, utilizing the complete Balthazar Scales of Adaptive Behaviour II (BSAB-II) in 6 ten-minute observation sessions for each subject. A Stereopathy Index was also computed for each subject. The Index was obtained from the Balthazar II Scales as follows:

Scale 2:   stereotyping, posturing, including objects
Scale 3:   nondirected, repetitious verbalization
Scale 7d: withdraws physically from others
Scale 1:   failure to respond (to others)
Scale 17d: noncompliance to instructions

RESULTS

All subjects demonstrated stereotypy and were grouped on the Stereopathic Index as follows: 18% were stereotypic only (Group 1), 7% demonstrated stereotypy and withdrawal (Group 2), 18% demonstrated stereotypy with both withdrawal *and* nonresponse (Group 3), and 57%, the stereopathic group, exhibited stereotypy and nonresponse with failure to withdraw from others (Group 4). Controls for vision and hearing were provided in all four groups.

Group 4 had a higher frequency of disruptive, nonsocial behavior, inappropriate behavior, and aimless exploratory and inactive behavior. Physical guidance was used more often for Group 4 residents, since they demonstrated higher scores in compliance to *and* resistance to physical guidance. Group 4 subjects established a statistical trend favoring social insulation. They demonstrated more elementary social behavior, including nonfunctional, inarticulate verbal behavior, and extremely low level "playful behavior." On a Verbal Index (Naor and Balthazar, 1975), Groups 1–3 engaged more frequently in *meaningful* verbal communication, and in games involving rules. They also handled and used objects more.

Group 4 demonstrated a lower rate of stereotypy. This seemed to be related to their high rate of aimless generalized activity. There is also the possibility that they may have experienced a higher rate of peer group victimization, and nonresponse and low frequency of withdrawal may have been the main reasons for this.

The behavior in Group 4 was found *not* to be related to chronological age, number of years institutionalized, or age at institutionalization. No differences in gender, presence of physical or neurological disability, seizure history, medical diagnosis, or medication were found. Their behavior was not related to mental or social age, or to self-care skills.

DISCUSSION

Because of the nature of this investigation, it is clear that our findings must be accepted cautiously, since causality relationships cannot be determined from observational evidence alone. It is true, however, that this study substantiates evidence for an arousal theory in Group 1, those who appeared to be alert to external stimuli, and a self-stimulation theory demonstrated by Groups 2, 3, and 4, with Group 4 being the highest stereopathic group. The frustration hypothesis was not directly tested. There is no reason to believe, in my view, that the frustration hypothesis is not acceptable.

The evidence of severe withdrawl and social isolation in a restricted environment encourages belief in both a frustration theory and in response overgeneralization or overselection of external cues. From the standpoint of reinforcement in a restrictive and all too frequently aversive, institutional environment, stereopathic individuals when compared to the other groups demonstrate a high degree of developmental arrest. To ameliorate the condition, extreme changes in direct intervention, including high priority placement in the community, should be made.

It would appear incorrect to characterize stereopathy in the more severely mentally retarded as a secondary disturbance after the manner of Anthony (1957) and Ward (1970). Nor can we resolve the question of the relationship between the "classical" form of the illness as it was described by Kanner, or possibly by Asperger, by viewing it as a direct outcome of a more or less discrete neuropathological process in the fashion of Ornitz and Ritvo (1968). While it is true that Group 3, and especially Group 4, exhibited some of the characteristics demonstrated by classical autistic individuals, differences in diagnosis, chronological age, mental age, and so on would seem to constitute fundamental differences between autistic, "autistic-like," and stereopathic groups. Action is needed now regarding the status of stereopathic individuals in residential centers who exhibit many of the salient behavioral characteristics observed in initial maze learning.

SUMMARY

The psychological and psychiatric literature of stereotyped acts and autism is explored. Studies of stereotyped acts, social isolation, and aimless exploratory behavior in a severely retarded, residential population using the Balthazar Scales are also offered. *Stereopathy* was inferred to account for certain behavior. The principle of *overgeneralization* is given along with frustration and/or self-stimulation hypotheses to account for stereopathic behavior in a restricted environment.

REFERENCES

Anthony, E. J. (1957) An experimental approach to the psychopathology of childhood: Encopresis. Brit. J. Med. Psychol. 30:146.

Asperger, H. (1944) Die Autistischen psychopathen in kindeshalter. Arch. Psychiat. NervKrankh. 117:76.

Balthazar, E. E. (1973) Balthazar Scales of Adaptive Behaviour II, Scales of Social Adaptation. Palo Alto, California: Consulting Psychologists Press, Inc.

Balthazar, E. E., and English, G. E. (1969) A system for the social classification of the more severely retarded. Amer. J. Ment. Defic. 74:361.

Balthazar, E. E., and Stevens, H. A. (1975) The Emotionally Disturbed, Mentally Retarded. Englewood Cliffs, New Jersey: Prentice-Hall.

Baumeister, A. A., and Forehand, R. (1973) Stereotyped acts. *In* International Review of Research in Mental Retardation, Vol. 6 (Ed. Ellis, N. R.). New York: Academic Press, p. 55.

Benda, C. (1952) Developmental Disorders of Mentation and Cerebral Palsies. New York: Grune and Stratton.

Bender, L. (1959) Autism in children with mental deficiency. Amer. J. Ment. Defic. 64:81.

Berkson, G., and Mason, W. (1964) Stereotyped behaviours of chimpanzees: Relation to general arousal and alternative activities. Percept. Mot. Skills 19:635.

Brody, S. (1960) Self-rocking in infancy. J. Amer. Psychoanal. Soc. 8:464.

Cleland, C. C., and Clark, C. M. (1966) Sensory deprivation and aberrant behaviour among idiots. Amer. J. Ment. Defic. 71:213.

Eisenberg, L., and Kanner, L. (1956) Early infantile autism: 1942–55. Amer. J. Orthopsychiat. 26:556.

Forehand, R., and Baumeister, A. A. (1971) Rate of stereotyped body rocking of severe retardates as a function of frustration of goal-directed behaviour. J. Abnorm. Psychol. 78:35.

Gerard, M. (1957) The Emotionally Disturbed Child. New York: Child Welfare League of America.

Hutt, C., and Hutt, S. (1965) Effects of environmental complexity on stereotyped behaviour of children. Anim. Behav. 13:1.

Ilg, F. S., and Ames, L. B. (1955) Child Behaviour. New York: Harper.

Kanner, L. (1943) Autistic disturbances of affective contact. Nerv. Child. 2:217.

Kaufman, M. E., and Levitt, H. A. (1965) A study of three stereotyped behaviours in institutionalized mental defectives. Amer. J. Ment. Defic. 69:467.

Keiper, R. R. (1969) Causal factors of stereotypes in caged birds. Anim. Behav. 17:114.

Klaber, M. M., and Butterfield, E. C. (1968) Stereotyped rocking—a measure of institution and ward effectiveness. Amer. J. Ment. Defic. 73:13.

Kubie, L. S. (1941) The repetitive core of neurosis. Psychoanal. Q. 10:23.

Levy, D. M. (1944) On the problem of movement restraint. Amer. J. Ortho-psychiat. 14:644.

Lourie, R. S. (1959) The role of rhythmic patterns in childhood. Amer. J. Psychiat. 105:653.

Mahler, M. S. (1945) Ego-psychology applied to behaviour problems. *In* Modern Trends in Child Psychiatry (Eds. Lewis, N. C. D., and Pacella, B. L.). New York: International Universities Press.

Naor, E. M., and Balthazar, E. E. (1975) Provision of a language index for severely and profoundly retarded individuals. Amer. J. Ment. Defic. 79:717.

Ornitz, E. M., and Ritvo, E. R. (1968) Perception inconstancy in early infantile autism: The syndrome of early infant autism and its variants including certain cases of childhood schizophrenia. Arch. Gen. Psychiat. 18:76.

Schroeder, S. R. (1970) Usage of stereotypy as a descriptive term. Psychol. Rec. 20:337.

Stone, A. A. (1964) Consciousness: Altered levels in blind retarded children. Psychosom. Med. 26:14.

Van Krevelen, D. A. (1971) Early infantile autism and autistic psychopathy. J. Autism Child. Schizo. 1:82.

Ward, A. J. (1970) Early infantile autism: Diagnosis, aetiology, and treatment. Psychol. Bull. 75:350.

RESEARCH TO PRACTICE IN MENTAL RETARDATION
Education and Training, Volume II
Edited by Peter Mittler
Copyright 1977 I.A.S.S.M.D.

TOWARD AN ETHOLOGY OF MENTAL RETARDATION
Quantitative Behavioral Observation in Residential Settings

G. P. Sackett and S. Landesman-Dwyer
Child Development and Mental Retardation Center,
University of Washington,
Seattle, Washington 98195, United States

Over the past decade, major advances have been made in instrumentation and research techniques for observing behavior under natural or structured conditions (e.g., Johnson and Bolstad, 1973; Kummer, 1968; Sackett, Stephenson, and Ruppenthal, 1973). This methodology has yielded quantitative data concerning the typical everyday activities of individuals as related to their social group structure and ecology. Examples of situations studied by observational methods include social and individual behavior of human and nonhuman primates tested in field and laboratory settings; behavior of human children in home, school, and institutional settings; teacher-pupil interactions; and interactions among family members in hospital, laboratory, and home environments. The purposes of these studies vary from pure description of behavior to testing specific hypotheses under controlled conditions.

Observational methods are generally used to ask questions concerning what individuals *actually do* while behaving under various environmental conditions, rather than what they might be capable of doing under ideal motivational and environmental conditions. The major difference between observational methods and more conventional paper-and-pencil or automated electronic measurement techniques lies in the fact that the observer's sense organs and judgmental abilities are the measuring instrument. When proper attention is paid to 1) choice of the behavioral categories to measure and 2) the reliability of observers in consistently using these coding categories, this measurement method should be as precise as any other.

Only a very few studies using observational procedures have been conducted on mentally retarded people. Almost all of the systematic research on mental retardation has employed scores on standard psychological tests, performance on tasks measuring specific intellectual or motor abilities, responses to questionnaires by professional workers associated with retarded people, and nonquantitative subjective evaluations. Many of these measures have yielded valuable information for identifying and defining abilities of particular individuals or etiological groups. However, none of these data can answer questions concerning what individuals actually do with their particular learning, communicative, motor, and social skills in real life situations. Furthermore, questionnaires and subjective evaluations have limited utility, at best, in identifying the specific social and nonsocial environmental factors that do and do not support adaptive behavior in real life settings.

The basic assumptions underlying the study reported in this chapter are that 1) quantitative, systematic observation can be reliably and validly performed in studying basic experimental research questions concerning mental retardation, and 2) such data can be valuable both for scientific investigation and for solving practical problems involving the education, residences, and life styles of retarded people. To state one of our own biases, we suggest that direct observation under everyday living conditions is the only measurement method that can yield valid information concerning the ethical, political, and economic decisions made by governmental and other institutions that affect the lives of retarded people.

This chapter will illustrate our rationale by presenting data from a recent study of resident and staff behavior in group homes for the retarded in Washington State (Landesman-Dwyer, Stein, and Sackett, 1976). As in most other parts of the United States, Washington State has implemented a major program to move institutionalized retarded people into community residential environments. This movement is based on a number of assumptions, including 1) community living will be less expensive for the state to support; 2) retarded residents will live a more normal life associating, at least in part, with nonretarded people; and 3) retarded residents will live a more independent life in the community and will, therefore, have a greater choice in their life style.

All of these premises require testing. In particular, this chapter will focus on three specific assumptions commonly made by people involved with the community residence movement, namely, 1) small homes are better than large homes in attaining the goal of an improved life style, 2) homes should be near parents or other family members so that they can participate in the lives of their retarded relatives, and 3) homes should contain a relatively heterogeneous grouping of residents in terms of their past histories so that residents will have more varied experiences to offer each other.

HOMES AND SUBJECTS

Twenty of the 43 group homes for retarded people in Washington State were studied. These were representative of all geography, neighborhood, size, resident age, resident retardation level, type of building, profit or nonprofit ownership, and sex of resident characteristics existing at the study time. Subjects included 351 residents and 55 staff. Residents ranged in age from 16 to 62 years, with 77% previously living in state institutions. Ten percent of the residents were borderline or not retarded, 28% mildly retarded, 41% moderately retarded, and 20% severely or profoundly retarded. Fifty-five percent of the residents were males, 45% females. Each resident or staff subject was observed for at least 40 hours on two separate 24-hour days, with an initial series of visits to familiarize observers with the home and to familiarize residents and staff with the observers.

OBSERVATION CATEGORIES AND PROCEDURE

Observational data were collected between 5 a.m. and 2 a.m. the next morning by two trained observers on two separate occasions. Observation proceeded by moving through every room in the home (excluding bedrooms and bathrooms) once every 15 minutes. All individuals found in each room were scored, using a pencil-paper coding sheet, for whatever activity they were engaged in at the time of observation.

Each observation contained information concerning ten independent behavior or environment categories. These were 1) subject, 2) time of day, 3) location in home, 4) major behavioral activity (see Table 1), 5) physical-gestural communication, 6) verbal communication, 7) assistance needed and/or received, 8) objects involved, 9) stereotyped movements, and 10) individuals interacting with the subject. Table 1 gives the 62 behavioral activities available for coding, while Table 2 gives the codes for communication and assistance. During the entire study, 16,000 hours of behavior were sampled. Whenever possible, an observer joined residents who left the home to go into the community, and observers kept detailed notes concerning details that could not be coded on the arbitrary coding categories.

In addition to the behavioral code data, observers mapped each home in terms of the floor plan and room sizes. A complete inventory of all resources and objects in each home was also made. Interview data were taken from staff concerning their perceptions of residents and their service needs. These data were collected to relate ecological variables to resident and staff behavior, and to assess the accuracy of staff perceptions concerning resident behavior and abilities. The detailed procedures and detailed presentation of results can be found elsewhere (Landesman-Dwyer, Stein, and Sackett, 1976). The results presented here are meant only to illustrate the potential information available from a study

Table 1. Listing of major activities in home observation code

I.   Basic sleep and wake behaviors

01   Sleep
02   Simple awake
03   Attentive looking
04   General movement
05   Specific transition
06   Specific waiting
09   Other (to be specified)

II. Self-care activities

10   Bathing
11   Grooming
12   Dressing
13   Toileting
14   Eating
15   Health-related activities
19   Other self-help behaviors
     (to be specified)

V.   Social activities

40   Affection and courting
41   Intimate contact
42   Approving or rewarding
43   Receiving approval or rewards
44   Assisting
45   Defending/protecting
46   Being defended/protected/consoled
47   Sharing resources
48   Teasing and joking
50   Initiates social interaction, general
51   Responds to social interaction, general
52   Mutual general social interaction
53   Disapproving or punishing
54   Receiving disapproval or punishment
55   Competition or aggression
56   Receiving competition or aggression
59   Other social interaction
     (to be specified)

III. Play, recreation, and fine motor skills

20　Unstructured activity
21　Focused activity
22　Gross motor/recreational skills
23　Externally structured activity
24　Specific handicraft/fine motor skills
25　Formal game or recreation
29　Other activities (to be specified)

IV. Educational and formal training activities

30　Transmitting information
31　Reception/observation of information
32　Active participation
33　Imitation/simple rote
34　Focused symbolic behavior
35　Specific problem resolution
36　Lack of or negative response to
　　learning situation
39　Other learning situation
　　(to be specified)

VI. Work and group maintenance activities

60　Cleaning
61　Organizing
62　Preparing and planning
63　Directing or supervising
64　Building/constructing
69　Other group activities
　　(to be specified)

VII. Unusual, asocial, or repetitive behavior

70　Abnormal-unusual
71　Repetitive body movement
72　Withdrawal
73　Mimicking or echolalic behavior
74　Persistent following

VIII. Unobservable or not in home

75　Could not find, should be in house
76　Left house—score purpose separately
77　Unable to observe—other reason(s)
78　Other (to be specified)

Table 2. Additional characteristics of behaviors in home observation code

Physical-gestural communication	Verbal communication	Assistance needed or received	Minor stereotypies
0 None	0 None	0 No assistance-appropriate	0 Absent
1 Directive	1 Directive		1 Present (to be specified further when observed)
2 Informative	2 Informative	1 No assistance-inappropriate	
3 Expressive	3 Expressive-conversational	2 No assistance-undeterminable	
4 Physical contact	4 Question	3 Assistance desirable	
5 Listening	5 Answer	4 Verbal assistance given but not essential	
6 Laughter-gleeful sounds	6 Singing	5 Verbal assistance given and needed	
7 Cry or distress sounds	7 Not understood by observer	6 Physical assistance given and needed	
8 Sign language	8 Repetitive	7 Verbal and physical assistance given and needed	
9 Other (to be specified)	9 Other (to be specified)	8 Physical assistance given, but not essential	
		9 Other (to be specified)	

such as this one. A full presentation is beyond the scope of time and space allowed for this chapter.

RESULTS

For purposes of statistical analyses the original 62 behavior category codes were collapsed into the 21 response types shown in Table 3. These data are the percentages of total 15-minute intervals observed for each resident in which each behavior occurred. The total distribution yields a profile of daily activities for residents in the 20 group homes studied. For example, social interaction behaviors of any sort occurred in 14.5% (behaviors 12–16) of the sampled intervals. Active learning occurred in less than 0.5% of the intervals. By far the largest percentage of time was spent in unstructured, nonsocial activities such as

Table 3. Means and standard deviations for major activity categories[a]

Major activity category (original codes)	Mean (%)	Standard deviation (%)
1 Sleep (1) excluding night sleep period	1.16	3.20
2 Inactive behaviors (2–9)	17.73	11.74
3 Self-care (10–13, 15–19)	4.21	3.61
4 Eating (14)	10.71	4.80
5 Unstructured activities (20, 21)	23.02	14.04
6 Organized activities (22–29)	4.46	6.68
7 Active learning (30, 32, 39)	0.45	1.76
8 Reading, writing, arithmetic (34)	1.85	4.53
9 Problem solving (35)	0.04	0.24
10 Observation-imitation (31, 33)	0.43	1.12
11 No learning response (36)	0.02	0.38
12 Affiliative behaviors (40, 41, 42, 44, 45, 47)	0.29	0.88
13 General social (48, 50, 52, 59)	13.11	9.43
14 Received general social (43, 46, 51)	0.70	1.35
15 Initiated negative social (53, 55)	0.13	0.59
16 Received negative social (54, 56)	0.25	0.92
17 Household maintenance (60–62, 64–69)	10.72	8.48
18 Supervising (63)	0.09	0.59
19 Undesirable behavior (70–74)	1.57	5.19
20 Leaving house (76)	2.74	1.56
21 Unobservable (75, 77–79)	9.03	6.80

[a]These means and standard deviations were calculated for 240 group home residents who were observed for a minimum of 26 time periods.

wandering about the home, or in inactive behavior such as sitting and doing nothing. (If an investigator had comparable data on these subjects, or on a matched group living in an institutional setting, it would be possible to test directly whether or not daily life was the same or different in a community versus an institutional environment.) In this study a number of behaviors varied as a function of retardation level, age, sex, time living in the home, and Down's syndrome versus other etiological groups. Only a very few of these effects are presented next in relation to home size, parent visitation, and heterogeneity of resident backgrounds.

Size of Home

Table 4 presents social behavior data for residents as a function of size of home. Scores on the four measures were calculated for each home and were then averaged over the homes in each size group. One general feature of social behavior concerns whether it occurs in two-person dyads or in larger groups. Measure 1 shows the percentage of total social behavior spent in dyad pairs. Medium homes had the highest percentage of dyadic behavior, with small homes

Table 4. Effects of home size on social behavior

	Home size[a]					
	Small $N = 5$		Medium $N = 6$		Large $N = 7$	
Measure	Mean	Standard deviation	Mean	Standard deviation	Mean	Standard deviation
Percent total social behavior in peer dyads	34.5	14.5	67.3	14.2	44.8	6.5
Number of peers interacted with in dyads/day	2.8	0.7	2.8	1.0	4.1	1.1
Percent residents having a mutual "best" friend	48.0	27.0	52.0	13.0	61.0	10.0
Number 15-minute periods spent with mutual "best" friend	3.4	1.8	3.7	1.5	6.3	2.2

[a]Small, 6–8 residents; Medium, 9–17 residents; Large, 18–20 residents.

lowest ($p < 0.05$). Large homes had a greater number of different peer dyads than either medium or small homes ($p < 0.05$).

Another major aspect of social behavior concerns whether a person living in a social group does, or does not, have a "best" friend. Best friends were defined as dyadic pairs who spent more of their social time with each other (on the part of both individuals) than with any other person. In large homes more residents had best friends, with little difference between medium and small homes ($p < 0.05$).

A final measure, the number of 15-minute sample periods in which the resident was observed interacting with his best friend, also revealed a higher score for the large home category ($p < 0.05$).

With respect to social behavior, these data question the validity of the assumption that small homes are better, unless one defines small as larger than 17 residents. Although we do not consider these data definitive in any way—more data in greater detail are required to answer this question—it does seem clear that the design of very small group homes for the retarded may be a poor choice if maximization of social behavior is of any interest.

Heterogeneity of Residents

Figure 1 presents curves fit by linear regression to the relationship between number of previous residences lived in by our subjects and the percentage of 15-minute intervals spent in 1) inactive behavior, 2) self-care behavior, and 3) social interaction. Linear regression coefficients for each function are also given in the figure. The range of prior residences was 1–6. Most of the individuals in a

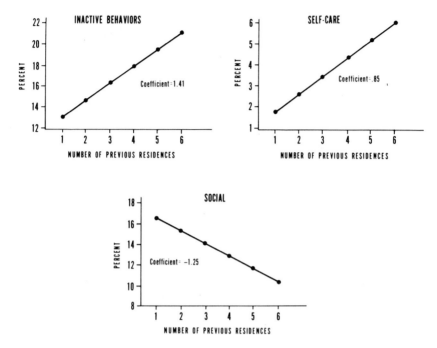

Figure 1. Linear regression functions for inactive, social, and self-care behavior related to number of previous residences lived in by group home subjects.

particular home that had only one prior residence were usually from the same institution as the other individuals in that home coming from only one prior environment. The data reveal a significant decrease in social behavior ($p < 0.05$) as residents lived in a greater number of past settings. Inactive behaviors occurred more frequently with a greater number of residences in the subject's background ($p < 0.05$). Self-care behaviors also showed the effect of occurring more frequently with a greater number of prior residences ($p < 0.05$).

Again, although these data are pilot in nature, it appears that bringing together a number of individuals who have heterogeneous backgrounds does not produce the anticipated effect of increasing social interaction or active participation in the daily routine of the home. The increase in self-care behavior is probably due to the need to learn such behaviors after having been shuttled about from one setting to another, and therefore not making friendships that can occupy a portion of the behavioral day.

Effects of Parent Visitation

Table 5 presents some suggestive data pertinent to the hypothesis that availability of parents is desirable when making decisions concerning where to place residents and where to build group homes. Inactive behaviors were found to be

Table 5. Effects of parent visitations

Behavior		Parents visit	Parents do not visit	Parents unavailable
	N	32.0	50.0	158.0
Inactive	$\bar{x}\%$	22.0	18.3	16.7
	SEM	2.2	2.1	0.8
Organized activity	$\bar{x}\%$	3.6	5.6	4.3
	SEM	1.0	1.1	0.5

SEM = Standard error of the mean.

significantly higher ($p < 0.05$) for residents who had visits from their parents than for residents whose parents did not visit (although they could have) or whose parents were unavailable (due to death or their own institutionalization). Organized behavioral activities, such as arranging flowers, putting away games and toys, or setting up items to start a project, were lower in residents whose parents visited than in the other groups, with residents whose parents did not visit (although they could have) being highest in organized activity ($p < 0.05$). If a more detailed study subsequent to these observations revealed the same basic effect on a wide range of behaviors, it would be clear that parent visitation is not only unnecessary for maintaining desired resident behaviors, but may actually be detrimental.

CONCLUSIONS

Although this chapter could present only a very few of the literally hundreds of specific comparisons made in this study, we hope that the value of observational data in understanding the behavioral and environmental interactions of retarded persons living their daily existences has been supported. The study was meant to be preliminary in nature. It had two major goals. The first was to determine whether or not it was possible to collect observational data in group homes for the retarded that made sense and that suggested important and meaningful hypotheses for further testing. The second goal was to see if such data would be useful for governmental agency policy decisions concerning placement of residents into homes, staffing of homes, and home construction. We conclude that our observational scheme and sampling technique does yield meaningful and interesting scientific data. We have also found that planners in the Washington State Department of Social and Health Services are using the full report in their decisions concerning group homes for the retarded. This was reinforced by granting of more funds by this state department to continue the work begun on the original pilot project.

SUMMARY

Quantitative methods for measuring behavior while individuals engage in their daily lives have been developed in human and animal research. These techniques measure what individuals *actually do* while behaving under various environmental conditions, rather than what they might be capable of doing as measured by a standardized testing instrument. The methodology and type of questions that might be asked are illustrated by a study of resident and staff behavior during 24-hour observations in 20 group homes for retarded people.

REFERENCES

Johnson, S. M., and Bolstad, O. D. (1973) Methodological issues in naturalistic observation: Some problems and solutions for field research. *In* Proceedings of the Fourth Banff Conference on Behavior Modification. (Eds. Clark, F. W., and Hamerlynck, L. A.) Champaign, Illinois: Research Press.

Kummer, H. (1968) Social organization of Hamadryas baboons: A field study. Bibl. Primatol. 6:1.

Landesman-Dwyer, S., Stein, J., and Sackett, G. (1976) Group Homes for the Developmentally Disabled: An Ecological and Behavioral Study. Technical report, Department of Social and Health Services, Olympia, Washington, February.

Sackett, G. P., Stephenson, E., and Ruppenthal, G. C. (1973) Digital data acquisition systems for observing behavior in laboratory and field settings. Behav. Res. Meth. Instru. 5:344.

RESEARCH TO PRACTICE IN MENTAL RETARDATION
Education and Training, Volume II
Edited by Peter Mittler
Copyright 1977 I.A.S.S.M.D.

FUNCTIONAL EXPECTANCY LEVELS FOR THE PROGRESS ASSESSMENT CHART OF SOCIAL AND PERSONAL DEVELOPMENT

J. M. Throne, R. L. Semrad, and R. E. Little
Lakemary Center for Exceptional Children,
100 Lakemary Drive, Paola, Kansas 66071, United States

The Progress Assessment Chart of Social and Personal Development (PAC) (Gunzburg, 1974) is a well-known clinico-educational instrument of English origin, providing data on the developmental status of mentally retarded children, adolescents, and adults of all ages and intelligence levels. Its administrative and programmatic usefulness, for planning, implementing, and evaluating Individual Program Plans (IPPs), which are required by the Joint Commission on Accreditation of Hospitals/Residential Facilities for the Mentally Retarded (JCAH/MR), was reported at the annual meeting of the American Association on Mental Deficiency earlier this year (Throne, Hand, Hupka, Lankford, Luther, McLennan, and Watson, 1976). The emphasis in that report was on how individualized programming for the mentally retarded who attend the Lakemary Center may be furthered by the Unified Programming Procedures (UPP) developed at Lakemary (Throne et al., 1976). The PAC is the linchpin of the UPP.

In line with the "developmental model" (NARC, 1972), it is accepted at Lakemary "that the development of all human beings . . . is susceptible . . . to environmental intervention" (Throne et al., 1976). It is also accepted that the chief justification for placing a child either in the residence or day care program at Lakemary is so the program can work purposefully toward "maximization of development of the mentally retarded as individuals" (Crosby, 1976). Hence the UPP and its developmental road map, the PAC.

Even the best of road maps usually do not give the whole story. Rarely do they present sound estimates of the time a trip should take. But the PAC is different. Gunzburg provides a simple method for calculating PAC expectancy levels, defined as "average levels of performance obtained by groups of people of similar age and intelligence" (Gunzburg, 1974, p. 15). These expectancy levels may be used for checking the efficiency of teaching, training, and treatment aimed at actual attainment of PAC objectives in comparison to expected attainment. Little if anything can be claimed for intervention if gains obtained through its employment do not exceed those expected in its absence. (Expectancy refers ultimately to time.)

Gunzburg's method involves adding up a particular group of PAC objectives (skills) mastered by a group of mentally retarded individuals of a given age and intelligence and dividing the sum by the number of individuals in the group to obtain the group's average performance level. For example, if 15 mentally retarded individuals score 60 successes in "Table Habits," their average performance level in this skill group is four. That is their expectancy level for "Table Habits." Other mentally retarded individuals of the same age and intelligence may be expected to perform in this skill group at the same level. Their successes, too, are added up and divided by the number of individuals in their own group, and it is noted whether the dividend is less than, equal to, or greater than the expectancy level, four. After teaching, training, or treatment aimed at remediating deficiencies in "Table Habits" in individual group members who fall below the expectancy level, the successes of the group are added up and divided by the number of individuals once again. The similarities of or differences in their scores between the first and second measurements indicate the efficiency of the intervention techniques employed with the group.

Gunzburg provided PAC expectancy levels for a sample of mentally retarded English children. The sample was neither random nor representative. But it need not have been, since the PAC does not purport to be a standardized test, but rather a developmental index. The PAC objectives are to be regarded as being more or less relatively, not absolutely, placed hierarchically with respect to one another—that is, on a developmental plane that is higher, lower, or the same. Even if some are misplaced, this is of small moment, because the PAC does not yield statistical scores on the basis of which deductions are to be made, but rather, performance scores, improvements in which are to be induced. The fact that the PAC sample's characteristics—of which their English nationality may be the least important—delimit the extent to which expectancy levels derived from their performances validly denote the performances to be expected for other mentally retarded children, is far less important for the PAC than it would be for a standardized test. PAC performances are intended to suggest improvements to be produced. Performances on tests as standardized tests are not supposed to provoke improvements, but predictions. A sample's performances must be valid for predictions of performances on their basis to be valid themselves (except by chance).

Gunzburg's PAC expectancy levels do have questionable functionality, however. Even *Individual* Program Plans must be undertaken in groups. What matters is not so much that efficiency of teaching, training, and treatment be established *after the fact* against benchmarks provided by others of the same age and intelligence. What matters is that efficiency be established *before the fact* by arrangements made to ensure that it exists.

At Lakemary we have developed alternative methods for calculating PAC expectancy levels functioning to aid in producing improved PAC performances by our residential and day care population. We have compiled PAC data for the residents of each of two residential units housing males and females. Teaching, training, and treatment of PAC objectives is a vital part of Lakemary's residential program; these activities are not the exclusive domain of teachers and other professional support staff. Each unit has 32 residents, 16 males and 16 females. One houses residents aged 3 to 12, the other, residents from 11 to 16. (There is some overlap in ages.) Subunits in each residence, corresponding to semi-private bedrooms, serve as sleeping quarters for four residents each.

The PAC data are calculated to reveal the PAC expectancy levels of the residents in each unit. The calculations do not describe the *average* levels of performance on PAC objectives by these groups, however; that is, the success rate of the mean child in each unit. Rather, the successful performances of 90% of the children in each unit are recorded. The reason for the higher cutoff point is that it is desirable in the close quarters of residential living for groups and subgroups to be as homogeneous as possible with respect to the PAC objectives on which they are taught, trained, and treated. It is more useful to know the *predominating* PAC performance levels of the children residing in the units and subunits than to know how the average individual performs—not only for purposes of PAC programming for the children already in residence but for deciding whether or not a child should be admitted to a residential unit or subunit in the first place, on the basis of his or her PAC scores.

PAC expectancy levels have also been compiled for our day care children, who attend our school and preschool together with the residential children. (During the current school year just started, there are 38.) PAC data are collected for each of eight classroom groupings plus the preschool. In these groupings there may be as few as one but as many as four PAC expectancy levels computed. In the preschool, PAC heterogeneity, rather than homogeneity, of children is the rule; PAC expectancy levels for four preschool subpopulations are required for determining both PAC programming goals for these children and appropriateness of placement there for possible new prospects. The school groupings, in which the tendency toward PAC homogeneity is greater than in the preschool, contain fewer PAC expectancy levels.

The whole point is this: what can be expected to be accomplished for a child by placing that child at Lakemary is Lakemary's principal administrative and programmatic concern. Help in determining what that expectation realistically can be is the purpose of obtaining PAC performance levels on groups and subgroups within Lakemary—the function that PAC expectancy levels, as calculated at Lakemary, are intended to serve.

42 Throne, Semrad, and Little

REFERENCES

Crosby, K. G. (1976) Essentials of active programming. Ment. Retard. 14:3.

Gunzburg, H. C. (1974) Progress Assessment Chart of Social and Personal Development. Birmingham, England: SEFA.

National Association for Retarded Citizens. (1972) Residential Programming for Mentally Retarded Persons. Vol. II. Arlington, Texas: NARC.

Throne, J. M., Hand, R. C., Hupka, M. L., Lankford, C. W., Luther, K. M., McLennan, S. L., and Watson, J. B. (1976) Lakemary Center's Unified Programming Procedures for the Mentally Retarded. Paper presented at the annual meeting of AAMD, Chicago, June.

RESEARCH TO PRACTICE IN MENTAL RETARDATION
Education and Training, Volume II
Edited by Peter Mittler
Copyright 1977 I.A.S.S.M.D.

LEVELS OF INTERACTION IN THE ASSESSMENT OF CHILDREN

M. N. Ozer
George Washington School of Medicine,
3000 Connecticut Ave. N.W.
Washington, D.C. 20008, United States

The assessment of children with developmental difficulties is to be considered in terms of the *process* by which data is generated as well as the *product,* or the particular data generated. Emphasis traditionally has been on the products of the assessment as a score or other description of the individual's behavior. Such products are used for classification in terms of degree and types of developmental difficulties. Level of function might be determined by the use of standardized tasks considered, on the basis of norms, to be predictive of function on a wider range of behaviors. Concurrently, behavior scales of various sorts are attempts to assess level of function in a sampling of more naturalistic situations and are criterion-referenced. The advantage of the behavior scales for the mentally retarded has been a more direct relationship to the development of programs for improvement in functional level, as well as more specific classification. Both such approaches arose in the context of classification in terms of functional level as the major goal of assessment (Kanner, 1964).

The purpose of this chapter is to explore the other parameter of assessment, that is, the process by which such data are generated. It is suggested that awareness of the process may have implications for a revision of what may be considered the proper goals for children with developmental problems.

The assessment process is to be considered in relation to the degree of interaction. The lowest degree of interaction is that of testing. Many, if not all, procedures in psychology and education have used the testing model. Such a model assumes that the interaction between the examiner and the "subject" is as limited as possible while still being consistent with getting the subject to perform. There is limited feedback to the individual about results. There is little opportunity for the examiner to vary the conditions for presentation of material. The idea has been to measure objective functions of the person without intrusion of that person or of the examiner in the collection of data.

43

The process of assessment in the testing model is thus considered to be one of noninteraction. Under ideal circumstances both the person and the examiner are somehow disembodied and do not participate as people in the testing model. In their concern for consistency and predictability of data concerning level of function, the testers no longer replicate the process of development they seek to predict. That process of development implies that change will occur, yet the traditional testing model seeks to fix the individual at a particular time and level of function.

More recently, the entire testing procedure has come under increasing attack as to its appropriateness for educational planning. Criticism has been voiced on two counts: 1) the unrepresentativeness of the tasks used as the context for assessment, and 2) the failure to reflect opportunities in life to vary both presentation and feedback (Bersoff, 1973). Measurement may then be taken of the child's behavior during actual teaching of tasks that relate directly to the issues in that child's environment. Thus, if the problem is in counting, one samples on that set of tasks. The conditions are also examined in terms of both presentation and feedback that might be varied so as to reach a particular goal in the teaching episode (Bijou and Peterson, 1971). Suggestions to be made to the child's teacher are made on the basis of what was actually done and found to work in the assessment setting.

The examination has then become a process. One samples the process of change in the child rather than the more static level of function. The concern is no longer merely determination of the problem areas but discovering possible solutions to the problem (Ozer, 1966; 1972). A higher level of involvement of the examiner is required. Indeed the product of the assessment now includes both some change in the child and an awareness on the part of the examiner of how such change came about. The child would also ordinarily become aware of the changes that had come about due to feedback of the results of the learning process. The examiner has become a teacher and is no longer disembodied from the process. The goal remains that of classification; classification not of product but of the means or styles by which teaching might go on.

The individual being taught, however, remains a relatively passive member of the dyad. In his/her concern for consistency and reliability of data, the examiner still fails to replicate the process of development. That process of development requires that change come about in the context of an interaction between two people. The focus has been on those who take the role of the teacher, whereas it is in the learner that the process of development must occur.

A third level of interaction is now being suggested, that of bilateral interaction. Both the examiner and the learner must be aware of what is being done. The product of assessment now includes the degree of awareness by the learner of how he learns. The assessment process now includes not only that the child learn something as a context but that he learn HOW that occurred, so that he can generalize such strategies to other situations.

The Child Development Observation (CDO) is the name given to the proto-col by which this bilateral assessment is carried out (Ozer and Richardson, 1974). One samples the process of learning in the context of a particular task or situation. The first objective is for the child to be able to carry out the task at issue. It may be to count or whatever seems to be appropriate based upon the needs of the child or his developmental level as established by testing or level of performance on a day-to-day basis as provided by his caregivers. The task used and his performance on that task is less relevant than in ordinary testing. The task is merely a vehicle for increasing the child's awareness of how he may learn.

The second objective to be determined by the examiner is the repertoire of strategies for modifying conditions for presentation and feedback to be used and eventually to be made part of the child's awareness. The choice of strategies may be derived from the previous experience of the examiner in relation to that type of task. It is preferable that this choice involve input from the child's primary caregivers as means of increasing their awareness of what works with the child. For example, it may have been elicited that it has been useful for the child not only to hear what he is to do, but also to go through the actual physical motion. The feedback conditions that worked have been positive feedback as to results, with the feedback of a physical nature, such as food, at high frequency. The character of the task limits to some degree the options to be used, but there are at least several options that may be tried.

The options for presentation may be generally categorized in terms of the *channel* of input, the *time* frame for input, and the *salience* of the stimuli. Each of these categories may be further divided. For example, the time frame may be varied in terms of amount of repetition, degree of accenting of sequence, duration of task to completion, degree of segmentation of the task, etc. The channel of input may be auditory-verbal, visual, kinesthetic, or combinations of these. The options for feedback may be similarly generally categorized as to *type, intensity,* and *degree of sharing.*

The number of options for modifying presentation and feedback are poten-tially large in number, but the goal for the child may be, for example, to use one such option during the assessment interaction as a model. Each of the options may be translated into a verbal statement to be used by the child. As examples, the child may begin to say "please repeat it" or "please show me." In nonverbal children, one may use the appropriate sign or point to a picture representing the concept. The size of the repertoire of options for use by the child may then be specified as the second objective of the interaction.

The third objective that may be specified is the level of independence or bilaterality to be sought in the use of these statements. The overall goal is for the child to have the experience of bringing about adaptation of his environment. Categories of bilaterality may also be specified. The lowest level of bilaterality would be nonverbal acquiescence, or saying "yes" in agreement to the suggestion made by the examiner. One may roughly estimate that the child is here contributing perhaps 20% to the decision. Verbal repetition of the examiner's statement when prompted may be estimated as a 40% contribution by the child. The child's verbal selection of an option from several alternatives may be considered as a 60% contribution and represents a significant shift in responsibility to the child. An independent free response from the child when asked "what might work" would be considered as 80%. The ultimate objective would be use by the child independent of the examiner, etc.

The procedure to be carried out in meeting these objectives would be similar to that used in language training of the usual sort. One is merely focusing on the development of a vocabulary by which he may communicate about his communication needs. The general procedures as outlined in the protocol emphasize the positive feedback given to the child not only for performance of the task but also for the specific ideas contributed toward the solution of the problem of understanding the task and the degree of contribution made by the child. A sample interchange would be as follows:

> If the task was not done correctly in its entirety, the examiner provides positive recognition of what had been done correctly and says "what would help you?" If the child is at the level of free independent statements, the response of the examiner would be "Thank you for telling me to show you so that you could see it with your eyes. That was a good idea you had."

It is important to specify the idea as one gives recognition for its use. The ultimate objective is for the child to internalize such statements and use such verbal control for himself. The verbalization by the child in the presence of the examiner provides an opportunity for the examiner to clarify and indicate, by feedback, the value of the idea contributed by the child. In this way, the child hears the idea more clearly as well. The more specific the idea, the more likely the child will be able to use it as an operational statement to control his actions.

This approach has been used with trainable mentally retarded individuals as well as with a range of other developmental difficulties. It is part of an entire system for problem-solving exploration by the child working with his parents and/or teachers (Ozer and Dworkin, 1974).

The emphasis of this chapter is on the implications of such a model of assessment for the educational needs of the retarded child. The assessment process has been designed as a model of child development and is part of an ongoing process. It focuses not only on the examiner's awareness of how to teach, but on the child becoming more aware of how to learn. Awareness of such strategies is felt to come about as the child is encouraged to verbalize ideas, receives recognition for such contributions, and observes the examiner being affected by such statements. The child learns by seeing himself teach another. The assessment is in itself part of the developmental process and helps enhance the child's sense of competence and confidence. The child learns both some "handles" by which he may more effectively interact with the environment and that he has the right to use them. Indeed it is this awareness of the right to use these handles that is one of the products of the interaction, rather than merely the specific statements that may be made.

The proper goal of assessment must ultimately be the enhancement of the individual's opportunities. Assessment may in itself represent an episode of such enhancement. When one focuses on the *process* of assessment, one begins to view it as providing a sample of the long-term treatment that is the increasingly more mutualistic interaction called human development. It is particularly appropriate that the assessment of the mentally retarded become concerned with the degree to which such procedures may contribute to the development of such individuals. For far too long, assessment in relation to the mentally retarded has been used as a means of confirming the limitations rather than the opportunities.

SUMMARY

Assessment is a sample not only of function but also of the *process* of learning. In the context of any task, one also explores "what works" for longer term planning. The child now also begins to learn for himself what works by having the experience of telling the examiner. A truly adaptive system is being modelled. The new objective is that the child begins to take control of the interaction as a model of the way he must take control of his own learning and life.

REFERENCES

Bersoff, D. N. (1973) Silk purses into sow's ears. Amer. Psychol. 28:892.

Bijou, S. W., and Peterson, R. F. (1971) Psychological assessment in children: A functional analysis. *In* Advances in Psychological Assessment (Ed. McReynolds, P.). Palo Alto: Science and Behavior Books, p. 63.

Kanner, L. (1964) A History of the Care and Study of Mentally Retarded. Springfield, Ohio: Charles C Thomas, p. 119.

Ozer, M. N. (1966) The use of operant conditioning in the evaluation of children with learning problems. Proc. Childrens Hosp. D.C. 22:235.

Ozer, M. N. (1972) Diagnostic evaluation of learning problems: A child development approach. Nebr. St. Med. J. 57:21.

Ozer, M. N., and Dworkin, N. E. (1974) The assessment of children with learning problems: An in-service teacher training program. J. Learn. Disabil. 7:539.

Ozer, M. N., and Richardson, H. B. Jr. (1974) The diagnostic evaluation of children with learning problems: A process approach. J. Learn. Disabil. 7:30.

RESEARCH TO PRACTICE IN MENTAL RETARDATION
Education and Training, Volume II
Edited by Peter Mittler
Copyright 1977   I.A.S.S.M.D.

A TECHNIQUE FOR APPRAISING THE VISION OF MENTALLY RETARDED CHILDREN

L. J. Lawson, Jr., J. S. Molloy, and M. Miller
Department of Ophthalmology,
Evanston Hospital, Evanston,
Illinois 60201, United States

There is a paucity of information relating to appraisal of the vision of mentally retarded children. Because of the children's intellectual handicap, it is of utmost importance that visual deficiencies be recognized and corrected, in order to ensure maximum potential for learning in educational settings. Unfortunately, many of these children have not had any appraisal of their vision, or if one has been performed, reliable data may have been difficult to obtain. Eye specialists usually find it difficult to deal with the mentally retarded child and frequently do not have a satisfactory method of examination. We were challenged to work with a group of children with mental handicaps and to develop a practical system of evaluation.

We started with a three-year program, the first year of which was primarily devoted to getting acquainted with the problems and to developing a satisfactory method of visual appraisal. The second year was spent collecting data and refining our techniques. During the third year, the program was transferred to the Evanston Hospital in order to allow maximum exposure of the system to the residents in opthalmology.

A group of 103 students from the Orchard School for Special Education of Skolie, Illinois, (now the Molloy Education Center) were examined. They were day students with a variety of etiologies (Table 1). Their ages ranged from three to twenty-two years, and each student had an intelligence quotient of approximately sixty or less. The tests were initially performed in the office, and in the

This work was supported by a grant from the Ben Levin Memorial for Retarded Children.

Table 1. Etiologies of mental retardation in the children in this study

Down's syndrome		33
Unknown		29
Brain damage:		13
Nonverbal	9	
Verbal	4	
Cerebral palsy		11
Cerebral dysgenesis		3
Encephalitis		4
Rh factor		3
Cerebral ataxia		3
Cranial dysostosis		2
Microcephaly		1
Battered child syndrome		1
Total		103

third year of the program were transferred to the Eye Clinic of the Evanston Hospital. The examinations were conducted in the clinic at a time when other activities were not scheduled so that there would be a quiet and nondisturbing environment. Each child was examined individually, with the nurse from the school in attendance for identification and reassurance. Frequently, an older child was examined first while a younger one was allowed to observe the procedure in order to indoctrinate the second child to the testing techniques. Because of the generally short attention span and easy distractability, the test procedures were performed rapidly. Those tests that were beyond the comprehension of the child were eliminated and the next procedure presented.

The initial approach was a general appraisal of the eyes, eyelids, and orbits. Visual acuity was then recorded. Lippman (1969) had stated that young children do not have the concept of direction and therefore illiterate "E" is usually unreliable. The use of various "pictographs" utilizing symbols was attempted, e.g., the American Optical projectochart, (Allen, 1957), children's eye chart, or the method proposed by Brauner and Brauner (1968), and Osterberg (1965). However, our children could not recognize these symbols, and therefore other methods were tried. We attempted the use of the Stycar test (Screening Test for Young Children and Retardates (Sheridan, 1960; 1963)). This test employs the use of cut-out symbols (T. H. O. V.) that are not read as letters but are placed on a table and matched with the same symbols placed at a distance. This system did not prove successful, however, because of the common failure among these children to comprehend the concept of "likeness" or similarities.

Vision testing "machines" have proven to be unsatisfactory for children with mental retardation.

Osterberg of Denmark (1965) stated that construction of optically correct pictorial charts is obviously impossible. In the past the optical principle of exact size was emphasized, but as the complexity of visual perception has been realized, newer ideas of visual tests have been introduced. The objects must belong to the child's world of ideas. With these principles in mind, we continued our experiment.

Since most of the children could recognize food items (and often no others), selected items from the Peabody series (Dunn and Smith, 1965) were photographed in color to provide a series of 2 X 2 slides to be used with the projector. Because of the resolution of the projected picture, smaller symbols could not be satisfactorily reproduced in reduced sizes. We therefore designed a wall chart using the most popular food items (apple, banana, hotdog, and ice cream cone) in color and calibrated for the standard twenty foot distance. Each symbol could be framed by an adjustable "framer" to stimulate attention. This method proved successful in a high percentage of our children. Lippman stressed the importance of the single-symbol exposure as the method of choice.

Ocular muscle coordination and the fusion status were then ascertained when possible, and measurement of the refractive error was made after using drops. The use of the refracting machine or trial frame was generally too frightening for the child.

Therefore, the use of loose lenses was the preferred method because of the rapidity of this technique. A fairly accurate measurement was possible in a majority of cases. The interior of the eyes was examined for defects by the indirect ophthalmoscope, which proved to be vastly superior to the direct method because of the ability to perform the examination without touching the child.

The exceptional child is very apprehensive when the need arises to visit anyone addressed as "Doctor." The ophthalmologist is no exception. The school nurse developed a routine of preparing the children by familiarizing them with the general procedure to be used in the examination. A period was set aside each day for role playing, in order to allow the child to become familiar with the particular examination that was forthcoming. During the morning period, conversation centered around the eye doctor—"Mary is going to the eye doctor. The eye doctor's name is Dr. _____; Who is going to the eye doctor? What is the doctor's name? Mary is going to the eye doctor in the school bus." The complete visit was incorporated into the exercise each morning.

The verbal children were taught to label correctly and the nonverbal children were taught to identify an apple, a hotdog, an ice cream cone, and a banana in a consistent way; a licking motion for the ice cream cone, a peeling motion for the banana, a tummy patting for the hotdog, and a biting action for the apple. This was done on a one-to-one basis with consistent primary reinforcement following each correct response.

A facsimile of the instrument used by the doctor was shown to the child. The way in which they were to be used was explained and demonstrated. Each child in the class took his turn first as the patient and then as the doctor. At the time of the actual testing, the administration of the drops is the fearful part of the examination. A bottle similar to the one used by the doctor was shown to the children and drops applied on the wrist of each child first by the nurse and then by the children in turn.

The day of the visit to the doctor was a happy experience rather than a fearful, traumatic one because of the time spent in "role playing" prior to the date. This approach resulted in a definite reduction of apprehension and created a more cooperative child, thus allowing a more thorough and accurate professional appraisal.

RESULTS

With the system described above, we could determine the visual acuity of a significant number of mentally retarded children (Table 2). By this method, rather than by the usual tests, a substantial number of children can be added to those in whom the visual acuity can be determined. Unfortunately, there remain some children for whom no system has been satisfactorily devised. In our series there were eighteen children who had less than 20/70 uncorrected vision in their better eye (sight-saving cut-off level), fifteen of whom could be corrected to better acuity. It is important to recognize that these children had not previously been identified as having any visual problems, and the significance of the benefit to their educational opportunities is stressed. Only 28% of our children were considered to have normal visual functioning, whereas in a general school population approximately 75% are usually found to be without ocular difficulties.

A total of forty-four children had significant need for glasses. Of these, twenty-five were previously not identified to the school or to the parents as requiring corrective lenses. Nineteen children already were wearing glasses, nine of whom needed significant changes in the power of their spectacles.

Of the 103 children there were thirty-three who had some degree of ocular coordination problem. This incidence is almost ten times that of a normal school population. There were nine students with an amblyopic eye who had never received treatment. A majority of the parents of these children had no previous knowledge of this condition. Two children had a history of previous eye surgery.

Table 2. Methods of determining vision

Technique	Number of children
Snellen	27
"E" game	14
Food pictures	36
Could not test	26

CONCLUSIONS

The results of our study demonstrate the need of an ophthalmological appraisal of every mentally retarded child (Lawson and Schoofs, 1971). These children have a high incidence (70%) of visual defects that may influence their level of functioning, especially in a learning situation. The need for treatment of a visual defect must be individually determined and the school alerted to the special problems and visual needs of the child, so that his education can be properly programmed.

A method of determining visual acuity in the retarded that has proven to be successful has been presented.

ACKNOWLEDGMENTS

The chart used in this study may be ordered from Milton Roy Company, Sarasota, Florida 33578, United States.

REFERENCES

Allen, H. F. (1957) A new picture series for pre-school vision testing. Amer. J. Ophthal. 44:38.
Brauner, F., and Brauner, A. (1968) Examen de L'Acuite Visuelle des Enfants Illettres ou Deficients Mentaux. Paris: Les Editions Sociales Francaises.
Dunn, L. M., and Smith, J. O. (1965) Peabody Language Development Kit. Circle Pines, Minnesota: American Guidance Service.
Lawson, L. J., and Schoofs, G. (1971) A technique for visual appraisal of mentally retarded children. Amer. J. Ophthal. 72:622.
Lippman, O. (1969) Vision of young children. Arch. Ophthal. 81:763.
Osterberg, G. (1965) A Danish picture chart. Amer. J. Ophthal. 59:1120.
Sheridan, M. (1960) Vision screening of very young or handicapped children. Brit. Med. J. 2:453.
Sheridan, M. (1963) Stycar tests. Brit. Orthop. J. 20:32.

COGNITION
AND LEARNING

RESEARCH TO PRACTICE IN MENTAL RETARDATION
Education and Training, Volume II
Edited by Peter Mittler
Copyright 1977 I.A.S.S.M.D.

IMPLICATIONS OF GENETIC STUDIES OF ABILITY FOR COGNITION AND LEARNING IN RETARDED CHILDREN

P. E. Vernon
Department of Educational Psychology,
University of Calgary, Alberta, Canada

This chapter will be confined to the mildly retarded, that is children whose subnormality can reasonably be ascribed to a combination of numerous small genetic factors and environmental deprivations. Psychologists are increasingly moving away from the notion of general intelligence as a unitary causal factor in mental retardation, which is recognizable and consistent from an early age. The work of Bayley and her colleagues (Jones et al., 1971) suggests rather that certain types of motor and perceptual skills mature with growth, and other more complex skills emerge out of these. But by the age of five to six years, we find a good deal of overlapping or correlation among the very varied information-processing skills, which justify us in measuring 'g' as an underlying general intelligence factor that is quite highly predictive of later educational and other kinds of achievement. This does not deny that abilities can, alternatively, be classified under several more specialized categories such as Thurstone's V, R, N, S, and other partially distinguishable factors. From five or six to say 18 years of age, there are still wide fluctuations in IQs, partly because of variations in the content of successive tests, and partly because children do develop irregularly, depending on environmental and personality changes that we know little about. Moreover, the predictive validity is limited, accounting only for about half the variance in educational achievements and a good deal less in adult occupational achievements. Hence the well-known findings of Baller (1936) and Charles (1953) that the majority of children who are retarded in elementary school nevertheless end up as self-supporting and reasonably well adjusted adults in a wide range of jobs.

Given then that this general intelligence is one important component in subnormality, how should we account for it? Probably most psychologists would agree that it depends in the first instance on genes that underly more effective brain structures in some individuals than in others, though some extreme environmentalist writers might deny this. However, we know that genes do not themselves determine any physical or mental attribute; their effects always also depend on environmental conditions. The phenotype—that is the intelligence we can observe and measure—results from the interaction between genetic endowment and favourable or unfavourable environmental stimulation, as has been argued by Hebb (1948), Piaget (1950), Hunt (1961), and even by Jensen (1969). The controversial question is how far should variations in phenotypic intelligence be attributed to genetic differences, and how far can they be modified by environmental differences and by any interventions we can make in children's upbringing and education?

As is generally known, the heritability ratio or genetic variance was estimated at 80% or more by Burt (1958) and Jensen (1975), mainly on the basis of analyzing the correlations between identical twins reared together or apart, or between other kinship groups that differ in their genetic resemblance. Such studies have been heavily criticized, especially in Kamin's recent book (1974). The trustworthiness of Burt's data has been questioned, and the applicability of analysis of variance to so complex and vague an attribute as general intelligence has been denied. In my view, many of the criticisms can be countered, although there is still considerable disagreement regarding the appropriate statistical model for specifying and estimating the various genetic and environmental components. It seems particularly difficult to assess adequately the extent of genetic-environmental covariance, which arises because children inheriting favourable genes are usually brought up in more stimulating environments, and conversely for those with poorer genes. Nevertheless, several recent heritability analyses, by Loehlin, Lindzey and Spuhler (1975), by Jencks et al. 1972 and by Jensen himself (1975), seem to be converging on a genetic variance around 65%. This would accord with the general trend of foster studies, indicating that the correlation of foster child with true parent ability tends to be higher, although probably not a lot higher, than the correlation with foster parent ability or foster home conditions.

Even this figure would seem, to many writers, to be contradicted by the very large rises in IQ reported when children are removed from severely deprived to good environments, as in Skeels' long-term follow-up (1966) and in Heber and Garber's study in Milwaukee (1975). However, changes equivalent to an average of 30 IQ points would be expected if the variance attributable to environment exceeds 30%, and if the difference between the children's initial and later environments amounts to say four sigma units on a scale covering the whole range from the best to the poorest environment within western cultures. Much more commonly the average changes attributable to fostering, or to early intervention programmes in the children's own homes, seem to be limited to some 15 points or less. We still have no recipe, as it were, for raising children's intelligence at will, though we are somewhat further on than we were at the time of the Head Start programmes.

The acceptance of a fairly large genetic component does not mean that intelligence is fixed once and for all either in the individual, or in an ethnic group. Not only is there great individual variability with growth, but also it is entirely possible that the discovery of some new, more effective, technique of mental stimulation could increase the all-round level of the population—just as the invention of printed books and public education must have undoubtedly increased the general intellectual capacity of civilized nations. Moreover, it is admitted that this 65% heritability, or any other figure, is a population statistic, which depends greatly on the extent of heterogeneity of environments. If a wider range of environments could be studied—as between, say, those of Australian aboriginals and those of upper class Americans—the environmental variance would be much larger, the genetic smaller. This is one of the reasons why it is difficult to reach agreement on whether or not there are genetic differences in intelligence between ethnic subgroups—a topic I do not intend to become embroiled in.

Another point that tends to be neglected both by environmentalists and by genetically inclined psychologists is that the level of IQ and of school achievement appear to stay relatively constant in the majority of pupils throughout their school careers, not merely because of the strength of genetic influences, but also because, in the preschool years, conceptual level, attitudes to learning, and strategies of perceiving and thinking, become implanted into the young child by the kind of stimulation and the reinforcements his environment provides. The middle class child is constantly being trained to become a successful learner and thinker, whereas children in highly deprived environments are more likely to be trained to be unintelligent—not to attend, analyze, generalize, and think rationally. These habits become so engrained before six years that it is extremely difficult for the schools to modify them, as shown in the results of Head Start. Indeed the school often continues this process of fixation at a low level. In so far as these habits and attitudes are as much motivational as cognitive, they probably affect scholastic learning even more than they do IQ. This fits in with the well-known finding that the heritability ratio for educational achievement is always much lower than that for IQ, probably only about half, meaning that home and school environment and child personality have considerably greater effects on his educability and trainability than they have on the generalized intellectual abilities measured by IQ tests.

One could say broadly that the greater the complexity of a cognitive skill, the more it involves coding into abstract and symbolic representations, the greater will be its dependence on 'g,' and therefore, usually, its heritability. Thus, rote memorization of paired associates or mechanical arithmetic skills can be trained fairly readily among retarded children, whereas logical understanding of social studies, or reasoning mathematics, are much less teachable. Speech and language are especially interesting, since many psychologists would agree with Chomsky and G. A. Miller (Miller and McNeill, 1969) that an inherited language acquisition device must underlie the astonishing capacity of young children to build up comprehension and usage; and this is to a large extent independent of 'g': many severely retarded people can acquire fairly effective speech and grammatical language, although they fail dismally in using it for conceptual purposes, that is for internal mediation, manipulation, and coding of experiences, and for self-regulation of behaviour, that is, functions that develop spontaneously in the child of average or above average intelligence. Many of the differences in the language of normal, and of retarded or seriously disadvantaged, children correspond to the distinction that Bernstein (1971) has drawn between what he calls the restricted and the elaborated codes; similar observations have been reported by Hess and Shipman (1965). They show also that these forms of speech are bound up with the values, attitudes, and interpersonal behaviour of advantaged and disadvantaged families—for example the appeals to reason and delayed gratification in the former, and the use of imperatives and dependence on immediate punishments and rewards in the latter.

There are several psychologists, of whom Denis Stott is a good example, who attempt to account for retardation entirely in terms of specific patterns or strategies of cognitive inefficiency, induced by early environment, and linked to personality differences. Stott (1971) entirely rejects any notion that backwardness may arise from insufficient genetic potentiality for intellectual growth, or to some other global cause such as a perceptual deficit. He lists 14 of these common maladaptive strategies, including the impulsive who does not stop to think, the highly distractible, those who avoid difficulties by withdrawing or playing more stupid than they are, and so on. He believes that these syndromes can be overcome by providing carefully regulated experiences, and reinforcing the appearance of more adaptive behaviours. While I would agree that professionally planned behaviour modification techniques might often be useful, it seems very unlikely that many teachers could devize and carry them out themselves while coping with the needs of a class of 30 children. It would also seem to me unwise to ignore basic individual differences in learning capacities. A good school psychologist recognizes both: that is, he does not merely give a retarded child an IQ test and dub him as irremediably dull; he usually does look for the existence of such syndromes in behaviour at school, and tries to advise the teacher how they might be handled, or—if he has time for remedial work himself—to plan his approach accordingly.

Another commonly expressed view is to distinguish between performance and capacity. Retarded children, it is said, may fail to learn in the classroom, and yet show good reasoning, quick learning, or fluent, grammatical speech in everyday social situations. William Labov is one who makes much of this distinction in his valuable linguistic studies of Negro English (1970). But to me, capacity has very little meaning other than performance under specified conditions. Of course, school psychologists recognize that performance may differ in different contexts. But it is up to those who deny that present tests measure capacity to produce new tests that will give better samples of performance in other situations.

Although insisting on genetic differences, and on cognitive differences deeply engrained during the preschool years, I certainly welcome current attempts to identify and develop deficient strategies of attending and thinking. But how trainable are they? We have all heard of Harlow's monkeys "learning how to learn," but then he was developing the ability to cope with a rather narrow range of problem-solving, and I fear that some of the work with retarded children may show disappointing transfer value. Jensen and some other writers on the topic stress that, because the retarded are usually unable to self-generate mediational and coding abilities, they require highly structured training of specific skills, and he cites Bereiter and Engelmann's work (1966). To quite an extent Sesame Street follows the same policy; but neither seem likely to stimulate the use of private speech for mediational purposes. On the other hand, Meichenbaum and Turk (1972) describes a programme, based on modelling, for training over-impulsive children to talk to themselves, and this did produce general improvement in reflectivity.

In conclusion, we still know far too little regarding the effectiveness of particular environmental changes in promoting cognitive skills, other than some of the broad influences of parental education and social class, and the probable importance of mother-child interactions even as early as the first year of life, as well as subsequently. However, I hope I have shown that admitting the importance of genetic potentialities in any kind of intellectual growth does not preclude us from fruitful investigations of how to stimulate certain kinds of achievement.

SUMMARY

Modern views regard intelligence as a collection of overlapping skills, the development of which depends on the individual's genetic potentialities, which interact with childrearing, educational and other environmental pressures. While many relatively specific intellectual and other skills can be trained in retardates, little is known of their generality or transfer to other tasks.

REFERENCES

Baller, W. R. (1936) A study of the present social status of a group of adults who, when they were in elementary schools, were classified mentally deficient. Genet. Psychol. Monogr. 18:165.

Bereiter, C., and Englemann, S. (1966) Teaching Disadvantaged Children in the Preschool. Englewood Cliffs, New Jersey: Prentice-Hall.

Bernstein, B. (1971) Class, Codes, and Control. London: Routledge and Kegan Paul.

Burt, C. L. (1958) The inheritance of mental ability. Am. Psychol. 13:1.

Charles, D. C. (1953) Ability and accomplishment of persons earlier judged mentally deficient. Genet. Psychol. Monogr. 47:3.

Hebb, D. O. (1948) The Organization of Behaviour. New York: Wiley & Sons.

Heber, R., and Garber, H. (1975) Progress Report II: An experiment in the prevention of cultural-familial retardation. Proc. 3rd Congr. IASSMD. 1973, 1:34. (See also this Congress, Volume I, p. 119.)

Hess, R. D., and Shipman, V. C. (1965) Early experience and the socialization of cognitive modes in children. Child Dev. 36:869.

Hunt, J. McV. (1961) Intelligence and Experience. New York: Ronald.

Jencks, C. et al. (1972) Inequality: A Reassessment of the Effect of Family and Schooling in America. New York: Basic Books.

Jensen, A. R. (1969) How much can we boost IQ and scholastic achievement? Harvard Educ. Rev. 39:1.

Jensen, A. R. (1975) The problem of genotype-environment correlation in the estimation of heritability from monozygotic and dizygotic twins. Acta Genet. Med. Gemell.

Jones, M. C., Bayley, N., MacFarlane, J. W., and Honzik, M. P. (1971) The Course of Human Development. Waltham, Massachusetts: Zerox Publishing.

Kamin, L. J. (1974) The Science and Politics of IQ. Potomac, Maryland: Lawrence Erlbaum.

Labov, W. (1970) The logic of non-standard English. In Language and Poverty (Ed. Williams, F.). Chicago: Markham, pp. 153—189.

Loehlin, J. C., Lindzey, G., and Spuhler, J. N. (1975) Race Differences in Intelligence. San Francisco: W. H. Freeman.

Meichenbaum, D. A., and Turk, L. (1972) Implications of research on disadvantaged children and cognitive training programs for educational television. J. Spec. Educ. 6:27.

Miller, G. A., and McNeill, D. (1969) Psycholinguistics. In Handbook of Social Psychology (Eds. Lindzey, G., and Aronson, E.). Reading, Massachusetts: Addison-Wesley.

Skeels, H. M. (1966) Adult status of children with contrasting early life experiences: A follow-up study. Monogr. Soc. Res. Child Dev. 23. No. 68.

Stott, D. H. (1971) Behavioural aspects of learning disabilities: Assessment and remediation. Experimental Publication System. 11:400.

RESEARCH TO PRACTICE IN MENTAL RETARDATION
Education and Training, Volume II
Edited by Peter Mittler
Copyright 1977   I.A.S.S.M.D.

UNDERSTANDING INTELLECTUAL DYSFUNCTIONS

J. P. Das
University of Alberta,
Edmonton, Alberta, Canada

For the last few years, there has been an increasing tendency to look at processes rather than differences in abilities. Global measures of intelligence have, at best, been treated as the beginning of understanding intellectually disparate groups of children rather than as the end. This shift from the study of abilities to an investigation of processes has necessitated the search for an integrative model of intellectual processes. We have used such a model, borrowing its essentials from Luria, in order to understand mental retardation and learning disability, particularly reading deficit.

First, the model: Luria (1966a, 1966b, 1969, 1973) has proposed a model that divides the human brain into three functional systems or blocks. The first block consists of the upper brain stem, the reticular formation and the oldest parts of the limbic cortex and the hippocampus. It is responsible for maintaining wakefulness and arousal. The second block of the brain includes the posterior cortex (parietal, occipital, and fronto-temporal lobes) and the underlying structures. It is responsible for the input, recoding, and storage of information and is organized hierarchically. Deeper tertiary (or overlapping) zones synthesize information from primary (modality-specific) zones. Both simultaneous and successive processing occur in this second block. The third block of the brain consists of the prefrontal lobes, and is responsible for the construction and execution of plans or programs. Through extensive connections with the other two blocks, it regulates and controls purposeful conscious action.

Simultaneous processing involves the synthesis of separate elements into groups that generally have spatial overtones, all portions of the synthesis being surveyable or accessible without dependence upon their position within the synthesis. This type of processing is required, for instance, in the formation of any holistic gestalt, or in the discovery of the relationships among two or more objects.

Simultaneous processing is impaired when the parietal-occipital regions of the brain are damaged. While the patient generally remains conscious and aware and retains narrative speech, he does exhibit deficits in certain kinds of tasks. Depending upon the depth and exact location of the lesion, the following may be impaired: understanding of logico-grammatical speech (e.g., who is your father's brother?), spatial orientation (confusing east and west), and executing spatial instructions (when told to "draw a square above a circle," the patient draws a square and then a circle, in no particular relationship).

Successive processing involves the integration of separate elements into groups whose essential nature is temporal. Portions of this synthesis are accessible only in the temporal order of the series—each element leads to only one other, and access to any element is dependent upon the preceding elements. Successive processing is necessary for the formation or production of any ordered series of events.

Disturbances of successive processing result from damage to the fronto-temporal regions of the brain. Again, depending upon the depth and location of the lesion, the following may be impaired: smooth serial actions (either perseveration takes place or order of actions is disrupted), retention and reproduction of rhythm and melody, and serial recall (though as many as ten items can be recalled, the patient cannot learn to order them correctly). The patient retains conscious awareness, but finds that he must make a voluntary effort to perform simple serial movements; these movements have become de-automatized.

In our modified form, we propose that information integration has four basic units: the input, the sensory register, the central processing unit, and the output unit.

A stimulus may be presented to any one of the receptors, extero-, intero-, or proprioceptors, and within exteroceptors to any one of the sense modalities. Further, the input may be presented in a parallel (simultaneous) or a serial (successive) manner. The stimulus is immediately registered by the sensory register. The information so registered is passed on for central processing.

The central processing unit has three major components: that which processes separate information into simultaneous groups, that which processes discrete information into temporally organized successive series, and the decision-making and planning component, which uses the information so integrated by the other two components. The processing in these components is not affected by the form of the sensory input—visual information may be processed successively as auditory information may be processed simultaneously. It is suggested, following Luria (1966a), that these components can be identified with the functions of specific parts of the cortex—the occipital-parietal area has evolved to specialize in simultaneous synthesis; the successive is located in the anterior regions, particularly in the fronto-temporal area. Both of these are concerned with coding and storage of information; they do not plan, regulate, or control conscious behavior. That function is carried out by the frontal lobe as suggested by Luria on the basis of clinical observations.

The model assumes that the two modes of processing information are available to the individual. The selection of either or both modes will depend on two conditions: 1) the individual's habitual mode of processing information as determined by sociocultural and genetic factors, and 2) the demands of the task.

The third component, which could be labelled thinking, utilizes coded information and determines the best possible plan for action. Perhaps it is also crucial for the emergence of causal thinking, which Hess (1967) describes as "an integrative activity which brings simultaneous and successive patterns of nervous excitation into a subjectively meaningful frame of reference (p. 1283)."

A theory of cognitive functions such as ours probably relates to Kant's theory of knowledge, especially to the part that discusses space and time. According to Kant, the outer world supplies the stimuli for sensation, but an individual's own psychic structure codes these in space and time. Spatial coding can be inferred from our experiences, but it does not form a part of the object that we experience. The same is true of temporal coding. Spatial ordering, according to Kant, is simultaneous, whereas temporal ordering is successive. However, we cannot attribute to Kant the notion that spatially presented materials can be ordered successively and, similarly, that temporally appearing experiences may be ordered simultaneously in groups as our simultaneous-successive model assumes. Nonetheless, in Kant's *Critique of Pure Reason,* ordering is done centrally, rather than at the level of sense experience. It is an integral mechanism of thought.

The philosopher's acute observation of human thought processes certainly finds a home in the functional areas of the brain. Luria's painstaking explorations for mapping cognitive functions indeed support the two basic coding processes, simultaneous and successive. Over and beyond coding are planning and decision-making. We have pictured these in the model, and following Luria, locate them in the frontal lobes. A parallel for these in Kant's system is judgment. Since judgment is closely related to acts, and the evaluation of the acts in terms of their effects, it is closely related to the old concept of volition. Switching back to brain localization, volition can be placed in the frontal lobe and its adjacent areas. Plans of behavior are guided by affective and ethical considerations as much as by their desired goals. Judgments in Kant's *Critique* can be similarly characterized. In the final analysis, then, the clinical investigations of Luria mesh nicely with the Kantian theory of knowledge; and in a genuinely modest manner, our factor analyses have established the invariance of simultaneous and successive processing of information.

In conclusion, however, it is fair to admit that we have merely begun to understand the complex question of intellectual dysfunctions in terms of processes. Conceptual clarity, such as between the notions of process and strategy, has not been achieved, and practical applications of the model are being tried out. However, we feel that process-oriented models such as ours delineate how performances come about. Therein lies their strength and usefulness.

REFERENCES

Hess, W. R. (1967) Causality, consciousness and cerebral organization. Science 158:1279.
Luria, A. R. (1966a) Higher Cortical Functions in Man. New York: Basic Books.
Luria, A. R. (1966b) Human Brain and Psychological Processes. New York: Harper & Row.
Luria, A. R. (1969) The origin and cerebral organization of man's conscious action. An evening lecture to the XIX International Congress of Psychology, London.
Luria, A. R. (1973) The Working Brain. Harmondsworth: Penguin.

RESEARCH TO PRACTICE IN MENTAL RETARDATION
Education and Training, Volume II
Edited by Peter Mittler
Copyright 1977 I.A.S.S.M.D.

SPECIFIC AND GENERAL COGNITIVE DEFICIT

N. O'Connor
MRC Developmental Psychology Unit,
Drayton House, Gordon Street, London WC1

Consecutive process learning models have made the implicit assumption that any weak link will break the chain of information processing and so lead to cognitive deficits.

Unfortunately, the consecutive model and the assumption concerning the interruption of the whole chain of events by the interruption of one process is inappropriate for children and for the mentally handicapped. The reason it is inappropriate is that in the case of the severely subnormal, neuropathology characteristically affects the cortex at or before birth either through biochemical anomalies or through congenital abnormalities, or by reason of birth accidents involving intravenous and intracranial bleeding and resulting in porencephaly or other massive lesions. In all subnormality, therefore, neuropathology is non-specific or sufficiently extensive to affect all functions. It also occurs before specialisation of function and therefore affects all functions by retarding them. As a result, a consecutive learning model such as that presented in Figure 1 is likely to be affected at all points and not just at one processing stage.

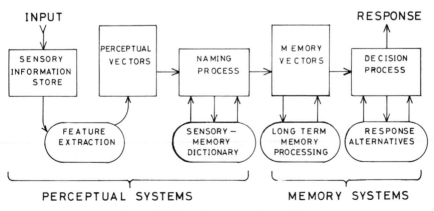

Figure 1. Information processing model.

An alternative paradigm, the subdiagnostic approach, for example, where Down's syndrome cases are compared with mental age—matched subnormals of unspecified diagnosis, brings out better differentiations from a psychological viewpoint. Work such as that of O'Connor and Hermelin (1961), Frith and Frith (1974), and Dodd (1975) in our laboratories is pertinent here. However, once again there are objections to such a model. They are threefold. First, few clearcut groups exist in numbers large enough to make group comparisons easy. Second, there are sometimes problems about diagnosis, for example in the borderland between autistic and psychotic children, between exogenous and endogenous subnormals, and in diagnosing hyperkinesis. The third, chief, and overriding objection, however, is that all kinds of neuropathology, whatever clinical subdiagnosis they indicate, have closely similar psychological consequences. Thus, although there are two or three hundred clinical subdiagnoses, the pattern of learning failure is nearly identical in all cases and it would not be useful, therefore, to follow either one of the above paradigms exclusively. Each may have some value in increasing information but each fails signally to surmount the basic obstacle in learning deficit analysis in relation to the subnormal. That is, each fails to account for the fact that learning failure in the subnormal follows a developmental pattern, a mental age progression, unlike, for example, developmental dysphasia, which retards only language, or autism, which may or may not be associated with subnormality, but which especially handicaps social responses. Subnormality does, however, resemble deafness in certain respects. Just as subnormal learning progresses developmentally—that is repeating all normal stages, but more slowly—so the acquisition of language by the deaf follows a similar pattern (Dodd, 1976).

This finding suggests that not only can 'central' or general handicap create a developmental kind of handicap but also a specific deficit with language can result in the same kind of developmental handicap as in deafness. It also leads us to ask how often such parallels occur and how many modality defects or specific output dysfunctions can simulate subnormality?

A corresponding set of studies that have been built up in the area of information processing provide us with an interesting parallel. The outline theory of these studies concerns the extent to which mental processing or cognitive operations such as selection, categorisation, and coding, are modality specific or modality independent. The question is important from the viewpoint of any comparison of the generally handicapped, e.g., the subnormal, and the specifically handicapped, e.g., deaf and blind children. Historically, the theory made its debut in relation to abnormal psychology through the observations so often quoted of von Senden (1932), and because of the subsequent work of Riesen (1947) and Gregory (1966). Gregory suggested that those who had been congenitally blind and had recovered their sight would need to relearn the significance of visual cues. Other workers such as Brown (1973), with the blind, and Furth (1966), with the deaf, have taken other views. These authors have often maintained, for example, that 'visual' concepts are innate and in a sense need no support from sight, or alternatively, that damage to one receptor leaves the functioning of others unimpaired. The relationship between peripheral handicap and more general handicap, may thus vary according to the operation in question.

To test this possibility, Dr. Hermelin and I have carried out a number of experiments, an outline of which is given here. In many of these, both specifically handicapped and generally handicapped subjects were involved. Usually the specifically handicapped were either the deaf or the blind; consequently the experiments are to some extent related to temporal, or alternatively to spatial perception.

The first experiments I will describe are concerned with space. One of the early experiments in this series (Hermelin and O'Connor, 1971) was concerned with the manner in which tactual and visual ordering in space were related. Severely retarded autistic children, blind children, and seeing adults, and blindfolded children and adults participated. Subjects were given a flat board with four points on it. They placed two fingers of each hand on the four positions and answered with a prearranged verbal response when any one finger was touched with a probe (Figure 2). When their responses achieved criterion, their

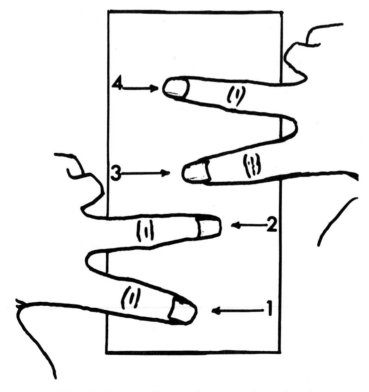

Figure 2. Position of hands in hand reversal experiment.

hands were switched and the task continued. Table 1 gives the results. It is clear that when blindfolded subjects responded, they did so with body-oriented responses whether the subjects were of high or low IQ and irrespective of previous visual experience. Blind children's behaviour, therefore, is not caused by lack of visual experience. Nor is intelligence relevant to the elected strategy adopted under these conditions. In the presence of sight, responses tend to be "location responses." In the absence of sight they tend to be "finger" identified responses. So the presence or absence of a sensory system determines in this case how space is represented in the internal coding system, as if each modality has its own coding system.

O'Connor and Hermelin (1975) subsequently asked subjects to decide whether or not two shapes examined by touch could form a square if the shapes were pushed close together. A blind group, a sighted group, and blindfold sighted group helped in this experiment (Figure 3). As can be seen, some shapes were rotated and some were not. Results are given in Table 2. They show that blind and blindfold children are identical in their results. Sighted children, of course, are much better, but considering the blind and blindfold only, a lifetime of experience of sight is once again of little value in a task that involves the mental manipulation of space. This result suggests that spatial intuition is innate rather than acquired in this case. It is regrettable that we have no controls for mental age in this experiment.

We can account for these findings by assuming that tactile-spatial parameters are given in cortical structure, independent of experience, or that touch or vision are spatially equivalent, both perceptually and mnemonically. The latter cannot be the case, of course, because a rotation effect occurs in vision, but not in touch. However, is the first proposition true? Can we find an experiment in which it is not? A third experiment to test this possibility was carried out. A right and a left plastic hand were presented tactually to blind and blindfold subjects. In this case, shape was not relevant because the two hands were the same shape, one being the mirror image of the other. Subjects had to say which hand was presented to them. The blindfolded obviously do better than the blind. Previous visual experience therefore counts in this instance (Table 3).

Table 1. Frequency of responses after hand reversal

	Finger response	Location response	Random response
10 seeing, normal children	158	239	3
10 seeing, autistic children	124	251	25
10 blindfolded adults	398	0	2
10 blindfolded normal children	297	85	18
10 blind children	276	116	8

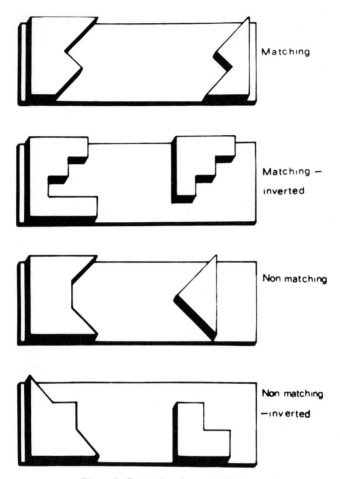

Figure 3. Rotated and unrotated shapes.

Table 2. Shapes (total error scores by groups and presentations)

	Rotated	Unrotated	Totals
Blind	139	124	263
Blindfold	154	159	313
Sighted	38	15	53
Totals	331	298	629

Table 3. Hands (total error scores by groups and orientations)

	Up	Down	Right	Left	Toward E	Away from E	Totals
Blind	39	39	39	38	44	46	245
Blindfold	19	26	23	22	13	26	129
Sighted	10	15	16	7	9	22	79
Totals	68	80	78	67	66	94	453

From all the experiments described so far, one could conclude that the mental reorganisation or recoding of spatial forms or order in space first recorded by touch or kinesthesis is not handicapped either by subnormality of intelligence nor by the congenital absence of vision. On the other hand, judged orientation may be based on visual experience.

Temporal ordering, as distinct from spatial ordering, is also influenced by specific or general handicap, and in some accounts of development, such as that of Piaget (1927), for example, the one is made to depend on the other. The following experiments report studies of temporal ordering in subnormal, deaf, and blind children.

The manipulation of time has at least two aspects, estimates of duration and estimates of, or memory for, order or sequence. We made our first observations with duration in which subjects were taught to differentiate intervals of two seconds and six seconds by touch. Children of mental age of eight years can do this task, and we trained deaf, blind, normal, and subnormal children to differentiate such intervals by touch, using a rotary probe in the palm of the hand and asking the subject to say whether or not two successive intervals were of the same or different durations. Having established the differentiation criterion, we transferred the task to sound or vision, using sounds with the blind or lights with the deaf subjects. Normal and subnormal controls were also included.

Irrespective of the type of handicap or lack of it, no transfer to the new modalities occurred. Coding in this instance (O'Connor and Hermelin, 1971) must have been modality-specific. Transfer did occur to different tactile stimuli but not across modalities. This particular test proved the specificity of estimates of duration and showed that despite very adequate verbal formulations on the part of nearly all subjects, indicating that they understood the principle of solution, no cross modal transfer occurred.

In another task in which digits were presented visually in a horizontal row, the first digit seen was not necessarily the one on the left. In other words, the sequential or temporal order was not necessarily the left to right, or "reading," order. Subjects in the first part of this study were asked to watch the display and to say, after it had finished, which was the middle digit. Deaf and hearing children chose the visually middle digit in this case, that is the second from the left in a set of three. When in the second part of the study they were asked to watch a display and then say, when it finished, what the three digits were, many deaf and many subnormal children gave visual or left to right read outs, as distinct from auditory successive read outs, when the two were incongruent. Hearing children with almost no exceptions gave auditory successive read outs.

We have repeated this experiment with subnormal children (Miklausic, 1976) and found that the election of auditory or visual coding was dependent on verbal IQ, with a cut off close to IQ 65. Deafness, therefore, parallels verbal IQ in affecting the choice of strategy involved. The results are also confirmed by presenting Latin and Arabic letters to young children between ages 6 and 11. With Latin letters, children show increasing verbal-sequential responses with age. With Arabic letters, which English children cannot code verbally, age effects are less marked. These experiments tend to confirm the inefficiency of subvocal "thought-speech" in both deaf and subnormal children.

Other experiments have shown that deaf children can remember sequential order but tend not to do so if alternative visual-spatial orders are available (O'Connor and Hermelin, 1973), and that deaf children tend to 'tag' the order of visually presented digits visually, and hearing children verbally, in such a way that reversed recall is easier for the deaf. Presumably, the motor habits of forward ordering in subvocal speech are more difficult to reverse than the visual inspection of a visual image (O'Connor and Hermelin, 1976). We have found the same freedom from interference phenomena in subnormals.

In these experiments we have shown that sometimes coding strategies are specific to the modality in which they occur, as in the three digits experiment. When visually presented material is recorded subvocally, output is auditory-verbal-sequential, the same as input. When recorded visually, it is left to right, and, therefore, output is not the same as input. In this experiment it turned out that deaf and subnormal children adopted similar strategies. We have also shown, however, that in other experiments, coding strategies appear not to be specific to the modalities involved, and, as a result, modality of input may be irrelevant so far as output is concerned. So, for example, shape or form recognition or manipulation is unaffected by congenital blindness and consequent lack of visual experience. Our experiments in this area are incomplete and so far do not include subnormal controls. However, O'Connor and Hermelin (1961) showed that there was little visual-perceptual impairment in severely subnormal patients so far as orientation was concerned when memory and motor output were not involved. In the current series of studies we have shown that the congenitally blind, on the other hand, and even the blindfolded individuals, are hampered in relation to orientation, although of course not in relation to form. It might be said, therefore, that form or shape is equivalent across modalities but that orientation is specific to visual input.

This series of comparisons of deaf, blind, and subnormal subjects has shown that a number of strategies, such as certain basic aspects of form perception, are unaffected by low mental age or absence of vision, perhaps because, as Kant

(1781) and William James (1890) thought, these are intuitive aspects of perception and are neither products of perceptual experience nor conceptual constructs. The fact that they exist in the severely subnormal shows in addition that they are present from an early age and "primitive" in a neuropathological sense of that word. Such a view would accord with T. G. R. Bower's (1974) view of the Gestalt-like character of the normal infant's visual development.

One could say, therefore, that some operations are modality-specific and that the loss of the modality for any reason leads to the adoption of a substitute encoding strategy. Others, however, are general or transferable. In some instances, therefore, specific handicaps force central coding changes and in others this does not occur. Where coding is specific to the modality involved, and alternative coding procedures are not possible, specific handicaps might create general deficits. An appropriate theory of perception or learning to account for this might be Hebb's (1949) phase sequence theory.

SUMMARY

Experimental studies of learning failure have used a consecutive processing learning model. This has limitations. In subnormality, neuropathology and psychopathology do not correspond. An alternative strategy would be to study a single psychological process across many diagnostic groups including subnormality. In this way specific and general handicaps could be compared.

REFERENCES

Bower, T. G. R. (1974) Development in Infancy. San Francisco: W. H. Freeman.

Brown, B. (1973) Spatial perception in the blind. Personal communication.

Dodd, B. (1975) Recognition and reproduction of words by Down's syndrome and non-Down's syndrome retarded children. Amer. J. Ment. Defic. 80:306.

Dodd, B. (1976) The phonological system of deaf children J. Speech Hear. Dis. 41:185.

Frith, U., and Frith, C. D. (1974) Specific motor disabilities in Down's syndrome. J. Child. Psychol. Psychiat. 15:293.

Furth, H. G. (1966) Thinking Without Language: Psychological Implications of Deafness. Canada: Collier-Macmillan.

Gregory, R. L. (1966) Eye and Brain. London: Weidenfeld and Nicolson.

Hebb, D. O. (1949) The Organization of Behavior London: Chapman & Hall.

Hermelin, B., and O'Connor, N. (1971) Spatial coding in normal, autistic, and blind children. Percept. Mot. Skills 33:127.

James, W. (1890) The Principles of Psychology. New York: Dover Publications, 1950. Originally published 1890 (Henry Holt. Copyright 1918. Alice H. James)

Kant, I. (1781) Kritik der reinen Vernunft. Riga: Hartknoch. (Translated by N. Kemp Smith. London: Macmillan, 1933)

Miklausic, K. (1976) The spatial and temporal organization of short term memory in the severely subnormal. Degree dissertation, University of London.

O'Connor, N., and Hermelin, B. (1961) Visual and stereognostic shape recognition in normal children and mongol and non-mongol imbeciles. J. Ment. Defic. Res. 5:63.

O'Connor, N., and Hermelin, B. (1971) Inter- and intra-modal transfer in children with modality specific and general handicaps. Brit. J. Soc. Clin. Psychol. 10:346.

O'Connor, N., and Hermelin, B. (1973) Short-term memory for the order of pictures and syllables by deaf and hearing children. Neuropsychologia 11:437.

O'Connor, N., and Hermelin, B. (1975) Modality specific spatial coordinates. Percept. Psychophys. 17:213.

O'Connor, N., and Hermelin, B. (1976) Backward and forward recall by deaf and hearing children. Q. J. Exp. Psychol. 28:89.

Piaget, J. (1927) The Child's Conception of Time. Translated by A. J. Pomerans (First published in Great Britain, 1969) London: Routledge & Kegan Paul.

Riesen, A. H. (1947) The development of visual perception in man and chimpanzees. Science 106:107.

Senden, M. von (1932) Raum und Gestaltauffassung bei operierten Blindgeborenen vor und nach der Operation. Leipzig: Barth.

RESEARCH TO PRACTICE IN MENTAL RETARDATION
Education and Training, Volume II
Edited by Peter Mittler
Copyright 1977 I.A.S.S.M.D.

PIAGET'S THEORY OF COGNITIVE DEVELOPMENT AND ITS RELATIONSHIP TO SEVERELY AND PROFOUNDLY RETARDED CHILDREN

J. V. Kahn
*University of Illinois at Chicago Circle, Chicago,
Illinois 60680, United States*

There have been a large number of recent studies on infant development that have made use of Piaget's sensorimotor period. Many severely and profoundly retarded children and adults can also be shown to be functioning cognitively at the sensorimotor level. However, there has been very little research relating Piaget's theory to these low functioning retarded children. Woodward (1959) first demonstrated that many profoundly retarded children and adolescents could be identified as functioning at one of the six stages of Piaget's sensorimotor period. Since Woodward's study there have been only a handful of research reports on this topic (Robinson, 1974; Wohlheuter and Sindberg, 1975; Bricker and Bricker, 1973).

EXPERIMENT 1

Much of the research, both with infants and with the retarded, has made use of one of the assessment instruments based on Piaget's writings. It appears from a review of the literature that the Uzgiris and Hunt (1975) scales are the most frequently used of the sensorimotor instruments. With the recent publication of these scales, they will probably be used even more frequently. The Uzgiris and Hunt scales are the most comprehensive available and have been shown to be both reliable and valid with infants (Uzgiris and Hunt, 1975). These scales of sensorimotor period development could be of great use in assessing the cognitive functioning of severely and profoundly retarded children. However, if the Uzgiris and Hunt scales are to be used with confidence with low functioning retarded children, we must be able to demonstrate reliability and validity for the scales with such a population. This is necessary because we cannot assume that a reliable and valid infant test will also be reliable and valid with a population that is replete with brain defects and experiential deficits. Therefore, this study was designed to investigate the reliability and validity of the Uzgiris and Hunt scales with just such a population.

Method

Subjects   The subjects were 30 institutionalized children and 33 children living at home and attending day care schools. These children were between 42 and 126 months of age with a mean of 67 months.

Procedure   Each of the subjects was individually assessed on each of the seven Uzgiris and Hunt (1975) scales. Thirty of these children were assessed a second time on these scales, 15 by the same examiner and 15 by a different examiner. The two testings were scheduled one week apart to control for the day of the week and time of day of testing. For statistical analyses, other than determining reliability coefficients, the scores from the first testing were used.

Results and Discussion

Interexaminer reliabilities ranged from 0.78 to 0.95, and test-retest reliabilities ranged from 0.88 to 0.96. Scalogram analyses were undertaken on six of the seven scales, no analysis being performed on the Development of Schemas scale. The results of the six scalogram analyses indicated ordinality of the items on each of the scales.

It appears that the seven Uzgiris and Hunt scales can be used reliably, and that six of the scales can be used validly, with severely and profoundly retarded children.

EXPERIMENT 2

The second study made use of the Uzgiris and Hunt Scales. This study was designed to investigate the relationship of stage six of Piaget's sensorimotor period and the development of expressive language.

A considerable body of research has been directed to the development of speech with children who have never exhibited expressive language (e.g., Bricker and Bricker, 1970; Guess, Rutherford, and Twichell, 1969; Sailor, Guess, and Baer, 1973; Sherman, 1965; Sloane, Johnson, and Harris, 1968). The procedures used in this research have emphasized operant conditioning techniques. While these studies have demonstrated considerable success for the operant procedures, they have been lacking in one area. That is, the attempts to develop speech with nonverbal retarded children have not, on the whole, been successful in generating generalization so that, after the training has been completed, the children will continue to increase their vocabulary and improve their grammatical structure (Sailor, Guess, and Baer, 1973). A plausible explanation for this lack of generalization, and for the failure of some children to acquire expressive language despite these operant conditioning efforts, is that these children might not have the cognitive structures necessary for the acquisition of expressive language.

According to Piaget (1951, 1963), language is acquired beginning during stage six of the sensorimotor period. Piaget's explanation of the transition from perceptual and motor behaviors to the verbal is based on his theory of the development of mental images. Piaget states that "During stages one to five of sensorimotor imitation there are no mental images. In stage six of this period, imaged representation makes its appearance" (1951, p. 74). This means that during stage six, the child acquires the ability to represent to himself objects and events that he is not directly perceiving. In other words, he has developed the necessary cognitive structures for representation and, therefore, is capable of acquiring expressive language.

Method

Subjects   The subjects in this study were living at home and attending day care schools for severely and profoundly retarded children. Eight of the children had demonstrated vocabularies exceeding ten words. They had chronological ages (CAs) ranging from 53 to 98 months, with a mean of 71 months. The other eight children studied had demonstrated a complete absence of expressive language at home and at school. They had CAs ranging from 47 to 92 months, with a mean of 67 months. There was no significant difference among the CAs of the two groups.

Procedure   All of the children were individually assessed using the Uzgiris and Hunt (1975) scales.

Results and Discussion

The findings indicated that all of the verbal children had achieved stage six of the sensorimotor period. Of the nonverbal children, only three demonstrated any evidence of having achieved stage six level functioning. In addition, correlations indicated moderate to strong relationships among cognitive functioning and verbal performance ($r = 0.51$ to 0.82).

These findings appear to support Piaget's contention that stage six of the sensorimotor period is prerequisite to the acquisition of meaningful speech. It was, therefore, concluded that stage six functioning is necessary, although not sufficient for the acquisition of expressive language.

The implications of these findings for the training of nonlanguage, profoundly retarded children to acquire language are potentially extensive. If, as these findings seem to indicate, the cognitive structures that develop during stage six of Piaget's sensorimotor period are necessary for the acquisition of expressive language, then training of nonlanguage, profoundly retarded children to develop language skills should begin with an assessment of their cognitive level. According to this position, those children who are at stage six could then reasonably be expected to learn expressive language with any reasonable degree of efficiency. These children would probably benefit more from training activities directed toward raising their cognitive level. After this is accomplished, so that they are functioning at stage six, it would then be reasonable to expect them to learn language from operant procedures with a much higher degree of efficiency. More research of this sort is necessary to verify these conclusions.

EXPERIMENT 3

If the implications of the preceding study are to be useful (i.e., if children should receive cognitive training to achieve stage six before expressive language training), it is necessary to demonstrate that training can accelerate the rate of cognitive development of severely and profoundly retarded children. This study attempted to demonstrate the feasibility of such a training procedure.

Method

Subjects   The subjects in the present study were eight children living in a residential facility for retarded children. None of the children in this study had ever demonstrated any expressive communication skills. These children were also all functioning well below the ceiling on each of the scales of the Uzgiris and Hunt (1975) instrument. The children were 43 to 78 months of age, with a mean of 57 months. The subjects were matched for age, etiology, and scores on the Uzgiris and Hunt scales and then randomly assigned to either the experimental group or the control group.

Procedure   Each of the subjects were individually given a pretest and a posttest using the four Uzgiris and Hunt scales. The four control subjects received only the pretest, and six months later the posttest, with no special training in the interim. The four experimental subjects received the pretest, followed by individual training in an isolated room for 45 minutes a day, three days a week, for six months and then the posttest. The training was individualized for each child and consisted of a concentrated effort to have the child demonstrate gains in his performance in the area of Object Permanence. Positive reinforcement (food and praise) was used to keep the children performing on the task. The steps followed in the training procedure were those of the Object Permanence scale of the Uzgiris and Hunt Instrument. This order was followed because the steps for this scale were found to be ordinal with severely and profoundly retarded children. The criterion for each step was considered achieved when the subject demonstrated success on the step, with no errors, for two consecutive sessions. Training then began on the next step through successive approximations of that step. If repeated efforts on the next step were unsuccessful, overlearning of the preceding step was begun.

To explain further the training procedure used in this study, two concrete examples are given. In the first case, the child could locate an object (a doll) when it was partially covered but not when totally covered. We started with the doll half covered (legs and feet showing) and slowly, step by step, covered more of the doll with the child finding it at each successive step. Eventually, the doll was totally covered. At this point, the doll was placed under the cover so as to present a large lump. The child was able to find the doll and the lump was gradually made smaller until the child could find the doll totally covered and laying flat.

The second example presents a simpler procedure though the procedure took as long as the one previously presented. In this case, the child could find an object when it was covered by one screen. When the object was alternately hidden under one of two screens, however, he did not always go to the correct screen first. Since the child did search under the second screen when wrong at first, just letting him practice this task would eventually lead him to accommodate his cognitive structures and solve the problem correctly. This was based on Piaget's theory that children develop cognitively through interacting with the environment.

Results and Discussion

All four of the experimental subjects achieved criterion for the highest item on the Object Permanence scale of the Uzgiris and Hunt (1975) instrument on the posttest. This represents gains from the pretest ranging from seven to 13 steps with a mean gain of 11 steps. In addition, three of the experimental subjects demonstrated improvement on five of the other six Uzgiris and Hunt scales, the other experimental subject gaining on four of the scales. These gains range from one to five steps.

Only one of the control subjects showed any change in functioning on these scales from the pretest to the posttest. This subject gained two steps on the Object Permanence scale and one step on the Means scale. However, he also lost two steps on the Spatial Relations scale.

The finding of generalization to scales other than the one on which the experimental subjects were trained is crucial to this study, although the generalization was, admittedly, limited. These findings are of potential importance to those involved with training severely and profoundly retarded children. However, this statement must be qualified for two reasons. First, this study appears to have two limitations. The number of subjects used in this study is admittedly small. While it seems unlikely that the dramatic improvements shown by the experimental subjects are just specific to the present study, replications need to be performed so as to nullify this argument. In addition, the use of a control group, rather than a placebo group, limits the generalization of these findings to other situations. The improvement could have been due to the specific training procedure utilized in this study or merely to the individual attention given the experimental subjects. However, the far greater improvement shown by the experimental subjects in the area of Object Permanence than in the other areas of sensorimotor intelligence, indicates that the training procedure did have some effect. Also, while the cause of the improvement may be in doubt, there was a good deal of improvement in a relatively short period of time. This finding by itself is significant.

The second factor, which could limit the importance of these findings, deals with the question of whether these findings are of any practical significance. The practical significance of these findings can at present only be hypothesized. More research is needed to resolve the many as yet unanswered questions before the full impact of this research can be known. It is necessary to determine if this sort of training leads to more efficient training in the various skill areas in which severely and profoundly retarded children are usually deficient (e.g., self-care skills, language skills, etc.).

CONCLUSIONS

This series of studies has increased the potential applications of Piaget's theory with severely and profoundly retarded children. The finding that the Uzgiris and Hunt scales are reliable and ordinal with severely and profoundly retarded children gives us an excellent instrument for assessing these children. These studies also support the contention that there are cognitive abilities that must precede certain skill acquisition and that the training of cognition is feasible.

Research is needed to pinpoint the precise areas and levels of sensorimotor functioning that are necessary for the learning of various skills.

SUMMARY

Three studies are presented here. One study investigated the reliability and validity of the Uzgiris and Hunt scales with retarded children. Another study explored the relationship of sensorimotor period functioning and the acquisition of language. The third study attempted to accelerate retarded children's development of the concept of object permanence.

REFERENCES

Bricker, W. A., and Bricker, D. D. (1970) A program of language training for the severely handicapped child. Except. Child. 37:101.
Bricker, D. D., and Bricker, W. A. (1973) Infant, Toddler, and Preschool Research and Intervention Project Report: Year III. IMRID Behavioral Science Monograph No. 23, Nashville, Tennessee: George Peabody College.

Guess, D., Rutherford, F., and Twichell, A. (1969) Speech acquisition in a mute, visually impaired adolescent. The New Outlook for the Blind, January.

Piaget, J. (1951) Play, Dreams, and Imitations in Childhood. New York: W. W. Norton.

Piaget, J. (1963) The Origins of Intelligence in Children. New York: W. W. Norton.

Robinson, C. (1974) Error patterns in level 4 and level 5 object permanence training. Amer. J. Ment. Defic. 78:389.

Sailor, W., Guess, D., and Baer, D. M. (1973) Functional language for verbally deficient children. Ment. Retard. 11:27.

Sherman, J. A. (1965) Use of reinforcement and imitation to reinstate verbal behavior in mute psychotics. J. Abnorm. Psychol. 70:155.

Sloane, H. N., Johnson, M. R., and Harris, F. R. (1968) Remedial procedures for teaching verbal behavior to speech deficient or defective young children. In Operant Procedures in Remedial Speech and Language Training (Eds. Sloane, H. N. and MacAulay, B. D.). Boston: Houghton-Mifflin.

Uzgiris, I. C., and Hunt, J. M. (1975) Assessment in Infancy: Ordinal Scales of Psychological Development. Urbana, Illinois: University of Illinois Press.

Wohlheuter, M. J., and Sindberg, R. M. (1975) Longitudinal development of object permanence in mentally retarded children: An exploratory study. Amer. J. Ment. Defic. 79:513.

Woodward, M. (1959). The behavior of idiots interpreted by Piaget's theory of sensorimotor development. Brit. J. Educ. Psychol. 29:60.

RESEARCH TO PRACTICE IN MENTAL RETARDATION
Education and Training, Volume II
Edited by Peter Mittler
Copyright 1977 I.A.S.S.M.D.

INTERPERSONAL COMPETENCIES OF THE MENTALLY RETARDED
A Piagetian Perspective

G. G. Affleck
University of Connecticut Health Center,
Farmington, Connecticut 06032, United States

In the recent literature on mental retardation, few issues have attracted more attention than the problem of social competence. Increasingly, we have come to recognize that one of the primary problems in the habilitation of moderately and mildly retarded persons in particular is, as one observer has put it, their "chronic lack of basic social skills, social immaturity, insecurity, and ineptness in interpersonal relations and situations" (McDaniel, 1960, p. 5). In this context, we have witnessed a proliferation of studies underscoring the significance of appropriate interpersonal behavior for an overall educational, vocational, and social adjustment of the mentally retarded student, worker, and citizen. Consequently, it was with some justification that, in 1968, Dunn challenged special educators to give the highest priority to the task of social skills development.

What have basic researchers contributed to our understanding of interpersonal phenomena among the mentally retarded? Basic to this problem is the controversy concerning the degree to which social functioning in its broadest sense is constrained by low intelligence. Some investigators (e.g., Capobianco and Cole, 1960; Goulet and Barclay, 1963) have reported significant relationships between mental age and social age among the retarded, and have appeared to be satisfied to conclude that observed differences in social-adjustment between retarded and nonretarded persons can be explained in terms of relative levels of general intellectual competence. This position has been criticized most recently by Kleck (1975) on the grounds that it reinforces the continuing "tenacity of the IQ" as the major dimension in the conceptualization and assessment of social adequacy in the mentally retarded.

In contrast, some authors, including Gunzburg (1965), have argued that much of the observed relationship between general intelligence and social performance is artifactual. Rather, what we observe as social immaturity among the retarded can be better explained by acknowledging our systematic failure to provide retarded persons with training in any but the most rudimentary skills for social living.

Whereas it would be difficult to deny that social skills development has received insufficient attention in our intervention programs with mentally retarded persons, it does not follow that we should ignore the intellective components of social/interpersonal functioning. Edgerton (1967) has argued convincingly that "the two competencies—intellectual and social—cannot be separated" (p. 216) in understanding the everyday lives of mentally retarded persons. Here, for example, the ability to deal with spatial, temporal, and numerical concepts may be quite important in achieving social effectiveness.

However, advocates of this position have paid little attention to what might be termed the "cognitive demands" of interpersonal behavioral competence per se. It is the central thesis of this paper that a sound analysis of the interpersonal competencies of mentally retarded persons must consider, among other factors, the role of cognitive functions in effective interpersonal interactions. What is being argued here is that we must begin to isolate and analyze the associations of specific cognitive skills with demonstrations of interpersonal effectiveness. In so doing we will reduce the emphasis on general intelligence (IQ) as the central marker in considerations of the social adequacy of retarded persons.

Preferably, this task will be guided by theories of cognitive development and social interaction. Kleck (1975) has evaluated the latter body of theory in an excellent discussion of Weinstein's model and its applications to the interpersonal problems faced by retarded persons (Weinstein, 1969). As a complement to Kleck's discussion, the remainder of the present chapter will focus on the contributions of cognitive-developmental theory.

THE PIAGETIAN PERSPECTIVE

One potentially heuristic but heretofore relatively ignored approach to the issue of interpersonal competence derives from Piaget's developmental framework. Whereas most of Piaget's work has dealt with developmental changes in the cognitive structuring of "nonpersonal" events (e.g., as in the conservation of number, mass, and volume), Piaget (1962) himself has assumed that there is no reason to believe that his work has no application to the interpersonal domain. Flavell (1963) agreed that there is some value in extending the Piagetian framework to the analysis of more "sanguine" developmental events, such as qualitative changes in the interpersonal behavioral repertoire. Later, Flavell (1968) underscored the significance of research on developmental changes in social cognition, or, the processing of information from the social/interpersonal environment.

In the Piagetian model, cognitive progress is characterized in part by the development (during middle childhood) of mental operations that serve to organize information about the environment and about oneself in relation to the environment. Essentially, mental operations are defined as internalized, reversible schemes, or logical plans, that impose some stability on the flux of perceived events. In effect, the appearance of operational thought marks the decline of childhood egocentrism. Gradually, the child develops the capacity to *decenter*, that is, to consider simultaneously more than one aspect of a situation. Decentration is observed in the child's growing differentiation between his and others' points of view as well as in his ability to compensate for the distortions engendered by changes in percepts (as observed in the well-known conservation experiments). In short, the child escapes the limitations of a singular and all-encompassing point of view and becomes competent at coordinating a number of perspectives in an organized, balanced manner.

Whereas a generally accepted formulation of decentration in the interpersonal domain is still lacking, Feffer and Suchotliff (1966) offered the following representative statement:

> The dovetailing of responses involved in effective social interaction requires that each participant modify his intended behavior in light of his anticipation of the other's reaction to this behavior. In order to accurately anticipate this reaction, one must be able to view his intended behavior from the perspective of the other. Modifying one's behavior in light of this anticipation further requires that one view the intended action from his own perspective at the same time. The cognitive organization of the individual capable of effective social interaction can accordingly be interpreted as one in which different viewpoints are considered in relation to each other such that the distortion engendered by a given perspective is equilibrated by a consideration of another perspective. (pp. 415–416)

In effect, Feffer regards social interaction as an implicit problem-solving situation requiring the "cognitive organization" of interpersonal perspectives. Elsewhere, Feffer (1970a) has expanded this hypothesis by elaborating the significance of a special social-cognitive scheme which he labels "role-taking ability." In the literature on child development, the construct of role-taking ability has taken on a variety of meanings, from the limited phenomenon of visual perspective-taking to the broad concept of social sensitivity. In Feffer's analysis, role-taking refers to the capacity of the person to recognize and coordinate self-other perspectives in the context of interpersonal interaction.

Much of the work of Feffer and his colleagues has been devoted to the delineation of stagelike achievements in role-taking proficiency. In this body of research, role-taking ability was measured with a specially designed projective-type instrument (Role-Taking Task) in which subjects provide stories from the perspectives of different characters (Feffer, 1959). In one study, Feffer and Gourevitch (1960) revealed various stages of role-taking development, culminating in the appearance of equilibrated social decentration at about the age of nine years. Perhaps the most significant finding was the demonstration of a specific relationship between level of role-taking performance and the presence of operational thought structures (as evidenced in classification and conservation behavior) among normal children.

Feffer (1970b) reported that role-taking development was associated with increasing mental rather than chronological age in a sample of mentally retarded children. This finding not only strengthens the validity of role-taking as a cognitive-developmental construct but also suggests that differences in role-taking performance between retarded and nonretarded children may be viewed in terms of a "developmental lag" hypothesis (see Zigler, 1973). This hypothesis, in which cognitive development among retarded children is seen as proceeding through universal stages but at a slower rate, may be a conceptually useful model for the explanation of differences between retarded and nonretarded persons in social-cognitive functions and their behavioral correlates.

The behavioral correlates of role-taking ability have been revealed in a number of investigations with intellectually normal persons. For example, role-taking proficiency was found to be related to cooperative behavior in children (Johnson, 1975) and to skillful communication behavior in adults (Feffer and Suchotliff, 1966).

ROLE-TAKING ABILITY AND
THE INTERPERSONAL COMPETENCIES
OF MENTALLY RETARDED PERSONS

Relatively less research has been done on the association of role-taking development with the achievement of interpersonal effectiveness among individuals who are mentally retarded. However, some preliminary findings pertaining to this question have been reported recently (Affleck, 1975a; 1975b; 1976). In the first of these studies, Affleck (1975a) found a significant relationship between role-taking ability (as measured by Feffer's Role-Taking Task) and the success with which mildly retarded young adults were able to resolve a number of everyday social conflicts presented in structured role-plays. Further, Affleck (1975b) reported that role-taking performance was a significant correlate of the extent to which dyads of retarded children were able to solve an interpersonal task requiring cooperative behavior in the form of reciprocal exchange.

In the most recent of these investigations, Affleck (1976) assessed the correlation between role-taking ability and a measure of interpersonal competence derived from Weinstein's analysis of the process of social interaction (Weinstein, 1969). Weinstein has argued that the interpersonally competent individual is able to exert some control over the responses of others—their thoughts, feelings, and actions. This achievement is mediated by the construction of a repertoire of manipulative tactics that enable the individual to accomplish personal goals in social encounters. "As such," according to Weinstein, "this concept is value free. . . . Competence is relative to the actor's purposes" (Weinstein, 1969, p. 755).

In the study by Affleck (1976), fifty mildly and moderately retarded children (ages 8–17) gave responses to two hypothetical situations involving the achievement of a personal goal that was dependent on changing the behavior of a target person (friend or subject's counselor). Specifically, each episode required a response on the part of the subject as to how he would convince the target person to allow him to watch his favorite television program when this objective was thwarted initially.

Among the responses of subjects to these episodes there was great variation in preferred strategies of interpersonal control. Only a few subjects were unable or unwilling to offer a line of action to secure the hypothesized goal. Many were content to rely on a simple request. Others believed that by begging or by threats of harm or punishment (negative sanctions), the goal could be achieved. A few were inclined to appeal to rules, fairness, or obligations (norm invocation) in order to change the other's behavior. Still others preferred the use of positive sanctions, or, offers of exchange, gifts, favors, or bargaining, in return for compliance with their requests.

The distribution of responses to both episodes were found to be related to subjects' relative levels of role-taking development. In particular, children above the median in role-taking ability tended to rely on the use of positive sanctions. According to Wood, Weinstein, and Parker (1967), this tactic is a relatively sophisticated one, in that it reflects an awareness of the "hedonic" motivations of others. Acting on this awareness helps to conserve the stability of future encounters with the other. In contrast, subjects low in role-taking ability were most apt to rely on a simple request to achieve their objectives. Wood, et al. (1967) viewed this tactic as a relatively primitive one for the accomplishment of many interpersonal goals.

Whereas, in this study, mental age and IQ were found to be associated with role-taking proficiency, neither general index of cognitive functioning was related to the distribution of tactical preferences. Accordingly, these preliminary findings provide some support for considering the role of social-cognitive competence in the achievement of interpersonal effectiveness by mentally retarded persons. Of course, no conclusions concerning the nature of this relationship between role-taking and interpersonal tactics were possible within the design limitations of this study. Whereas some investigators (Feffer, 1970a; Chandler, 1973) have argued that role-taking and other social-cognitive operations regulate interpersonal effectiveness, it is tenable that the development of effective tactics, perhaps through modeling and reinforcement processes, enables the child to maintain relationships that provide the necessary experiences for role-taking development to proceed.

CONCLUSION

The problem of social competence has received much attention in the recent literature on mental retardation. In his evaluation of this area, Zigler (1966) concluded that "we must abandon some simplistic notion of social competence in favor of a variety of continua theoretically based on the cognitive demands of the social requirements involved" (p. 116). The developing theoretical perspective outlined in this chapter may be viewed as a preliminary response to this challenge. Specifically, there may be some heuristic value in analyzing the interpersonal behavior of retarded individuals from a Piagetian perspective. One construct derived from Piaget's developmental framework—role-taking ability—has been shown to have a relationship with differential social performance among retarded children and adults.

It should be noted that one of the benefits of this approach is that it promotes a "positive" view of the behavior of mentally retarded persons. Its value lies in the fact that "it forces us to shift from looking at what retarded persons are not to looking at what they are" (Robinson and Robinson, 1965, p. 356). If future research confirms the validity of the notion that interpersonal functioning is at least in part regulated by the development of social-cognitive operations, then we will be in a better position to devise individualized and theory-based social skills curricula for the mentally retarded.

SUMMARY

The importance of social-cognitive development for the achievement of interpersonal competence among the mildly and moderately retarded is discussed. Research data bearing on the association of social role-taking ability with strategic interpersonal behavior are presented. Discussion focuses on the profitability of employing the Piagetian model in conceptualizing the social strengths and weaknesses of mentally retarded persons.

REFERENCES

Affleck, G. G. (1975a) Role-taking ability and interpersonal conflict resolution among retarded young adults. Amer. J. Ment. Defic. 80:233.

Affleck, G. G. (1975b) Role-taking ability and the interpersonal competencies of retarded children. Amer. J. Ment. Defic. 80:312.

Affleck, G. G. (1976) Role-taking ability and the interpersonal tactics of retarded children. Amer. J. Ment. Defic. 80:667.

Capobianco, R. J., and Cole, D. A. (1960) Social behavior of mentally retarded children. Amer. J. Ment. Defic. 64:638.

Chandler, M. J. (1973) Egocentrism and anti-social behavior: The assessment and training of social perspective-taking skills. Develop. Psychol. 9:326.

Dunn, L. M. (1968) Special education for the mildly retarded—Is much of it justifiable? Except. Child. 35:5.

Edgerton, R. B. (1967) The Cloak of Competence. Los Angeles: University of California Press.

Feffer, M. H. (1959) The cognitive implications of role-taking behavior. J. Pers. 27:152.

Feffer, M. H. (1970a) A developmental analysis of interpersonal behavior. Psychol. Rev. 77:197.

Feffer, M. H. (1970b) Role-taking behavior in the mentally retarded. (Final Report No. 42-2029). New York: Yeshiva University.

Feffer, M. H., and Gourevitch, V. (1960) Cognitive aspects of role-taking in children. J. Pers. 28:383.

Feffer, M. H., and Suchotliff, L. (1966) Decentering implications of social interaction. J. Pers. Soc. Psychol. 4:415.

Flavell, J. H. (1963) The Developmental Psychology of Jean Piaget. Princeton, New Jersey: Van Nostrand.

Flavell, J. H. (1968) The Development of Role-Taking and Communication Skills in Children. New York: Wiley & Sons.

Goulet, L. R., and Barclay, A. (1963) The Vineland Social Maturity Scale: Utility in assessment of Binet MA. Amer. J. Ment. Defic. 67:916.

Gunzburg, H. C. (1965) A "finishing school" for the mentally subnormal. Med. Offr. 114:99.

Johnson, D. W. (1975) Cooperativeness and social perspective-taking. J. Pers. Soc. Psychol. 31:241.

Kleck, R. E. (1975) Issues in social effectiveness: The Case of the mentally retarded. *In* The Mentally Retarded and Society: A Social Science Perspective (Eds. Begab, M., and Richardson, S.) Baltimore: University Park Press.

McDaniel, J. (1960) Group action in the rehabilitation of the mentally retarded. Group Psychother. 13:5.

Piaget, J. (1962). Comments on Vygotsky's critical remarks concerning The Language and Thought of the Child and Judgment and Reasoning in the Child. Attachment to Thought and Language (L. S. Vygotsky) Cambridge, Mass: M.I.T. Press.

Robinson, H., and Robinson, N. (1965) The Mentally Retarded Child: a Psychological Approach. New York: McGraw-Hill.

Weinstein, E. A. (1969) The development of interpersonal competence. *In* Handbook of Socialization Theory and Research (Ed. Goslin, D.) Chicago: Rand McNally.

Wood, J. R., Weinstein, E. A., and Parker, R. (1967) Children's interpersonal tactics. Sociol. Inq. 37:129.

Zigler, E. (1966) Mental retardation: Current issues and approaches. *In* Review of Child Development Research, Vol. II (Eds. Hoffman, L. W., and Hoffman, M. L.) New York: Russell Sage Foundation.

Zigler, E. (1973) The retarded child as a whole person. *In* The Experimental Psychology of Mental Retardation (Ed. Routh, D. K.) Chicago: Aldine.

RESEARCH TO PRACTICE IN MENTAL RETARDATION
Education and Training, Volume II
Edited by Peter Mittler
Copyright 1977 I.A.S.S.M.D.

PATTERNS OF CROSS-MODAL AND INTRAMODAL MATCHING AMONG INTELLIGENCE GROUPS

R. F. Jarman
The University of British Columbia,
2075 Wesbrook Place, Vancouver, B.C., Canada V6T 1W5

The study of information processing in children has been characterized in recent years by an increasing interest in the functions of sensory modalities (e.g. Chalfant and Scheffelin, 1969; Freides, 1974). The present study represents a new contribution to this area of research in four respects. First, it utilizes a multivariate research design in contrast to the simple designs used previously. Second, new instruments were developed for this study in order to overcome many of the difficulties in the tests used in earlier investigations. Third, and more substantially, performance on the tasks administered is interpreted and compared through use of a recent model of information processing that has been developed on the basis of Russian clinical research. Finally, the functions of sensory modalities are studied in three different intelligence groups, thus explicitly examining the importance of individual differences in cognitive adaptation to sensory systems.

Information processing tasks may be presented either cross-modally or intramodally. If the task requires matching of stimuli, as opposed to discrimination or transfer tasks (Ettlinger, 1967; O'Connor and Hermelin, 1971), the subject is 1) aware of the possible relationships between the stimuli in the two modalities and that the expectation of the experimenter is for the subject to judge the equivalence of the stimulus in the first modality compared with that of the second modality, 2) learning is minimal and transfer is not of major interest, and 3) the time interval is very brief: the subject is presented with a stimulus in the first modality and then is asked immediately to compare it with a stimulus in the second modality.

Very little research has been conducted on the relationship between performance in sensory modality matching and psychometric intelligence (IQ).

Despite this lack of empirical information, some substantial claims have been made regarding the significance of cross-modal and intramodal matching performance as an indication of intellectual development (eg., Birch and Belmont, 1964; Jensen, 1969).

In order to examine the significance of sensory modality matching tasks in the context of individual differences in intelligence, it is necessary to broaden the perspective beyond that taken in the research literature to date and examine both cross-modal and intramodal matching with a model of information processing. The model chosen in the present study has been proposed by Das, Kirby, and Jarman (1975) as an extension of clinical research by Luria (1966a, 1966b, 1973). Luria proposes that the processing of the cognitive content of the brain is accomplished via the employment of a series of exteroceptive, proprioceptive and interoceptive analyzers, which collectively synthesize input into two basic forms: simultaneous synthesis and successive synthesis. Simultaneous synthesis refers to the integration of separate elements of information into groups, often through spatial representation. Successive synthesis is characterized by serial ordering of events or sequencing of information.

The present study uses this model to address the following problems: 1) the relative importance of cross-modal and intramodal matching performance as indicators of intelligence and 2) the forms of information integration used by different intelligence groups in cross-modal and intramodal tasks.

METHOD

Subjects

The major focus of this research is the study of the characteristics of subjects of varying levels of cognitive adaptation as defined by IQ. In establishing the ranges of IQ, it was necessary to hold chronological age constant, that is to meet the requirements of a chronological age (CA) matched design (Ellis, 1969; Heal, 1970).

The main selection criteria for the subjects were verbal and nonverbal Lorge-Thorndike intelligence test scores. Three IQ groups were used in order to assess trends over the range of intelligence. The limits of verbal IQ for the low (LIQ) group were set at 71–90, for the normal IQ (NIQ) group the range used was 91–110, and for the high IQ (HIQ) group the verbal IQ range was defined as 111–130. A survey of the IQ data suggested that 66–95, 86–115, and 106–135 were the most feasible ranges of performance IQ for the low, normal and high IQ groups, respectively.

Three additional criteria that were necessary aspects of the identification of the subjects were sample size, sex, and socioeconomic status. Sample size was set at 60 for each IQ group, the sex of the subjects was restricted to males for all IQ groups, and SES was randomized within a middle range through omitting subjects from exclusively high or low SES population areas.

Tests

Auditory-auditory Matching   This task involves matching a stimulus pattern of 1,000 cycle tones with a comparison pattern of tones. All tones are of 0.15 seconds duration, with variation in patterns created by short pauses of 0.35 seconds and long pauses of 1.35 seconds. A score of one is given for each of the 30 items in the test.

Auditory-visual Matching   The items in this test utilize an auditory pattern as a stimulus as in the auditory-auditory test, but this is matched with a comparison visual display of dots. For a dot of 1 unit in diameter, a short gap is 0.80 units in length, and for a long gap is 7.17 units in length. Each of the 30 items in the test is scored as one mark.

Visual-auditory Matching   This test is the converse of auditory-visual matching; the visual display is the stimulus portion of each item and the comparison section is a set of tones.

Visual-visual Matching   This test is comprised of sets of visual patterns, where the first pattern of each set is compared to the second pattern, with a score of one given to each correct response for a test total of 30.

Simultaneous and Successive Syntheses   These tests have been described previously (Das, Kirby, and Jarman, 1975):

1. Raven's Progressive Matrices
2. Figure copying
3. Graham-Kendall's Memory for Designs
4. Serial recall
5. Free recall
6. Visual short-term memory
7. Word reading

Procedure

The set of four cross-modal and intramodal matching tests was administered in a balanced design within each IQ group in order to compensate for possible transfer effects from a given sequence of administration. The tests of simultaneous and successive syntheses were administered in random order within each IQ group.

RESULTS

Descriptive Statistics

The means and standard deviations for verbal and performance IQ for the IQ groups were found to be quite symmetric due to the sampling procedure. The NIQ group in this study has a verbal IQ mean of 101.03, and the LIQ group mean for verbal IQ is approximately 19 points below the population mean, and the HIQ group is approximately 19 points above the population mean, with standard deviations approximately equal for all groups. Performance IQ data was also characterized by this symmetry.

Performance Among the IQ Groups

The means and standard deviations for each of the IQ groups on the 11 variables demonstrated a uniform rank ordering of performance on the 11 tests as a function of IQ. The tests that appeared to indicate the greatest discrepancy in group performances are auditory-visual matching and Raven's Progressive Matrices. The least discrepancy between the groups appeared in visual short-term memory. A three-group one-way fixed effects multivariate analysis of variance (MANOVA) was performed on the data from the 11 tests to test the significance of these differences (Tatsuoka, 1971). The results of the MANOVA indicated significant differences between the groups, with a Wilk's Lambda of 0.44, and F $(22, 334) = 7.70, p < 0.01$.

Cognitive Strategies in Cross-modal and Intramodal Matching

In order to identify the processes involved in each of the tests, the individual responses were intercorrelated and factor analyzed by principal components. In the factor analytic results for each group, the same set of reference factors, namely simultaneous and successive syntheses and speed, was identified.

In the factor matrix for the low IQ group, Factor I has strong test loadings from visual-auditory matching, visual-visual matching, and serial recall. This factor apparently represents a form of coding. The second factor for the low IQ group was clearly simultaneous synthesis, and Factor III represents successive synthesis. Factor IV of the matrix for the LIQ group is the speed factor often found by Das (1973). For the LIQ group it is apparent that speed aids serial recall, probably through cumulative rehearsal of the word lists as they are presented.

The results of the principal components analyses for the normal IQ group demonstrated some variation from those of the LIQ group. Most notably, the use of the Scree test gave a three-factor solution, rather than the four factors given from the LIQ group. Factor I of the NIQ matrix appeared to be a similar coding factor to the one found for the LIQ group. In contrast, however, Raven's Progressive Matrices and Memory for Designs, rather than serial recall, have some relationship to this factor. Also, the auditory-auditory matching test has a shared loading between this and the second factor. The second factor of the matrix appears to be a combination of successive synthesis and speed. The two marker tests for successive synthesis, serial recall and visual short-term memory, have high loadings on this factor, in conjunction with a high negative loading for word reading and a moderate positive loading for auditory-auditory matching. Factor III of the matrix for the NIQ group is clearly simultaneous synthesis, with a slightly reduced loading for Raven's Progressive Matrices. Similar to the results for the LIQ group, auditory-visual matching has a shared loading between this factor and the coding factor.

The matrix for the high IQ group has four factors. Factor I of the matrix, which has been designated as a coding factor previously, is very interesting, because for this level of IQ the factor is made up almost solely of the sensory modality matching tests built by the investigator. The second factor of this matrix is simultaneous synthesis, and Factor III is successive synthesis. The fourth factor in the matrix is a bipolar speed factor.

DISCUSSION

The results of the study indicate that in mean levels of performance the sensory modality matching tests were ordered from easiest to the most difficult as: visual-visual (V-V), visual-auditory (V-A), auditory-visual (A-V), and auditory-auditory (A-A). This order of difficulty in the tests was identical for each of the IQ groups.

In terms of group discrimination, however, the tests were ordered differently. A-V matching demonstrated much stronger group differences than the other three tests, which were roughly equal in strength of discrimination. In fact, A-V matching was the major discriminator of all of the tests administered, including the simultaneous-successive tests. Only the Raven's Progressive Matrices, which itself has been used in some research as a test of intelligence, demonstrated comparable group discrimination.

The results of the factor analyses indicated some very clear patterns in the strategies used by the subjects in the sensory modality matching tests. These patterns are particularly interesting when combined with the data on levels of performance on each test.

A-A matching demonstrated less group differences than the other tests, but also differential strategies. For the low IQ group it was performed successively, for the normal IQ group a combination of successive synthesis and coding was used, and for the high IQ group the task was coded. Thus, although performance level differences were not strongest on this test relative to the others, different strategies were still in evidence.

The A-V matching task demonstrated very strong group differences, and a different strategy was used in the task by the HIQ group relative to the LIQ and NIQ groups.

The remaining two tasks, V-A matching and V-V matching, discriminated the groups less powerfully than the A-V task, but were completed by the subjects in all of the groups by the same coding strategy.

SUMMARY

This study examined patterns of performance and cognitive strategies in cross-modal and intramodal matching for three intelligence groups at the grade four level. Differences were interpreted in terms of a model of cognitive abilities, known as simultaneous and successive syntheses.

REFERENCES

Birch, H. G., and Belmont, I. (1964) Auditory-visual integration in normal and retarded readers. Amer. J. Orthopsychiat. 34:852.

Chalfant, J. C., and Scheffelin, M. A. (1969) Central Processing Dysfunction in Children: A Review of Research. NINDS, No. 9. Washington, D.C.: US Department of Health, Education and Welfare.

Das, J. P. (1973) Structure of cognitive abilities: Evidence for simultaneous and successive processing. J. Educ. Psychol. 65:103.

Das, J. P., Kirby, J., and Jarman, R. F. (1975) Simultaneous and successive syntheses: An alternative model for cognitive abilities. Psychol. Bull. 82:87.

Ellis, N. R. (1969) A behavioral research strategy in mental retardation: Defense and critique. Amer. J. Ment. Defic. 73:557.

Ettlinger, G. (1967) Analysis of cross-modal effects and their relationship to language. In Brain Mechanisms Underlying Speech and Language (Eds. Millikan, C. H., and Darley, F. C.) New York: Grune & Stratton.

Freides, D. (1974) Human information processing and sensory modality: Cross-modal functions, information complexity, memory and deficit. Psychol. Bull. 81:284.

Heal, L. W. (1970) Research strategies and research goals in the scientific study of the mentally subnormal. Amer. J. Ment. Defic. 75:10.

Jensen, A. R. (1969) How much can we boost IQ and scholastic achievement? Harvard Educ. Rev. 39:1.

Luria, A. R. (1966a) Human Brain and Psychological Processes. New York: Harper and Row.

Luria, A. R. (1966b) Higher Cortical Functions in Man. New York: Basic Books.

Luria, A. R. (1973) The Working Brain. London: Penguin.

O'Connor, N., and Hermelin, B. (1971) Inter- and intra-modal transfer in children with modality specific and general handicaps. Brit. J. Soc. Clin. Psychol. 10:346.

Tatsuoka, M. M. (1971) Multivariate Analysis: Techniques for Educational and Psychological Research. Toronto: Wiley & Sons.

RESEARCH TO PRACTICE IN MENTAL RETARDATION
Education and Training, Volume II
Edited by Peter Mittler
Copyright 1977 I.A.S.S.M.D.

METAMEMORY AND MENTAL RETARDATION
Implications for Research and Practice

M. Friedman, A. Krupski, E. T. Dawson, and P. Rosenberg
University of California,
Los Angeles, California 90024, United States

This chapter is concerned with an alternative to traditional approaches used to study memory in the mentally retarded. Our particular concern is with the measurement of metamemory, a term coined by Flavell to refer to an individual's awareness of the way memory works (Flavell and Wellman, 1976). For example, most adolescents of normal intelligence are aware that different materials may require different plans of study for apprehension and also that some materials may simply be forgotten over time unless special strategies are used to prevent forgetting. Younger children demonstrate less awareness of such strategies (Kreutzer, Leonard, and Flavell, 1975). Thus, metamemory processes, or one's awareness of the way memory works, appear to be an important component of competence in a variety of tasks that require memory. Although there have been few studies of metamemory processes in the mentally retarded to date, the work with normal children suggests that such information would be useful in the assessment of competence in the retarded.

Metamemory can be assessed through a structured interview where the participant is asked to respond to a series of questions about memory. For example, in the study to be presented here, mentally retarded adolescents were asked questions such as, "Would it be easier to remember five things or ten things?" "Would you remember more if you studied for one minute or five minutes?" and so on.

It is important to note that most American research on memory processes is based on laboratory tasks and paradigms (such as the learning of lists of words or paired-associates) that are of limited scope and doubtful validity for the life of the retarded person. These same criticisms have also been made of standard intelligence tests. We share the opinions of other researchers (e.g., Paris and Haywood, 1973) that global IQ scores do not capture the range of cognitive competence shown by retarded persons in their daily lives. For example, a child of moderate intelligence may fail to learn a five-item list of paired-associate words in the laboratory, yet demonstrate in his casual conversation that he can remember the names of a large number of baseball players, their teams, and a good deal about their histories. Neither his laboratory performance nor his IQ score capture this memory competence. It was observations such as this that led us to explore the nature of memory processes within a broader perspective than those suggested by more traditional approaches.

The value of broadening our view of memory is illustrated in the following example. It is frequently assumed that laboratory-administered serial learning tasks tap processes that underlie everyday activities, such as remembering telephone numbers. However, when normal children are asked how they remember telephone numbers, they frequently state that they write them down (Kreutzer et al., 1975). This is clearly a functional strategy for remembering telephone numbers or any other list of unrelated items, yet few if any laboratory tests of serial learning allow subjects this option. As a result, writing things down has seldom been studied as a viable storage-retrieval strategy.

The question of memory for telephone numbers relates in an important way to differences between normal and retarded subjects' performance on a short-term memory task. Frequently, such differences have been interpreted in terms of a cognitive deficit model. In our initial work on metamemory, we asked some moderately retarded children how they remembered telephone numbers in order to compare their answers with those obtained by Kreutzer et al. (1975). We quickly learned from the nature of their answers that this question was not relevant to their life experiences. Many of these children simply did not use the telephone at all in their daily lives or else used it in a different manner from the children studied by Kreutzer et al. (1975).

This example points to the necessity of using a cross-cultural perspective in comparing the memory competencies of normal and retarded persons. The argument can be made that the retarded individual really lives in a different culture, and this culture determines what he learns about memory and the strategies and coping mechanisms he employs in his cognitive behavior. Cole and Bruner (1971) have noted that in comparing competencies in different cultures, "One must inquire, first, whether a competence is expressed in a particular situation, and second, what the significance of that situation is for the person's ability to cope with life in his own milieu." Few investigators of memory processes in the retarded have addressed themselves to this issue in spite of its obvious relevance to interpretation of cognitive deficits.

This brief overview suggests that traditional laboratory investigations of memory processes tell us little about the level of competence retarded persons display in activities involving memory in their daily lives. These investigations can best be characterized as limited in scope and of doubtful validity for the life of the retarded person. Such considerations, coupled with the informal observation that even moderately retarded individuals frequently display a higher level of memory competence in their daily activities than one would expect from either their IQ or laboratory performance, led to the design of the present study.

The present study was conceived as an exploratory approach for obtaining descriptive information about retarded individuals' awareness of the way memory works. The study involved interviewing young adult retarded students enrolled in a public school for the trainable mentally retarded. We attempted to formulate interview questions that were relevant to the everyday activities of the participants. Because the methodology is new, we regard the results as tentative and suggestive. We offer them as illustrations of the potential of metamemory research. This study was modeled after the investigations of Kreutzer et al. (1975), who studied 5-, 7-, 9-, and 11-year-old, normal children. However, a number of modifications made in the present study precludes direct comparisons of the results.

Our sample consisted of 22 students whose mean age was 18 and mean IQ was 49. Because of the nature of the task, participants were required to have some verbal skills.

Flavell and Wellman (1976) have suggested a taxonomy of metamemorial knowledge. Three classes of variables are postulated as probable influences on memory performance in particular situations. These include, memory characteristics of the person, memory characteristics of the task, and strategies that might be used for particular situations. Examples in each of these variable classes will be presented.

In an initial attempt to assess person characteristics related to metamemorial knowledge, participants were asked about the overall quality of their memory. Specifically, the interviewer asked, "I sometimes have a problem remembering things. I forget things. Do you ever have that problem? Do you ever forget anything?" Although it was by no means the most common response, a few of our retarded participants insisted that they never forgot anything. This is to be compared with the results of Kreutzer et al. (1975), who asked the same question of normal children, of age 5 to 11, and found denials of forgetting only for the youngest children. We observed this sort of posturing behavior to occur repeatedly. Another important person variable we attempted to assess was the extent to which our participants were aware that memory may decay over time. The interviewer asked the following question: "Suppose you were in the principal's office and he gave you the names of five kids he wanted you to bring to the office from some classroom. You were trying real hard to remember these five names so that you could get the kids and send them to the office. Do you think that it would make any difference in how well you did the job and remembered the names if you stopped and talked to a friend on the way to get the five kids?" After an initial response was given, the interviewer probed with further questions to assess the reason for the answer and the understanding of the concept. Our initial scoring indicates that eight of our 22 participants understood the question, and their answers suggested that they understood that stopping and talking with a friend might cause them to forget some of the names. Three answered that they should not talk to their friend and should go straight to the classroom. However, their rationale was that they would get in trouble if they stopped, not that they would forget. Seven were judged not to understand either the question or the concept. Four said that they would remember just as well if they stopped and talked with friends; however, this may well have been another example of "posturing," i.e., it seemed that they were coping with the interview situation by attempting to impress the interviewer with their good memory.

Several situations were used to assess understanding of task characteristics that affect memory performance. About half of our sample seemed to understand clearly that ten objects were harder to remember than five objects. However, our statement of the problem might have led some participants to say that ten objects were easy to remember in order to impress the interviewer with their own memory ability. The understanding of the role of study time in memory was also assessed. Fifteen of the 22 students understood that studying a set of 16 pictures for five minutes would yield better memory than study for one minute. An interesting aspect of the results for this question was that several of the students understood the general role of study time in memory, but said that someone who studied for only one minute might remember more than another person who studied for five minutes. They reasoned that the person who studied for only one minute obviously had a superior memory, or as one of our students noted, "he knew how to do it." This again illustrates the importance of understanding retarded persons' social cognitions in memory tasks. When asked whether they would study for one minute or five minutes, thirteen said five minutes. Five of those who said one minute indicated that the task would be very easy for them.

Our retarded subjects demonstrated a great deal of competence in describing strategies they would use in some specific situations. For example, one situation was set up as follows: "Suppose your friend told you that he wanted one of your class pictures. You told him that you would bring the picture to school the next day so that he could have the picture. What would you do to be sure and remember to bring the picture?" Twelve of our students said that they would remember by doing such things as putting the picture in their shirt pocket the night before, six would remember by asking someone to remind them, and three said they would remember by simply cuing themselves, e.g., "I would remember in my mind." Similarly, most of the students demonstrated that they could think up appropriate strategies for remembering to watch a special TV show and strategies for finding a jacket that they had lost during recess.

We are encouraged by these preliminary results. It seems to us that meta-memory research may allow us to make a more complete assessment of the memory competence of retarded persons.

It is frequently argued that retarded persons do not spontaneously produce strategies to assist them in storing and retrieving information (Brown, 1974). This may indeed be true for many laboratory tasks, but our results suggest that even rather severely retarded individuals are able to generate functional strategies within the context of their daily lives. We should note that our hands are not entirely clean and that we did test our sample on a standard laboratory learning task using classifiable stimuli. Here we found the sort of deficit reported in previous research: not one subject in our sample generated a study strategy using the conceptual structure of the cards. These results reinforce our argument that it is important to consider a wider variety of tasks than has traditionally been employed in the analysis of retardate memory.

One of the most interesting findings of recent cross-cultural research (Cole and Scribner, 1974) is that strategic behavior in some laboratory memory tasks is positively correlated with the amount of Western schooling a child has received. Might it be that at least some of the problems of retarded persons on laboratory tasks are "instructional deficits" due to the curriculum to which they have been exposed?

We noted over and over again in our interviews that subjects in our sample interpreted tasks within their cultural frame of reference. Their answers to the interview questions about memory often reflected inappropriate and maladaptive social responses, such as the frequent posturing behavior that we observed. As Zigler (1973) and others have pointed out, some of the coping strategies that retarded persons adopt interfere with the effectiveness of their cognitive activity. Most investigators of memory in the retarded try to separate the basic memory and cognitive processes from social factors. On the other hand, Meacham (1972) has stressed the theme that memory is a social skill that develops as a function of the interaction of the child with his environment. We agree with this view. It is probably impossible to separate social and cognitive processes. To study the memory of the retarded person, it is important to study how he uses memory in his own world. The study of metamemory offers an entry into this world.

SUMMARY

Metamemory refers to an individual's awareness of memory processes such as the need for planning and effort and the factors that influence memory in various tasks. Topics discussed are the nature of the metamemory abilities of the mentally retarded and the relationship between metamemory judgments and memory behavior.

REFERENCES

Brown, A. (1974) The role of strategic behavior in retardate memory. *In* International Review of Research in Mental Retardation, Vol. 7. (Ed. Ellis, N.) New York: Academic Press.

Cole, M., and Bruner, J. (1971) Cultural differences and inferences about psychological processes. Amer. Psychol. 26:867.

Cole, M., and Scribner, S. (1974) Culture and Thought. New York: Wiley & Sons.

Flavell, J., and Wellman, H. (1976) Metamemory. *In* Perspectives on the Development of Memory and Cognition. (Eds. Kail, R., and Hagen, J.) Hillsdale, New Jersey: L. Erlbaum Associates.

Kreutzer, M., Leonard, C., and Flavell, J. (1975) An interview study of children's knowledge about memory. Mongr. Soc. Res. Child Dev. 40 (1, Serial No. 159).

Meacham, J. (1972) The development of memory abilities in the individual and in society. Hum. Dev. 15:205.

Paris, S., and Haywood, H. (1973) Mental retardation as a learning disorder. Pediatr. Clin. North Amer. 3:641.

Zigler, E. (1973) The retarded child as a whole person. *In* The Experimental Psychology of Mental Retardation. (Ed. Routh, D. K.) Chicago: Aldine Publishing Co.

RESEARCH TO PRACTICE IN MENTAL RETARDATION
Education and Training, Volume II
Edited by Peter Mittler
Copyright 1977 I.A.S.S.M.D.

MEDIATED LEARNING EXPERIENCE
A Theoretical Basis for Cognitive Modifiability During Adolescence

R. Feuerstein
*Hadassah-Wizo-Canada Research
Institute, Youth Aliah Child Guidance
Clinic, Bar Ilan University , Jerusalem, Israel*

In this chapter, a theoretical basis is suggested and empirical evidence is presented for the significant cognitive modifiability of the retarded performer at the age of adolescence. The material is presented against the background of an illustrative case study and a brief analysis of suggested etiological determinants of differential cognitive performance.

Cognitive modifiability is here defined as a transformation in the structure of the intellect of the individual, which will reflect a change in the expected course of his development. Thus defined, modifiability as opposed to "change" sui generis (as is produced by developmental and maturational processes) represents a noticeable departure from the normal developmental course of the individual as directed by his genetic or neurophysiological constitution and/or his experiential and educational background.

Such a departure, even when it is in the desired direction, is conceived by many developmental and behavioral scientists as an aberration of the organism and, as such, not to be considered a phenomenon one can produce at will or rely upon. A disbelief in the power of intervention to produce modifiability,—as distinguished also from sheer modification, probably explains the reluctance of clinical psychologists to enter the area of mental retardation. And yet, instances are numerous in which changes in the expected course of development are reported, but scientists adhering to the ideas of an immutable, predictable sequence and goal of development show little readiness to accept these instances as evidence of modifiability. In practice, very few attempts have been

This research presented in this and the following chapter has been supported by the NICHD under Grant IROI HDO4634-01 for Instrumental Enrichment, and the Ford Foundation for the Learning Potential Assessment Device.

made to create conditions for the induction of modifiability during adolescence; this, in turn, has also limited the opportunity to research the theoretical meaning of such phenomena.

There is, in sum, a strong need for a theory that will provide an explanatory and predictive basis for modifiability, not only in order to understand the phenomenon, but also as the sole means to gain control over it, and produce it to the benefit of those in need. The successful outcome of such an effort is likely to change the current approach towards this segment of the population, marked today by a passive acceptance reflecting the belief that the individual, if he cannot be changed and made adaptable to life, should be accepted as he is, and that conditions of life, rather than the individual, should be modified in such a way as to make them suitable to his level of functioning (Feuerstein, 1969).

Three etiological hypotheses have been advanced to account for (retarded) cognitive functioning, each one emphasizing a particular aspect of the organism: 1) the genetic constitution, 2) deviations in its neurophysiological substrata, and 3) interaction with the environment. The question is posed: In what way do these determinants produce the final outcome: retarded performance? What are the mechanics by which genetic endowment, organic conditions, or environmental deprivation affect the capacity of the individual to use representational abstract thinking? The fact that one finds a great variability in outcome, despite relative uniformity of etiological factors, makes a causal relationship between them highly questionable.

Before discussing the three etiological hypotheses and the notion of cognitive modifiability in general and its occurrence at late stages of development in particular, both as a desirable phenomenon and as a process that can be elicited experimentally, we would like to present a case study, which, in terms of all the three etiological hypotheses, seemed to give very little hope for betterment and change.

CASE HISTORY

A fifteen-year-old, severely retarded boy with an IQ in the 35–45 range, referred to us 11 years ago may serve as an illustration of our concept of cognitive and behavioral modifiability. Martin was referred to the author by the welfare department of a European country for life-long placement in custodial care in Israel, in response to the will of his Jewish mother.

The second of three brothers, Martin was born into a pathogenic family. His father, a schizophrenic, alcoholic, poorly adjusted Foreign Legion soldier, met and married the mother during his service in North Africa. The mother, herself primitive, illiterate, and cognitively retarded, died as a hospitalized, diagnosed, psychotic. Heredity has affected Martin and a brother. In addition, Martin suffered from brain damage produced by prematurity and low weight (2½ lbs) at birth, requiring prolonged incubator care. Infancy and childhood were marked by nutritional difficulties and by repetitive and prolonged separations with placements in crêches and foster families. Early adolescence was largely spent in socially and educationally restrictive environments.

When first seen, Martin manifested a level of functioning even lower than the one anticipated by his IQ. He showed an almost total lack of constituted language (we counted 40–50 words on the expressive level), severe impairment of spatio-temporal orientation, imitation, retention, and social behavior. Echolalia, echopraxy, and echomimy were observed, but no psychotic-autistic signs were detected. Trainability having been considered very poor, custodial care seemed unavoidable.

Dynamic assessment of Martin using the Learning Potential Assessment Device (LPAD, see below) provided us with an index of modifiability giving unexpected hopes for radically changing his destiny. Based upon the assessment, Martin was placed in a foster home group care treatment program for the redevelopment of severely disturbed and low functioning adolescents (Feuerstein, Krasilovsky et al., 1967). The program implied a considerable investment and consisted of a variety of strategies for mediating the world to Martin by selecting stimuli, framing them for him, providing them with meaning—reinforcing and equipping him with learning sets of which he was initially totally devoid.

This concerted effort over 11 years has resulted in the development of an independently functioning individual oriented in time and space with a fully and richly constituted language (Hebrew), humor and social skills and goal orientations enabling him to be almost completely self-subsistent as an upkeeper of a huge public indoor swimming pool. He is reading and writing and uses complex inferential and conceptual levels of thinking. Surprisingly, he has learned to speak French and some German, following his mastery of Hebrew. He still has difficulties in mathematics. Thus, despite adverse conditions of pathogenic conditions, heredity, organicity, early separation, hospitalization, traumata and continuous stimulus and social deprivation, modifiability proved possible through powerful and systematic intervention. This has radically changed the course of development from anticipated placement in life-long custodial care to a life path of an autonomous, independent, contributive, socially adaptive young man looking forward to building his own family.

Cases such as Martin's are much more numerous than one tends to believe. Clarke and Clarke (1976) summarize a wealth of relatively little-known research, surveys, and follow-up studies that provide solid evidence of modifiability in cases where intervention started at the latency period. They conclude that ill effects of many kinds of adverse early experience can be wiped out simply by the discontinuation of the depriving conditions and even more so by the establishment of the intervention necessary for the redevelopment process to take place. In fact they found that "the worse the early social history, the better the prognosis for change" (p. 72).

Yet, none of the three predominant etiological hypotheses explaining retarded performance is as optimistic regarding the possibilities for instituting meaningful change, as would seem to be indicated by a case such as Martin's. The heritability hypothesis of differential cognitive development implies not only quantitative but also qualitative immutable differences between individuals and groups said to differ by their genetic endowment. The dichotomy suggested by Jensen (1969) of Level I and Level II types of intelligence divides humanity into those who, by virtue of their greater capacity to transform, elaborate, organize, and conceptualize incoming data—attain Level II and those who, limited to Level I, function on a purely reproductive, imitative level structurally no different from mental activity ascribed to subhuman species. Jensen's suggestion to limit educational goals and investments to the manifest level of functioning of individuals and groups is a blatant illustration of a passive-acceptance approach—"since you cannot do what you want, better want what you can do."

This kind of dichotomy is dangerous on both theoretical and practical grounds. The question is asked: Can one—and should one—derive an approximation of heritability from data which *at best* represent the *manifest* level of functioning reflected by static "inventory" types of data produced by conventional IQ tests? Moreover, why should genetic endowment be considered immutable? Would it not be more adequate to consider the genetic factor as producing variations in the level of responsiveness of the organism to learning situations requiring corresponding variations in the quantity and quality necessary for the production of growth? Formulated this way, the nurture/nature controversy may be resolved by considering it as a ratio of investment/outcome rather than as setting limits on the future development of the organism.

A second etiological determinant for differential cognitive development in individuals and groups is considered to be linked to differential frequency of neurophysiological conditions affecting the organism's cognitive development. Reproductive risks, resulting in CNS damage are thought to be differently distributed among various socioeconomic and ethnic/racial subgroups and, although preventable, are thought to be unmodifiable once the ill effects become established. Indeed, retrospective studies have often given the impression of having established a causal relationship between pre-, para-, and postnatal incidents and later developmental deficiencies. Sameroff and Chandler (1975) point out that very limited links are found between reproductive risks and their presumed outcomes once prospective research methodology is applied. It appears, therefore, that it is the interactions between the reproductive risk and the caretaking environment that should be considered the determinants of differential cognitive development.

The third etiological category is the interaction between the child and his environment. By far the most optimistic, important aspects of the interaction are regarded as accessible not only to prevention but also to remediation. Yet, retarded performance is considered to be produced largely by early deprivation and to be modifiable only by intervention occuring within limits of hypothesized critical periods. This strict interpretation of "critical" as contrasted with "optimal" periods is a basic antecedent of the notion of irreversibility.

Early intervention programs have undoubtedly done much in the way of prevention and remediation, but they leave neither reason nor hope for a return on investment at any later stage, and have resulted in substantial neglect of adolescents. Also, the one-shot types of intervention based on the strict interpretation of critical periods is hardly a strategy for establishing immunity and safeguards from the ill effects of exposure to the depriving conditions of life.

The critical period hypothesis such as formulated by Hebb (1949) and elaborated by Hunt (1961) has served as the theoretical basis for infancy and preschool intervention programs. The neurophysiological substrata of the critical periods hypothesis setting limits to modifiability at later stages of development has been questioned in a recent paper by Konrad and Melzack (1975). These authors have interpreted the deficiencies of animals reared in isolation as reflecting a reaction to "novelty enhancement," which is a temporary and highly modifiable condition once the animal is subjected to stimulation. In sum, the data indicate that the critical periods concept is better understood as optimal periods affecting development, but not definitively and not irreversibly.

The presentation of the case of Martin and our discussion of the etiological determinants described above receive strong support from authors questioning the possibility of perceiving any single etiological factor as directly responsible for a given outcome. An interactional approach taking various factors into account is conceived to be more adequate, but there is a need for a much improved understanding of finer grain environmental processes if more powerful explanations of interaction are to become possible.

We, therefore, propose to consider two categories of etiological factors: distal and proximal. Distal etiologies are defined as determinants that neither directly nor invariably lead to certain and specific outcomes. Proximal etiologies are determinants that directly and invariably lead to specific outcomes. The relationship between distal and proximal etiologies is such that the distal etiology can, but may or may not, trigger the proximal one. When the distal factor does trigger the proximal determinant, then the specific outcome will appear.

Our cognitive map (see Figure 1), shows a selection of distal determinants, including *genetic factors, organicity, poverty of stimulation, disturbance of child or parents,* and *socioeconomic disadvantages.* The proximal etiology includes Mediated Learning Experience (MLE), its presence or absence. Retarded performance will be elicited whenever lack of MLE is caused by one or more distal determinants. However, if, despite heredity and/or organicity and/or other distal factors, the child is provided with MLE, and if the barriers obstructing mediation are overcome and by-passed by special strategies or by increasing the intensity of exposure to MLE, then the expected deficiency from the distal determinant will not necessarily follow. The concept of MLE is briefly presented in the following discussion.

The organism develops through two major modalities, 1) maturational and growth processes built into the system of the organism itself and, 2) interaction with its environment. For this latter source of development and change, we

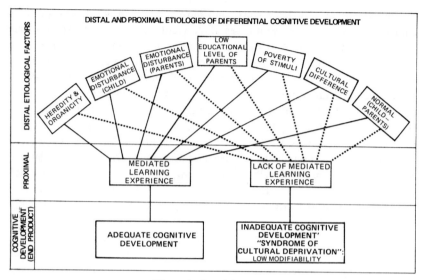

Figure 1. Cognitive map.

would like to suggest the distinction between direct and mediated exposure. The organism is from the very beginning of life affected and changed by stimuli impinging on it. This direct exposure, transforming as it does the organism's reactions, is to be equated with learning, because of the lasting effects it produces on the behavioral repertoire of the organism. This modality includes the activities and manipulations the organism imposes on the stimuli, and is to be equated with the process described by 'S-R students' and as 'S-O-R' in Piaget's theoretical framework.

However, in the mediated exposure, by which the organism also is changed, modified and learns, the organism is no longer directly exposed to the stimuli. Between him and his sources of stimuli, an experienced, intentioned, and active human being interposes himself and mediates the stimuli in such a way that each stimulus is changed as it reaches the organism. In the Mediated Learning Experience the experienced and intentioned adult selects certain stimuli, frames them, orders them in a given sequence of "before and after," representing causal as well as teleological systems, schedules them on both temporal and spatial dimensions (e.g., "Not now, later" and "Not here, there") and provokes anticipatory behaviors, provides meaning to certain stimuli by emphasizing them through repetition, wipes out others by discontinuing their appearance, produces categories of behavior by associating certain stimuli with others, and eliminates certain associations between them. This mediation occurs at a very early stage in the development of the child at the preverbal level and continues into early childhood on verbal levels in those areas that are novel to the organism.

It is our contention that MLE provides the organism with instruments of adaptation and learning in such a way as to make the individual who has been exposed to MLE able to use efficiently the direct exposure for learning and to become modified. The organism that has not received such a mediation is characterized mainly by limited capacity to become modified through direct exposure and experience, perceptual, motor, and emotional.

Lack of MLE leaves the organism a passive receiver of information, with an episodic grasp of reality, lack of comparative behavior, lack of need to establish relationships between events, and sum up and a host of other deficiencies on the input, output, and elaborational levels of the mental act that will limit the impact of further experience on the organism.

The reason for the lack of MLE can be either one or both of the following: the environment fails to mediate the world to the child or the organism itself produces barriers to attempts at mediation. Reasons for the failure of the environment to mediate include poverty, apathy of parents, and emotional disturbance of parents resulting in weak emotional ties with the child, limiting their responsibilities to its bare physical needs. When the organism produces barriers, it may make attempts at mediation on the part of parents, or other possible mediators, temporarily or permanently futile, laborious, and difficult. Thus, the responsiveness of the child may differ because of genetic factors, organicity, hyperkinesis, or traumata, requiring increased intensity and frequency of exposure to mediation in order for this barrier to be penetrated. In such a case, the very limited responsiveness of the child may lead to a reduced effort of mediation on the part of the parents, instead of an increased effort: "He does not need us; it does not really matter to him."

According to this model, many so-called retarded children manifest low mental functioning not necessarily because of a particular distal etiology but because of a lack of MLE. The deficiencies produced by a lack of MLE are mainly in the realm of attitude, orientation, and habits of the organism toward the world and toward himself. We have been able to identify an inventory of deficient functions that are considered to be responsible for the inefficient use of exposure to stimuli. It follows from the MLE model that: 1) deficits produced by the absence or insufficiency of MLE can be modified with relative ease and limited investment, 2) even though early childhood is the optimal period for MLE, there are no time limits to remedial and redevelopmental processes, and 3) cultural deprivation, as produced by lack of MLE, can be found in a great variety of socioeconomic and cultural backgrounds as a determinant for differential cognitive development.

If this theoretical model is accepted, one may explain the instances of modifiability observed in relatively late stages of development reflected in sharp changes in the courses of life otherwise dictated by heredity, organicity, or early childhood deprivation.

Three sources of empirical support are available for the theoretical framework outlined above. Deriving from both clinical and experimental work, the empirical support includes the results obtained through the extensive use of the Learning Potential Assessment Device (LPAD), follow-up studies over a period of 25 years of high risk adolescents, and the study of the effects of an active interventional program termed Instrumental Enrichment. Research in all of these areas is still in progress, but a great deal of material is already available in final form.

THE LEARNING POTENTIAL ASSESSMENT DEVICE

The LPAD is both a clinical and an experimental method aimed at measuring in vitro the cognitive modifiability of retarded performance. This method, which entails a test-teach-test strategy was developed by the author over the last 25 years of his work with culturally different and socioeconomically deprived adolescents immigrating to Israel under the auspices of Youth Aliyah. It has proved its efficiency inasmuch as it has enabled us to consider adolescents functioning in the range of EMR (educable mentally retarded) as meaningfully modifiable and therefore eligible for investment in order to increase their academic proficiency. In contradistinction to the static goal of conventional assessment techniques, which predict development on the basis of an inventory of the individual's manifest level of functioning, the LPAD uses a dynamic approach focusing its interest, investment and interpretation on the first provoked and then measured changes in the individual's functioning during the assessment procedure. This shift from a static inventory type of evaluation toward a dynamic goal necessitates a change in the nature of the instruments employed for assessment. They have to provide the examiner and the examinee with tasks that can be taught; tasks by the help of which one can evaluate the effect of the teaching process on the capacity of the individual to deal with new situations.

Figure 2 shows a model for constructing such instruments. By the same token, this shift from a static to a dynamic goal implies a change in the test situation turning the examiner into a teacher-observer and the examinee into a learner-performer. Such a change entails the establishment of a two-way communication process, instead of the usual situation in which the examiner is the questioner and the examinee the responder. It entails mutual feedback and a variety of teaching and reinforcing strategies, followed by ways to evaluate their efficiency. A third change is the great emphasis on process orientation as the final criteria for assessment of capacity and modifiability. Finally, the interpretation of results uses the peak of functioning of the individual as a measure of his capacity rather than a combined score, which obscures it.

The LPAD enables us to answer questions such as the capacity of the examinee to grasp a set of principles, rules, and prerequisites for their generaliza-

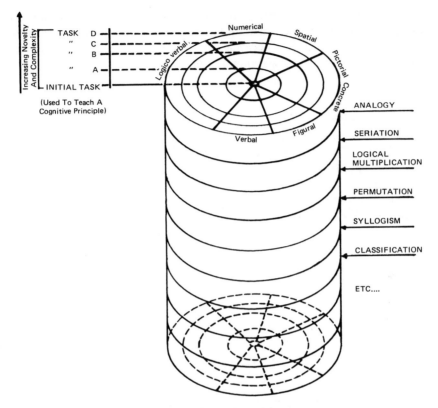

Figure 2. LPAD model.

tion; the quantity of investment necessary for him to reach mastery; and the changes in his capacity to adapt himself to situations that are becoming progressively newer and more complex. Finally, instruments are built in such a way as to point out the preferential modalities for learning characteristic of the individual.

A battery of tests has been constructed with the help of this model, all requiring the use of representational, transformational, and abstract conceptual behavior defined by Jensen (1969) as Level II intelligence. Most of the tasks are difficult for the initiated, normal functioning individual, so training as used in the LPAD is beneficial even for them. Thousands of children, among them retarded performers ranging from 40–80 IQ assessed with this method, have shown varying degrees of modifiability above and beyond their manifest low level of functioning. Following the assessment, programs aimed at the realization of their modifiability have been instituted. Follow-up studies have shown the efficiency of the LPAD to predict, as well as to orient investment towards preferential areas of modifiability and the most appropriate modalities of intervention (Feuerstein et al., 1971). In addition to measuring modifiability, the LPAD becomes a very rich source for clinical observations—out of which we have derived knowledge and understanding of the dynamics of failure in cognitive behavior of the culturally deprived child.

FOLLOW-UP STUDIES

In addition to the many children examined and aided by the LPAD, we also have extensive evidence of modifiability from a large population of adolescents studied over a 35-year period beginning with their post-World War II acceptance into the Youth Immigration Department of the Jewish Agency. This agency was and is charged with in-gathering of Jewish children and adolescents into Israel and placement in total care programs, such as kibbutzim, youth villages, foster homes, etc. The follow-up studies indicate that children of this population who initially showed levels of functioning in the range of EMR and even lower had a very high rate of modifiability at as late a stage of development as adolescence following their placement in enriching, stimulating and powerful environments. A study comparing graduates of Youth Aliyah with their non-Youth Aliyah siblings indicated that the initially more advantaged siblings were lower on all measures of performance administered, supporting the hypothesis of modifiability under enriching conditions (see Table 1).

INSTRUMENTAL ENRICHMENT

Modifiability studied with the help of LPAD and follow-up studies have been seminal not only in the search for a better theoretical framework for understanding such observed changes, but also in orienting our efforts in producing optimal conditions for modifiability to take place. Among a variety of other strategies, such as placement of the retarded performer in total care programs, or enriching his environment with stimuli and Mediated Learning Experience, Instrumental Enrichment is an attempt to provide a focused, systematic, and powerful attack

Table 1. Israel defense force recruits by subgroup and level of intelligence[a]

Subgroup	High (7—9) %	Average (5—6) %	Low (1—4) %	Mean	Standard deviation	N
Youth Aliyah	17	53	30	5.12	2.55	83
Non-Youth Aliyah	17	40	43	4.80	1.72	92
Treatment group	24	44	32	5.27	1.52	34
Day center	7	34	56	4.09	1.53	70
Residential center	2	59	39	4.44	1.38	59
Disturbed residential	11	44	45	4.72	1.53	18

[a]Comparative data of results obtained by Youth Aliyah graduates at the time of the army draft by different treatment conditions.

on those functions considered to be directly responsible for the failure of the culturally deprived to use direct exposure to stimuli for learning. Instrumental Enrichment is structured in such a way that it exposes the student to a systematic and age-specific substitute for Mediated Learning Experience. The program consists of approximately 400 hours of intensive paper-and-pencil exercises used in both classroom and individual sessions over a period of two or more years. Sixteen instruments of content-free exercises, such as orientation in time and space, organization of dots, syllogistic thinking, etc., involve the student in tasks structured to fulfill six basic subgoals:

1. Correction of deficient functions characteristic of the retarded performer, such as blurred perception, impaired spatial and temporal orientation, lack of comparative behavior, lack of need for logical evidence and accuracy, and impulsive behavior.
2. Providing the learner with the mental skills (concepts and relationships) necessary to master the highly complex tasks presented in Instrumental Enrichment.
3. Turning acquired principles, skills, and problem-solving strategies into organized schemata through habit formation, by offering ample opportunity for repetitive exposure to the same task presented in a great number of variations and situations.
4. Creation of insight processes as a way of enabling the learner to generalize the acquired principles by understanding the meaning of the processes that take place during his interaction with the task.
5. Production of strong task-intrinsic motivation, which is accomplished by making the tasks both challenging and accessible to progressive mastery.
6. Instrumental Enrichment is in its construction aimed at a change of the individual's perception of himself from the image of a passive recipient into the active producer of information. Each task in Instrumental Enrichment is designed so as to produce a feeling of mastery in the learner, and the self-image of one who is capable of selecting and actively organizing the world of stimuli impinging on him.

Results of the two-year IE experiment are presented in the next chapter. However, the results obtained from the follow-up study are of importance to this chapter in as much as they bring clarity into the dynamics of our concept of modifiability. Results obtained two years after the termination of the IE program show a difference in favor of the experimental group that is meaningfully bigger than the difference found in favor of the same group immediately upon termination of the experiment. The fact that we find a divergent effect over time indicates that the program produced a change in the cognitive structure of the individual rather than a sheer increase in information and specific skills. This enables the individual to use direct exposure to stimuli, to formal and informal sources of learning, to experiences and to life events for his further development and growth.

SUMMARY

MLE is conceived as the interaction between human environment-child, marked by the intention of the experienced adult to mediate the world to the child and transmit to him HIS culture, values, and cognitive skills. MLE enhances the individual's capacity to use direct exposure to stimuli. Lack of MLE produces deficiencies in functions—prerequisites of cognitive development. Redevelopment is conceived possible in adolescence under conditions of MLE adapted to age characteristics. Instrumental Enrichment is an attempt to substitute MLE for cognitive redevelopment in adolescence.

ACKNOWLEDGMENTS

The authors express their gratitude to many collaborators, especially to Professor Abraham J. Tannenbaum, Professor Martin Hamburger, and Mendel Hoffman, for their assistance in outlining the theory and elaboration of the findings. A special thanks to Mogens Reimer Jensen for his editorial work.

REFERENCES

Clarke, A. M., and Clarke, A. D. B. (1976) Early Experience: Myth and Evidence. London: Open Books.

Feuerstein, R. (1969) The Instrumental Enrichment Method, an Outline of Theory and Technique. Jerusalem: Hadassah-Wizo-Canada Research Institute.

Feuerstein, R. (1970) A dynamic approach to the causation, prevention and alleviation of retarded performance. In Social-Cultural Aspects of Mental Retardation. (Ed. Haywood, H.C.) New York: Appleton, p. 341.

Feuerstein, R., and Krasilovsky, D. (1967) The Treatment Group Technique. Israel Annals of Psychiatry and Related Disciplines 5:1, Spring.

Feuerstein, R., Krasilovsky, D., Hoffman, M., Rand, Y., and Tannenbaum, A. J. (1973) The Effects of Group Care on the Psychosocial Habilitation of Immigrant Adolescents in Israel with Special Reference to High Risk Children. Jerusalem: Hadassah-Wizo-Canada Research Institute.

Feuerstein, R., and Rand, Y. (1974) Mediated learning experiences: An outline of the proximal etiology for differential development of cognitive functions. International Understanding, 9/10:7.

Hebb, D. O. (1949) The Organization of Behavior. New York: John Wiley.

Hunt, J. M. (1961) Intelligence and Experience. New York: Ronald.

Jensen, A. (1969) How Much Can We Boost IQ and Scholastic Achievement? Educ. Rev. 39:1.

Konrad, K., and Melzack, R. (1975) Novelty-Enhancement effects associated with early sensory social isolation. In The Developmental Neurophysiology of Sensory Deprivation. New York: Academic Press.

Sameroff, A. J., and Chandler, M. J. (1975) Reproductive risk and the continuum of caretaking casualty. In Child Development Research, vol. 4 (Ed. Horowitz, F. D.) Chicago: University of Chicago Press.

RESEARCH TO PRACTICE IN MENTAL RETARDATION
Education and Training, Volume II
Edited by Peter Mittler
Copyright 1977 I.A.S.S.M.D.

AN ANALYSIS OF THE EFFECTS OF INSTRUMENTAL ENRICHMENT ON DISADVANTAGED ADOLESCENTS

Y. Rand, R. Feuerstein, A. J. Tannenbaum, M. R. Jensen and M. B. Hoffman
Hadassah-Wizo-Canada Research Institute, 6 Karmon Street,
Beit Hakerem, Jerusalem, Israel

Based on a set of theoretical assumptions pertaining to the nature of human development and cognitive functioning (Feuerstein, 1977, this volume), a program for the remediation of cognitive deficiencies was developed and researched for its impact on a population of low functioning adolescents. The results of the controlled experiment are set forth and discussed following a brief presentation of the main theoretical assumptions, the targeted population, and the Instrumental Enrichment program.

Seven theoretical assumptions formed the underlying basis of the study:

1. The human individual is an open system, susceptible to environmental influence and consequently modifiable.
2. There is internal permeability among subsystems of the individual so that interventions in one area will produce changes in adjacent areas of functioning.
3. The cognitive modifiability of the retarded performer through direct exposure to stimuli is limited, because of absences or restrictions in the nature of the Mediated Learning Experience (Feuerstein and Rand, 1974). Any attempt to modify the cognitive structure of the retarded performer will have to be geared to the remediation of the deficit produced by the absence of Mediated Learning Experience.
4. Cognitive modifiability is not limited to critical periods for the redevelopment of the individual.
5. The greater the impact of a planned cognitive strategy, the higher the efficiency with which the individual can use it in both a versatile and an

117

adequate way, a continuous and multisource type of intervention is called for in order to obtain a meaningful modification.

6. The individual's active involvement in the process of modification enhances quantitative and qualitative aspects of modification.

7. Cognitive operations are basically of a transferable nature, implying the encouragement of their applicability to a great variety of situations, areas, contents, and aspects.

Feuerstein's Instrumental Enrichment program (1969) is a multifaceted strategy for intervention involving direct attacks on the deficiencies in cognition and auxiliary competencies exhibited by the low-functioning performer. The program aims at nurturing proper learning sets and systematic data-gathering behavior on the input level, inducing comparative behavior and other cognitive functions on the elaborational level, and removing attitudinal inhibitions on the output level, as well as a host of behavioral dysfunctions typically operating in low-functioning children. The multiple emphases of the program are made salient through the grouping of exercises according to particular skill areas. An integral part of the program is teacher training in the underlying theory, constructs, and methods of administration. The program is administered on an hour per diem basis as part of the regular classroom program for a two year duration. Teacher-training is emphasized within a context of bridging the remediational effort with conventional school curricula and, ultimately, problems of living.

DESIGN

A research design was constructed in order to assess the program's modificational impact on, especially, the cognitive functioning of adolescents typically viewed as deprived and as poor school performers. A sample of this target population was obtained, the experimental and comparison groups being composed of Israeli youngsters, aged 13–16, who were extremely low performing on scholastic achievement measures, with a gap of about three to four years from their normal peers and psychometrically scoring at levels ranging between the borderline and the educable mental retardates (EMR). Subjects originated from groups of North African or Asian origin that in Israel have been described as low-functioning, disadvantaged and socioculturally deprived. In the controlled experiment, Instrumental Enrichment (IE) was contrasted with General Enrichment (GE) (General Enrichment is the term used to designate a regular school curriculum.) Subjects were located in two residential and two day centers (RC and DC, respectively). One of each type of setting was reserved exclusively for Instrumental Enrichment, while the two remaining settings, one of each type, were reserved for General Enrichment and functioned as comparison groups. The contrasting of educational settings reflects differences in the research sample studied, with subjects of the residential facilities displaying relatively more dependency, lower scores on scholastic achievement tests, and a higher frequency of crisis in family life focusing on the need perceived by welfare agencies, parents, or relatives to place the child outside the home. Children in day centers are most often referred by school officials who believe that the child cannot continue his studies in regular classes with any hope of success.

HYPOTHESES

Four main hypotheses were formulated within this simple 2×2 research design:

1. Socially disadvantaged adolescents, functioning poorly at school and participating in residential and day centers programs, show greater gains on intellective and nonintellective criterion measures after exposure to Instrumental Enrichment than after exposure to General Enrichment.
2. Participation in Instrumental and General Enrichment programs produces better performance on criteria measures for adolescents in residential centers, where special intervention is administered in the context of total care, than in day centers, which have relatively limited contact with the student.
3. There is an interaction effect between treatment (IE vs GE) and setting (RC vs. DC) with the Instrumental Enrichment program and residential facility having a mutually reinforcing impact.
4. Exposure to the Instrumental Enrichment program produces changes in the aptitude profiles of the target population, while General Enrichment does not.

MEASURES

The research design called for obtaining test data on intellective and nonintellective criterion measures administered once before and once following the intervention period (pre- and postlevel testing). The measures employed included the eight subtest and five factor Thurstone PMA tests (Thurstone, 1962), the twelve subtest Project Achievement Battery, the Levidal Self-Concept Scale, and a teacher rating inventory—the Classroom Participation Scale (CPS)—with one part being a trait check list (CPS I) and the other employing brief behavior descriptions (CPS II). The last four instruments were specifically developed and researched for this study. In addition to the PMA, three nonverbal measures of general intelligence were administered at the postlevel: the Terman test (Terman, 1942) the D-48 (Gough and Domino, 1963) and the Porteus IQ (Porteus, 1965). Four measures of dimensions relating to specific cognitive functions emphasized in the Instrumental Enrichment program were also obtained only at the post level: global versus analytic cognitive style measured by the Embedded Figures

Test (EFT) (Witkin, 1950) and the Human Figure Drawing test (HFD) scored by Marlens' sophistication scale (Witkin et al., 1962), spatial orientation measured by a revised and expanded version of the Kuhlman-Finch Postures test (Kuhlman-Finch, 1953) and, finally, precision-rapidity as measured by the Lahy Test (Zazzo, 1964). All postlevel data were treated by the analysis of covariance method. The covariate for each test administered pre and post was the score obtained at the prelevel of testing. For measures administered only at the postlevel, covariates were introduced drawing on the total PMA prescore, and also, in most cases, one or more PMA subtests were introduced as additional covariates on their face validity. Thus, a single statistical model was used to test the first three hypotheses. For the final hypothesis, profiles were drawn contrasting the experimental and comparison groups on scores obtained on the five-factor PMA and examined by simple inspection.

Comparable baselines for the statistical analysis were ensured for 57 pairs of IE versus GE subjects who were selected from the Total Research Population (N = 218) and matched separately within residential centers (24 pairs) and day centers (33 pairs) on the basis of age, sex, ethnicity, and the total score obtained on the PMA at the prelevel of testing. Adding more matching variables would have critically reduced the number of pairs that could be matched. In this chapter results are presented for this matched pairs sample only.

RESULTS

The results indicate a very substantial support for Hypothesis 1 with four out of the eight PMA subtests (Numbers, Addition, Spatial Relations, and Figure Grouping) being significantly better for IE subjects than for their GE counterparts. Significance was obtained also for the PMA total score. This result is highlighted by the fact that subjects were matched on the PMA total score obtained at the prelevel of testing (see Table 1).

IE subjects also scored significantly higher than their GE counterparts on two out of the three additional intellective measures, on the Terman Test and on the D-48 Test. Although the IE group performed better than the GE group on the Porteus IQ test, this difference did not reach the accepted level of significance (see Table 1).

IE subjects uniformly performed better than GE subjects on the tests administered to evaluate the impact of Instrumental Enrichment on specific measures of performance. The data on the Embedded Figures Test indicate that while IE subjects spent significantly less time on average working on the tasks they produced significantly more correct responses. Significant differences were likewise revealed in the Human Figures Drawing Test (HFD), taking into account articulation of body image as well as elements centering on form level, extent of identity and sex differentiation and level of detailing. Similarly, the Experimental groups significantly outperformed the control groups on the Postures test indicating superior Spatial Orientation. The scores on the Lahy Test indicate an insignificant difference on the total number of items attended to during the testing interval. The IE group however had a significantly higher proportion of correct responses while the GE group had a significantly higher proportion of incorrect responses.

On the Project Achievement Battery only two out of twelve subtests (Bible and Geometry) showed the IE subjects performing significantly better than GE subjects. It should be noted, however, that on this measure as well as on all measures presented above, no instance was recorded in which a significant result was indicated in the direction opposite to that hypothesized.

The tendency towards more successful development among experimental groups is confirmed by results on some of the nonintellective criteria. On the CPS II behavior descriptors, significant differences were observed between groups exposed to contrasting treatments, regardless of setting. The Instrumental Enrichment group improved more on Factor B, "Self-Sufficiency," which includes ratings of the subjects' ability to start and to finish work independently, as well as their persistence in work. Similar results favoring the Instrumental Enrichment group were obtained on Factor C, "Adaptiveness to Work Demands," which includes such behaviors as helping other children, sharing, and caring for materials and using them safely. The General Enrichment group, on the other hand, scored significantly higher on Factor A, "Interpersonal Conduct"—which includes behaviors such as interacting aggressively with classmates, disruptive behavior, and lack of deportment in class. That is, the GE subjects were more likely to be seen by their teachers as developing (or maintaining) these negative behaviors over the two-year period than were their IE counterparts. No significant differences were observed in either direction on the CPS I trait check list factors and the Levidal self-concept factors.

The second hypothesis predicted that subjects studying at residential centers (RC) would score higher on the criterion measures than subjects studying at day centers (DC), irrespective of their program of studies. This hypothesis received credible support, albeit less dramatically. Two subtests of the PMA (Numbers and Addition) and the total score on this test revealed significant differences in favor of the RC group. The RC group was also superior on the Porteus IQ Test, while a significant difference in the direction *opposite* to the hypothesized, was obtained on the D-48 Test. On the Terman Test, DC subjects scored higher, but this difference failed to reach the accepted level of significance. No significant differences were observed on any of the tests checking specific cognitive dimensions. On the Project Achievement Battery, significant differences in favor of RC subjects were obtained on the Bible and Geometry subtests and on three out of the four arithmetic operations, with only subtraction not reaching significance. As to the nonintellective measures, significance was obtained for Factor B of the CPS I trait check list, "Unsocialized Behavior," which includes such traits as depression, tension and withdrawal. The residential center children were thus far

Table 1. Significant F ratios from analyses of covariance on PMA, project achievement battery, CPS I, CPS II, Levidal and additional postlevel measures, for pairs of IE versus GE subjects matched separately within RC and DC settings on PMA total prescore, age, sex and ethnicity by setting and treatment ($N = 114$)

Variable Effect	Primary mental abilities (PMA) Subtest	F ratio	Project achievement battery Subtest	F ratio	Classroom Participation Scale I and II Levidal Factor	F ratio	Additional postlevel measures Test	F ratio
IE versus GE	Numbers	15.34[a]	Bible	6.98[a]	CPS I B	NS	Terman[e]	6.57[a]
	Addition	4.22[b]	Geography	NS	CPS II A	3.77[b]	D - 48[c]	22.89[a]
	Spatial relations	22.02[a]	Geometry	5.28[b]	CPS II B	22.45[a]	Porteus IQ[c]	NS
	Figure grouping	3.79[b]	Reading comprehension	NS	CPS II C	10.92[a]	EFT: Average time[a]	28.75[a]
	Total	13.66[a]					EFT: Total correct[a]	16.68[a]
			Addition	NS	Levidal	NS	HFD[c]	5.07[b]
			Multiplication	NS			Postures[a]	13.38[a]
			Division	NS			Lahy: Proportion correct[c]	7.51[a]
							Lahy: Proportion wrong[c]	4.41[b]
RC versus DC	Numbers	7.60[a]	Bible	5.70[b]	CPS I B	17.23[a]	Terman[e]	NS
	Addition	6.38[a]	Geography	10.19[a]	CPS II A	NS	D - 48[c]	5.15[b] (p)
	Spatial relations	NS	Geometry	NS	CPS II B	NS	Porteus IQ[c]	5.61[b]
	Figure grouping	NS	Reading comprehension	NS	CPS II C	NS	EFT: Average time[a]	NS
	Total	6.90[a]			Levidal	NS	EFT: Total correct[a]	NS
			Addition	4.88[b]			HFD[c]	NS
			Multiplication	16.23[a]			Postures[a]	NS
			Division	36.15[a]			Lahy: Proportion correct[c]	NS
							Lahy: Proportion wrong[c]	NS

Interaction						
Numbers	NS	Bible	NS	CPS I B	5.09[b]	Terman[e] 9.17[a]
Addition	NS	Geography	NS	CPS II A	NS	D - 48[c] NS
Spatial relations	NS	Geometry	NS	CPS II B	NS	Porteus IQ[e] NS
Figure grouping	NS	Reading comprehension	11.37^a	Levidal	NS	EFT: Average time[d] NS
Total	NS	Total				EFT: Total correct[d] NS
		Addition	NS			HFD[c] NS
		Multiplication	NS			Postures[d] NS
		Division	NS			Lahy: Proportion correct[c] NS
						Lahy: Proportion wrong[c] NS

Covariates			
Pre PMA score for each variable	Prescore for each variable	Prescore for each factor	

[a] Significant at the 0.01 level or better. (p) Significant in the direction opposite the hypothesized.
[b] Significant at the 0.05 level.
[c] Covariate: PMA total prescore.
[d] Covariate: Prescores on PMA total, spatial relations and perceptual speed.
[e] Covariate: Prescores on PMA total, spatial relations and figure grouping.

more likely to be seen by their teachers as developing or maintaining these unsocializing tendencies than were their counterparts in the day center facilities. No significant findings were observed on the CPS II behavior descriptors and on the Levidal self-concept factors.

The third hypothesis predicted an interaction effect between treatment (Instrumental Enrichment versus General Enrichment) and setting (residential versus day center) with the Instrumental Enrichment program and the residential facility having a mutually reinforcing impact. No support was found for this hypothesis on any of the intellective measures, except the Terman Test. Here, however, students from the *day center* receiving Instrumental Enrichment scored highest, and not, as hypothesized, students from the residential center receiving this treatment. On the Project Achievement Battery, an interaction effect was observed on the Reading Comprehension subtest, but again, this finding was in support of the *day center* students receiving Instrumental Enrichment. A third interaction effect was obtained on Factor B on the CPS I trait check list in support of the hypothesis, i.e., Instrumental Enrichment produced more salutary results on this Factor in the residential setting, while the opposite is true for General Enrichment in the day center setting. The few and constrasting findings on interaction indicate that the third hypothesis is untenable.

The fourth hypothesis stated that the exposure to Instrumental Enrichment produces changes in the aptitude profiles of the target population while General Enrichment does not. This hypothesis was tested by plotting profiles on PMA factor scores, using the normative Israeli sample ($N = 1,117$) on which the factors were originally extracted as the baseline population (see Figure 1).

Comparing the Instrumental Enrichment group pre and post there is no change in profiles. However, comparing the profiles of experimental and comparison samples, it is obvious that they are more alike at the point of preintervention than at postintervention. The change that has taken place is clearly in the General Enrichment sample, possibly reflecting what amounts to a normal change over time or a regression towards the mean, neither of which is noted in the experimental group.

A similar comparison of residential and day center samples showed no profile changes over the two year period for both groups (see Figure 2).

DISCUSSION

It is clear from the outcomes of the controlled experiment that Instrumental Enrichment enabled the children to cultivate more efficiently those cognitive operations that are usually tapped in tests of general intelligence, judging by the highly noteworthy results on the PMA total score and on the Terman and D-48 tests. These results and the unequivocal IE superiority on measures of specific cognitive skills and style aspects (i.e., the EFT, HFD, the Porteus and the Lahy), suggest the presence of a broad base of extra intellective power, broader

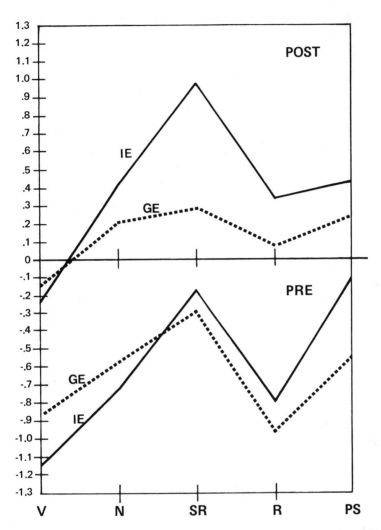

Figure 1. Comparative profiles on PMA factor scores, pre and post, for pairs of IE (*solid line*) versus GE (*broken line*) subjects matched separately within RC and DC settings on PMA total prescore, age, sex, and ethnicity by treatment (*N* = 114).

psychological differentiation and variegated intellectual adequacy in the experimental subjects in comparison to the controls. Neither do these findings appear to be limited to noncontentual areas, although only modest support was obtained for IE superiority in achievement-oriented areas. The modesty of these results has to be viewed in the light of the fact that IE places relatively little emphasis on the verbal factor and proportionately more on figural concepts.

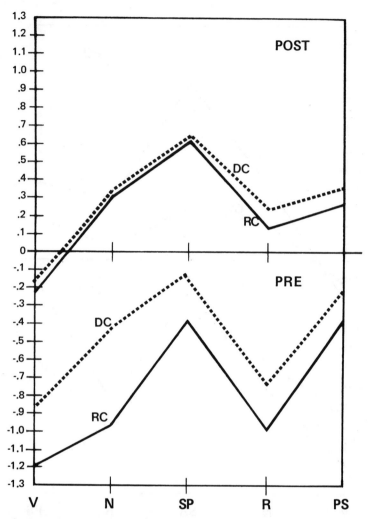

Figure 2. Comparative profiles on PMA factor scores, pre and post, for pairs of IE versus GE subjects matched separately within RC (*solid line*) and DC (*broken line*) settings on PMA total prescore, age, sex, and ethnicity by setting (*N* = 114).

Comparison groups, moreover, profited from about 300 additional hours of instruction in the usual school curriculum and were compensated with further assistance in these areas when encountering difficulties.

Instrumental Enrichment also appears to have a beneficial effect on adjustment, with a significant impact on attitudinal variables relating to self-sufficiency, adaptiveness to work demands and interpersonal conduct. The findings of the study suggest, moreover, that residential center care is superior to day center care in generating cognitive modifications, but the support for this conclusion was less unequivocal than the support obtained in favor of Instrumental Enrichment versus General Enrichment. So, while the residential center does have a positive impact on some areas of personal development and cognitive functioning, children can benefit from Instrumental Enrichment irrespective of the setting in which the program is administered. Moreover, no combination of treatment and setting was found to generate a mutually reinforcing impact.

The lack of any observed change in self-concept is possibly attributable to self-concept either being very resistant to change or needing a longer time span for changes to be accommodated and expressed. It is still an open question whether Instrumental Enrichment can make qualitative changes in subjects' aptitude profiles. It is possible that the intercorrelations between the PMA factors force some stability into the profiles, which could thus account at least in part for the lack of radical changes in the profiles.

CONCLUSIONS

It is clear that Instrumental Enrichment has had a beneficial effect on the targeted population in terms of its overall cognitive functioning and its growth in particular scholastic aptitudes, achievement skills, and classroom behaviors. The evidence is consistent enough along intellective and nonintellective dimensions to suggest the likelihood that such a program merits adoption in redevelopment efforts for low functioning children comparable in background and handicap to those evaluated. The conclusion that may be drawn is that a systematic approach to mediated learning such as the one exemplified by Instrumental Enrichment can have an impact on the cognitive development of educational retardates even after they have reached adolescence. There is no need to withhold special services for this age group, nor is there need to place our hope almost entirely on early intervention on the grounds that once the child has graduated beyond his preschool years it is too late for an equitable return on investments in mediated learning. Results of the present study should lead to a far more optimistic view of the responsiveness of the older child to educational stimulation.

SUMMARY

Instrumental Enrichment (IE) is an intervention program aimed at cognitive redevelopment of sociocultural disadvantaged adolescents. It consists of 400 hours of paper-pencil exercises, taught by trained teachers. A two-year comparative study shows significant positive effects of IE by criterion measures of intelligence, academic achievement, and cognitive style. No effects on self-image have been observed.

REFERENCES

Feuerstein, R. (1969) The Instrumental Enrichment Method, an Outline of Theory and Technique. Jerusalem: Hadassah-Wizo-Canada Research Institute.

Feuerstein, R., and Rand, Y. (1974) Mediated learning experiences: An outline of the proximal etiology for differential development of cognitive functions. International Understanding 9/10, 7:37.

Finch, F. (1953) Kuhlman-Finch Intelligence Test Manual. Philadephia: Educational Testing Bureau.

Gough, H. C., and Domino, G. (1963) The D-48 test as a measure of general ability among grade school children. J. Consult. Psychol. 27:344.

Porteus, S. D. (1965) Porteus Maze Test: Fifty Years of Application. Palo Alto, California: Pacific Books.

Terman, E. L. et al. (1942) Non Language Multi-Mental Test. Bureau of Publications, Teachers College, Columbia University.

Thurstone, T. G. (1962) SRA Primary Mental Abilities. Chicago, Illinois: Science Research Associates.

Witkin, H. A. (1950) Individual differences in ease of perception of embedded figures. J. Pers. 19, 1:15.

Witkin, H. A. et al. (1962) Psychological Differentiation. New York: Wiley & Sons.

Zazzo, R. (1964) Le Test de Deux Barrages. Neuchatel, Switzerland: Delchaux et Niestle.

RESEARCH TO PRACTICE IN MENTAL RETARDATION
Education and Training, Volume II
Edited by Peter Mittler
Copyright 1977 I.A.S.S.M.D.

UPDATE ON RESEARCH INTO INCREASING INTELLIGENCE LEVELS OF MENTALLY RETARDED CHILDREN

J. Farb, A. W. Cottrell, J. C. Montague, and J. M. Throne
Lakemary Center for Exceptional Children,
100 Lakemary Drive, Paola, Kansas 66071, United States

This chapter presents an update on our research into increasing the intelligence levels of mentally retarded children through training. Intelligence is conceptualized by us to be, purely and simply, behavior: observable, measurable, manipulable (Throne, 1970). To us, intelligent behavior should be as susceptible to training as any other behavior. We use as clues to its components the performances tapped by the subscales of the Wechsler Intelligence Scale for Children (WISC) (Wechsler, 1949). Our training procedures are derived from the science of operant conditioning (Skinner, 1938) and its technological arm, applied behavior analysis (Baer, Wolf, and Risley, 1968). In essence, they involve reinforcing correct responses or successive approximations of them by deliberately and systematically arranging circumstances such that reinforceable responses can—and do—occur.

MEMORY

Improving mnemonic performances, or memory, was the aim of our first training program (Farb and Throne, 1974; Farb, unpublished). The first child trained was a Down's syndrome girl six years and seven months old at the onset of training, a student at the Lakemary Center for Exceptional Children. Her IQs on standardized intelligence tests consistently clustered around 50. Digit span items like those found on the WISC were the mnemonic performances selected for training. The WISC items themselves were never trained, only items like them were. That is, items with numbers of digits equal to those in each WISC series.

The digits to be trained were divided into item classes on the basis of length, i.e., number of digits. Hence, two-digit items formed the basis of the two-item class, three-digit items the three-item class, etc. Each item class also contained probe measures—untrained items serving to measure the generalized effects of training. Initially, two probes were employed: other digit items, including those on the WISC, and grammatical sentences. In both cases, the probes corresponded in length to the digit span item classes that were trained. That is, the number of digits or syllables in each probe class equalled the number of digits in each training class. The number of item classes to which a child was exposed extended from the child's baseline level—i.e., the highest item class attained prior to training—to the level at or just above the item class attained by a normal child of the same chronological age.

For the first child, the item classes extended from the three-item (three digits) to the five-item (five digits) class, at which level her mnemonic performances would be normal for her chronological age. Following the recording of baseline across all measures, training and probe, training proceeded progressively from one item class to the next higher class as gains were achieved on both the training and probe items. The training procedure involved the modeling of digit span items with reinforcement contingent upon correct digit span responses or incorrect digit span responses, which, through repeated modeling, became increasingly more correct. Reinforcement consisted of praise, and on occasion, candy or potato chips.

Two forms of presentation of items were tried out. In the first, five digit span items in an item class were trained at the same time that ten probes—five digit span items and five grammatical sentence items—in that class were examined for generalized training effects. While this procedure resulted in correct responses to the training items quickly reaching 100%, there was only limited generalization to the probes. In order to produce greater generalization, a second training procedure was introduced.

In the second procedure, a wide variety of digit span items, as opposed to merely five, were trained. These were drawn from an item pool previously prepared, and presented in a continually varying order. Generalization was measured by responses to items from another pool, probes also being presented in continually varying order at the same time training was taking place.

Also, when the second procedure was introduced, two more probe items were added. They were nongrammatical sentences and match-to-sample tasks in which letters of the alphabet were to be matched to samples. The nongrammatical sentence probes were added to control for initially high levels of correct responses to the grammatical sentence probes and also to provide evidence of even broader generalization effects. The match-to-sample probes were added to determine whether or not trained mnemonic improvements would generalize to mnemonic performances not involving imitation; on all the other items, training and probe, the performances involved imitation. The child was asked to point to the letters on a probe card matching those on a sample card removed when the probe card was presented. The number of letters to be matched corresponded to the various digit span item classes. (An example of a match to sample probe was presented at the Congress. Space limitations prohibit inclusion of the 29 figures and tables in the Proceedings. Interested readers may receive copies of these by writing the first author.)

The second procedure proved superior to the first, with performances on all items, training *and* probe, increasing to levels at or near 100%. To ascertain further the comparative effects of both procedures, all item classes were trained initially under the first procedure, then under the second. In each case, the results were the same, with the first procedure producing improvement in the training items at or near 100% correct but few or none in the probes, but the second producing improvements to 100% in both.

Occasioned by the successes of the initial mnemonic training program with the single child, the program was expanded to include two more children, two boys (Farb, Throne, Sailor, and Baer, 1974). One of the boys was a 12-year-old Down's syndrome child whose IQs clustered around 45. The second was 10 years old and diagnosed as culturally deprived as well as retarded. His IQs clustered around 70. For the first child, the training program involved item classes two through five. For the second child, item classes five through seven were introduced. Only the second training procedure, the superior effectiveness of which has been demonstrated previously, was used with the two boys. Along with the digit span training items, probes of untrained digit span items, grammatical sentences, nongrammatical sentences, and match-to-sample items were presented.

Again, the second training procedure resulted in performances on all items, training and probe, increasing to levels at or near 100% correct. For the first boy, training was terminated with the five-item class—slightly below normality for his chronological age. For the second boy, training terminated with the seven-item class—normal for his chronological age.

A follow-up probe session was conducted with all three children seven months after the end of training. All gains showed maintenance over this extended period, during which no training sessions were conducted. Thus, the second training procedure as applied to these three children appears to represent an effective and efficient means of improving generalized mnemonic performances to normal levels according to chronological age.

VOCABULARY

While research in the memory training program was underway at Lakemary, a program to improve vocabulary performances in mentally retarded children was initiated at the University of Arkansas at Little Rock (Cottrell, unpublished; Cottrell, Montague, Farb, and Throne, 1976).

The program began with an initial study conducted with a single girl and was subsequently expanded to include two other girls. The first child was a Down's syndrome girl who was six years and six months old at the beginning of the program. Her IQ on the Peabody Picture Vocabulary Test was 42. Her WISC IQ was 52.

The first eight words of the WISC vocabulary subscale were used as the basis for eight semantic classes. For instance, *bicycle* was treated as a member of the class *vehicles; knife* as a member of the class *cutting instruments; hat* as a member of the class *clothing;* etc.

The WISC word itself in each of the semantic classes served as a probe, never receiving training. In each class, three different words served as vocabulary training words. That is, in each class there were three words that received training and a WISC vocabulary word serving as a generalization measure.

All words in each class were treated in terms of both identification and definition (e.g., "Show me the car" and "What is a car?" respectively). Identification was included 1) because there would be relatively little utility in teaching a child to define something that he would be unable to identify and 2) in order to determine the relationship between identification and definition. Training in identification was conducted together with training in definition. Trials consisted of the trainer asking the child for an identification or a definition response in the manner noted above. The same procedure was conducted for the probe words. The percentage of correct responses was recorded on identification and definition for each word, both training and probe. After baseline was recorded across all items, training and probe, training proceeded progressively from one semantic class to the next as the percentage of correct responses to training words in the previous class and its respective probe word increased through training.

The training procedure involved immediate reinforcement for correct responses to the training words and/or successive approximations of a correct response. The reinforcer consisted of a combination of praise and candy. Incorrect responses resulted in the trial being presented again, with the correct response being modeled for the child by the trainer. Closer and closer approximations of the correct response were reinforced over repeated trials until an unaided correct response was emitted and reinforced. Responses to probe words were never repeated or reinforced regardless of the response.

The procedure resulted in rapid, generalized gains within each semantic class as it was applied. Frequently, the training of the first two words in a given class resulted in the immediate generalization of correct responses to the remaining training word and the WISC probe. It was also demonstrated that the child could often identify the pictorial referents of terms although he was initially unable to define them. At no time was correct identification at a lower level than correct definition. Neither identification nor definition was trained for the WISC probes of each class, but correct responses on both measures occurred in every case. In other words, generalization effects of training were obtained.

A follow-up probe session conducted after 90 days demonstrated that all training and probe gains were being maintained. Similar improvements in vocabulary performance were obtained when the program was extended to include two other children, thus replicating the effects of the program obtained for the first child.

SPATIAL RELATIONS

Block design is the spatial relations subscale of the WISC. A program was conducted to train two retarded children in block design performances. The program involved two girls who are students at Lakemary. The first girl was 10 years and eight months old at the beginning of the program. Her IQs clustered around 70. The second girl was 14 years and five months old. Her IQs clustered around 50. In both cases brain damage was indicated.

The program involved one set of block design training items and four sets of probe measures. The training items consisted of block design tasks similar to but different from the block design items on the WISC. The primary probes consisted of untrained block design items similar to but different from the training items and included the block design items on the WISC. The block design training items and probes were presented on index cards showing a given block design. The block design was constructed by the child using the nine blocks of the WISC block design subscale. A correct response consisted of the child constructing the pictured design within a time period of 65 seconds for training items and probes or within the maximum time criterion set for WISC block design items. The second set of probes consisted of two-dimensional block constructions also presented on index cards. The third set of probes consisted of three-dimensional block constructions that were otherwise exactly like the two-dimensional probes. The number of blocks involved in all these probes was determined on the basis of the individual child's baseline performances. The two- and three-dimensional probes involved seven blocks for the first child and five blocks for the second child. A correct response to either of these probes involved the child duplicating the pictured block construction within 65 seconds using the blocks from the Stanford-Binet Intelligence Scale. The fourth probe was a "figural-reasoning" match-to-sample task in which the child was given a card showing three abstract figures and was required to choose from among three other figures on a second card the one that belonged with those on the sample card.

After baseline measures were recorded across all items for both children, training was begun for the first child. The second child continued in the baseline condition. Training consisted of immediate reinforcement in the form of praise presented for correct responses, or successive approximations of them, on the block design training items. All items, both training and probe, varied from day-to-day. The probe items served as measures of generalized improvements within the block design performance category.

The introduction of the training procedure resulted in rapid generalized improvements in block design performances for the first child, with the percentage of correct responses to both training items and all probes increasing to levels far above baseline. Seven days after the beginning of training for the first child, training was initiated for the second child, producing similar rapid, generalized improvement. A probe session with the WISC block design subscale was conducted for the first child on her eleventh day of training. The results showed the child's performance to be well within the normal range for her chronological age. A WISC probe session conducted for the second child on her ninth day of training showed her performances to be within the normal range for her chronological age.

GENERATIVE INTELLIGENCE

Factor analysis of the WISC points to a threefold breakdown of its subscales into sequential, conceptual, and spatial performance tasks (Rugel, 1974). The programs reported above fall into those factorial categories, one into each. Digit span falls into the sequential category, vocabulary into the conceptual, and block design into the spatial. All three of these programs have proved to be successful in generating increased intelligence levels, as measured, of mentally retarded children. On the basis of our success with these three programs, we are now ready to turn our attention to generating the same kind of results across the nine other performance categories constituting intelligence according to the WISC. But the fact that each of our three programs falls into one of the factorial categories, sequential, conceptual, and spatial, suggests a research strategy that may enable improvements in these nine other categories to occur as effectively but more efficiently than is permitted by a strategy enabling only one performance category at a time to be trained.

Just as we have demonstrated within-performance generalization from training to probe items in the three training programs previously described, the factorial evidence gives us reason to suspect that between-categorical generalization may also occur. It may not be necessary, therefore, to train performance items in each performance category one-by-one in order to get generalized improvements of the performances in each category. It may prove possible to train items in but one of the performance categories subsumed under each of the three factorial categories to get generalization to the other performance categories in the same factorial category. Our combined research findings have demonstrated that the intraperformance categorical relationships are functional—that they are yoked. If the intrafactorial categorical relationships are functionally related to one another also, the same generalized effects of training producing increases in probe levels within each performance category should produce intrafactorial categorical increases as well.

Accordingly, we have proposed a research design (Throne and Farb, 1975) that should enable us to determine these functional effects not only within but across performance categories in the course of training them (Throne and Farb, 1976a). All 12 training programs, corresponding to the 12 performance categories of the WISC, will be introduced together for a given child, and will form a total intelligence training package. The tasks of all 12 programs will be presented to the child. After baselines have been recorded across all measures, training and probe, in all of the 12 performance categories, training will be directed at one performance category (digit span). The measures in the remaining 11 performance categories will remain in the baseline (i.e., pretraining) condition. As gains are obtained in the first performance category, the 11 categories remaining in the baseline condition will be examined for evidence of any generalized effects from the ongoing training. After training gains have been obtained in the first performance category, training will be directed at a second category (vocabulary), with the 10 remaining categories continuing in the baseline condition and being continuously monitored for evidence of generalized improvements. Then, training will be directed at a third performance category (block design). At this point training will have been conducted across the three factorial categories of the WISC with an accompanying analysis of the generalized effects of these training procedures across the entire gamut of performance categories tapped by the WISC. To the extent generalization within and between performance and factorial categories is obtained, we will demonstrate our ability to generate intelligence (Throne and Farb, 1976b) irrespective of past or present environmental or organismic variables prevailing. The overall effect might be a reconsideration of the long-held assumption that mental retardation is essentially irreversible (Throne, 1975).

REFERENCES

Baer, D. M., Wolf, M. M., and Risley, T. R. (1968) Some current dimensions of applied behavior analysis. J. Appl. Behav. Anal. 1:91.

Cottrell, A. W. (1975) An operant procedure for improving the vocabulary performances of a mentally retarded child. Unpublished master's thesis, University of Arkansas, Little Rock.

Cottrell, A. W., Montague, J. C., Farb, J., and Throne, J. M. (1976) An operant procedure for improving the vocabulary performances of a mentally retarded child. Paper presented to the annual meeting of the Arkansas Speech and Hearing Association, Jonesboro, Arkansas.

Farb, J. (1976) Operant investigative training of generalized mnemonic performances of a Down's syndrome child. Unpublished master's thesis, University of Kansas, Lawrence.

Farb, J., and Throne, J. M. (1974) Operant investigative training of generalized mnemonic performances of a Down's syndrome child: A preliminary report. Paper Presented to the joint meeting of the American and Canadian Associations on Mental Deficiency, Toronto, June.

Farb, J., Throne, J. M., Sailor, W., and Baer, D. M. (1974) Improving generalized mnemonic performances of mentally retarded children. Paper presented to the annual meeting of Region V of the American Association on Mental Deficiency, New Orleans, October.

Rugel, R. P. (1974) WISC subtest scores of disabled readers: A review with respect to Bannatyne's recategorization. J. Learn. Dis. 7:57.

Skinner, B. F. (1938) The Behavior of Organisms: An Experimental Analysis. New York: Appleton-Century-Crofts.

Throne, J. M. (1970) A radical behaviorist approach to diagnosis in mental retardation. Ment. Retard. 8:2.

Throne, J. M. (1975) Raising intelligence levels of the mentally retarded: An overlooked educo-legal implication. J. Educ. 157:43.

Throne, J. M., and Farb, J. (1975) An operant alternative to multivariate statistics: A proposal. Educ. Technol. 15:43.

Throne, J. M., and Farb, J. (1976a) Operant investigative training (in preparation).

Throne, J. M., and Farb, J. (1976b) Generative intelligence (in preparation).

Wechsler, D. (1949) Wechsler Intelligence Scale for Children. New York: The Psychological Corporation.

NOTE ADDED IN PROOF:

Partial support for this research was provided by a National Research Service Award HD 07066 from the National Institute for Child Health and Human Development to the Kansas Center for Mental Retardation and Human Development.

RESEARCH TO PRACTICE IN MENTAL RETARDATION
Education and Training, Volume II
Edited by Peter Mittler
Copyright 1977 I.A.S.S.M.D.

FLEXIBILITY TRAINING WITH MODERATELY AND SEVERELY RETARDED CHILDREN AND YOUNG ADULTS

V. Parmar[1] and **A. D. B. Clarke**[2]
[1]*Psychology Department, St. Ebba's Hospital,
Epsom, Surrey, England*
[2]*Psychology Department, The University, Hull,
Yorkshire, England*

There has been much discussion of rigidity as an essential feature of mental retardation. Even now, the concept remains unclear. Very few studies have been concerned with developing cognitive assets in the retarded and, in particular, establishing conditions that maximise learning transfer. One of the exceptions in this area is the research reported by Corter and McKinney in 1968. Their work on flexibility training with the educable retarded and bright normal children will be briefly outlined.

They defined "flexibility" as the ability to modify ongoing behaviour, and "cognitive flexibility" as the sum total of scores on the "flexibility tasks." They attempted to improve cognitive flexibility by providing a process-orientated training programme. Their training was designed to provide subjects with reinforced practice in making cognitive shifts. The effect of the training was then evaluated on "flexibility tasks" developed by these authors and also on the Binet scale. The three areas of their flexibility studies were perceptual, conceptual, and spontaneous. The study included 32 mildly retarded children attending special education classes and 32 normal children in kindergarten. Both groups of children were split further into two subgroups and were randomly allocated to teaching and control conditions. The two groups were matched for mental age and sex.

These teaching groups received cognitive flexibility training for 20 days. Each session lasted between 30 and 45 minutes. The control groups participated in their usual classroom activities. At the end of the training period, experimental and control groups were retested on the Stanford-Binet and on the Cognitive Flexibility Test battery. The retests on the Stanford Binet were carried out by three experienced examiners, who did not take part in the experiment. Their results show that the experimental groups improved highly significantly in their flexibility scores. The control retarded group had very little change between their pre- and postflexibility test scores. However, the normal controls obtained significantly higher flexibility score without any training. The retarded experimental group had mean IQ increase of about six, while the normal experimental group had mean IQ increase of about ten points, both increments being significant. The controls did not show any IQ gains.

Corter and McKinney consider that their results support the earlier findings from literature that retardates have greater difficulty in concept shifting compared to normals. They also pointed out that their normals were "bright" and the two groups were not matched for social class. Therefore, the results are somewhat equivocal. However, the training was effective in producing significant increases in flexibility. It is interesting to note that their study showed that retardates and normals responded similarly to the training programme. The trained groups had significant increases in their IQs compared to the controls. This suggests that there was some generalisation from training to other areas of cognitive functioning. Corter and McKinney rightly list limitations of their study and are cautious in their interpretations. However, an important point that emerged is that retardates gained significant increases in flexibility from the training programme. Normal children subjected to the same programme gained even more.

McKinney and Corter (1971) repeated the above study on 56 mildly retarded children. Their results showed that training was effective in increasing cognitive flexibility in the instruction group. However, there was no increase in IQ scores, as had been reported in their earlier study. They also indicated that transfer was specific rather than general.

PROBLEM

The authors of the present study felt that Corter and McKinney's research warranted a follow-up study with the more severe grades of retardation. The few studies reported so far suggest that there has been a widespread underestimation of what can be achieved with children and adults below IQ 50. The present study was a deliberate attempt to develop cognitive flexibility in moderately and severely retarded children and young adults. We will describe this study as follows:

1. transfer and training tasks used
2. design and procedure adopted
3. results obtained.

Transfer and Training Tasks

The Cognitive Flexibility test developed by McKinney (1966) was used as the transfer task. This test covers three different areas of 'flexibility'—namely, perceptual, conceptual, and spontaneous. Perceptual flexibility has two sub-tests—Embedded Figures and Figure Ground Reversal. The Conceptual Flexibility part has two subtests—Form Classification and Picture Classification. Spontaneous Flexibility has two subtests—Classification and Tell About This. The Cognitive Flexibility test, as used by Corter and McKinney, yields raw scores ranging from 7–80 for the six subtests. In order to equate the weighting of subtests for the groups, these raw scores were converted on a scale ranging from 0–10 so that more useful comparisons could be made. The original training programme by Corter and McKinney included 42 exercises, 14 for each of the three areas of flexibility—perceptual, conceptual, and spontaneous. For the present experiment it seemed a priori that a number of these exercises would prove to be too difficult for moderately and severely retarded subjects. Hence they were reduced to a total of 28 of the easier ones, nine for the perceptual area, nine for the conceptual area, and ten for the spontaneous flexibility.

Design and the Procedure

Two groups of 12 subjects each were formed in matched pairs. They were originally selected from a larger institutional group of 46 with IQs between 25–53 on the Stanford Binet. Very close matching was achieved on total pretest score on the Cognitive Flexibility test; profiles on the six subtests of the transfer task gained at the pretest; chronological age and IQs on the Stanford-Binet. An example of some of the matching data of six profiles on the Cognitive Flexibility test is given in Figure 1.

The subjects were randomly allocated to experimental and control conditions. The former had flexibility training, while the latter were seen individually for play sessions over 20 days. These included participating in card games, painting, colouring, cutting out pictures, and so on. Thus the exposure to the experimenter was identical for experimental and control groups.

Each subject in both groups spent about ten minutes per day with the experimenter. On average, the experimental subjects attempted three exercises per day with training individualised for particular weaknesses. Each subject moved on to the next exercise if he passed three successive trials or if after several sessions he failed to grasp it. The research design of our experimental procedure is summarised in Figure 2. After training, the subjects were reassessed on the criterion task. They were exposed to a further six learning trials and then reassessed after three to nine months of nonpractice respectively.

On average, experimental subjects were able to complete 66% of the perceptual training tasks, 48% of the conceptual and 62% of the spontaneous flexibility tasks.

Results

Figure 3 (p. 142) shows the overall progress at various stages of the experiment. After 20 days training, the retest showed highly significant differences between experimental and control groups. The difference between the groups widened during the six direct learning trials on the transfer task and only decreased slightly at a further three monthly retest. After a further nine months, the difference between groups decreased even further and there is little doubt that a further period of nonpractice would result in an extinction of the effects induced by the training programme.

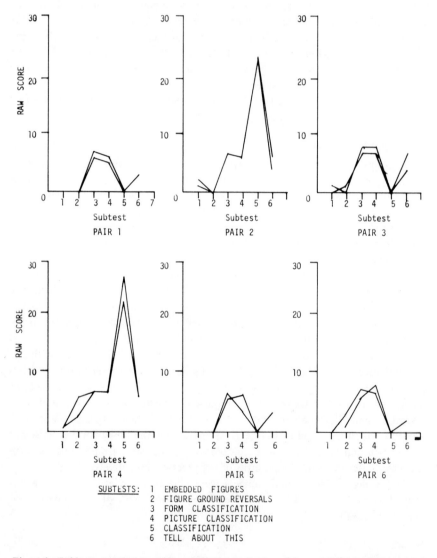

Figure 1. Subjects matched in pairs on individual subtests of the cognitive flexibility test.

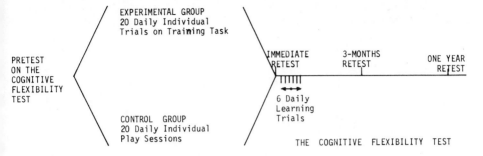

Figure 2. Experimental design.

The other points that emerged from our investigation are that no significant relationships existed between the number of training exercises completed and the gain on retest, nor between age and gain. However, a growing relationship emerged between number of training exercises completed and score on learning trials subsequent to retest. Thus correlations were 0.63 by learning trial 3, 0.75 by trial 4, 0.71 by trial 5, and 0.67 on trial 6. On trials 7 and 8 the values have declined slightly to 0.62 and 0.61, respectively. These correlations are significant at various levels. They show tendencies for the initially more responsive to profit by further experience.

A significant relationship existed between pretest score on the Cognitive Flexibility test and amount of gain at retest, indicating that the better the initial ability, the greater the response to training.

It is interesting to note that most improvement occurred in the Conceptual Flexibility and the Spontaneous Flexibility areas. Very little effect was apparent on the Perceptual Flexibility tasks. This is also reported by McKinney and Corter in their 1971 study.

We would like to point out some of the differences between our investigations and the research reported by Corter and McKinney. Apart from the obvious differences in the sample employed and equal time spent by the experimenter with teaching and control groups, there are other differences to which attention should be directed. Corter and McKinney found greater training effects on immediate retest with the mildly retarded than were present in our more handicapped sample. However, their daily training period was at least four times longer than our experiment. Also, Corter and McKinney employed group training, whereas our approach was individual, and therefore made less economical use of our time. In our experiment, we checked the stability of the changes induced during the training period, i.e., the subjects were retested at three months and also at nine months after the training was completed without any practice. No such retests were reported in Corter and McKinney's study.

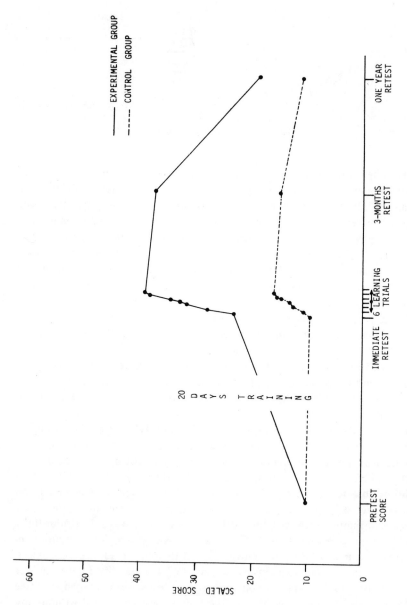

Figure 3. Average scores on cognitive flexibility test for experimental and control groups at various stages of experiment.

Unlike Corter and McKinney, we did not use a repeat Stanford-Binet in which more generalised cognitive changes might be assessed. Thus, the transfer that the present results yielded was relatively specific and we lacked opportunities to test for more general nonspecific transfer. It is important to stress here the point that our study indicated that there is potential difference between capacity and competence, when changed conditions of demand are imposed.

We also repeat the fact that the potential performance of persons below IQ 50 has been widely underestimated, leading to the circularity of poor care, poor training opportunities, if any, and hence poor outcome.

Twenty years of experimental work has shown that the skills of the moderately and severely retarded, can, to varying extents, be improved. Indeed, virtually no failures to do so are reported. What is increasingly needed, is a move out of the laboratory and into properly evaluated, lengthy and "real life" programs, founded upon such work.

SUMMARY

This study to improve the cognitive flexibility of severer grades of retarded is a follow-up of Corter and McKinney's research with the educable retarded and bright normal children. The results report the immediate and very significant effects of a 20-day training programme and also retests at three months and one year to check the stability of the changes induced during the training period.

REFERENCES

Corter, H. M., and McKinney, J. D. (1968) Flexibility training with educable retarded and bright normal children. Amer. J. Ment. Defic. 72:603.
McKinney, J. D. (1966) Cognitive flexibility training with educable retarded and bright normal children of the same mental age. Unpublished master's thesis, Dept. of Psychology, North Carolina State University.
McKinney, J. D., and Corter, H. M. (1971) Flexibility training with educable retarded children. J. Sch. Psychol. 9:455.

ADAPTIVE
BEHAVIOR

RESEARCH TO PRACTICE IN MENTAL RETARDATION
Education and Training, Volume II
Edited by Peter Mittler
Copyright 1977 I.A.S.S.M.D.

ADAPTIVE BEHAVIOR AND ITS ASSESSMENT

K. F. Kennett
College of Cape Breton, Sydney, Nova Scotia, Canada

Utilization of the concept of adaptive behavior as the focal dimension of normal and adequate mental development led the American Association on Mental Deficiency (AAMD) in 1959 to sponsor a program investigating adaptive behaviors and assessment techniques relevant to the mentally retarded. The emphasis on adaptive behaviors concentrated on the real issues of mentally retarded people developing skills of daily living, that is, the basic coping strategies necessary as prerequisites for the successful encountering of the natural and social demands of the environment.

This program, Measurement of Adaptive Behavior, essentially meant the empirical development of a schedule to measure numerous dimensions or sub-domains of behavior relating to social competence. The effort culminated in the publication of the Adaptive Behavior Scales (ABS) by Nihira, Foster, Shellhaas, and Leland (1969), which are described as:

> prototype scales for the purpose of measuring adaptive behavior in institutional populations and enhancing and furthering research with retarded populations within community-based agencies (Leland, 1972, p. 72).

The ABS attempts to ascertain the retardate's level of behavioral efficiency in terms of both his social awareness and his social competence.

In particular, the scale development, based on measures to assess the individual's ability to adapt to environmental demands, focused on three major behavioral formations, namely:

1. *independent functioning,* involving tasks demanded by the general community in terms of critical community survival demands and specific age expectations
2. *personal responsibility,* involving willingness and accomplishment in assuming individual responsibility (including decision-making) for his own behavior
3. *social responsibility,* involving the acceptance of responsibility as a member of a community by demonstrating appropriate behaviors in line with group expectations.

Part I ABS items cover personal care habits, eating skills, cleanliness, appearance, travel experiences, money handling, and shopping skills. Such skills are essential for independent socially acceptable functioning in a community. Part II of the ABS concentrates on maladaptive behaviors (e.g., violence, destructiveness, or antisocial tendencies) that may result in rejection by others in the environment. Thus, adaptive behavior for the mentally retarded meant "matching between the resources of the individual and the demands of his environment" (Nihira, 1973). This matching meant that skills of daily living were projected to the forefront and emphasized the need for normalization programs in order to facilitate adequate development among mentally retarded people.

These competencies for normal living listed as behavioral formations seem to move across and beyond cultural boundaries and appear to be basic essentials for mature living. Each culture expects of its members a set of behaviors (including decision-making) that infer normal or usual ways of doing things. Nonetheless the ways of obtaining and the overt demonstration of such competencies vary from culture to culture.

In all parts of the ABS the mentally retarded individual is examined under subdomains that reflect acceptable modes of conduct and value judgments about behavior that are integral components of the family, the socioeconomic status group, the community, and the culture as a whole. Researchers in different cultures have utilized the ABS for the betterment of the mentally retarded. For example, in Canada Kennett (1973) has developed an assessment technique, the Family Behavior Profile (FBP), for examining the adaptive behavior climate of the home environment.

As the ABS gains wider use for evaluating adaptive behavior in retarded individuals living in the community, the significance of the home environment as a direct influence on the learning of social competence increases. Again, such competencies seem to move beyond cultural boundaries, while at the same time focusing attention upon the fact that in each culture differing from general mainstream expectations may not necessarily be seen as maladaptive, and workers (e.g., in social work) may gain preparation in order to reduce susceptibility to subculture bias.

The home environment is an important determinant of human behavior (Kennett, 1974; Kennett and Cropley, 1970; Kennett and Grant, 1975). Baumrind and Black (1967) reported that pertaining competent behaviors in relation to parents' rearing practices is as applicable to parents of a mentally retarded child as they are to parents of normal children.

The ABS assesses the level of social awareness and social competence demonstrated, the FBP assesses the behavioral tendencies of all members of the family in order to show the ongoing daily experiences within the home. This assessment involves a rating of adaptive behavior for each member of the family on the subdomains of the ABS (those relevant at the present time and those of developmental stages). Initial data indicated highly satisfactory inter-rater reliability.

Both sets of information can contribute to understanding when "the learning environment" in the home is studied, and programming aimed at developing adaptive behavior is facilitated. Thus, guidance essential for the minimization of conflict between training and home environment is possible. The needs of the family may become more obvious, providing possible tactics for intervention. The FBP can complement information from the ABS.

Others have utilized and amended the ABS for examining adaptive behavior in cultures other than an "American culture." Translations and modifications have occurred; for example, El Ghahit (1973) worked in Egypt, Magerotte (1974) in Belgium, and Tomiyasu, Marakami, Matsuda, and Emi (1974) in Japan. In all cases the ABS has acted as "an evaluative measure of social awareness scored by an assessment of varying levels of social competence" (Kennett, 1975, p. 2)

As these researchers worked in different cultural settings, adaptive behavior has been defined in terms of how the individual copes with the total demands of his culture and in particular the social demands of his immediate environment, including his home. Adaptation or maladaptation is meaningful only in relation to the demands of a particular social system to which the individual seeks full membership. Thus, within each social system or culture, descriptions of normal environmental demands made on mentally retarded individuals is an essential prerequisite for any assessment of adaptive behavior, and, subsequently, for the development of all sound and meaningful rehabilitation programs.

REFERENCES

American Association on Mental Deficiency (1959) A Manual on Terminology and Classification in Mental Retardation. (Ed. Heber, R.) Amer. J. Ment. Defic. (Monogr. Suppl.)

Baumrind, D., and Black, A. E. (1967) Socialization practices associated with dimensions of competence in pre-school boys and girls. Child Dev. 38:291.

El Ghahit, Z. (1973) Adaptive Behavior Scales, Manual (translated into Arabic) Cairo: American University of Cairo.

Kennett, K. F. (1973) The Family Behavior Profile. Sydney: Saint Francis Xavier University.

Kennett, K. F. (1974) Creativity, family size and socioeconomic status. Proceedings of the XV Interamerican Congress of Psychology, (Columbia), p. 125.

Kennett, K. F. (1975) Mental retardation and family conditions: Further applications of the Adaptive Behavior Scales. Paper presented at the Eighty-third Annual Convention of the American Psychological Association, Chicago.

Kennett, K. F., and Cropley, A. J. (1970) Intelligence, family size and socioeconomic status. J. Biosoc. Sci. 2:227.

Kennett, K. F., and Grant, E. (1975) Family environment, socioeconomic status and academic achievement. Paper presented at the Eighty-third Annual Convention of the American Psychological Association, Chicago.

Leland, H. (1972) Mental retardation and adaptive behavior. J. Spec. Educ. 6:71.

Magerotte, G. (1974) Important aspects in the evaluation of mental handicaps: intelligence and adaptive behavior. Rev. Psychol. Sci. Educ. 9:3.

Nihira, K. (1973) Importance of environmental demands in the measurement of adaptive behavior. *In* Socio-behavioral Studies in Mental Retardation (Eds. Eyman, R. K., Meyers, C. E., and Tarjan, G.). Los Angeles: Mongr. AAMD, No. 1.

Nihira, K., Foster, R., Shelhaas, M., and Leland, H. (1969) Adaptive Behavior Scales. Washington, D.C.: AAMD.

Tomiyasu, Y., Marakami, E., Matsuda, S., and Emi, Y. (1974) Structure of the adaptive behavior of the mentally retarded. A factor analytic study. Jap. J. Spec. Educ. 12:1.

RESEARCH TO PRACTICE IN MENTAL RETARDATION
Education and Training, Volume II
Edited by Peter Mittler
Copyright 1977   I.A.S.S.M.D.

ADAPTATION, COPING BEHAVIOR, AND RETARDED PERFORMANCE

H. Leland
*Department of Psychology, Nisonger Center,
The Ohio State University, 1580 Cannon
Drive, Columbus, Ohio, 43210, United States*

The concept of adaptation, not a new one in psychology, was first introduced as a classification dimension into the area of mental retardation in 1959 (Heber, 1959). At that time, the concept, which was said to include the ideas of "maturation," "learning," and "social adjustment," was related to the manner in which the individual coped with the natural and social demands of his environment. Since that time, the measurement dimension "adaptive behavior" has been organized, systematized, and developed into a variety of scales and planning concepts that have made it a specific part of our more general consideration of mental retardation and developmental disability. As a result, the current AAMD definition, as well as the laws of many of our various states, now insist that the label of mental retardation be based on elements besides the IQ or psychometric test results, and that that label should, in fact, include evidence of a "deficit in adaptive behavior" (Grossman, 1973).

However, the process of adaptation is basic to the growth and development of the organism and the human must be considered essentially as an adaptive organism. In most respects, the human organism is somewhat more adaptive than other living organisms. Faced with what is essentially an environment that contains other living organisms, all struggling for survival, the human must find some means of survival, through the utilization of the surrounding environment on the one hand, and through the adjustment and accommodation to environmental forces on the other. The process of adaptation in any organism is the very delicate balance that it is able to achieve in this interaction with its immediate environment. The human must take from the environment the cues and behavioral guides critical to the successful comprehension of the demands of that environment, and having comprehended these demands, he must, through his own processes, adjust his behavior and modify his approaches to develop individual strategies to deal with those demands; in short, he evolves "coping behavior."

This human evolution of coping behavior becomes part of what might be described as a clinical concept of intelligence. That is, the multitude of interdependent factors that, when operating as a unit, direct the individual's mental behavior, seem to include the sensorimotor development of the organism, the evolution of cognitive processes, the adoption of a personal rate of learning, and the development of varying levels of social awareness. Alongside these four elements, the human organism also learns to adapt, and this coping behavior becomes part of the total process of higher nervous activity within the organism that we describe in terms of behaviors related to intelligence. Thus, while all organisms may be said to cope with their environment, the human organism must cope intellectually as well as physically.

The necessity for the human organism to cope "intellectually" comes from that aspect of behavior that seems almost uniquely human, namely, the fact that as a cognitive animal he develops a mechanism for storage of information that traverses the centuries. He is thus able to use the experiences and knowledge gained from the history of the species as a basis for producing successful adjustment within the structure of the ongoing environment. Most of this accumulation of lore and information takes the form of adjusting the environment to his needs primarily through the development of what can best be described as a prosthetic environment; that is, the inabilities inherent in the organism to make an appropriate adaptation to the everyday needs of the environment has led him to invent ways of helping this adaptation along. Over the centuries, these prostheses have finally come down as airplanes, motor cars, televisions, rockets to the moon, etc., all of which establish for us a prosthetic world that makes it possible for members of the species to survive in spite of their inherent weaknesses as biological organisms.

Retarded performance must be looked at in terms of the individual's relative inability to develop appropriate coping strategies. Those individuals who cannot utilize the stimuli and behavioral guides that the environment offers in order to either adapt to the environment, to utilize the prosthetic devices already created to help such adaptation, or to develop new prosthetic devices to deal with new situations, are said to be unable to develop appropriate coping strategies. Society, looking at the performance of those individuals describes them as mentally retarded, mentally deficient, feeble-minded, or whatever label is current, on the basis that their level of performance is not consistent with the minimal demands of the community or personal milieu in which they must personally survive (e.g., family, neighborhood, school, etc.).

Thus, we have a phenomenon in which the individual displays behaviors that make him socially visible. Under the guise of mental retardation, these behaviors cause society to isolate him from his community, although in point of fact it was the maladaptive behavior that brought about the social decision. This same maladaption maintains him in the institution or in the isolated setting because it is the nature of the setting to increase the unsuccessful coping or to continue to delimit the knowledge necessary to adapt to the community. Thus, the possibility of correcting or reversing the situation becomes increasingly smaller as the individual ages. This gives us as a product a much more severely retarded individual than we would have had, had he not been so socially visible in the first place. Because coping and adaptation are reversible elements within the growth pattern of the individual, we can conclude that had there been appropriate help available in the beginning, when the unsuccessful coping was first observed, it is entirely possible that some of those elements could have been reversed, and, as a result, the individual would not have become as retarded as he later did.

The foregoing underlines the necessity of developing some sort of adaptive diagnosis. Diagnosis, used in this frame of reference, is considered a combination of 1) knowledge of the individual's current level of functioning as determined by various behavioral observations, 2) comparing the current functioning with information available from the history of the individual, 3) judging areas of expected change in growth, and 4) comparison with "typical" behaviors of other persons of the same age and community background and with the critical or survival demands of the family, the community, or other social groups (Leland and Smith, 1974).

There is a certain logical organization to human behavior patterns, and failure to perform in one area should not occur if performance requiring the same kind of ability is present in an alternative area. Thus, "what the individual is doing instead" becomes part of the diagnostic process, and if we find, for example, that an individual is throwing a rock through a window, he obviously does not need training because the rock got through the window. What he needs is a regrouping of those behaviors so the same capacities and skills, e.g., motor control, can be rechanneled into more prosocial forms. An adaptive diagnosis must contain the elements described above with a view toward the fact that there are behaviors present that require skills, and that if it is possible for the individual to have utilized these skills in a maladaptive manner, then he certainly can be trained to discover and use similar skills for more adaptive performance.

With this in mind, there have been developed a number of adaptive behavior measures that identify both the necessary and the desirable behaviors, and that serve, in turn, as diagnostic and evaluative tools to help in developing life plans for the individual who has demonstrated problems in his coping behavior.

These life plans can be based on adaptive skills. These types of skills must include new and additional social and living experiences if he is going to maintain optimal relationships with the rest of his community. These experiences should occur at the same time they occur to other persons his age in that community; if they cannot, they have to be built into a training curriculum. They should be experienced with individuals with whom he can communicate, on the one hand, and whom he can watch perform on the other. There should be a group of other persons who have already had these experiences who can, in a sense, serve as models for the appropriate manner of dealing with situations, and they should be related in some sort of a time sequence with the levels of physical growth and development that are occurring within the individual at any one time.

There are three general types of uses for adaptive behavior measurement. First, it may be used as a direct report of behavior skills and coping strategies for the purpose of program planning, training, behavior modification, etc. The important information is what the individual does currently, what the usual antecedent behavior is to the current behavior, and what the expected succeeding behavior should be. In a general sense, little else need be known about the handicapped person beyond this basic information regarding whether or not he can perform a desired function or is exhibiting maladaptive behavior. As soon as this information can be gathered, the trainers can be taught what is involved in performing at the next higher functional level, and they will be able to establish from the measurement instrument a series of intervening steps or a procedure to modify or extinguish an undesirable behavior.

The second use of adaptive measurement is to serve as a functional instrument for program evaluation. Here, very little need be known about the specific individual except that he performs certain behaviors producing a profile. From the profile, the agency has to establish priority areas on the basis of the critical demands of the environment the measures are representing. The major question is, are the procedures being used by the agency the appropriate procedures for producing the necessary change in the priority areas? This question can be asked either in terms of individual programs for specific handicapped persons or for all of the programs of the agency as they relate to the total population with which they are working. On the basis of changes within the individual profile or the agency profile, the agency can determine whether or not results are consistent with their program goals. This will permit them either to re-evaluate the goals in terms of behavior priorities or to reappraise procedures in terms of their ability to accomplish desired ends. The agency can thus determine what major program modification or overhauling of goals is required to bring a program to a higher level of efficiency along the lines of establishing independence or a "roadmap" for deinstitutionalization and for a more "normalized program of community integration of the handicapped."

The third use of adaptive measurement is its function as an aid to diagnosis and classification. This use includes the possible interpretations of the relationship between various aspects of adaptive measurement and particularly in terms of the three major factors that the AAMD Adaptive Behavior Scales (Nihira, Foster, Shellhaas, and Leland, 1975) seem to measure. These are levels of personal independence, levels of personal responsibility, and levels of social maladaptation. The diagnostic use of the scale emerges as a valuable adjunct to better understanding of persons who are failing to perform in the expected manner or who are carrying out undesirable maladaptive behaviors. Interpretation of the material is not to create new labels or to enhance old labels, but rather to provide additional information leading to the learning of new skills and modification of inappropriate behaviors.

Thus, measurement in the area of adaptation permits the development of planning, evaluation, and diagnosis for persons performing at a retarded level, and this, in turn, helps them reverse the behaviors that would otherwise put them at odds with the rest of their community. If the information concerning their personal independence or personal responsibility can be used for either agency or program placement or personal planning, then the additional information concerning social maladaptation can become a very important aid in determining what kinds of program priorities can be established and what types of results, with regard to the rapidity of rehabilitation success, can be anticipated. Failure to utilize the information from these three factors has been one of the long-term problems in the institutional picture, and this failure has led, as stated previously, to an actual increase in the general problem of retarded mental abilities. If an adaptive behavior approach to change is adopted, it is possible to develop an integrated program plan that will take into consideration the priority needs of both the community and the individual for whom the plans are being made. And this, in the long run, will help us gain much higher levels of personal independence at a much more rapid pace.

In this short overview, I have attempted to outline how the processes of adaptation and the development of coping behaviors relate to the broad areas of intellectual growth, and how, when they fail to develop properly, they may lead to retarded performance, which, in turn, increases the problems of subaverage intellectual functioning. From this it should be apparent that one of the most important aspects of our judgment of the intellectual and social level of an individual relates to his adaptive behavior. This, rather than psychometrically derived intelligence quotients, should be the major base for all decisions concerning the development of rehabilitation, training, and treatment programs for developmentally disabled persons.

REFERENCES

Grossman, H. (Ed.) (1973) A Manual on Terminology and Classification in Mental Retardation. Special Publication Series No. 2. Washington, D.C.: AAMD.

Heber, R. (Ed.) (1959) A Manual on Terminology and Classification in Mental Retardation (1st edition). Amer. J. Ment. Defic. 66 (Mongr. Suppl.)

Leland, H., and Smith, D. E. (1974) Mental Retardation: Present and Future Perspectives. Worthington, Ohio: Charles A. Jones.

Nihira, K., Foster, R., Shellhaas, M., and Leland, H. (1975) AAMD Adaptive Behavior Scale. (revised) Washington, D.C: AAMD.

RESEARCH TO PRACTICE IN MENTAL RETARDATION
Education and Training, Volume II
Edited by Peter Mittler
Copyright 1977 I.A.S.S.M.D.

DEVELOPMENT OF ADAPTIVE BEHAVIOR IN THE MENTALLY RETARDED

K. Nihira
*Neuropsychiatric Institute, University of California
at Los Angeles, 760 Westwood Plaza, Los Angeles,
California 90024, United States*

In recent years, there have been significant changes in the provision of services for mentally retarded persons. A major trend has been the development and use of smaller community facilities as an alternative to large public institutions. Although this trend has considerable intuitive appeal, the scientific evaluation of its efficacy presents many challenging tasks to our profession. One of these tasks is assessment of the development of adaptive behavior.

Limited information is now available on the acquisition of self-care skills and the maturation of adaptive behavior in mentally retarded populations. The lack of baseline data on the development of adaptive behavior through maturation or "standard" treatment represents one of the roadblocks in program assessment (Eyman, Tarjan, and Cassady, 1970). The effect of care programs upon adaptive behavior development must be evaluated in terms of an individual's subsequent behavioral change over and beyond the development normally expected of his age and the type of disabilities. A positive change in adaptive behavior may represent an accelerated development for one individual, while the same rate of development may merely indicate normal maturation for another individual. This is the basic assumption upon which a longitudinal study of a large sample of retarded individuals in institutions and community care facilities has been conducted by the UCLA Neuropsychiatric–Pacific State Hospital research group.

In this chapter, the developmental change will be described in terms of three salient dimensions, or factors, of adaptive behavior. Recent factor analytic studies of the AAMD Adaptive Behavior Scale demonstrated the existence of three general dimensions of adaptive behavior in Part I and two general dimensions of maladaptive behavior in Part II of the scale. These dimensions have been repeatedly delineated by several studies using different samples of mentally retarded individuals in residential institutions and in public schools (Lambert, 1976; Nihira, 1976; Tomiyasu and Matsuda, 1975). This chapter compares cross-sectional development with the longitudinal development of retarded persons in terms of the first three dimensions of adaptive behavior:

Factor I: Personal Self-Sufficiency—eating, toilet use, cleanliness, dressing and undressing, and motor development.

Factor II: Community Self-Sufficiency—money handling and budgeting, shopping skills, expression, comprehension, social language development, numbers and time, cleaning, kitchen duties, other domestic activities, travel (locomotion), and general independent functioning.

Factor III: Personal-Social Responsibility—initiative, perseverance, leisure time, responsibility, and socialization.

Personal Self-Sufficiency consists of essential skills and abilities that contribute to how well the individual handles his immediate personal needs. It is considered a basic dimension of adaptive behavior for an individual as an independent social unit, with emphasis being on his self-sustaining adequacies in his predominantly personal sphere. *Community Self-Sufficiency* represents skills and awareness of the individual toward the achievement of 1) personal independence beyond his immediate personal needs, and 2) self-sufficiency as reflected in his relationship with other members of his social environment. It is considered a higher extension of Personal Self-Sufficiency toward the attainment of self-sufficiency as an independent social unit in the sphere of community living. *Personal-Social Responsibility* represents a broad cluster of personality attributes, including initiative to engage in purposeful activities, self-direction, motivation to manage one's own affairs, responsibility for others, and interest in interpersonal relationships. It is considered an important dimension of the traditional notion of social competency.

A series of factor analyses demonstrated that these three dimensions are invariant across a wide span of ages from childhood to senility. These studies were based upon over 3,000 residents from 68 state institutions for the mentally retarded representing 39 states in the United States. Table 1 presents the distribution of sample population by age and IQ. Approximately half of the subjects were male in all age groups. The distribution of mean IQs and standard deviations across different age groups are similar to the statistics derived from the total population of residents in state institutions for mentally retarded in the United States in the late 1960s. Therefore, it is safe to assume that our sample population is a representative sample of the total residents of state institutions in this country of that period.

In order to observe the development of adaptive behavior, factor scores were estimated for each subject. Mean factor scores were then computed for each of the ten separate age groups. Figure 1 depicts the cross-sectional growth curves for mildly retarded population, i.e., IQ between 67–52. Each line represents the development of a specific factor as expressed by mean factor scores for ten separate age groups. For ease of inspection, the smoother curves are presented

Table 1. Distribution of subjects by age and IQ (*N* = 3,354)

| Ages | Number of subjects | Intelligence quotients | |
		Mean	Standard deviation
4	222	29.3	17.1
5	186	30.3	16.9
6–7	486	31.2	17.7
8–9	393	37.3	19.7
10–12	528	40.5	20.4
13–15	323	44.2	21.1
16–18	340	45.8	21.5
19–29	304	44.0	20.8
30–49	278	43.6	21.9
50–69	294	45.2	21.1

here by the method of running average and interpolation. The vertical axis represents factor scores in the standard score unit with the mean of zero and standard deviation of 1.0.

Note that Personal Self-Sufficiency and Personal-Social Responsibility show an initial rapid growth during childhood followed by relatively slow and gradual increment during adolescence. On the other hand, the Community Self-Sufficiency curve shows an initial slow growth during early childhood followed by the accelerating growth during late childhood and early adolescent periods. In other words, the initial rapid growth of Personal Self-Sufficiency and Personal-Social Responsibility during early childhood is gradually replaced by the accelerating growth of Community Self-Sufficiency. This trend is observed more dramatically in the borderline level of retardation, i.e., IQ between 83–68.

The crossover of developmental gradients between Community Self-Sufficiency and the two other factors seems to occur earlier, at age eight to nine years, for the borderline group than the mildly retarded group. More accelerated early growth in all three factors is predicted for a group of normal children.

Figure 3 depicts the developmental trends of moderately retarded persons, i.e., IQ between 51–36. This group is distinguished from borderline and mildly retarded groups in the development of Community Self-Sufficiency. This factor shows a somewhat slower rate of growth during childhood. It does not reach the level of two other factors until late adolescence, and it never rises above the level of the two other factors. Personal Self-Sufficiency and Personal-Social Responsibility of the moderately retarded also grow slower during childhood and do not reach the level of the mildly retarded group until young adulthood.

Figure 4 depicts the developmental trends of the severely retarded population, i.e., IQ between 30–20. In all three factors, the growth is considerably slower in rate and lower in level than in the previous groups across the various age ranges.

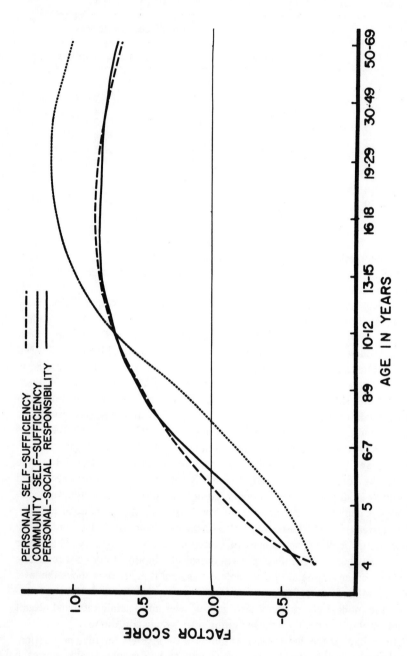

Figure 1. Developmental trends of the three factors in measured intelligence level II (mild) group.

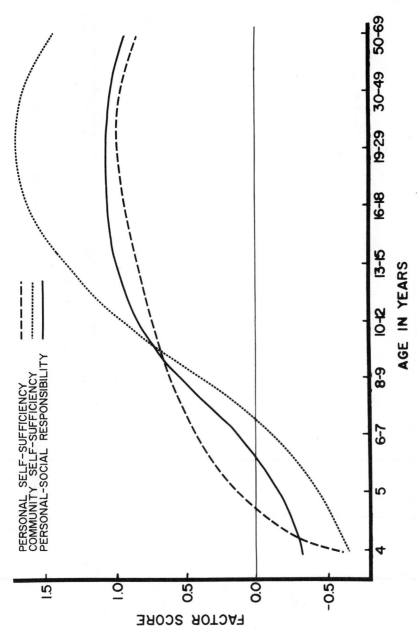

Figure 2. Developmental trends of the three factors in measured intelligence level I (borderline) group.

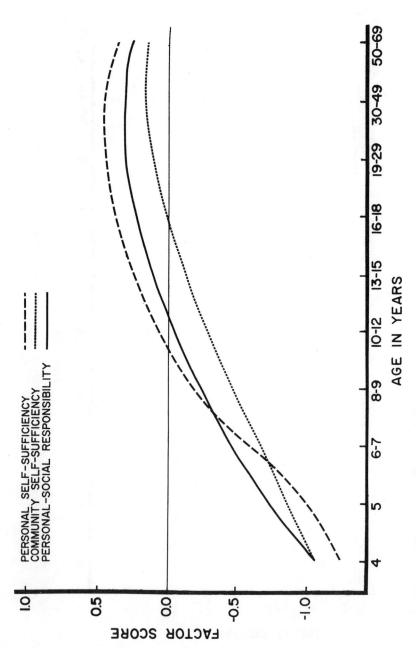

Figure 3. Developmental trends of the three factors in measured intelligence Level III (moderate) group.

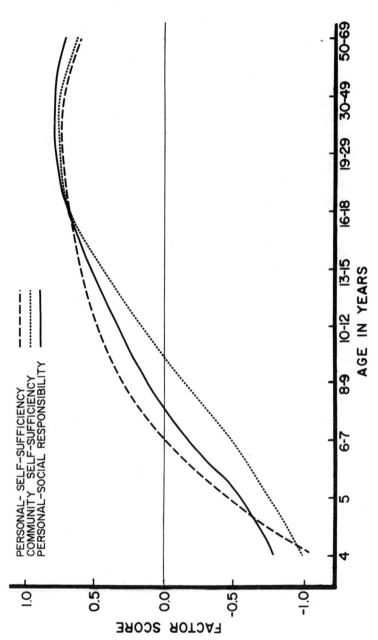

Figure 4.   Developmental trends of the three factors in measured intelligence level IV (severe) group.

Note that Community Self-Sufficiency never reaches the level of the two other factors.

It should be noted that the developmental trends observed in these figures are based upon cross-sectional observations of the residential population in public institutions. Therefore, if cohort effects are present, these developmental trends cannot be interpreted as a function of age alone. For example, the slow but constant growth in the severely retarded group throught most of the adult years may be the result of selective attrition, since among the severely or profoundly retarded population those with fewer handicaps tend to live longer than those with more handicapping conditions. In a borderline or mildly retarded population, those who have achieved a higher adaptive behavior level may have a greater chance of being discharged from residential institutions. Therefore, the observed trends may indicate a slower rate of growth than the true rate of maturation. Thus, the growth curve, as a function of age alone, can only be estimated from longitudinal studies with different cohort of subjects at each age level (Baltes, 1968; Schaie, 1965).

Such a longitudinal study of adaptive behavior is currently underway. Our longitudinal population consists of a total of over 2,000 residents in state institutions, and approximately 600 residents in community care facilities in five Western states. Retarded individuals between the ages of three and 21 are the major target population. The complete analysis of this massive data will take us some time yet.

In the following section of this chapter our longitudinal data will be compared with the cross-sectional data in an attempt to illustrate the importance of developmental baseline data for proper program evaluations. Table 2 lists a part of the longitudinal samples in state institutions and community residential facilities. The subjects have been evaluated twice within a maximum period of two years. The total sample includes a large number of profoundly retarded individuals in state institutions. However, they were not included in this paper because there were not enough profoundly retarded subjects in community residential facilities. The analysis of variance for repeated measures gave us the following results.

Table 2.   Longitudinal   samples: age range 10–15 years[a]

M.I. Level	Institutional residents	Community residents
Mild	$N = 50$	$N = 52$
Moderate	$N = 80$	$N = 165$
Severe	$N = 161$	$N = 97$

[a]Two repeated evaluations within 1 to 2 year period.

1. Significant positive change was observed between the first and second evaluations in Personal Self-Sufficiency (p=0.006) and Community Self-Sufficiency (p=0.000).
2. There was a significant interaction effect between the two evaluations and MI levels, indicating that the mildly retarded residents have shown greater positive change than the severely retarded residents in the above two factors (p=0.005 for PSS; p=0.011 for CSS).
3. The interaction effect between the two evaluations and the type of residence was not statistically significant although the community residents have shown somewhat greater positive change than the institutional residents in Community Self-Sufficiency (p=0.341 for PSS; p=0.80 for CSS).
4. The third factor, Personal-Social Responsibility, presented somewhat complex results. The overall change between the two evaluations did not reach the statistical significance at 0.05 level (p=0.085). There was some degree of triple interaction between the two evaluations, MI levels, and the type of residence (p=0.137). In the institutional samples, greater positive changes were observed in the mildly and moderately retarded groups than in the severely retarded group. On the other hand, in the community sample, the mildly and moderately retarded groups suffered a slight regression while the severely retarded group indicated considerable positive change.

From these results, one might hastily conclude that the rehabilitation programs have been more effective for the higher level residents than for the lower level residents in both institutions and community, and that the type of residence has differential effects upon the development of Personal-Social Responsibility for different levels of retardation.

However, the cross-sectional data in the previous figures have shown a generally higher rate of development in the higher level individuals than in the lower level individuals during childhood and adolescent periods. Therefore, the longitudinal change, although statistically significant, should be closely examined in terms of the growth normally expected of a specific group of individuals.

Table 3 compares the mean factor scores between the longitudinal sample and the cross-sectional sample for ages 10 through 15 years. The mean factor scores for longitudinal sample came from the first evaluation conducted during the period of 1973–1974. The table indicates the following significant trends.

1. Mean factor scores for the institutional samples in the 1973–74 period are considerably lower than the institutional samples of equivalent IQ levels in the 1968–70 period.
2. Within the longitudinal samples, mean factor scores for the community samples are considerably higher than the institutional samples of equivalent IQ levels.
3. The combined means for institutional and community samples in the 1973–74 period are not significantly different from the institutional samples of equivalent IQs in the 1968–70 period.

Table 3. Mean factor scores[a] (age range, 10–15 years)

Factor	M.I. level	Longitudinal[b] (1973–1974)			Cross-sectional (1968–1970)
		Institution	Community	Combined	(Institutions)
PSS	Mild	0.61	0.76	0.69	0.77 ($N = 165$)
	Moderate	0.21	0.65	0.46	0.55 ($N = 188$)
	Severe	−0.14	0.28	0.07	0.12 ($N = 151$)
CSS	Mild	0.59	0.91	0.75	0.87
	Moderate	0.11	0.48	0.30	0.20
	Severe	−0.53	−0.15	−0.34	−0.25
PSR	Mild	0.58	1.02	0.80	0.85
	Moderate	0.18	0.78	0.48	0.37
	Severe	−0.34	0.17	−0.08	−0.11

[a]Standard score unit
[b]First evaluation

The above trends seem to reflect the results of the strong emphasis placed on the development of community care systems for mentally retarded persons since the early 1970s. During recent years, individuals with higher adaptive functioning have been placed in various community facilities, while those with lower adaptive functioning have remained in the state institutions even though their IQ levels were equivalent. For the purpose of this paper, it is important to note that the initial evaluation of the longitudinal sample, when institutional and community samples are combined, is not significantly different from the cross-sectional data derived from the sample of institutional population before the mass exodus of residents from large public institutions since the early 1970s.

A comparison between the longitudinal changes and the cross-sectional growth curves revealed the following trends. In the mildly retarded population, the institutional residents developed at about the same rate expected from the cross-sectional developmental curves in all three factors, while the community residents developed at a rate greater than expected in Personal Self-Sufficiency and Community Self-Sufficiency factors. In the moderately and severely retarded populations, the rate of longitudinal development was at the level expected or less than expected from the cross-sectional growth curves in both institutional and community residents. In these instances, the statistically significant changes may merely indicate the normal maturational phenomena.

This chapter illustrates the importance of baseline developmental data in research concerning the effect of environmental factors or program interventions on behavior changes. In spite of the limitations in cross-sectional data in developmental research, the study indicated the utility of the cross sectional data when it is interpreted as the age-related function in special populations, e.g., specific levels of retardation, or when it is interpreted as the interaction of age and population change, e.g., change in the characteristics of institutional populations. This is not to say that the present cross-sectional data is an adequate baseline data for the evaluation of adaptive behavior development. Kessen (1960), in his excellent discussion of research designs for developmental problems, specified a behavioral change in a developmental model as being a function of age, special population, and environment. He suggested that the most meaningful approach will be to study the simultaneous interactions of the age-related function with difference in population and environment. Schaie and others (Baltes, 1968; Schaie, 1965) argued that neither cross-sectional nor longitudinal data in the conventional sense will reveal purely age-related developmental baseline data.

In addition, longitudinal studies are not only expensive but also time consuming. In these days of rapid social change, results of longitudinal studies often contribute more toward the development of archives than toward the development of appropriate behaviors. More rapid approximations of developmental baseline are needed most in the area of behavioral assessment, since social changes alter the value and implications of studies of culturally anchored adaptive behavior variables. The need for methodological innovations is critical to further advancement of our knowledge concerning the effect of environmental factors on the development of adaptive behavior.

SUMMARY

This study aims to describe the development of mentally retarded individuals in terms of three salient dimensions of adaptive behavior delineated by factor analyses. Both cross-sectional and longitudinal developmental data are examined in relation to the subject's level of measured intelligence and the type of residential environments.

ACKNOWLEDGMENTS

The author is grateful to the *American Journal of Mental Deficiency* for permission to reproduce his Figures 1–4, originally published in Nihira (1976).

REFERENCES

Baltes, P. (1968) Longitudinal and cross-sectional sequences in the study of age and generated effect. Hum. Dev. 11:145.

Eyman, R., Tarjan, G., and Cassady, M. (1970) Natural history of acquisition of basic skills by hospitalized retarded patients. Amer. J. Ment. Defic. 75:120.

Kessen, W. (1960) Research design in the study of developmental problems. *In* Handbook of Research Methods in Child Development (Ed. Mussen, P.) New York: Wiley & Sons.

Lambert, N. (1976) Dimensions of adaptive behavior of retarded and non-retarded children attending public schools. Amer. J. Ment. Defic. 81:135.

Nihira, K. (1976) Dimensions of adaptive behavior in institutionalized mentally retarded children and adults: Developmental perspective. Amer. J. Ment. Defic. 81:215.

Nihira, K., Foster, R., Shellhaas, M., and Leland, H. (1974) AAMD Adaptive Behavior Scale: 1974 Revision. Washington, D.C.: AAMD.

Schaie, W. (1965) A general model for the study of developmental problems. Psychol., Bull. 64:92.

Tomiyasu, Y., and Matsuda, K. (1975) Assessment Method of Adaptive Behavior. Tokyo, Japan: Nihon Bunka Kagakusha, p. 69.

RESEARCH TO PRACTICE IN MENTAL RETARDATION
Education and Training, Volume II
Edited by Peter Mittler
Copyright 1977 I.A.S.S.M.D.

SOCIAL ADJUSTMENT OF PREVIOUSLY UNASCERTAINED ADULTS

S. Granat
Mental Retardation Project,
Psychiatric Research Clinic, Ulleråker Hospital, Uppsala, Sweden

This chapter describes a part of a larger research project that attempts to illustrate epidemiology, structure of intelligence, and social adjustment of previously unascertained mentally retarded adults (Granat and Granat, 1973, 1975). The group to be considered consists of mentally retarded adults at the levels of borderline and mild retardation. From studies of prevalence rate and the assumption of normal distribution of intelligence, one can presuppose a considerable number of individuals who, in spite of their mental handicap, manage fairly independently without special support. Because of difficulties in identifying these individuals after completion of school, comparatively few studies have been made of this group, in contrast to institutionalized individuals of the same intellectual level.

PROBLEMS

This part of the project was carried through in three studies with different problems.

Study 1

How large is the group of individuals who are on the same intellectual level as institutionalized mentally retarded without being institutionalized or labeled mentally retarded?

Study 2

Does the profile of intelligence of the group of nonlabeled intellectually subaverage adults deviate from institutionalized mentally retarded in such a way that it is in line with the profile of a group with an average level of intelligence?

Study 3

How should we describe social adjustment at this level of intelligence? Is there, within this group of nonlabeled adults, a latent group that will not manage in the future without special support?

METHOD

Subjects

For about 300 years, Sweden has had a carefully conducted system for registration of all inhabitants. This registration forms the basis for enlistment of all 19-year-old male Swedish citizens for compulsory military service. This group is homogeneous from an ethnic point of view. About 0.7% of the age group are not enlisted, as they have a medical certificate stating that they are mentally retarded. A further 0.4% are not enlisted for other reasons, mainly medical, which have no systematic relationship to low intelligence. The remaining 99% all undergo the examination for placement in the military system.

Of the 2,000 men who underwent the enlistment procedure, 217 with the lowest scores for the enlistment tests (one or two points on a standardized scale based on the sum and representing the lowest 11%) were chosen for further examination. Of these men, 128 were finally selected as comparable to those on mildly and borderline levels. None of the men in this group had ever been under special services for the mentally retarded according to information obtained from psychologists and the enlistment authorities who had interviewed them. They can therefore be defined as a group of nonlabeled intellectually subaverage persons.

Variables

The group to be studied is described by the following variables:

1. Intelligence tests given upon enlistment for military service.
2. Nine tests from a battery specially constructed for measuring the intelligence profile of the mentally retarded (Ulleråker Sjukhus battery, Kebbon, 1965).
3. Data on personal and social adjustment obtained from interviews.
4. Data on adjustment and social background from questionnaires filled in by all enlistees.
5. Data on income, criminality and contact with social authorities obtained from different civil authorities.

Study 1

In most studies of prevalence the main criterion for mental retardation is an IQ below 70, measured by a test such as the Stanford-Binet. None of the men from the enlistment procedure was given such a test. The IQ of this group was estimated in order to make this study more comparable with others. Kebbon (1965) had given both the Ulleråker Sjukhus battery and a Stanford-Binet to the same group of retarded persons, thus making it possible to estimate multiple regression coefficients for the four Ulleråkers Sjukhus tests against IQ. The multiple correlation coefficient was 0.77. The prediction of IQ = 70 should be especially precise as it was near the average for Kebbon's group of retarded subjects.

According to this comparison the prevalence of 19-year-old men with low intelligence, but not previously labeled as mentally retarded, was estimated to be 1.50 ± 0.56% for the whole of Sweden. The 95% confidence interval was estimated with consideration of the special methods used in this study. Together with the 0.71% who were not enlisted because they were already labeled mentally retarded, the prevalence of 19-year-old men in Sweden fulfilling the psychometric criterion for mental retardation was estimated to be 2.21%.

This figure is interesting because the men are beyond school age and the estimation is based on an almost complete registration of all inhabitants of the country. The prevalence rate obtained for school ages is often near 2.21%, but the rate at the age of 19 is nearly always lower. This fact supports the theory that the paradoxical decline in prevalence after school age is at least partly due to differences in accessibility. A survey using conventional methods to estimate the country-wide prevalence of retardation in young adults would probably reach mainly the 0.71% who are not enlisted because of labeled mental retardation, and this figure corresponds well to earlier findings from different countries (Gruenberg, 1964).

Study 2

In this study, 104 institutionalized mentally retarded individuals were studied to obtain a group for comparison (Group I). From the tests used in the enlistment procedure 54 subjects (Group II) were chosen to be compared with group I. Eighty-one subjects (Group III) were selected, who, according to the enlistment tests, were of average intelligence.

The three groups mentioned above were given the Ulleråker Sjukhus battery, which, according to previous factor analysis (Kebbon, 1965), measures five factors (see Figure 1). Perceptual speed was measured with only one test, remaining factors with two tests. Variance analysis on the shape of the profiles regardless of level shows that all differ significantly as far as shape is concerned (5% between groups I and II, 1% between groups I and III, and II and III).

The main result is that the shape of the profile of group II differs significantly from that of group I and deviates in the direction of the profile of the average group. The hypothesis is therefore confirmed, and the general conclusion is that the intelligence profile found in intellectually subaverage persons in institutions cannot be generalized to refer to the whole population of intellectually subaverage persons at the mild and borderline levels.

It is important to remember that group II is to be considered most representative of the intelligence level in question. Group I, on the other hand, is selected in different ways by processes in the social system. The differences in profile found between groups I and II can be explained in terms of both selection and environmental effects. Obviously, no definite conclusions as to cause can be made in this type of study. Factors influencing the profile of the labeled group only seem to be present in the nonlabeled group to a limited extent, however.

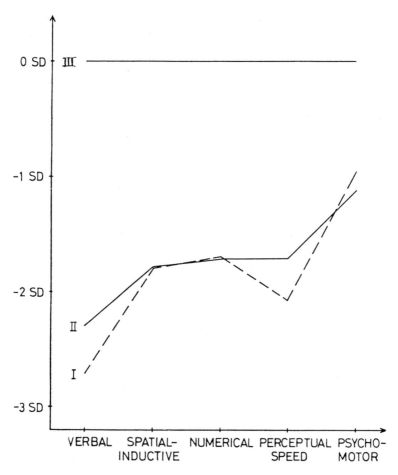

Figure 1. Deviations from the average group of mean subscale scores expressed as within-group standard deviations. I, institutionalized subjects (N = 104). II, unascertained subjects (N = 54). III, normal subjects (N = 81).

Study 3

To obtain a description of social adaptation for the studied group a cluster analysis was carried out on 22 dichotomous variables. These were within the areas of work, economy, criminal activity, addiction, health, personal problems, and social contacts. They were obtained through interviews, medical examinations, questionnaires, and records from different authorities.

The cluster analysis shows with surprising clarity that the 128 subjects can be divided into four subgroups (clusters) with respect to their adjustment (see Table 1). The *well-adjusted cluster* is recognized by better adjustment than the other clusters in all variables. Subjects included in this group show signs of

Table 1. Adjustment variables on which the clustering is based (percent negative deviation within each group)

	Clusters			
Variables	Well-adjusted $N = 66$ %	Personal problems $N = 32$ %	Crime $N = 15$ %	Working problems $N = 15$ %
Adjustment				
Extremely unqualified work	5	22	20	47
At least three different jobs	15	6	20	73
Give up easily	6	9	0	93
Criminality	6	6	100	33
Alcohol abuse	2	3	40	7
Dislike responsibility	5	75	27	40
Several psychosomatic complaints	9	69	7	47
At least two somatic illnesses	20	53	0	13
Background				
From a large city	42	31	87	47
Parents known by social authorities	14	19	73	13
Disliked school	8	28	27	67
Absent at least once a week	2	16	13	33

maladjustment only in occasional variables. They constitute approximately half of the whole group. The *personal problems cluster* consists of persons who consider themselves to have difficulties in taking responsibility, and claim several psychosomatic symptoms. A high frequency of illness is noted. One positive aspect is that few of them have extremely low salaries. Thus, they adjust well socially despite some personal problems. They constitute a quarter of the whole group. The *crime cluster* is characterized by the fact that all the subjects have seriously violated the law, which in most cases resulted in sanctions. Alcoholic problems are frequent in this group and many have extremely low income. With reference to health and psychosomatic symptoms they are the opposite of the former group. These subjects constitute the most maladjusted group socially. The *working problems cluster* consist of those who see themselves as giving up very easily, who have had many jobs, who have lost them because of neglect, and who frequently have low salaries and extremely low-qualification jobs. None of them is receiving any education. Furthermore, they claim a regular and high consumption of alcohol, a fact which is not, however, recognized by the social authorities as abuse. These are probably passive and low performing persons. They have difficulties on the job, but infrequently initiate crime or are arrested for intoxication.

To sum up, one can say that all signs of lack of adjustment are not concentrated in a small group, but occur in approximately half of the subjects, some of whom are characterized by personal problems, some by violations of the law, and some by difficulties on the labour market. A comparison with a corresponding group of average intellectual functioning subjects shows that negative deviations are consistently considerably less; a corresponding cluster analysis of this group is therefore not possible.

Background Variables

The cluster analysis thus distributed the subjects with respect to their present adjustment. Four background variables were selected to check whether their background is related to their current adjustment (Table 1). The rates of all the background variables differ significantly between the groups, according to chi-square analysis, on the 1% level. Background variables show that the crime cluster is extreme in two respects: nearly all of the individuals come from big towns, and the parents are, irrespective of the children, known by social welfare authorities. The working problems cluster had problems in school, probably of the same type as they now experience on the job.

CONCLUSION

The results show that among mildly retarded unascertained 19-year-old males there is at least a small group, which in the future runs the risk of being regarded as mentally retarded. The social authorities tend to be arbitrary in deciding whether or not this group should be considered mentally retarded or be placed under the jurisdiction of different social agencies, such as social welfare, employment, and probation. It is a problem for the social authorities but it also affects the self-esteem of the mentally retarded. Clinical observations show that to be stigmatized as a social welfare recipient or a criminal is considered less humiliating by the person concerned than to be stigmatized as mentally retarded. The continuous process of urbanization and higher demands of efficiency in industry is likely to make it more difficult for the mildly mentally handicapped to get along. Rising social demands should be seen as relevant in deciding how this group can best be supported.

SUMMARY

Nonlabeled retarded adults were identified in connection with conscription for military service and their scores in ordinary school. Interviews, register data, and testing show that about half the group are considerably well-adjusted in spite of retardation. Three groups with different adjustment problems were those with personal problems, difficulty in retaining employment, and minor criminality.

REFERENCES

Granat, K. and Granat, S. (1973) Below-average intelligence and mental retardation. Amer. J. Ment. Defic. 78:27.

Granat, K. and Granat, S. (1975) The generalizability of patterns of intellectual performance from institutionalized to non-labelled intellectually subaverage adults. J. Ment. Defic. Res. 19:43.

Gruenberg, E. M. (1964) Epidemiology. *In* Mental Retardation (Eds. Stevens, H. A. and Heber, R.) Chicago: The University of Chicago Press.

Kebbon, L. (1965) The Structure of Abilities at Lower Levels of Intelligence. Stockholm: Skandinaviska Testförlaget.

RESEARCH TO PRACTICE IN MENTAL RETARDATION
Education and Training, Volume II
Edited by Peter Mittler
Copyright 1977 I.A.S.S.M.D.

MEASUREMENT OF ADAPTIVE BEHAVIOR IN JAPAN
A Factor-analytic Study

Y. Tomiyasu

*Institute for Developmental Research, Aichi Prefectural
Colony, Kamiya-Cho, Kasugai, Aichi 480-03, Japan*

The first edition of the AAMD Adaptive Behavior Scales (Nihira et al., 1969) was translated into Japanese with slight modifications by this author and his colleagues, and published for general use in Japan (Tomiyasu et al., 1973). For standardizing the Scales in Japan, adaptive behavior ratings for 6,092 retarded persons (i.e., 1,971 children under twelve years of age and 4,121 adolescents or adults older than twelve years) were collected from various regions across this country. Most of the subjects were cared for and trained in the residential institutions for the retarded (Tomiyasu et al., 1972; Tomiyasu and Matsuda, 1974b).

In order to make clear the nature of adaptive behavior and to improve its measuring techniques, several factor-analytic studies were carried out on 27 subdomain scores in Part I and/or 13 domain scores in Part II of the Scales. Thus, as far as factor patterns were concerned, several important trends were uncovered:

1. Three orthogonal factors in Part I and three factors in Part II were disclosed. These factors were named from the subdomains or domains having relatively large loadings for each of them. The three factors in Part I are "Personal Independence," "Social Adjustment," and "Personal-Social Responsibility," and the three factors in Part II are "Antisocial-Aggressive Behavior," "Self-Stimulating Behavior" and "Deficits in Interpersonal Behavior." These factor patterns were confirmed as emerging repeatedly in series of analyses in each of the groups divided in terms of age or MI level (Tomiyasu et al., 1974). The factor pattern in Part I was replicated in a study in the United States using an oblique solution (Nihira and Mink, 1975).

2. A systematic developmental change in the factor pattern in Part I was observed. The weight of contribution of the "Personal Independence" factor decreases with age. On the contrary, however, the weight of the "Social

Adjustment" factor increases gradually. Thus, the factors providing the largest contribution among these three factors are "Personal Independence" for the younger age level and "Social Adjustment" for the older age level. When the similar analyses were made for groups divided by MI Level, the changeover in the order of these two factors appeared with the increase in intelligence level. The MI Level at which the changeover takes place is lower for the older retarded than for the younger (Tomiyasu and Matsuda, 1974a).

3. This tendency was parallel with the change of factor scores. The factor score for "Personal Independence" increases in younger ages or lower MI Levels, while the factor score for "Social Adjustment" increases in older ages or higher MI Levels (Tomiyasu et al., in press a).

4. When further analyses were performed for the matrices of correlations among subdomains or domains from the two Parts together, the factors revealed in the analyses in each of the Parts re-emerged, except for the factor of "Deficits in Interpersonal Behavior." It was clearly shown that the factors were retained without mixture of the two Parts of the Scales (Tomiyasu et al., in press b).

In addition to these findings, it is especially noteworthy that the subdomains, such as "Locomotion" and "General Independent Functioning," which are included in the domain of "Independent Functioning" in the Scales have consistently relatively large loadings for the factor of "Social Adjustment" (Tomiyasu et al., 1974, in press a and b; Tomiyasu and Matsuda, 1974a) or "Community Self-Sufficiency" (Nihira and Mink, 1975). It seems to be reasonable to consider behaviors such as having a "Sense of Direction," using "Public Transportation," and "Telephone," to be "Social Adjustment" rather than "Personal Self-Sufficiency." These findings seem to suggest that there is room to look for another way to classify items in Part I of the Scales. Therefore, a further factor-analytic study based on item scores in the Part was executed to reveal a new system for classification of the items. This chapter is a report of the study.

METHOD

To find a new system for classifying items in Part I, factor analyses were performed separately for a group of children (from six to 12 years of age) and a group of adolescents (from 13 to 20 years of age). The product-moment correlation matrix of 67 items in the group of children and the matrix of 69 items in the group of adolescents were analyzed by the principal factor solution; the factor matrices obtained were then rotated by the direct oblimin method. These computations were conducted, using the SPSS, by a FACOM 230-60 computer at Nagoya University. In the factor solution by the principal factor method, the largest coefficient in each column of the matrix was selected as the initial diagonal estimate.

Because it was made clear in a previous investigation (Tomiyasu et al., 1974) that behaviors of the retarded at MI Level V were distinctly different from those at higher MI Levels, and that some items were inappropriate for identifying individual differences among the retarded at the lowest level of measured intelligence, the retarded at MI Level V were excluded from the subjects for this study. Furthermore, the retarded younger than six years or older than 20 years were excluded because the younger ones seemed to have various problems with themselves or their families that might have led to their early admission into residential institutions, and the older ones seemed to have special problems that might have prevented them from being released from the institution for such a long time. Therefore, the final subjects for the analyses in this study were 1,037 children and 1,780 adolescents.

RESULTS

To identify the most psychologically meaningful factor pattern across the two age groups, matrices of patterns of various numbers of common factors from three to eight, for various values of delta from −2.0 to 0.5 in increments of 0.5, were compared with one another. Although the first significant drop in eigenvalues obtained after successive iterations on refactorings took place between the first factor and the second one, and the eigenvalues were greater than 1.0 only for the first six factors in the principal factor solution, the pattern of seven common factors, rotated with delta = 0.0, was considered simplest and most meaningful for each of two age groups. These seven factors together accounted for 45.5% and 49.2% of the total variance in the correlation matrix for children and adolescents, respectively.

For the convenience of describing the factor pattern common to two different age groups, seven pairs of factors considered as corresponding to each other were arbitrarily labeled factors A, B, C, D, E, F, and G.

The correlations among these seven factors are presented in Table 1. The correlation matrix for children appears in the upper triangle and the matrix for adolescents appears in the lower triangle in the table. Although correlations for adolescents are somewhat larger than those for children, these matrices of correlation resemble each other in respect to the relative magnitude of coefficients among each of the matrices. Thus, the identification of the corresponding pairs of factor can be considered valid.

These factors and the items that have relatively large coefficients (i.e., over .300) for each of factors are graphically presented in Figure 1. In the following description about the factors, the names of items, subdomains and domains are adopted from the 1974 version of the Scale (Nihira et al., 1974) as far as they are included also in the revision for the convenience of current readers.

Factor A is defined as "Motor Skills" by seven items enclosed with solid lines at the upper left hand side in the chart because these variables are relevant

Table 1. Correlation among seven primary factors[a]

Factor	A.	B.	C.	D.	E.	F.	G.
A. Motor skills		0.368	0.163	0.285	0.320	0.177	0.244
B. Personal self-sufficiency skills	0.417		0.208	0.365	0.200	0.377	0.295
C. Community self-sufficiency skills	0.139	0.324		0.374	0.198	0.249	0.242
D. Academic skills	0.185	0.347	0.431		0.271	0.239	0.481
E. Communication skills	0.233	0.282	0.269	0.285		0.161	0.179
F. Self-regulation in personal activity	0.253	0.535	0.390	0.260	0.183		0.323
G. Self-regulation in group activity	0.174	0.310	0.459	0.253	0.227	0.414	

[a]Correlations for 1,037 children appear in the upper triangle and correlations for 1,780 adolescents appear in the lower triangle.

to how neatly, effectively, and/or purposefully individuals are able to move and control every part of their bodies. In children, the item of "Undressing at Appropriate Times" has also a relatively large coefficient for this factor. It is especially noteworthy that the item "Use of Table Utensils," which has been considered to belong to the behavioral category of "Independent Functioning," seems to have the nature of "Motor Skills" rather than "Self-Sufficiency Skills."

Factor B is named "Personal Self-Sufficiency Skills" from ten variables having large coefficients for this factor. As shown in the box of broken lines at the lower left of the chart, these items are originally included in the subdomains of "Toilet Use," "Cleanliness," "Appearance," "Care of Clothing," and "Dressing and Undressing" in the Scales. In children, two other items, that is, "Undressing at Appropriate Times" and "Toilet Training," and, in adolescents, three other items, that is, "Table Manners," "Laundry," and "Personal Belongings," are added to the item list for this factor. Therefore, in children, Factors A and B overlap not only on the item of "Dressing," as in adolescents, but also on the item of "Undressing at Appropriate Times."

Ten items having significant coefficients for Factor C are shown in the broken-line box at the upper middle part in the chart. These items are originally classified into such subdomains as "Travel," "Other Independent Functioning," "Eating," "Money Handling and Budgeting," "Shopping Skills," "Kitchen," and "Leisure Time" in the Scales. Except for "Eating" and "Leisure Time," most of these subdomains had loadings primarily for the factor of "Social Adjustment" in our previous orthogonal analyses (Tomiyasu et al., 1974; Tomiyasu and Matsuda, 1974a) and the oblique factor of "Community Self-Sufficiency" in an American study (Nihira and Mink, 1975). Therefore, this factor may be named "Community Self-Sufficiency Skills." It is particularly interesting to note that behaviors such as "Eating in Public," "Sense of Direction," "Telephone," and "Public Transportation," which are originally classified into the domain of "Independent Functioning" in the Scales, are included in the list of items for this factor. The items such as "Table Setting," "Table Clearing," and "General

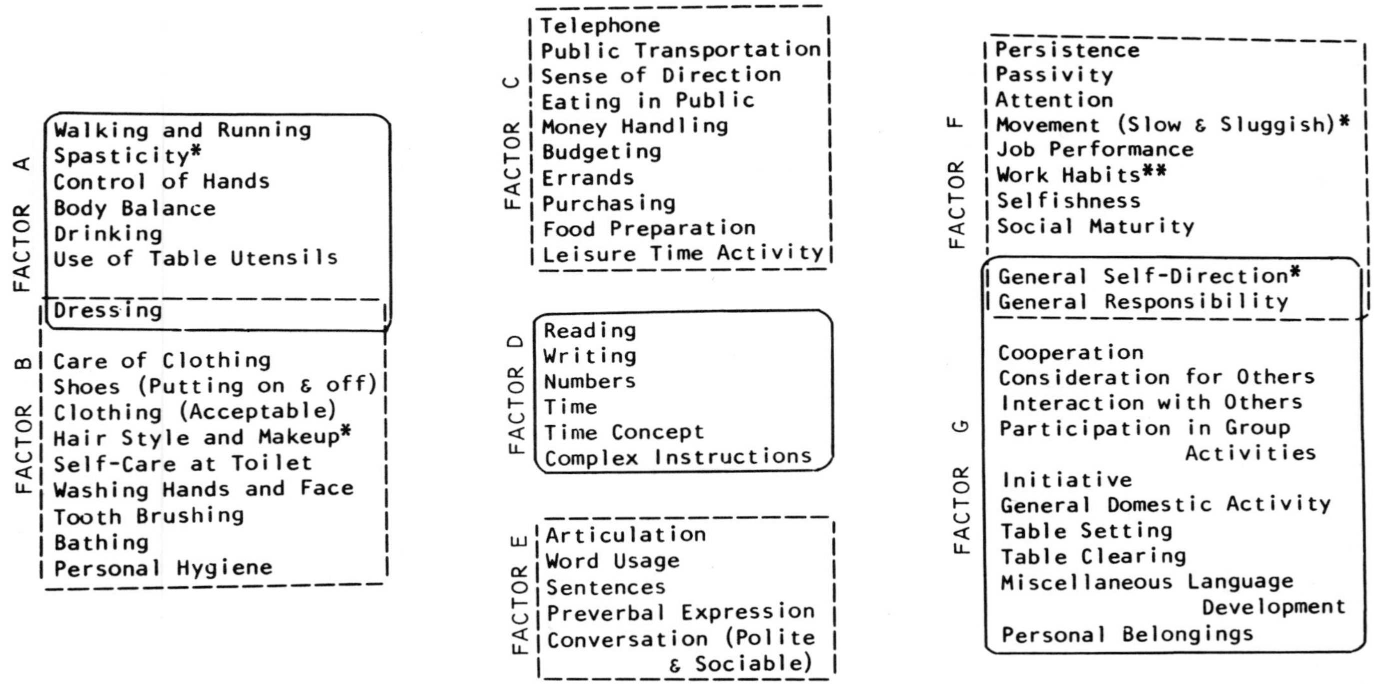

FACTOR A
Walking and Running
Spasticity*
Control of Hands
Body Balance
Drinking
Use of Table Utensils

FACTOR B
Dressing
Care of Clothing
Shoes (Putting on & off)
Clothing (Acceptable)
Hair Style and Makeup*
Self-Care at Toilet
Washing Hands and Face
Tooth Brushing
Bathing
Personal Hygiene

FACTOR C
Telephone
Public Transportation
Sense of Direction
Eating in Public
Money Handling
Budgeting
Errands
Purchasing
Food Preparation
Leisure Time Activity

FACTOR D
Reading
Writing
Numbers
Time
Time Concept
Complex Instructions

FACTOR E
Articulation
Word Usage
Sentences
Preverbal Expression
Conversation (Polite & Sociable)

FACTOR F
Persistence
Passivity
Attention
Movement (Slow & Sluggish)*
Job Performance
Work Habits**
Selfishness
Social Maturity

FACTOR G
General Self-Direction*
General Responsibility
Cooperation
Consideration for Others
Interaction with Others
Participation in Group Activities
Initiative
General Domestic Activity
Table Setting
Table Clearing
Miscellaneous Language Development
Personal Belongings

Figure 1. The chart of items with relatively large coefficients for each of seven oblique factors across two age groups. *Factor A*: Motor skills, *Factor B*: Personal self-sufficiency skills, *Factor C*: Community self-sufficiency skills, *Factor D*: Academic skills, *Factor E*: Communication skills, *Factor F*: Self-Regulation in personal activity, *Factor G*: Self-Regulation in group activity. *The item is only in the first edition of Adaptive Behavior Scales. **The item is only for adolescents or adults in the first edition.

Domestic Activity" in children, and "Writing," "Time," "Time Concept," and "Miscellaneous Independent Functioning" in adolescents, also have significant coefficients for this factor.

Factor D can be clearly interpreted as "Academic Skills" by the nature of the six items having larger coefficients for this factor. Literally, these items relate to cognitive development in skills for writing and reading and to concept formation of numbers and time, all of which are usually seen as the basic subjects during elementary education. In children, six other items, "Sentences," "Word Usage," "Money Handling," "Miscellaneous Language Development," "Miscellaneous Independent Functioning," and "Attention," have large coefficients for this factor.

Factor E may be defined as "Communication Skills." As shown at the lower middle section of the chart, five items have high coefficients for this factor. These items are useful to describe the level of individuals' efficiency for the interpersonal exchanges of feelings, needs, thoughts, and others. It is noteworthy that the item of "Hearing" also has a large coefficient for this factor in children.

As shown at the upper right hand side in the chart, in the case of Factor F, the significant coefficients appear for the ten variables that are relevant to the behaviors required for uninterrupted attention for some length of time, for continuing activities to completion without being forced by others, and for being entrusted with personal matters. This factor is therefore named "Self-Regulation in Personal Activity." In addition to the variables listed in the chart, three other items, that is, "Table Manners," "Posture," and "Clothing" in children, and the item of "Personal Belongings" in adolescents, also have large coefficients for this factor.

Finally, Factor G and twelve items having important coefficients for this factor in both age groups are shown in the box of solid lines at the lower right section in the chart. Since the items of "Cooperation," "Consideration for Others," "Interaction with Others," "Participation in Group Activities," and "Initiative" play major roles for this factor, and these variables are relevant to the ability for the self-control or self-direction needed in social life, this factor is named "Self-Regulation in Group Activity". Two other items, i.e., "Passivity," and "Awareness of Others" in children, and the item of the "Room Cleaning" in adolescents, are joined with this group of items. It is remarkable that the Factors F and G are simultaneously given weight by the items of "General Self-Direction" and "General Responsibility" which have been conclusive for defining the factor of "Personal-Social Responsibility" in previous studies on the basis of subdomain scores (Nihira and Mink, 1975; Tomiyasu et al., 1974; Tomiyasu and Matsuda, 1974a).

Sixty-four items for children and 62 items for adolescents, including 56 common to the two age groups, are differentiated according to the factor space mentioned above. Some items, however, do not have a significant coefficient. They are the items such as "Vision," "Room Cleaning," "Laundry," and "Job

Complexity" for children, and "Toilet Training," "Menstruation," "Posture," "Vision," "Hearing," "Job Complexity," and "Awareness of Others" for adolescents. Although these items can be classified into one of three categories, i.e., categories of items undifferentiated only for children, only for adolescents, or for both age groups, a more thorough study is now in progress.

CONCLUSION

Seven meaningful oblique factors of adaptive behavior were uncovered on the basis of item scores in Part I of the AAMD Adaptive Behavior Scales. These findings seem to suggest a new classification system and/or an alternate scoring system of adaptive behavior measured by the Scales.

REFERENCES

Nihira, K., Foster, R., Shellhaas, M., and Leland, H. (1969) Adaptive Behavior Scales. Washington, D.C.: AAMD.

Nihira, K., Foster, R., Shellhaas, M., and Leland, H. (1974) AAMD Adaptive Behavior Scale; (1974 revision). Washington, D.C.: AAMD.

Nihira, K., and Mink, Iris (1975) Development of adaptive behavior: A comparison between cross-sectional and longitudinal data. A paper presented at the annual meeting of the American Academy of Mental Retardation, Portland, Oregon.

Tomiyasu, Y., and Matsuda, S. (1974a) A factor-analytic study on adaptive behavior: The structure and its developmental change. A paper presented at the annual meeting of the American Association on Mental Deficiency, Toronto, Canada.

Tomiyasu, Y., and Matsuda, S. (1974b) Seishin hakujaku-sha no tekiou koudou no sokuteihou (Measuring techniques of adaptive behavior for the mentally retarded). Tokyo: Nihon-bunka-kagaku-sha. (In Japanese.)

Tomiyasu, Y., Matsuda, S., Murakami, E., and Emi, Y. (1974) Structure of the adaptive behavior of the mentally retarded: I. A factor-analytic study. Jap. J. Spec. Educ. 12:10. (In Japanese with an English summary.)

Tomiyasu, Y., Matsuda, S., Murakami, E., and Emi, Y. (in press a) Structure of the adaptive behavior of the mentally retarded: II. Analysis on the developmental change. Jap. J. Spec. Educ. (In Japanese with an English summary.)

Tomiyasu, Y., Matsuda, S., Murakami, E., and Emi, Y. (in press b) Structure of the adaptive behavior of the mentally retarded: III. The adaptive behavior and the maladaptive behavior. Jap. J. spec. Educ. (In Japanese with an English summary.)

Tomiyasu, Y., Murakami, E., Matsuda, S., and Emi, Y. (1972) An attempt to construct Japanese revision of adaptive behavior scales for the mentally retarded. Bulletin of the Faculty of Education—the Department of Educational Psychology—at Nagoya University, 19:151 (In Japanese with an English summary.)

Tomiyasu, Y., Murakami, E., Matsuda, S., and Emi, Y. (1973) Tekiou koudou shakudo (The Japanese version of Adaptive Behavior Scales). Tokyo: Nihon-bunka-kagaku-sha. (In Japanese.)

RESEARCH TO PRACTICE IN MENTAL RETARDATION
Education and Training, Volume II
Edited by Peter Mittler
Copyright 1977 I.A.S.S.M.D.

ADAPTIVE BEHAVIOR
Concepts
and Trends
in India

S. Upadhyaya
Department of Psychology, University of Jodhpur, India

The concept of adaptive behavior relates to the individual's ability to adapt to environmental demands that decide his success or failure in a cultural setting. It becomes especially important in the case of the mentally retarded because their various handicaps restrict their adaptive functioning in society. It is considered a failure on the part of the individual if he is not meeting the demands of the environment effectively, or if he is showing behavior that is not tolerated by the community at large. Unfortunately, it would appear that manifestations of behavior are not fully taken into account by the professionals when the subject's diagnosis and management are considered.

Like other countries, India has relied heavily on IQ assessment for information on the degree of mental retardation, and has given labels for categorizing the mentally retarded that become the basis for grouping them for education and training purposes. A common distinction is 'educable' and 'trainable', which is once again based on IQ assessment. Studies conducted in India having direct or indirect bearing on adaptive behavior fall into two categories. Under the first category come developmental studies conducted on normal children. Two such studies (Murlidharan and Topa, 1970; Verma et al., 1969) were conducted to obtain developmental norms, using Gesell's developmental schedule and Bayley's infant schedule.

Under the second category come those studies that have been conducted on retarded persons in order to know their potential and their problems of adjustment with a view to helping them and their parents. In such studies, the Vineland Social Maturity Scale (Shastri and Mishra, 1974; Verma et al., 1969), Gesell's developmental schedules (Teja et al., 1970; Verma et al., 1969) and adjustment inventories (Shukla and Khoche, 1974) have been used. One of these studies (Teja et al., 1970) concluded that measurement of IQ levels is not adequate for a complete assessment of the capacities and limitations of the mildly retarded group. However, a high correlation was obtained for moderate, severe, and profound groups of retarded between motor functions, impairment of social functions, and measured intelligence. A study by Mohan and Menon (1968) compared persistence in performance between normal and mentally retarded. They found the mentally retarded slightly superior in comparison to normals. Thus it indicated that in adaptive functions like persistence, the retarded can be better than normals. Some other studies like those of Ganguli (1968) investigated problems that affect social and economical adjustment of the retarded. Prabhu (1968) recommended participation of the parents in the services for the retarded.

The overall view of these studies indicates that the Vineland Social Maturity Scale and Gesell's developmental schedules have been much in use with the retarded. It is also evident that the inadequacy of IQ has been realized, and that the need of other kinds of assessment in mental retardation has been felt.

STUDIES IN ADAPTIVE BEHAVIOR

Study I

A systematic beginning in the study of adaptive behavior and its measurement was made by Upadhyaya (1974) and Upadhyaya and Borikar (1974) in connection with a rehabilitation project in which the AAMD Adaptive Behavior Scale was used. Interviews with parents of the mentally retarded, teachers, and professional workers led to an understanding of the cultural demands upon and expectations for the individuals in our society. This formed the basis for modifications in the AAMD Adaptive Behavior Scale to suit Indian conditions. Such modifications had to be made mostly in the areas of independent functioning and domestic occupation. The necessity for such changes was due to certain cultural patterns which could be classified as follows.

Customary Habits 1) Usually eating is done with the help of fingers, with occasional use of a spoon. Use of knife and fork is either absent or limited to restaurants and westernized homes. 2) Eating in public is encouraged less. It is limited to taking cold drinks and snacks, etc. Having lunch or dinner out is done only occasionally, starting at the college level. 3) Cleaning of teeth is done with the finger or with the tender stem of certain trees. However, the tooth brush and tooth paste are also used.

Different Expectations from Boys, Girls, and Women Boys and girls of school or college age are expected to concentrate on their studies and not bother about other things. However, there is differentiation in regard to boys attending to jobs outside, like running errands, and girls attending to jobs at home, like helping mothers with house chores. It is usually the ladies' job to do the cooking, serving food to other family members, cleaning, taking care of clothes, making beds, etc.

Certain functions, such as travelling on unfamiliar journeys and long distance travel, either by train or bus, are not expected of boys and girls below 18 years.

Although they may perform such functions, they are not supposed to be fully capable of taking care and protecting themselves. Girls usually are not allowed to take such journeys alone.

Dependence on Parents For some functions such as money handling, budgeting money, and making purchases, children usually depend on their parents. Once again, although children at a certain age may perform such functions, parents still have their say in these things. These functions are mostly in existence only in middle and upper class homes. Making use of bank facilities, using telephones, consulting with a doctor for medical care, and similar functions are considered to be an adult's job. In Indian culture, at least in a social sense, a person is not considered capable of managing his affairs until and unless he is married and has a job.

The above mentioned points come under the purview of independent functioning and personal responsibility. "Social responsibility" is only expected from boys or girls when they grow up, get married, or work. Otherwise for them social responsibility is limited to an educational career, civic responsibilities, and proper interaction with due regard for elders and others.

Study II

The study reported here deals directly with the application of adaptive behavior in the assessment and teaching/training of the mentally retarded. Over the years it has been our observation that IQ scores obtained on standardized intelligence tests, and assessment of personality through projective tests, do not yield much information on the potential of the mentally retarded. Designing training programmes for them thus becomes very difficult (Upadhyaya and Sinha, 1974).

Study II is based on observation and ratings of 32 mentally retarded people who attended the rehabilitation unit for special education and vocational training. They were in the age range of 14–21 years, with admission IQ (Stanford Binet, 1960 revision) varying from 19 to 59. All the cases were rated on the Adaptive Behavior Scale by two raters who were also in charge of special education and vocational training, thus having direct contact with the mentally retarded. The ratings were obtained at the time of admission to the program and also at intervals of six to nine months while rehabilitation cases were under training. Interrater reliability obtained for the first rating had a mean reliability coefficient of 0.83, with reliabilities ranging from 0.98 for "Number and Time Concept" to 0.61 for "Responsibilities" (Table 1).

Out of the 32 cases studied, ratings were available for four stages for 18 cases, three stages for 27 cases, and two stages for 32 cases. These ratings were then analyzed to see whether or not growth, occurring in mentally retarded individuals due to exposure to special education and vocational training, also increases their adaptive behavior. Since the different ratings were obtained on the same individuals, the Sandler's A Test was used in order to assess changes occurring over a period of time on various areas of the Adaptive Behavior Scale.

Table 1. Reliabilities for adaptive behavior domain scores

Domains	Mean reliability
1. Independent functioning	0.93
2. Physical development	0.70
3. Economic activity	0.82
4. Language development	0.96
5. Number and time concept	0.98
6. Occupation domestic	0.70
7. Vocational abilities	0.78
8. Self direction	0.84
9. Responsibilities	0.61
10. Socialization	0.95
Mean reliability for the scale	0.83

The analysis was done by working out the differences between two observations and then finding the A values, which is similar to t, except that in the A test the smaller the value, the higher the significance of the difference (Table 2).

From Table 2 it can be noted that changes in a positive direction have occurred among mentally retarded individuals over a period of time when they undergo a training program. This is reflected in their adaptive behavior scores in different areas. Such increase in adaptive behavior scores is comparatively more between I–II, I–III, and I–IV stages of observation, where A values are statistically significant in all areas of adaptive behavior. However, it is not the same between the II–III or III–IV stages of observations. Between the II and III stage of observation there is significant change only in the areas of Economic Activity, Language Development, Number and Time Concept, and Self-Direction.

Table 2. Significance of difference in different areas of adaptive behavior over different periods of study, using Sandler's A Test

Areas	I - II	I - III	I - IV	II - III	II - IV	III - IV
1. Independent functioning	0.0459	0.0481	0.0686	0.2322^a	0.0902	0.0892
2. Physical development	0.0453	0.0649	0.0714	1.0867^a	0.2198^a	0.7216^a
3. Economic activity	0.0408	0.0453	0.0744	0.0752	0.0939	0.2936^a
4. Language development	0.0523	0.0469	0.0660	0.1289	0.1094	0.2959^a
5. Number and time concept	0.0388	0.0398	0.0646	0.1106	0.0836	0.1181
6. Occupation domestic	0.0366	0.0476	0.0642	0.2250	0.1376	0.3125^a
7. Vocational abilities	0.0451	0.0493	0.0684	10.0500^a	0.1065	0.1580
8. Self-direction	0.0392	0.0414	0.0693	0.1328	0.1552	0.2857^a
9. Responsibilities	0.0454	0.0541	0.0830	0.1925	0.1413	5.5000^a
10. Socialization	0.0318	0.0405	0.0693	0.2159^a	0.1460	0.1436

^{a}Values not significant. Significance levels: 0.116 ($p = 0.001$); 0.168 ($p = 0.01$).

Similarly, it is significant only in the areas of Independent Functioning, Number and Time Concept, Domestic Occupation, Vocational Abilities, and Socialization between III and IV stages of observation. This has to do with the emphasis given at different stages of training. These cases underwent a training that emphasized personal-social skills and general work skills in the initial stages, work-specific skills in the middle stage, and job-oriented training in the third stage.

Use of the Adaptive Behavior Scale in such a program seems to have served two purposes. First, it indicated the level of functioning of the mentally retarded at a time in training. Second, it indicated whether particular education or vocational training was effective in bringing about changes in adaptive functioning of the individuals. This helps in having a second look at the program for making necessary changes and modification.

SUMMARY

The IQ has been used in India both for the diagnosis of mental retardation and for placement of the mentally retarded in training. However, inadequacies of the IQ have also been pointed out, and the need for understanding of adaptive behavior and adjustment problems has been expressed. In understanding the adaptive behavior of the mentally retarded, the basis has been cultural expectation and demands made on them. A modified form of the AAMD Adaptive Behavior Scale was used for the same purpose in a rehabilitation programme. It was found that changes occurring due to exposure to training also brought significant improvements in adaptive behavior. In this context the utility of adaptive behavior was demonstrated.

REFERENCES

Ganguli, D. (1968) Problems involving social and economical adjustment among the mentally retarded children. Indian J. Ment. Retard. 1:29.
Mohan, J., and Menon, D. K. (1968) Mental retardation and physical persistence. Indian J. Ment. Retard. 1:63.
Muralidharan, R. (1970) Home stimulation and child development. Indian Educ. Res. 5.
Murlidharan, R., and Topa, V. (1970) Need for achievement and independent training. Indian J. Psychol. 45:1.
Prabhu, G. G. (1968) The participation of parents in the services for the retarded. Indian J. Ment. Retard. 1:4.
Shastri, A. S. I., and Mishra, A. K. (1974) Assessment of social functioning of 56 mentally retarded children. Indian J. Ment. Retard. 7:31.
Shukla, T. R., and Khoche, V. (1974) A study of adjustment problems of mentally retarded children. Indian J. Ment. Retard. 7:4.
Teja, J. S., et al. (1970) A comparative study of motor and social milestones and their relationship with the intelligence test results in mentally retardates. Indian J. Ment. Retard. 3:75.

Upadhyaya, S. (1974) Evaluation of Adaptive Behavior. Paper presented at the All Indian Conference on Developmental Approach in Occupational Therapy, Ahmedabad, December.

Upadhyaya, S., and Borikar, A. M. (1974) Adaptive Behavior Scale: Implications in Rehabilitation Programme for the Mentally Retarded. Paper presented at the 5th All India Convention of Clinical Psychologists, New Delhi, November.

Upadhyaya, S., and Sinha, A. K. (1974) Some psycho-diagnostic findings with young retarded adults. Indian J. Clinc. Psychol. 1.

Verma, A., Poffenberger, T., Pathak, P., Shah, J. M., and Shah, H. B. (1969) Motor and Mental Growth of Baroda Babies, Research Report No. 3. Baroda: Dept. of Child Development, M.S. University.

RESEARCH TO PRACTICE IN MENTAL RETARDATION
Education and Training, Volume II
Edited by Peter Mittler
Copyright 1977 I.A.S.S.M.D.

ASSESSMENT OF ADAPTIVE BEHAVIOR IN BELGIAN SPECIAL SCHOOLS

G. Magerotte
Interuniversity Center for Psychological and Educational Research
and Training in Mental Retardation,
Mons State University, Belgium

In the adaptive behavior movement, two main aspects have been stressed by researchers and professional staff: first the need to use assessment techniques for planning better intervention (Lambert et al., 1975; Leland, 1964; Magerotte, 1976a, 1976c; Nihira et al., 1969, 1974) and, on the other hand, the need to obtain in-depth knowledge of the concrete and specific adaptive demands of diverse environments and of taking these more into account. Two investigations carried out in Belgian special schools for the mentally retarded tried to shed some light on these two requirements.

Providing better assessment for a more accurate intervention and education is the first goal of the AAMD Adaptive Behavior Scale (Nihira et al., 1969, 1974). Our French adaptation of this scale (experimental version, 1972) was carried out as closely as possible in this perspective. Unlike the original Adaptive Behavior Project, we used a representative sample of mentally retarded pupils attending day schools; they were assessed by their own teachers. Furthermore, we did not try, as did Lambert et al. (1975), to investigate several samples of subjects attending different school systems; we were not interested in preparing norms for classifying purposes.

Four hundred and twenty-eight mentally retarded children (237 boys and 191 girls) from six to 13 years of age, served as subjects (mean CA, 9.11; mean IQ, 59). They were selected to form a representative sample of mentally retarded pupils attending special day schools.

As a result of our research, some changes were deemed necessary to obtain a more accurate relationship with the school population assessed and with the intervention goal. As far as the first aspect is concerned, this was done by scrutinizing the factor analysis results and from the information gathered when meeting the teachers at the "assessment sessions.'

The detailed factor analysis results have been reported elsewhere (Magerotte, 1976a and 1976b). Only the main conclusions will be summarized here. In respect to Part 1, the major changes concern the area of physical development. The motor development subcategory checks independence in daily living activities associated with basic motor skills, and would therefore be better placed in the independence domain. Furthermore, sensory development was removed from the scale and placed in the general information heading.

Part 2 was completely restructured under eight categories: physical aggressiveness, socially unacceptable behaviors, verbal aggressiveness, rebellious behavior toward authority (these four aspects have a clear antisocial orientation), withdrawal behavior (and peculiar habits), socially unacceptable vocal or motor hyperactivity, unacceptable sexual behavior, and psychological disturbance (this last area needs more refinement, too).

On the other hand, the adequacy of some items in the school system and environment was frequently questioned during "assessment meetings"; behaviors such as brushing teeth, using public transport, phoning, and domestic activities were evaluated with difficulty in so far as they did not match "traditional" school activities. Lambert et al. (1975) made similar observations. However, in accordance with our basic goal, we did not remove these items from the scale, but excluded them only from the norms. The reasons for this were that we noticed important differences between the schools and we did not necessarily wish the scale to be an accurate image of current school practices insofar as, in our experience, special schools imitate the normal school practices too closely and then ignore specific but essential needs of mentally retarded children, mainly in the social area.

This introduces us to the use of the scale for action and for appropriate changes. First, we translated some negative items into positive ones, i.e., into educational goals (personal hygiene and clothing). The Adaptive Behavior Scale Manual was deliberately rewritten in simple, nontechnical language in order to be more suitable for the teacher. It was also restructured to lead directly to the design of intervention programs. Finally, we designed a set of sheets to use in connection with the inventory, itself printed in a reusable booklet, so that the teacher who is in charge of 6–12 children does not have to handle a mass of documents. The individual answer sheet collects, on page 1, the identification data and general information translated from the central personal file in terms of adaptive behavior (e.g., influence of medication, sensory defects on daily living activities). On page 2 the teacher's observations are recorded by shading (in green for the acquired skills and in red for maladjusted behaviors). Pages 3 and 4 are reserved for the preparation of intervention. An individual scoring sheet may be added inside the answer sheet; it permits computation of the raw scores per domain, as well as comparison with the main sample.

If the Adaptive Behavior Scale is to be used efficiently to facilitate an effective intervention, it needs to summarize the basic requirements for adaptation to social life. As noted by Lambert et al. (1975), it does not try to cover the whole range of adaptive requirements but limits its scope to the minimum. We made a preliminary investigation in the special school to get an idea how this environment considers these demands. The critical incident technique already used by Nihira in devising the Scale (Nihira and Shellhaas, 1970; Nihira, 1973) was also used here. Each observer was invited to give a written report of two critical behaviors for each of the three following conditions:

1. behavior that shows that the child does not derive any benefit from the classroom or school activities proposed to him to improve his independence and social adaptation (our aim was to get a complete list of specific activities in adaptive behavior education) (Type I)
2. behavior difficult to tolerate in a normal environment but not causing too much trouble in the classroom or school (Type II)
3. behavior difficult to tolerate both in a normal environment as well as in the classroom or school. (Type III)

These last two kinds of critical incidents would permit a study of the gradation of requirements from the least to the most intolerable.

To explain the results more fully, some other questions were asked about the causes of the behaviors and about the degree of tolerance.

The investigation, carried out in eight day schools and one residential school, afforded 376 critical incidents from 70 observers. These incidents were distributed amongst the items and areas of the Adaptive Behavior Scale. We shall now review the results.

RESULTS

The most frequently referred items were decreasingly:

No. 13 Resists instructions, requests, or orders (71 times—rebellious behavior 115 times)
No. 1 Threatens or does physical violence (45 times—violent and destructive behavior 83 times)
No. 39 Reacts poorly to frustration (30 times)
No. 32 Has hyperactive tendencies (28 times)
No. 11 Uses profane or hostile language (20 times)
No. 38 Reacts poorly to criticism (20 times).

The most prevalent requirements therefore concern behavior against adult authority and physical aggression toward others. Notice that two items from the psychological disturbance domain were frequently mentioned.

Part 1 items most frequently cited were Perseverance (14 times), Passivity (12 times), and Toilet training (8 times). These behaviors are not specific, except Toilet training. Does it mean that the observers were sensitive to general attitudes and reactions of the retarded rather than to specific and concrete behaviors? Does it mean also that only a few specific activities are proposed to develop adaptive behaviors? Probably, but this needs a more in-depth study of school environments. The wording used in our investigation may also be imprecise.

The comparison of Type II and Type III incidents is supposed to distinguish between two levels of requirements. In fact, the analysis indicates that physical aggressiveness and behaviors hostile toward authority represent an absolute norm (Type III). At a second level (Type II), the less disturbing behaviors are found, the main characteristic of which seems to be the frequency of appearance, i.e., hyperactive tendencies and unacceptable vocal habits. It is worthwhile noting that this dichotomy also appears in the factor analysis.

The difference between school and normal environmental requirements is explained by three factors: 1) the teacher is accustomed to this kind of behavior, 2) he knows each child intimately, and 3) this behavior does not have too disturbing an influence on other children. This disturbing effect is frequently evoked with Type III incidents, and explains the intolerable characteristic of these behaviors.

Answers to questions concerning the causes of critical behaviors may be consider under two headings:

1. psychological explanations, e.g. "the need to have his value acknowledged," "the need of security," an unrepressed drive, and so on
2. global external explanations relating to the familial, schooling, or other handicapping conditions.

In spite of our insistence upon the precise description of concrete behaviors and events, most explanations were a-situational, and did not make any reference to current observable events: the here-and-now environment is quite absent and the critical behaviors are often, as one educator wrote, "beyond the scope of educational action"! This appeared most obviously in the Type III incidents, where "nothing" was sometimes the only explanation given by the observer. The event is described as inexplicable and unpredictable.

This investigation had an exploratory purpose only and the observations discussed and conclusions need to be more fully analyzed and confirmed by other researchers with different techniques and in other milieus. Nevertheless, it allows us to shed some empirical light on the concrete demands of the environment. It further confirms the need for more accurate observation, and fully justifies the effort to devise an adaptive behavior scale more suitable to the school environment and the intervention perspective.

ACKNOWLEDGMENT

This investigation was carried out with the assistance of one of our students, Y. Bawin, whose contribution is greatly appreciated.

REFERENCES

Bawin, Y. (1976) Les Exigences Adaptatives du Milieu. Louvain: Faculté de Psychologie et des Sciences de l'Education. Unpublished masters thesis.

Lambert, N., Windmiller, M., Cole, L., and Figueroa, R. (1975) AAMD Adaptive Behavior Scale—Public School Version, 1974 Revision—Manual. Washington, D.C: AAMD.

Leland, H. (1964) Some thoughts on the current status of adaptive behavior. Ment. Retard. 2:171.

Magerotte, G. (1976a) L'évaluation du comportement adaptatif des écoliers arriérés mentaux. Revue Neuropsychiat. Infant. 24:127.

Magerotte, G. (1976b) Adaptive behavior of mentally retarded pupils. A factor analysis of the AAMD Adaptive Behavior Scale. Submitted for publication.

Magerotte, G. (1976c) L'échelle de Comportement Adaptatif. Inventaire des Comportements d'Adaptation à la Vie Quotidienne. Adaptation française de l'AAMD Adaptive Behavior Scale. Liège-Mons: Groupe Interuniversitaire de Recherche et de Formation Psychologique et Pédagogique dans le domaine de l'arriération mentale. (Mimeograph).

Nihira, K. (1973) Importance of environmental demands in the measurement of adaptive behavior. In Sociobehavioral Studies in Mental Retardation (Eds. Eyman, R. K., Meyers, C. E., and Tarjan, G.) Washington, D.C: AAMD, p. 101.

Nihira, K., and Shellhaas, M. (1970) Studies of adaptive behavior: Its rationale, method and implication in rehabilitation programs. Ment. Retard. 8:11.

Nihira, K., Foster, R., Shellhaas, M., and Leland, H. (1969, 1974) AAMD Adaptive Behavior Scale—Manual. Washington, D.C: AAMD.

LANGUAGE
AND COMMUNICATION

RESEARCH TO PRACTICE IN MENTAL RETARDATION
Education and Training, Volume II
Edited by Peter Mittler
Copyright 1977 I.A.S.S.M.D.

SOME CURRENT PERSPECTIVES ON TEACHING COMMUNICATION FUNCTIONS TO MENTALLY RETARDED CHILDREN

D. E. Yoder and J. E. Reichle
Department of Communicative Disorders
University of Wisconsin–Madison
Madison, Wisconsin 53706, United States

Our earliest attempts at language intervention with mentally retarded children who had not acquired speech, language, or communication skills at a normal rate seemed to be an attempt to answer Roger Brown's imposing question "how shall a thing be called?" Our assumption was that the child should be taught labels for a variety of things. Then he should be taught a variety of action words describing what the things did. Next the child was taught to label simultaneously both the object and the traditional action that the object performed. Our problem was not to be found in teaching mentally retarded children to perform in this paradigm, but was to have the children use the forms we taught at an appropriate time, in an appropriate setting, with appropriate individuals. How, when, and where names of things shall be used is a problem that continually haunts those of us attempting to teach speech, language, and communication skills to mentally retarded persns.

The reasons mentally retarded children fail to generalize trained language behavior may be several. Miller (1976) has indicated that the content of our original programming assumed that 1) "the child was not able to use those processes employed by normal children to acquire language" and 2) the assumption was made that "the child had not learned language because he had not been given sufficient exposure." With local children, some of these failures have been dealt with in the programming strategies, described by Miller and Yoder (1974), Blank (1973) MacDonald (1975) and Stremel and Waryas (1974).

These latter intervention paradigms use content derived from the data available on language development in the normal child, the grammatical acquisition along with cognitive and the semantic base of language structure. Consequently, the normal child is considered the ideal speaker-hearer at any given developmental level. This approach is possible as a result of a long and fruitful line of research of language in mother-child interaction (Snow, 1972; Phillips, 1972; Broen, 1972; and on and on) and of the evergrowing data base in normal language acquisition (Bloom, 1973; Bowerman, 1973; Braine, 1976). But successful as it may be in teaching sounds, words, grammar, and meaning, one bridge that has not been crossed with any regularity of success is the programming of early communication acts. Dore (1973), Bruner (1975), and Bates (1976) suggest that early routines of motor and/or vocal behavior express early communicative sequences between mother and child. Both Bruner (1975) and Bates (1976) describe sequences of mutual attending. Bates (1976) has additionally described sequences in which the infant attempts to reach for an object that could not be displaced from the adult's hand, after which the infant seeks to obtain eye contact with the adult. This type of behavior might be analogous to an early form of requesting or demanding behavior. Other behaviors noted in normally developing children prior to the acquisition of vocal communicative skills include: showing off objects to obtain attention, showing objects for referential value, giving objects to another person that have just been shown off, and pointing to objects as an act of reference. Children have also been observed to display motor communicative behavior with respect to agents, actions, and objects prior to exhibiting such relations in their verbal output.

Bates (1976) has described children in Piaget's sensorimotor Stage 5 as following observable sequences of development in their interactions with objects in the environment. First, children may be observed to utilize objects to operate on other objects; then they begin to use human agents either to obtain or to operate on objects. Eventually, they begin to manipulate objects to obtain human attention. The verification of these early communicative strategies offers a rationale for the content of an early communicative curriculum. The work of investigators Dore (1973), Bates (1976) and Bruner (1975) also suggests that our starting point in language training curriculum has concentrated too much on the form of language syntax rather than on the function.

Until now, our definition of function in intervention has stressed the specific vocabulary item and not what knowing this content is going to get for the child when the interventionist is not monitoring the child's performance.

The functions that Bates, Bruner, and Dore address may be viewed as transdisciplinary target behaviors. Early attention, visual and auditory localization, reaching, giving, showing, and pointing are all skills of equal interest to all individuals interested in the learning of children. These behaviors, however, emitted spontaneously by the child, represent the basis of communication and the foundations of reference that are the initial end to which the majority of programming attempts need to be directed.

This, however, is not the direction we have been taking with regard to teaching speech and language skills to retarded children.

Today, the vast majority of language intervention programs for mentally retarded children use a respondent training paradigm. The clinician acts as the initiator (show me ____; you say ____ where's the ____) in most training programs for the severely impaired (Guess, Sailor, and Baer, 1977; Kent, 1974; Tawney, 1972). In this paradigm the child may be taught a number of vocabulary items, syntactic rules, and perhaps even several semantic functions. It is a misnomer, however to contend that the child is learning communication.

Very early in respondent paradigms the child is taught "I do" and then "you do." In such a paradigm it is no surprise that children in a program designed to ask questions fail to generalize question asking. In the typical question asking program, the interventionist holds up an object. If the child knows the label he responds with the label. If, on the other hand, he does not know the label, he is taught to ask "what is it?" It is obvious that in asking the question, the child is functioning as respondent because: 1) we have no indication that the child actually wanted to know what the object was, and 2) even if he wanted to know, he is being trained that "I wait until the interventionist signals me to ask" (similar to "the teacher will call on me, otherwise I remain silent").

Under the above paradigm one would predict one of two response patterns. 1) The child might see the use of the "What's that?" as a way to achieve an adult's attention and use it as an arousal statement (e.g., walking up to adult, tugging at sleeve and saying "what's that?"). 2) The other probable response pattern would be one in which the child never initiates the questioning behavior unless prompted by the adult. This illustration is not meant to suggest that question asking behavior cannot be taught. Instead it is an example of an all too usual program designed to teach form without establishing communicative function.

So what is communicative function and what is its relationship to teaching communicative skills to mentally retarded children? Individuals who have relegated themselves to the task of deciphering the pathways that lead the child from signal to sophisticated verbal communication agree that an utterance including motor behavior can account for more than it means in a strict semantic sense. Achieving communicative competence entails not only the encoding and decoding of messages in isolation, but also learning how to use these messages to perform communicative functions. These functions are based, to a great extent, upon the environmental context of the utterance.

Bates (1976) has suggested that contextual rules may assist in the observation of early communication behavior. The study of communicative intentions on the part of the speaker and interpretation on the part of the listener(s) has been ascribed the nomenclature "pragmatics."

The intent of early communicative behavior has been defined by Dore (1974) as the overt effort to induce in a listener the recognition of the speaker's expectation. In early communicative behavior during the first several months of life, it is very likely that we actually study adult interpretation and only at a later point in time do we begin effectively to evaluate the child's communicative intent. Brown (1973) has described early communicative attempts in infancy as being "narrowly adapted" because effective communication could not be completed unless there was someone who was as Muma (1975) has said "sufficiently aware of the child's verbal repertoire and particular context" to interpret the utterance.

Regardless of the defining attributes, the general consensus among investigators is that, over time, signals emitted in a consistent context and interpreted in a consistent fashion during early life come to influence phonological, semantic, and syntactic acquisition (Bruner, 1975). Chapman (1976) has indicated that parents of infants approximately one year of age who are just beginning to learn to talk are often reported to understand everything spoken to them. Chapman goes on to point out several comprehension strategies used by the child. Most of these strategies rely upon some aspect of context to cue a response rather than the verbal utterance itself. It is also reasonable to assume that adults have interpretation strategies based on the context of the child utterance, the time of day, etc.

The backbone of all communicative function is context. Even though context is often the best indicator of purpose in early communication it is ripe with ambiguities. Some contextual variables are not observable unless one has had prior experience with the participants. Attitudes of the speaker and beliefs about the listener greatly shape the potential use of contextual features of the environment by both speaker and listener. Other potential features include the environmental setting, the age of the respective participants, the number of participants, the task, the time of day, the language age of the participants, sex, socioeconomic status, and countless other as yet unspecified variables.

If one views communication function as thread for the beads of motor, cognitive, semantic, syntactic, and, to a certain extent, social development, it is only natural that the distinctions between pragmatics and several of these disciplines are somewhat ambiguous. While it is appropriate to speculate upon the relationship between these skills, there is little evidence supplying a causal link.

If one goes to the environment and explores what the basic functions of communication are for coping with everyday problems one can come up with a rather long, exhaustive list. Dore (1974, 1975) has distinguished 32 communicative intentions performed by normal three-year-olds. These major functions of language are of real importance to us because they provide a framework from which we can begin to observe the child's use of language in various situations. This is of particular importance to those of us who are attempting to put together intervention strategies for young retarded children based on communicative need and basic communicative function within a developmental model. Since communication function is the goal of our language teaching programs, functions become important not only to assess but to teach. Major functions of communication may ultimately become the criteria for success in language training programs. As of now, however, we lack specific operational procedures for measurement (if they can be constricted) and we must rely on behavioral observation for their analysis.

Allow us to suggest major communicative functions that should be considered in establishing a program for young mentally retarded children. This is a composite of functions taken from Dore (1974), Chapman (1975), Hymes (1972) and Yoder.

If the target behavior is functional communication, then the content of the program should be focused on the functions of communication. In turn, if we expect the child to use these functions, they need to be taught within the environment where they have the probability of being used. We are suggesting that all communication is for problem-solving purposes. This may be a simple problem of coping with an everyday need, such as signaling the need to go to the toilet, or it may be a more sophisticated (a value judgment) problem of believing that Jimmy Carter really will make a better president than Jerry Ford. Regardless of the problems the child will have to solve in everyday life, the efficiency in doing so with a communication system is the important point (see Table 1).

Functional communication, as we have implied, is not accomplished basically through the oral/aural system. There is sufficient evidence today to indicate that

Table 1. Functions of language in the communication process—
the overriding function is to solve problems

Methods of problem-solving
1) Giving information
2) Getting information
3) Describing events
4) Getting listeners to:
do something
believe something
feel something
5) Expressing one's own:
intentions
beliefs
feelings
6) Indicating desire for further communication (interaction)
7) Entertainment
8) Learning new behavior
rehearsal
reinforcement
feedback
9) Interactional
10) Personal gratification (fantasy and day dreaming)

Table 2. Our basic concerns at this point

A. Focus on the communication functions of the young child first. Current evidence would support the notion that communication functions develop prior to the structure of the language system. (Bates 1974, 1975; Bruner 1975).

B. Focus on the functions we know are used in communication by the speakers of the community language. We now have some good ideas of what these are from the work of Dore, Chapman, Hymes, and others.

C. Focus on nonverbal as well as verbal communication modes. The literature of Bates, Dore, and others indicate that communication functions are taking place long before oral verbal behavior is used by the child.

D. If we are to develop functional communication systems for the mentally retarded person we must focus on the functions of communication.

E. The structure of the language is not to be neglected. In a fine work by Waryas and Stremel-Campbel (in preparation) the authors have reexamined the place of grammatical training for the language delayed child. They concur with Jon Miller, Robin Chapman, and us, that we have no intent of suggesting that syntax and semantics are no longer important. They are as important as they always were. We are, however, at a place in our understanding of the development of speech, language, and communication of placing it more appropriately within the teaching paradigm later in the system.

F. Mentally retarded children at all developmental levels are acquiring communication systems. They will continue to develop more efficient and effective systems as the interventionist becomes more knowledgeable with the system we are attempting to teach. We have a pretty good handle on the technology; the content of the system continues to give us some struggles.

G. We are now at a point where we are as concerned with the *why* of communication as with the *how* and the *what*. When we've got all the pieces of the puzzle put together we may be able to provide the mentally retarded citizen with the communication system completely commensurate with his community, but then the question may be: "But should we?"

---

alternative and augmentative systems are also effective in communication. Those are being discussed in other chapters of this volume and we do not go into them here, except to say that the functions of communication are the same for all persons regardless of the mode for receiving and expressing the information (see Table 2).

Another point one should keep in mind in putting together a program for teaching communication functions is that, at present, we do not yet have the information on the developmental strategies used in acquiring these functions, nor do we know which functions may be precursors to others. We do know, however, that there is a horizontal developmental pattern within functions, and our observations tell us that there is also some developmental strategy for vertical development.

REFERENCES

Blank, M. (1973) Teaching Learning in Preschool: A Dialogue Approach. Columbus, Ohio: Merrill.

Bruner, J. S. (1975) From communication to language: A psychological perspective. Cognition 3:255.

Chapman, R. (1974) Developmental relationship between receptive and expressive language. *In* Language Perspectives: Acquisition, Retardation and Intervention. (Eds. Schiefelbusch, R. L., and Lloyd, L.) Baltimore: University Park Press.

Chapman, R. (1976) Language development charts. *In* Procedures for Assessing Children's Language: A Developmental Process Approach. (Ed. Miller, J.) Unpublished manuscript, University of Wisconsin-Madison.

Chapman, R., and Miller, J. (1975) Word order in early two and three word utterances: Does production precede comprehension? J. Speech Hear. Res. 18:355.

Dore, J. (1974) A pragmatic description of early language development. J. Psycholing. Res. 4:343.

Guess, D., Sailor, W., and Baer, D. (1977) A behavioral-remedial approach to language training for the severely handicapped. *In* Educational Programming for Severely and Profoundly Handicapped. (Eds. Sortag, E., Smith, J., and Certo, N.) Special publication of Division in Mental Retardation, The Council for Exceptional Children.

Hymes, D. (1972) *In* Functions of Language in the Classroom. (Eds. Cazden, C., John, V., and Hymes, D.) New York: Teachers College Press.

Kent, L. (1974) Language Acquisition Program for the Severely Retarded. Champaign, Illinois: Research Press.

MacDonald, J. (1975) Ready, Set, Go. The Nisonger Center, Ohio State University.

Miller, J. (Ed.) (1976) Procedures for assessing children's language: A developmental process approach. Unpublished Manuscript, University of Wisconsin-Madison.

Stremel, K., and Waryas, C. (1974) A behavioral-psycholinguistic approach to language training. Amer. Speech Hear. Monogr. 18:96.

Tawney, J. W., and Hispsher, L. (1972) Systematic Instruction for Retarded Children: The Illinois Program. Experimental Edition: Part II. Systematic Language Instruction. Danville, Illinois: The Interstate Printers and Publishers.

RESEARCH TO PRACTICE IN MENTAL RETARDATION
Education and Training, Volume II
Edited by Peter Mittler
Copyright 1977 I.A.S.S.M.D.

COMMUNICATION ASSESSMENT IN THE MENTALLY RETARDED
Current Practices in the United States

M. Fristoe
Department of Audiology and Speech Sciences,
Purdue University, Heavilon Hall,
West Lafayette, Indiana, United States

Language is like love:

It is experienced almost universally.

A person can survive without it, but the quality of life is diminished.

It cannot be defined satisfactorily, but we all can recognize it when we experience it; if we have not experienced it we do not know what it is like.

We would like to know how to trigger and enhance its development.

It is very difficult to measure.

The purpose of this paper is to discuss the current status of assessment of the retarded in the United States with regard to placement in language intervention programs. The primary basis for this report is a recent survey of speech, hearing, and language services for the retarded (Fristoe, 1975).

In the past decade and a half, marked changes have occurred in attitudes and practices concerning provision of speech, hearing, and language services for the retarded, especially the lower level retarded. Formerly, clinicians-in-training were told in essence, "Don't waste time working with the retarded. They cannot be helped very much, if at all. There are others who need your services more because they *can* benefit from them and they can be helped to become normal, productive citizens." It was even said that spending time providing therapy for the retarded could border on the unethical—taking money for providing training when the prognosis for progress was nil. (This we would now call a matter of accountability.) Assessment generally was done for the purpose of determining whether or not a given individual was retarded and thus ineligible for speech and hearing services.

Now we are aware that the lack of progress that was experienced in therapy did not occur because the retarded lacked potential for change but because they were not being provided with the most beneficial procedures. Now that pioneers have shown the way, many other people are developing means for promoting progress in acquisition of communication skills by retarded persons.

The present survey grew out of a desire to select the best possible language program or set of programs for use at the Lurleen B. Wallace Developmental Center—an outstanding new facility for the severely and profoundly retarded in Decatur, Alabama—and in its surrounding community. No comprehensive collection of information about original structured programs that are presently available or in process of development could be found, so it was decided that a national survey should be done to locate and identify such programs. In the process, a wealth of information was obtained about almost 700 service programs offering speech, hearing, and language evaluation and treatment for the retarded, and over 200 original language systems being used with the retarded were located. A description of the survey, a directory of speech, hearing, and language services for the retarded in the United States, a list of materials being used and their sources, and detailed information, mostly from the authors, on 187 original structured language systems have been presented by Fristoe (1975).

In examining some of the findings of the survey, let us look first at the types of population served by the respondents (see Figure 1). Thirty-three percent (33%) of them had residential programs, 82% had day programs; 14% had both.

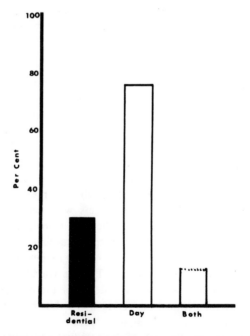

Figure 1. Survey of speech, hearing, and language services for the retarded. Type of population served in facilities, given in percent of replies received.

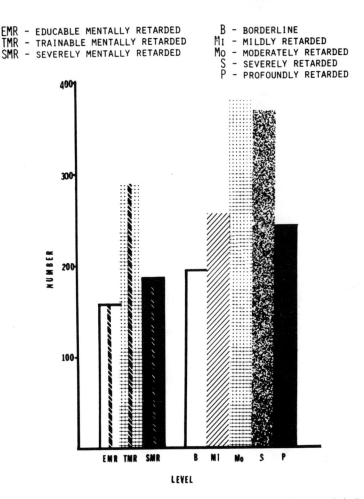

EMR - EDUCABLE MENTALLY RETARDED   B - BORDERLINE
TMR - TRAINABLE MENTALLY RETARDED   Mi - MILDLY RETARDED
SMR - SEVERELY MENTALLY RETARDED   Mo - MODERATELY RETARDED
                                        S - SEVERELY RETARDED
                                        P - PROFOUNDLY RETARDED

Figure 2. Survey of speech, hearing, and language services for the retarded. Level of functioning (according to the classification system preferred at each facility) of persons receiving language intervention services, given in number of replies received.

Now let us look at the level of retardation for which each program reported provision of language training (see Figure 2). This was to be stated according to the classification system used or preferred at each facility. Most used either an *educational* categorization or a *degree of retardation* categorization. Both are represented here. (Note that this does not give the number of clients served but rather the number of facilities providing services.) The TMR and moderately-to-severely retarded groups were served by the most respondents. The severely and profoundly retarded seem to be getting the attention of more respondents than was anticipated in view of the commonly expressed observation that language training for these groups is almost nonexistent. This suggests that the effect of the zero-reject policy already is being felt strongly in many areas of the United States.

Figure 3 shows the diagnostic (evaluation) and therapeutic (training) services provided in speech, hearing, and language. It is given in terms of the number of facilities that provide each type of service. With regard to both hearing and speech, more facilities offered diagnostic than therapeutic services. This is to be expected; it is the usual finding. The surprising finding was that, for language, therapeutic services were offered by more facilities than diagnostic services. This reversal of the expected diagnostic-therapeutic relationship probably is due in part to the difficulty in diagnosing language disorders by some neat, quick means that gives a quantitative representation of ability in the language area (Siegel and Broen, 1976). It also reflects recognition of a need for providing language training, even though assessment means may be inadequate. This finding may be due in part to a lack of sophistication that allows the inclusion of language stimulation programs and remedial programs in the same category, with no distinction between clients who show language development that is below that expected for their chronological age but is similar to their overall level of functioning, and those with language development that is at a lower level than their functioning in other areas.

An appalling finding is the difference between the number of facilities providing speech and language assessment services and those providing hearing assessment services. Since it has been reported repeatedly that the prevalence of hearing impairment in the retarded is relatively high—15% to 20%, or three to

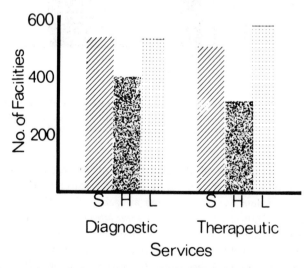

Figure 3. Survey of speech, hearing, and language services for the retarded. Diagnostic and therapeutic services provided in speech/hearing/language, given in number of replies received.

five times what is found in the population as a whole (Lloyd, 1970)—and since hearing loss has a deleterious effect on communication and on learning in general, it is shocking to find that this vital area of assessment is apparently overlooked in many facilities. Comfort cannot be found in assuming that hearing assessment is provided by other agencies, because this arrangement was seldom mentioned. This is one area of assessment that we cannot afford to ignore.

Survey respondents indicated that a wide variety of assessment approaches were being used for varying purposes in their language training programs. These included intelligence tests, developmental scales, articulation tests, concept tests, developmental scales in the social, language, self-help, and sensorimotor areas, imitation skill assessments, memory evaluations, language sampling (evaluated in a variety of ways, including mean length of utterance, structural analysis, and vocabulary measurement), study of syntax use, testing for understanding of syntax rules, tests of receptive language competence, tests of expressive language competence, information processing tests, computations of rate of vocal emissions, binary speech-versus-no-speech ratings, and sensory evaluations (usually hearing and vision).

Intelligence or intelligence-type tests were most often named, but apparently the results of such tests are used in a wide variety of ways. The most common use was to establish that a child is indeed retarded and thus is eligible for aid. Many reported that they included all retarded children in their programs since "they all need it." Some reported that they tried to concentrate on the less retarded children "since they benefit most," while others indicated they concentrated on those with the greatest degree of retardation since their communication problems gave them the greatest need. Regardless of which philosophy was followed, the decision regarding candidacy for language intervention programs was dependent primarily on the results of intelligence tests, such as the Stanford-Binet (Terman and Merrill, 1973), or intelligence-type developmental tests, such as the Bayley (Bayley, 1969), which yield intelligence quotients or mental age equivalents. The results of the tests were used to show that children are retarded and in many cases to determine the degree of retardation.

Other tests were used to determine degree of deviancy in speech and language development, or the type of problem present, or the level of communication ability of the client.

The wide range in philosophies of assessment that was demonstrated, as well as what seemed in many cases to be an apparent lack of philosophy, suggests that individuals providing service programs would profit from reviewing their rationale for using different types of assessment in terms of what can be gained by using each type.

When most people refer to evaluation they think of "testing" in the formal sense. They have reference to standardized tests that have been developed, based on psychometric theory. These tests are normative; the results will tell how deviant a person is on the attribute that is being measured, or how severe a problem a person has in this area. This type of information is usually necessary for classification purposes and in some cases is helpful in grouping children. Quite often, funding regulations are written so that the amount of money budgeted depends on the numbers of persons who fall within categories determined by results of testing with standardized tests. Performance on such tests also is frequently used to determine which professional will have the major responsibility for providing training for the child. This type of assessment and classification and its effect on both clients and training programs have recently been closely examined by Hobbs (1975).

The problem with most standardized tests is that while they provide an indication of the severity of a problem they rarely give information about specifics of a problem, and, what is more important, they give little direct information about what should be done to alleviate the problem. Thus they are of little direct use in planning an intervention program.

Many standardized tests are developmental in nature, particularly tests of language, but the results of standardized language tests are not particularly valuable when they yield little information that can help in planning an intervention program. As Siegel and Broen (1976) have pointed out, language has many more components that can be tested in a relatively short period of time. Nelson (1976) and Bowerman (1976) have emphasized that there are many differences in rate and sequence of language development among otherwise "normal" children. The more we study language acquisition the more we realize that we know relatively little as yet about what the necessary and sufficient antecedents are for different stages of language development.

One of the most widely used tests of language is the Illinois Test of Psycholinguistic Abilities (Kirk, McCarthy, and Kirk, 1968). The ITPA consists of ten subtests (plus two additional optional tests) that are designed to sample communication at the representational and automatic levels. It measures relative deviance in the targeted areas but does not provide an analysis of specific competencies within these areas. The ITPA yields age-related scores, but since it was standardized on children with average intelligence its application to the retarded is open to question. Although the validity of the ITPA has yet to be satisfactorily established, according to Cicciarelli, Broen, and Siegel (1976), it has become a standard in special education. The model is compelling and many language programs have been based on it.

Tests of language and speech development in the severely and profoundly retarded pose particular problems. It is difficult to separate language delay from overall developmental disability. Tests that are designed to go below the thirty-six month level sample language behavior grossly but certainly are not exhaustive. They can tell us that the individual being tested is far below normal, but not what can be done to modify this condition, or what specifically needs to be worked on next. Although we may know what is typical for a number of normal children in that mental age range, we are still uncertain what to expect of the severely and profoundly retarded who have achieved the same general mental age level. Most language development tests were based on performance of children with normal intelligence from white, middle class homes from a limited geographical area. This makes reference to norms highly questionable for most of the severely and profoundly retarded population. Also, it is not uncommon to find several individuals who achieve the same "language age" but have markedly different communication skills. For example, a person may demonstrate no apparent comprehension of language but produce a stereotyped speech output consisting of high frequency emission of a small number of wh-questions and declarative sentences serving no apparent communicative purposes except when part of the output occurs by chance in situations that make it appear to have some communicative intent. (One child of my acquaintance frequently says, "How much did it cost?" an utterance that often seems to be an appropriate question in many contexts, but it is emitted also in equally nonappropriate situations with the same frequency.) Another person may make no attempts to communicate, demonstrate no expressive output, but be able to follow instructions and thus show a degree of language competence (knowledge of language rules) not possessed by the previous individual. On a number of language tests in common use, both individuals could achieve the same "language age," or the first could even be rated at a higher level. For reasons such as this, care must be taken in the interpretation of test results.

"Assessment" is the term that is usually reserved to indicate evaluations of a less formal nature than standardized tests. These are often criterion referenced rather than normative. Their use is usually for diagnostic purposes—to look for a pattern of performance. The focus is on the content of performance; for example, one important type of language assessment is the determination that a child has knowledge of the rules of some aspect of syntax, such as pronoun case. Because assessments of this type are criterion referenced, they have potential for helping the intervener determine what needs to be done to bring about desired changes. Unlike formal tests, which are usually done at set intervals (for example, every year, or in the first, fourth, and sixth grades), not only are assessments done in a less formal manner but also they usually are ongoing in nature and closely linked to therapy.

One example of an assessment tool that is getting increasing use nationally is the BCP, the Behavioral Characteristics Progression (Office of the Santa Cruz County Superintendent of Schools, 1973). The BCP was not designed to be a finished assessment tool, but to serve as a model for the development of an assessment, instructional, and communication tool that can be tailored to meet individual needs. It consists of 2,400 "behavioral characteristics" or observable traits grouped into "behavioral strands" or categories of behavior. Each strand has up to 50 characteristics. Each strand also has a checklist of "identifying behaviors" that helps the user set priorities by focusing on areas needing attention the most. Provisions are made for expanding the number of behavioral strands and the number of characteristics in each strand that are necessary to aid the individual in advancing toward the final goal of each behavioral strand, displaying the behavioral characteristics which society deems appropriate adult behaviors in that category. For most retarded persons it will be necessary to generate many additional strands and additional characteristics within each strand, according to individual needs. This is particularly true of the strands most closely associated with language (see Table 1). Sue Porter's group at the Day Service Centers in Arkansas is presently engaged in such a project to aid the retarded citizens of that state in communication development (Porter, 1976). The "strands" of this instrument are arranged so that they indicate in relatively small steps what the person being tested needs to accomplish next in a given area of development. Although the BCP strands tell *what* needs to receive attention next they do not tell *how* to teach it, leaving that up to the creativity, resourcefulness, and training of the teacher. Results of assessments such as this do not lend themselves easily to statistical summarization or to classification of clients and thus they are probably publicized less than they are actually used, but they can be extremely useful.

Table 1. Behavior characteristics progression: strands most closely associated with language development

Strand number	Strand name	Number of characteristics
13	Auditory perception	47
18	Prearticulation	50
19	Articulation	48
20	Language comprehension	29
21	Language development	50
22	Listening	39
46	Sign language	50
57	Articulation I	45
58	Articulation II	42

An example of a test that looks for knowledge of language rules is the Programmed Conditioning for Language Test (PCLT) of the Monterey Language Program (Gray and Ryan, 1971). By using this test the clinician knows with fair precision where to begin on the Monterey Language Program. The Monterey Program serves as a good example of a program that integrates assessment and training. Performance is constantly assessed in light of criteria for advancing to the next level, repeating the same level, or going to a branching program that covers an area in much more detail with smaller increments in task difficulty. A task analysis approach is used, with no reference to age equivalents or quotients.

Children's communication development is being subjected to an ever finer analysis. Nelson (1976) has arranged in developmental order Halliday's (1973, 1975) identification of the various types of speech acts that have been observed in young children:

A. Pragmatic—related to interpersonal relationships; appear in Phase I (Brown, 1973)
  1. *Instrumental:* This category is used for demands and desires—it is the child's effort to achieve his ends through speech. It is the "I want" function.
  2. *Regulatory:* In this mode the child attempts to regulate the actions of others, and thus it goes beyond the instrumental, using language to achieve ends through others as intermediaries. Its prototypical form is "Do as I tell you."
  3. *Interactional:* In this mode the child uses speech to form a bond or for purely social or affective communication. It expresses the relationship "You and me."
  4. *Personal:* With this function the child informs others of his own actions, for example, "Here I come." ("Now I'll . . .").

B. Mathetic—related to learning or knowing, ideational.
  5. *Heuristic:* In this mode the explanation behind a statement or events is focused on. In the use of this function, the child separates the actions and intentions of others from his own. Halliday's example is "Tell me why."
  6. *Imaginative:* This function is self-explanatory; it is the "Let's pretend" function.
  7. *Informative:* Uses language to import information not apparent to the listener from his own direct experience; it is the "I've got something to tell you" function.

(Based on Nelson, 1976, pp. 28–29)

This is an example of the expanding knowledge of the specifics of communication development with which we will be dealing in the future. Such analyses may lead eventually to the discovery of the necessary and sufficient prerequisites for optimum language development. These developments will serve both to broaden and to focus our language assessment efforts.

The more we learn the more we realize how little we know about the incredibly complex subject of normal language development. Assessment of language abilities and problems becomes more and more challenging.

Ideas, understandings, and theories change. We would not have it otherwise. It is important that we view the assessment tools that we have now and will have in the future as offering only a very small contribution to our understanding of the language and communication skills of the child. We should not throw out assessment tools in general but should regard them as providing only a very limited view of the domain that they purport to sample. Users must keep abreast of developments in this rapidly changing field and familiarize themselves with commentaries and reviews concerning the many tests and assessments that are available, such as those in Buros (1972) and those by Siegel and Broen (1976), Vernon (1976), and Cicciarelli, Broen, and Siegel (1976). Only when we understand the limitations of our tools will we actually be able to get maximum benefit from their use.

REFERENCES

Bayley, N. (1969) Bayley Scales of Infant Development. New York: Psychological Corporation.

Bowerman, M. (1976) Word meaning and sentence structure: Uniformity, variation and shifts over time in patterns of acquisition. Paper presented at the NICHD-sponsored conference on early behavioral assessment of the communicative and cognitive abilities of the developmentally disabled. Rosario, Orcas Island, Washington.

Brown, R. (1973) A First Language: The Early Stages. Cambridge, Massachusetts: Harvard University Press.

Buros, O. K. (1972) The Mental Measurement Yearbook, Vol. 7. Highland Park, New Jersey: Gryphon Press.

Cicciarelli, A., Broen, P. A., and Siegel, G. M. (1976) Language assessment procedures. In Communication Assessment and Intervention Strategies. (Ed. Lloyd, L. L.) Baltimore: University Park Press.

Fristoe, M. (1975) Language Intervention Systems for the Retarded: A Catalog of Original Structured Language Programs in Use in the US. Montgomery, Alabama: State of Alabama Dept. of Education. (Available from Language Intervention Systems, Lurleen B. Wallace Developmental Center, Box 2224, Decatur, AL, USA 35602.)

Gray, B. B., and Ryan, B. P. (1971) Monterey Language Program (Programmed Conditioning for Language). Palo Alto, California: Monterey Learning Systems.

Halliday, M. (1973) Explorations in the Functions of Language. London: Edward Arnold.

Halliday, M. (1975) Learning How to Mean. London: Edward Arnold.

Hobbs, N. (1975) The Futures of Children: Categories, Labels and their Consequences. Nashville: Vanderbilt University.

Kirk, S. A., McCarthy, J. J., and Kirk, W. D. (1968) Illinois Test of Psycholinguistic Abilities. Urbana, Illinois: Board of Trustees of the University of Illinois.

Lloyd, L. L. (1970) Audiologic aspects of mental retardation. In International Review of Research in Mental Retardation, Vol. 4. (Ed. Ellis, N. R.) New York: Academic Press.

Nelson, K. (1976) Early speech in its communicative context. Paper presented at the NICHD-sponsored conference on early behavioral assessment of the communicative and cognitive abilities of the developmentally disabled. Rosario, Orcas Island, Washington.

Office of the Santa Cruz County Superintendent of Schools (1973) Behavior Characteristics Progression. Palo Alto, California: VORT Corp.

Porter, S. (1976) Personal communication.

Siegel, G. M., and Broen, P. A. (1976) Language assessment. In Communication Assessment and Intervention Strategies. (Ed. Lloyd, L. L.) Baltimore: University Park Press.

Terman, L. M., and Merrill, M. A. (1973) Stanford-Binet Intelligence Scale. Boston: Houghton Mifflin.

Vernon, M. (1976) Psychologic evaluation of hearing-impaired children. In Communication Assessment and Intervention Strategies. (Ed. Lloyd, L. L.) Baltimore: University Park Press.

RESEARCH TO PRACTICE IN MENTAL RETARDATION
Education and Training, Volume II
Edited by Peter Mittler
Copyright 1977 I.A.S.S.M.D.

THE ASSESSMENT OF AUDITORY ABILITIES

L. L. Lloyd
Chairman, Special Education Section
Purdue University, West Lafayette, Indiana 47907
United States

A speech and language assessment is incomplete unless the client's auditory abilities have been evaluated. Normal auditory ability is a prerequisite to normal speech and language development. Except in the case of purely manual communication, the treatment of communication disorders is inefficient at best, and possibly unethical, if the clinician does not know about the auditory abilities and limitations of the client. Knowledge of the client's auditory abilities is also critical to other educational and habilitative programming. In light of the critical role of hearing and the high prevalence of hearing impairment among the retarded in general, it would seem that reliable and valid audiological assessment would be of the highest priority in habilitative programming for the retarded. Unfortunately, this is not the case. Many retarded individuals have not had the benefit of even a puretone screening test, or a puretone threshold test of auditory sensitivity. As Fristoe (this volume) has pointed out, many programs fail to provide diagnostic services in hearing.

Why do we find this sad state of affairs? Is it because we do not have the technical capabilities of obtaining reliable and valid measures of the auditory sensitivity of most retarded individuals? Or, is it the lack of application of our currently available technology? I fear it is the latter.

In reviewing the literature on the audiologic aspects of mental retardation, it is clear that we have at present the technology to ascertain accurately the auditory sensitivity and to detect middle ear pathologies in most retarded individuals (e.g., Lloyd, 1970; Lloyd and Moore, 1972). With only minor modifications, behavioral audiometry can even be used to define a number of significant auditory functions that are deemed critical in habilitative planning. While there is still a need for considerable research in the area of speech discrimination and speech processing by retarded individuals, we have at present the capability of providing considerable service for all but the more severely and profoundly retarded in this area. The major problem has not been one of a lack of available technology, but of lack of application. I hope that through meetings such as this one, more administrators and other professionals concerned with providing the best possible habilitative service to the retarded will understand the significance of hearing and will demand the best possible audiologic information on all of the retarded individuals they serve.

Because time limitations do not permit a discussion of the application of all audiologic procedures to the retarded, I have elected to present a brief presentation of operant audiometry for testing auditory sensitivity, and then to discuss the extension of such procedures along with other considerations to obtain speech discrimination information.

APPLICATION OF OPERANT PRINCIPLES

I have previously emphasized the careful application of operant principles such as: 1) simplicity of responses, 2) selection of reinforcers, 3) reinforcement contingencies, 4) immediate reinforcement, 5) reinforcement schedules, and 6) reinforcement shifting with a number of audiometric procedures, including a) conventional or standard hand raising, b) ear choice, c) play (e.g., dropping blocks in a box, putting rings on a peg), d) visual reinforcer (e.g., peep show and slide show), and e) TROCA (Tangible Reinforcement Operant Conditioning Audiometry) (Cox and Lloyd, 1976; Lloyd, 1966; 1975a; 1975b). All of these principles are critical in testing the retarded, but this portion of the chapter will discuss TROCA as a procedure for testing the more severely retarded, with the primary focus on the first two principles—responses and reinforcers. More extensive presentations on TROCA have been presented previously (e.g., Cox and Lloyd, 1976; Lloyd, 1975a and 1975b; Lloyd and Cox, 1975; Lloyd, Spradlin, and Reid, 1968; Spradlin, Lloyd, Reid, and Hom, 1968). The following part of this section has been modified from a recent presentation on the use of operant procedures to obtain thresholds of infants (Lloyd, 1976).

To minimize tester or observer bias and increase reliability, the response to be used should be one that is both easily observed and unambiguous. The response should be simple and a behavior that is easily within the motor and eye-hand coordination of the particular individual being tested. It should be something that is already within the individual's behavioral repertoire. For example, many retarded individuals have the eye-hand coordination required for play audiometry, but play audiometry also requires the grasping, moving, and releasing behaviors all to be associated and sequenced with the auditory stimulus. While play audiometry has been quite successful with many retarded individuals, it has not been useful with the more severely retarded. Therefore, the law of parsimony indicates we should use a simpler response that is easier to bring under stimulus control. For example, the simple hitting of a relatively large response button would be an easier task that is within the capabilities of most retarded individuals.

One of the most common bits of misinformation about operant procedures is the nature of a reinforcer. Too frequently the clinician thinks that giving someone an M & M (a candy-coated chocolate) is giving positive reinforcement.

An M & M may be reinforcing to some of the individuals some of the time, but not all of the time, and it is not reinforcing to all individuals. Actually, with some retarded individuals we found M & Ms were not positive reinforcers. For many (but not all) retarded individuals, sugar-coated dry breakfast cereal was a good reinforcer. Like candy, sugar-coated cereal is sweet and in some cases it has an appealing color and shape (e.g., the breakfast cereal called Froot Loops). It has the advantage, however, of resisting satiation better than some of the richer, more filling items such as M & Ms. Such cereal also has the advantage of being something that does not last long; it is rapidly consumed.

I have previously emphasized (Lloyd, 1966; 1976) three points in the selection of a reinforcer. First, *it must be reinforcing* for the particular individual and not just be assumed to be reinforcing. (This will be discussed later in the paper.) Second, *it must not interfere with the task.* The reinforcing stimulus (or consequence) must not be an event that can compete or be confused with the discriminative stimulus or test signal, and must not be an event that will serve as a masker, or that will fatigue the sensory system being tested. For example, music has been found to have reinforcing properties for some individuals and has been used quite effectively in sheltered workshop settings for the retarded, but music (and especially some of the loud music that seems so reinforcing to our teenagers) would be a totally inappropriate reinforcer for audiometric testing. Likewise, in the name of parsimony, the reinforcer should not take a long time to consume. Third, *it should not make habilitation difficult.* This point is of relevance when considering punishment. A strong aversive consequence that is used to extinguish false positive responses (i.e., responses when no test signal is present) may be generalized to the audiologist, the clinic, and/or earphones, any of which could be crucial to the subsequent habilitative program. For example, years ago I saw young children who had readily worn earphones in the past return to the clinic after being tested with GSR or EDR audiometry and reject the earphones. This required us to take time to reorient the child to earphones before we could continue with auditory training.

The point that the consequent event must truly be a reinforcer to that particular child cannot be overemphasized in testing infants and other difficult-to-test individuals. The clinician cannot assume that because some young children like play activities such as putting blocks in a box, that all children will like that activity, or that a given child likes that activity all the time.

Selecting the appropriate reinforcer may be the most crucial step in operant audiometry. In developing TROCA for the profoundly retarded, we (Lloyd, Spradlin, and Reid, 1968) used a cafeteria procedure to see what the child preferred in a wide choice of edibles. Once the child indicated a preference for one item, we did a simple test to see if the child would work for that item. As the child reached for the item, we would close the hand and see if the child would make an effort to get the item out of the closed hand.

Once a reinforcer has been determined, the clinician must watch for the initial signs of satiation, such as decrease in response strength, increase in response latency, and even obvious lack of interest in the reinforcer such as not retrieving it or consuming it more slowly.[a]

AUDITORY ABILITIES

Threshold testing is just one aspect of the audiologic assessment which each retarded citizen deserves. A complete audiologic assessment includes much more than just audiometric data (ASHA, 1974; Cox and Lloyd, 1976; Lloyd, 1972), but for this presentation I will limit my remarks to audiometric data. As a minimum, the audiometric assessment should provide information about abilities (or behaviors) and aspects of the type of pathology that have major implications for communication programming, including the following data: 1) auditory sensitivity across the frequency range, 2) stability of the auditory

Relatively easy to
specify and control:
"most analytic"

Low human
communicative
value

Pure tones, clicks, narrow band noise
White noise, "sawtooth" noise
Several bands of noise
   (Environmental sounds)
"Isolated" speech sounds
   (Environmental sounds)
Nonsense syllables
   (Environmental sounds)
Monosyllabic words
Disyllabic words
Phrases and word chains
Sentences and longer word chains
Continuous discourse
"Normal conversation"
"Everyday speech"

Relatively difficult to
specify and control:
"least analytic"

High human
communicative
value

Figure 1. Continuum of acoustic stimuli relative to specificity and control. Since various environmental sounds may fall at a number of points along the continuum, they are shown in parentheses at their three simplest levels. Sounds from noise-makers, toys, musical instruments, and animals have been omitted to simplify the table, but they may be considered along with environmental sounds. It should also be noted that for speech-type stimuli, synthetic speech such as that produced by the Bell or Haskins Laboratories for experimental purposes would rank higher in specificity or control than human speech. The stimuli may also be considered along a continuum of human communicative level. (From: Cox and Lloyd, 1976; Lloyd, 1972; Lloyd and Cox, 1975).

[a]At this point a six-minute video-tape demonstrated the use of TROCA to obtain thresholds from a seven-month-old. This was one of the original three infants tested by Lloyd, Spradlin, and Reid (1968).

sensitivity, 3) dynamic range and tolerance, 4) recruitment or distortions of loudness, 5) basic auditory discrimination, 6) speech discrimination, 7) habituation and fatigue, and 8) interaural differential of the above measures. A wide variety of acoustic stimuli may be used in the audiometric assessment, as is shown in Figure 1. These stimuli range over a continuum of degree of specificity or control (listed from easiest to most difficult to specify or control acoustically). The stimuli may also be considered along a continuum of human communicative value representing the frequency of human use in aural/oral communication and a general approximation of the ordering of the stimuli in terms of communicative importance. It will be noted that the two continua run counter to each other or have a negative relationship. For some fundamental auditory abilities (e.g., sensitivity, recruitment, or habituation), an easily specified stimulus is quite appropriate, but for other high level auditory abilities (e.g., speech processing), the more difficult to specify stimuli have the highest face validity. Therefore, the audiologist sometimes makes a compromise between specificity (or reliability) and communicative value (or validity). In each case, the choice of stimuli is the one with the highest degree of reliability and validity. It should be noted that at least six of the first seven auditory abilities listed above as critical for habilitative planning may be quite reliably and validly assessed with pure tone or noise stimuli. The only one that would definitely require a speech type stimuli for higher face validity is that of "speech discrimination." The interaural differentiation of the seven measures is naturally based upon the measures used to assess the ability. Using pure tone and/or noise band stimuli with currently available behavioral audiometry and impedance audiometry procedures, it is possible to assess the auditory sensitivity across the frequency range, the stability of this auditory sensitivity, and the possible recruitment (or distortions of loudness) and the interaural differential of these measures on most retarded individuals. Also, pure tone and noise band stimuli can be used to test the dynamic range and tolerance, and the auditory habituation and fatigue of many retarded individuals. (See: Fulton, 1974; 1975; Katz, 1975; Lamb, 1975). Although there is a need to further improve such assessment procedures, the major need is for the application of currently available clinical tools.

SPEECH AUDIOMETRY

Now that I have reiterated a basic point about how much information of value for habilitative planning we can get with simple pure tone (or noise band) stimuli I would like to conclude this chapter by referring to some developments in speech reception testing, which I hope will point the way to improved speech audiometry for the retarded.

For many years audiologists depended upon the use of the so-called spondaic and phonetically balanced word list as developed at the Harvard Psychoacoustic

Laboratory (Egan, 1948; Hudgins, et al., 1947) and revised at the Central Institute for the Deaf (Hirsh, et al., 1952). These word lists and their typical administration procedures involving verbal responses of the subject have been of only limited value in testing the retarded and other difficult-to-test subjects. Therefore, speech reception threshold and speech discrimination tests have been developed using limited vocabularies that are more appropriate for use with children, and a point-to-the-picture response (see Giolas, 1975), of which probably the four most commonly used are the Threshold by Identification of Pictures (TIP) and the Discrimination by Identification of Pictures (DIP), developed by Siegenthaler and Haspiel, 1966); the Word Intelligibility by Picture Identification (WIPI) by Ross and Lerman (1968; 1970; 1971), and the Goldman-Fristoe-Woodcock (G-F-W) Tests of Auditory Discrimination (Goldman, Fristoe, and Woodcock, 1970). These tests have several features that might be considered in developing and/or selecting tests for use with the retarded:

1. They all have broken the old tie to the so-called spondee and phonetically balanced word lists.
2. The TIP and G-F-W recommend that you make sure the child can identify each of the pictures used to represent the test words before starting the test. The child is taught unfamiliar items.
3. They all use practice before testing.
   A. The TIP and WIPI use different words and pictures than are subsequently used in the test.
   B. The DIP uses four of the words and pictures subsequently used in the test.
   C. The G-F-W uses all of the words and pictures subsequently used in the test.
4. They all use relatively familiar words that can be represented by pictures but have differing approaches to the repeated use of words in different forms or lists.
   A. The TIP and WIPI use different words in each list.
   B. The DIP uses some of the same words but also has some different words on each of the three forms.
   C. The G-F-W uses the same 30 words (in different order) on both the quiet and noise tests.
5. They all use a close-message set but they vary in the degree of constraint (or size of set).
   A. The DIP has a choice of two pictures per stimulus.
   B. The G-F-W has a choice of four pictures per stimulus.
   C. The TIP has a choice of five pictures per stimulus.
   D. The WIPI has a choice of six pictures per stimulus.
6. The G-F-W uses prerecorded stimuli to administer the test in quiet and with a 9 dB S/N cafeteria noise background.

7. The scoring on the DIP and G-F-W are designed for error analysis.
   A. The DIP for voicing, influence, and combinations of these acoustic factors.
   B. The G-F-W for the distinctive features of voicing and manner (plosives, continuants, and nasality).
8. The test administration and scoring of the WIPI is designed to test auditory, visual, and combined auditory-visual speech reception. Therefore, in addition to testing auditory discrimination you can get an index of visual speech reception or speechreading ability.

These tests were standardized on normal children as young as three years of age and have been used with some older retarded individuals. Unfortunately, there has been very little research reported on the use of these tests as originally developed or in modified form with the retarded. It would seem that the above tests could be successfully used with more retarded individuals and younger children if the procedures were modified to include the operant principles previously discussed. This is especially true of contingent reinforcement, which has been recently used with point-to-the-picture (Beckwith and Thompson, 1976); Sidman, 1971, this volume) and head-turning (Eilers, Wilson, and Moore, 1977; Wilson, 1978) responses. These two response-reinforcement procedures are worthy of mention. The point-to-the-picture response to an auditorially presented word procedure is just one of several stimulus-response tasks in Sidman's (1971; this volume) cross-modality procedure.

Recently, Beckwith and Thompson (1976) developed a point-to-the-picture procedure with visual reinforcement for testing the vocabulary comprehension of children between the ages of 17 and 30 months of age. They project 35-mm slides of real objects or events on two 25-cm square rear view screens. The child sits on a small chair or on his/her parent's lap facing the response and reinforcement apparatus which has a 15-cm rabbit face located above each screen. The examiner sits to the side and slightly to the rear of the child to present the stimulus items live voice and to operate remote control switches to present the pairs of response pictures on the screens and to illuminate the eyes and mouth of the rabbit above the correct screen when the child makes a correct response. Thirteen trials are used before beginning the test as an operant training procedure to teach the child to touch the picture that is named by the examiner. Both in the training and in the test the illumination of the rabbit's eyes and mouth is assumed to be a reinforcer.

The Beckwith procedure could be immediately used for clinical speech discrimination testing by using words and pictures such as those in the DIP designated for speech discrimination. It could also be modified to use a larger set such as four pictures per stimulus (e.g., G-F-W) or six pictures per stimulus (e.g., WIPI). (With a deviation from the standardized administration of a test such as the DIP or G-F-W, the published norms may no longer be valid and new norms may need to be established.) The procedure may also be improved by developing more appropriate word lists, using prerecorded stimuli (and controlling the level of presentation), and automating the reinforcement delivery.

Wilson and his colleagues (Eilers, Wilson, and Moore, 1977; Wilson, 1978) have developed a Visually Reinforced Infant Speech Discrimination (VRISD) paradigm that uses a head-turning response and visual reinforcement to test infants six to eight months of age. The infant is seated on the parent's lap and entertained at the midline while prerecorded speech sounds at the rate of one syllable per second at 50 dB SPL are presented. Then a contrastive syllable is presented, and when the infant makes a normal localizing response to a change in auditory environment by looking at the speaker, an illuminated, animated toy provides visual reinforcement. During the training phase the contrastive (or figure) syllable is presented 10 to 20 dB above the referent (or ground) syllable. The reinforcement maintains the head-turning response to the intensity and/or syllable difference. When the infant is consistently responding to the change, the stimulus levels are equated and the speech discrimination is assessed with three presentations of the contrastive syllable and three control periods with no syllable change.

VRISD is presented as an illustration of combining operant principles with the stimulus paradigm previously used to obtain infant speech perception information from groups of infants (see Butterfield and Cairns, 1974; Eimas, 1974; Eimas et al., 1971; Morse, 1974, 1978). VRISD provides speech discrimination data on individual infants. Procedures such as this offer exciting possibilities for testing the speech discrimination abilities of retarded and other difficult-to-test individuals.

There are other procedures that could be presented, such as asking the child to point to a picture *when* it is correctly labeled rather than to the picture that was named. This procedure is used in the Washington Speech Sound Discrimination (WSSD) Test (Prather et al., 1971) and more recently in a "preference procedure" described by Waryas and Waryas (1974).

SUMMARY

In summary I have: 1) provided a brief review of the major audiological movements in the area of mental retardation, 2) presented a method for obtaining measures of the auditory sensitivity of most retarded individuals, 3) commented on the auditory abilities that should be examined in an audiological assessment, and 4) considered the use of various speech discrimination procedures with the retarded. Although there is a need for more research, the major need is for the application of already available audiometric assessment procedures.

REFERENCES

ASHA Committee on Rehabilitative Audiology (1974) The audiologist: Responsibilities in habilitation of the auditorily handicapped. Asha, 16:68.

Beckwith, L., and Thompson, S. K. (1976) Recognition of verbal labels of pictured objects and events by 17- to 30-month-old infants. J. Speech Hear. Res. 19:690.

Butterfield, E. C., and Cairns, G. F. (1974) Summary—Infant reception research. *In* Language Perspectives—Acquisition, Retardation and Intervention (Eds. Schiefelbusch, R. L., and Lloyd, L. L.) Baltimore, Md.: University Park Press, p. 75.

Cox, B. P., and Lloyd, L. L. (1976) Audiologic considerations. *In* Communication Assessment and Intervention Strategies (Ed. Lloyd, L. L.) Baltimore, Md.: University Park Press, p. 123.

Egan, J. P. (1948) Articulation testing methods. Laryngoscope, 58:955.

Eilers, R. E., Wilson, W. R., and Moore, J. M. (1977) Developmental changes in speech discrimination of three-, six-, and twelve-month old infants. J. Speech Hear. Res. 20 (in press).

Eimas, P. D. (1974) Linguistic processing of speech by young infants. *In* Language Perspectives—Acquisition, Retardation, and Intervention. (Eds. Schiefelbusch, R. L., and Lloyd, L. L.) Baltimore: University Park Press, p. 55.

Eimas, P. D., Siqueland, E. R., Juoczyk, P., and Vigorito, J. (1971) Speech perception in infants. Science, 171:303.

Fulton, R. T. (1974) Auditory Stimulus-Response Control. Baltimore: University Park Press.

Fulton, R. T. (1975) Bekesy audiometry. *In* Auditory Assessment of the Difficult-to-test. (Eds. Fulton, R. T., and Lloyd, L. L.) Baltimore: Williams and Wilkins Co., p. 71.

Giolas, T. (1975) Speech audiometry. *In* Auditory Assessment of the Difficult-to-test (Eds. Fulton, R. T. and Lloyd, L. L.) Baltimore: Williams and Wilkins, Co., p. 37.

Goldman, R., Fristoe, M., and Woodcock, R. (1970) Goldman-Fristoe-Woodcock Test of Auditory Discrimination. Circle Pines, Minn.: American Guidance Service.

Hirsh, I. J., Davis, H., Silverman, S. R., Reynolds, E., and Benson, R. W., (1952) Development of materials for speech and audiometry. J. Speech Hear. Dis. 17:321.

Hudgins, C. V., Hawkins, J. E., Karlin, J. E., and Stevens, S. S. (1947) The development of recorded auditory tests for measuring loss of speech. Laryngoscope 57:57.

Katz, J. (1975) Differential diagnosis of auditory impairments. *In* Auditory Assessment of the Difficult-to-test. (Eds. Fulton, R. T., and Lloyd, L. L.) Baltimore: Williams and Wilkins. p. 120.

Lloyd, L. L. (1966) Behavioral audiometry viewed as an operant procedure. J. Speech Hear. Dis. 31:128.

Lloyd, L. L. (1970) Audiologic aspects of mental retardation. *In* International Review of Research in Mental Retardation, Volume 4 (Ed. Ellis, N. R.) New York: Academic Press, p. 311.

Lloyd, L. L. (1972) The audiologic assessment of deaf students, Report of the Proceedings of the 45th Meeting of the Convention of American Instructors of the Deaf. (Little Rock, Arkansas: Arkansas School for the Deaf, 1971) Washington, D. C.: U. S. Government Printing Office, p. 585.

Lloyd, L. L. (1975a) Behavioral audiometry with children. *In* The nervous system, Volume 3: Human communication and its disorders (Ed. Tower, D. B.) New York: Raven Press, pp. 173–179. (An invited paper in this three-volume work in commemoration of the NINCDS 25th anniversary.)

Lloyd, L. L. (1975b) Puretone audiometry. In Auditory Assessment of the Difficult-to-test (Eds. Fulton, R. T., and Lloyd, L. L.) Baltimore: Williams and Wilkins, p. 1.

Lloyd, L. L. (1976) Behavioral audiometry for obtaining thresholds of infants. *In* Proceedings of the VII World Congress of the World Federation of the Deaf (Ed. Carmmatte, A. B.) (Washington, D. C., August 5, 1975). Washington D. C.: National Association of the Deaf (in press).

Lloyd, L. L. and Cox, B. P. (1975) Behavioral audiometry with children. *In* Glasscock, M. J., (Guest Ed.), The Otolaryngology Clinics of North America: Symposium on sensorineural hearing loss in children: Early detection and intervention. Philadelphia: W. B. Sanders, p. 89.

Lloyd, L. L., and Moore, E. J. (1972) Audiology. *In* Mental Retardation: An Annual Review (Ed. Wortis, J.) New York: Grune & Stratton, p. 141.

Lloyd, L. L., Spradlin, J. E., and Reid, M. J. (1968) An operant audiometric procedure for difficult-to-test patients. J. Speech Hear. Dis. 33:236.

Lloyd, L. L., and Wilson, W. R. (1976) Recent developments in the behavioral assessment of the infant's response to auditory stimulation. Proceedings of the XVI World Congress for Logopedics and Phoniatrics (Interlaken, Switzerland, August 26, 1974). Basel, Switzerland: Karger Verlag, p. 301.

Morse, P. A. (1974) Infant speech perception: A preliminary model and review of literature. *In* Language Perspectives: Acquisition, Retardation and Intervention (Eds. Schiefelbusch, R. L., and Lloyd, L. L.) Baltimore: University Park Press.

Morse, P. (1978) Infant speech perception. *In* Communicative and Cognitive Abilities: Early Behavioral Assessment of the Developmentally Disabled. (Eds. Minifie, F. D., and Lloyd, L. L.) Baltimore: University Park Press (in press).

Prather, E., Miner, A., Addicott, M. A., and Sunderland, L. (1971) Washington Speech Sound Discrimination Test. Danville, Ill.: The Interstate Printers and Publishers.

Ross, M., and Lerman, J. (1968) A picture-identification test for hearing impaired children. U. S. Office of Education, Cooperative Research Project No. 7-8038, Univ. of Connecticut, Storrs, Conn.

Ross, M., and Lerman, J. (1970) A picture identification test for hearing-impaired children. J. Speech Hear. Dis. 13:44.

Ross, M., and Lerman, J. (1971) Word Intelligibility by Picture Identification (WIPI). Pittsburgh: Stanwix House, Inc.

Sidman, M. (1971) Reading and auditory-visual equivalences. J. Speech Hear. Res. 14:5.

Siegenthaler, B., and Haspiel, G. (1966) Development of two standardized measures of hearing for speech by children. U. S. Office of Education Project No. 2372, Contract No. OE-5-10-003.

Waryas, C. L., and Waryas, P. A. (1974) The "preference procedure" as an instrument for speech reception assessment and training. Acta Symbolica 5:83.

Wilson, W. (1977) Auditory assessment. *In* Communicative and Cognitive Abilities: Early Behavioral Assessment of the Developmentally Disabled. (Eds. Minifie, F. D., and Lloyd, L. L.) Baltimore: University Park Press (in press).

RESEARCH TO PRACTICE IN MENTAL RETARDATION
Education and Training, Volume II
Edited by Peter Mittler
Copyright 1977 I.A.S.S.M.D.

THE DEVELOPMENT OF SPEECH PERCEPTION

E. C. Butterfield
Ralph L. Smith Mental Retardation Research Center,
University of Kansas, Kansas City, Kansas 66103, United States

The question I would *like* to answer in this chapter is whether the language and communication problems of mentally retarded people depend to any extent on deficits in speech perception processes. Unhappily, I cannot answer that question, because the relevant comparative research between normal and retarded people has not been done. The question I will try to answer *instead* is whether or not there is any reason to perform that research. Is there any reason to believe that aberrations in the processes that underlie speech perception might account for any language and communication deficits?

My premise is that most cases of mental retardation are developmental problems. To see whether any particular process might account for any part of most mentally retarded people's behavior, one should see whether that process develops. Unless it develops, a process should not be considered a fruitful target for research that compares normal and retarded people. Evidence for development can be sought directly, by looking for changes with age, or indirectly, by looking for behavioral changes that result from experiences of the sort that accompany aging. Accordingly, I will devote most of my paper to research that considers whether or not speech perception changes with age or experience. If it changes with either, then it would be appropriate to study mentally retarded people to see whether or not their mechanisms of speech perception are different than those of normal people. If it were found that normal and retarded people perceive speech in different ways, then one could entertain the hypothesis that training speech perception would reduce the language problems of the retarded. Research to test that hypothesis would be eminently worthy of this audience.

Let me begin by noting that the acoustic properties of speech suggest that perception of its phonetic features should develop. This is illustrated well by spoken English, the acoustic characteristics of which have been analyzed with both spectographic and oscillographic techniques. Several cues isolated by such analyses have been mechanically synthesized and built into speech-like stimuli. Even though such synthetic stimuli seldom sound like natural speech, English adults discriminate and classify them phonetically. Such analytic and synthetic procedures have revealed acoustic variables that are sufficient for phonetic perception, but acoustic analysis and synthesis have revealed only a few invariant correlates of the linguistic features of any language. Instead of invariance, they have shown, first, acoustic cues that can signal different phonetic messages in different linguistic contexts. For example, cues that are sufficient to signal /b/ in one context, signal /p/ in another. They have also shown different cues that can signal the same phonetic message in different contexts. Thus, the perception of /d/ can be signalled by one set of cues in some acoustic environments, and by a completely different set in other environments. Such contextually conditioned variation seems the rule for phonetic elements of speech: acoustic invariance is the exception.

Acoustic studies of speech have also found that cues for several different phonetic segments can be coded in a single part of the signal. Thus, cues for the initial /b/ and for the terminal /g/ are both carried on the same portion of the acoustic signal that also carries the middle /a/ for the word "bag." As a result of such spillover from neighboring segments, phonetic boundaries are nearly impossible to find in the speech signal. Moreover, this complex coding seems not to be achieved by any kind of multiplexing, through which the neighboring carrier segment might be readily discerned. Instead, the coding of adjacent segments onto a phonetic element can cause changes in what seems its basic nature. Simultaneously mutiple, complexly interacting codes seem the rule in speech; singular, transparent codes are the exception. All of this should spell perceptual difficulty early in life.

The discoveries of poorly defined phonetic boundaries, contextually determined variation, and simultaneous acoustic coding of events that are perceived sequentially have elicited different responses from students of the acoustics of speech. Some have continued to accept the hypothesis that each phonetic contrast is associated with at least one acoustic invariant. They argue that these invariants may be complex and abstract, but that acoustic analysis will eventually reveal them. Others have abandoned the hypothesis that every phonetic contrast has its acoustic invariant. These theorists argue that precise phonetic messages are extracted from variable acoustic signals by what amounts to cognitive computation based on internal knowledge of the physical constraints of the human vocal system. Having perceived the articulatory constraints of a speech passage from its few acoustic invariants, a listener is said to infer the articulatory gestures that must have produced its ambiguously coded remainder. The ambiguity in the acoustic signal is thus said to be resolved by inferences about articulation, which gives phonetic meaning directly. No matter which of these interpretations ultimately prevails, we know enough now to conclude that decoding the acoustic properties of speech requires sophisticated feature detection mechanisms. Whether these perceptual mechanisms rely on high order acoustic invariants or a knowledge of articulatory constraints probably matters little as regards the need for experience, unless speech perception and visual perception are entirely different. If speech were visual, there seems little doubt that the feature detection mechanisms necessary to resolve its perceptual complexities would require some years of experience for their perfection. By analogy to vision, we should expect phonetic perception to develop.

Seemingly contrary to this expectation, recent findings suggest that phonetic discrimination is good during the first few months of life. Thus, four different experiments have shown that young infants discriminate /b/ from /p/, and one has shown that they discriminate /v/ from /s/. Infants have also been shown to discriminate /b/ and /d/ from /g/, /d/ from /t/, /s/ from /sh/, and /i/ from /a/ and /u/. Not all English phonetic contrasts have been studied, but the data are compelling: young infants discriminate many stimuli that differ phonetically.

Findings concerning the stop consonants /b/, /p/, /d/ and /t/ have also been taken by some to mean that young infants somehow know the phonetic identity of speech stimuli. Eimas (1974) and Morse (1974) have concluded that infants not only discriminate phonetic differences, they also equate tokens of particular phonetic categories, even though those tokens are acoustically distinct from each other. This equation is said to be phonetic despite the fact that it occurs before the age when infants could have learned the phonology of their language. We should look closely at the experiments that prompt such arguments. They may be showing us that speech perception does not require extensive experience and does not develop as visual perception does. They may be showing that at or near birth infants extract equivalents of phonetic features from speech by relying on the same complex cues that adults use when they perceive phonetically. Speech perception may not develop, and nonexperiential principles may be needed to account for its subtleties. If so, then studying the speech perception of retarded people would seem pointless.

The phonetic features of speech are not conveyed directly. They are indirectly cued by acoustic variations. But not every acoustic variation in the speech signal has phonetic significance. We can usually judge a speaker's mood, age, sex, and sometimes his unique identity from his speech, but when we can't judge any of these things, we may still perceive his phonetic message. So we should ask about the particular acoustic properties of stimuli used to study infants' speech perception. Could the stimuli have been discriminated acoustically as if they had contained no phonetic cues? No one can say for certain, but that seems probable for the several infant experiments that used natural speech segments. None of these experiments has satisfactorily established that its natural speech tokens are acoustically equal with respect to their nonphonetic features. Indeed, it is not clear that such equality could ever be established with analytic tools that are currently on the market. So there is reasonable doubt that infants respond to any phonetic cue when they discriminate /v/ from /s/ and /s/ from /sh/, /a/ from /i/ and /i/ from /u/, since these contrasts have only been studied with natural speech segments.

To ensure that infants respond only to acoustic cues that are correlates of phonetic features, some experimenters have used synthetic speech. But since cues for phonetic features are generally complex and multivariate, the question must arise whether infants discriminate only one acoustic element or the whole phonetically-sufficient synthetic complex. Presenting complexly varying stimuli to infants, on the grounds that adults do not perceive simply varying ones phonetically, may not prevent infants from responding nonphonetically to some simple acoustic element in the stimuli. No one *knows* which, nor how many, other phonetic cues are absent from synthetic stimuli used in infant experiments. There may be many sets of minimal cues that adults can use to make phonetic discriminations among stop consonants. For example, when adults discriminate /b/ from /g/, they may use burst cues, which usually have not been included in the synthetic stimuli presented to infants. Therefore, even if it were shown that infants discriminate some particular set of minimal cues as adults do, that would not eliminate the possibility that they come to discriminate others only much later in life.

We know from the study of visual perception that less experience is required for the discrimination of gross stimulus properties than for the development of the ability to discriminate subtle and more abstract stimulus characteristics. We also know that the speech signal is exceedingly rich and complex, and that its acoustic analysis, although extensive, is far from complete. Every analytic effort in the history of science has revealed increasingly specific and more abstract physical properties of its subject matter as it has been pursued longer. And the synthesis of physical properties generally lags behind their analytic discovery. This is true at least in the early phases of any scientific endeavor, and the acoustic analysis of speech is certainly in its early phases. The tape recorder, upon which speech analysis and synthesis are both absolutely dependent, was first built only 30 years ago, and it is still being refined in important ways. It follows that experiments using synthetic stimuli have studied infants' discrimination of gross features of speech, and it is these features that are likely to develop very early in life and to require minimal experience for their perception.

If the speech cues that have so far been studied are the grosser cues upon which people rely, then it should require only a little experience very early in life to promote their discrimination. Since practically all studies of infant's speech discrimination have used children who were at least two months old, the role of experience may have already been played before the children were studied. To evaluate this idea, Butterfield and Cairns (1974) examined the effects of experience upon newborn infants. Consistent with this analysis, the amount of prior stimulation with a relevant voicing cue predicted the degree of discrimination by newborn infants. Findings like these suggest that the place to seek evidence for a larger role of experience in the development of speech perception is in the study of more complex cues. For example, there is now evidence collected at Haskins Laboratory that the particular value of formant onset discrepancy, that is VOT, which signals the English voicing contrast, varies widely with the rate of initial formant transition. Adults' classifications and discriminations of VOT stimuli change systematically with rate of transition at the beginning of the formants, indicating that they perceive VOT relationally. If this were also true for very young infants, then experience would seem to play a minor role in prompting discriminative capacity for speech, and we would have a sounder basis for discounting any possible role of speech perception processes in the language problems of retarded people. As it stands now, the vast bulk of the data on speech discrimination is consistent with the view that there is no important development in speech perception.

It could be that infants make every particular phonetically-relevant acoustic discrimination at or near birth. What they may acquire as a consequence of experience is the knowledge of how the various individual cues or features are combined into phonemes. Infants might discriminate every minimally sufficient cue from birth, but not recognize the various bundles of such cues that signal particular phonemes in their language until they have had considerable experience with it. To test this possibility we must go beyond studies of speech discrimination. Studies of how infants classify synthetic speech stimuli are required, and procedures for measuring infants' classifications have not yet been developed. Developing techniques to fill this gap is necessary to an adequate test of whether or not speech perception develops. It is also necessary for students of speech to move beyond the research strategy of isolating minimally sufficient cues and to determine instead the complexes of cues which taken together adequately specify the bases of particular phonetic concepts.

It is conceivable, of course, that infants holistically discriminate bundles of minimally sufficient cues from birth. If so, the best guess is that they do that with acoustic mechanisms analogous to the feature detectors isolated in the visual systems of cats and frogs. But it seems unlikely that the outputs of such analyzing mechanisms would have phonetic meaning early in life. How they might acquire phonetic meaning is uncertain, but experience should play a role in that process. Studdert-Kennedy (1975) has suggested that the child gradually discovers relationships between the acoustic analysis of his own speech and the articulatory gestures with which he creates it. His suggestion is that the child's acoustic analyzers provide templates against which he compares the sounds he produces, much in the fashion of some birds who refine their singing against auditory templates. The phonetic meaning of the outputs of acoustic analysis thus might arise from, and in some sense be, the understanding of how to produce sounds that activate different acoustic feature analyzers. The assertion that acoustic analysis becomes phonetically relevant thus means that at some point in development the outputs of the acoustic analysis system are given articulatory meaning. Prior to the learning that makes that possible, the infant might nevertheless use the results of his acoustic analyses to discriminate amongst acoustic events, whether they are speech or not.

This analysis by Studdert-Kennedy suggests another place to look for the development of speech perception. It is in the childs' knowledge of articulatory constraints. It has recently been shown that adults use their knowledge of what speakers can do to guide their interpretation of what they hear. When two stop consonants are arranged sequentially on magnetic tape so that the period of silence between them is too brief for them to have been produced by a single speaker, the second consonant is perceived only when it is produced by a second speaker. This suggests that we should look to see whether such allowances for the articulatory capabilities of speakers depend upon substantial experience, or whether they are made very early in life.

Studdert-Kennedy's analysis also suggests that we should more closely examine the vocal productions of infants throughout the first year of life. If the critical experiences with respect to speech are the matchings of one's own vocalizations against his feature-detecting templates, then a careful tracking of infants' productions should suggest developmental sequences of perceptual capabilities. I am calling here for improved versions of the work begun by Irwin (1949), for more refined observations of infants' vocalizations.

I began this chapter by proposing to answer the question: Is there any reason to believe that aberrations in the processes underlying speech perception might account for any language and communication deficits? The bald answer to the question is "No," but "Not yet" may be the more appropriate answer. All of those studies that might have shown that speech perception develops have studied speech discrimination, and they have examined what are probably exceptionally gross acoustic correlates of phonetic distinctions. There is still a reasonable possibility that speech discrimination develops, but that its development is confined to those aspects of the acoustic code that have yet to be discovered. Moreover, there is far more to speech perception than the discrimination of segments. I have suggested three places where developmental research might reasonably focus its efforts in order to shed more light on whether or not perceptual processes could underlie language deviance. First, there is the study of the ways infants classify speech stimuli, particularly synthetic ones that are differentially complete in their acoustic features. Second, there is the study of infant's and children's knowledge of articulatory constraints. Third, there is the study of prelinguistic vocalization and its development. When these matters have been investigated it should be clear whether or not there is any reason to explore the possibility that mentally retarded people's language problems stem in any extent from perceptual disturbances.

REFERENCES

Butterfield, E. C., and Cairns, G. F. (1974) Discussion summary—infant reception research. *In* Language Perspectives—Acquisition, Retardation and Intervention (Eds. Schiefelbusch, R. L., and Lloyd, L. L.) Baltimore: University Park Press.

Eimas, P. D. (1974) Linguistic processing of speech by young infants. *In* Language Perspectives—Acquisition, Retardation and Intervention (Eds. Schiefelbusch, R. L., and Lloyd, L. L.) Baltimore: University Park Press.

Irwin, O. C. (1949) Infant speech. Sci. Am. 181:22.
Morse, P. A. (1974) Infant speech perception: A preliminary model and review of the literature. *In* Language Perspectives—Acquisition, Retardation and Intervention (Eds. Schiefelbusch, R. L., and Lloyd, L. L.) Baltimore: University Park Press.
Studdert-Kennedy, M. (1975) Speech perception. *In* Contemporary Issues in Experimental Phonetics (Ed. Lass, N. J.) Springfield, Illinois: Charles C Thomas.

RESEARCH TO PRACTICE IN MENTAL RETARDATION
Education and Training, Volume II
Edited by Peter Mittler
Copyright 1977 I.A.S.S.M.D.

DEVELOPMENT OF PSYCHOLINGUISTIC ABILITIES IN MENTALLY RETARDED AND DEVELOPMENTALLY BACKWARD CHILDREN

V. I. Lubovsky
*Research Institute of Defectology, Pogodinskaya 8,
Moscow G–117, U.S.S.R.*

Research on verbal control in mentally retarded and developmentally backward children has called for a special study of speech comprehension and production. These processes, defined as psycholinguistic abilities, determine to a great extent the ability of a child to follow verbal instructions as well as to verbalize his own actions. Kirk and others have shown that psycholinguistic abilities reflect the level of mental development.

Concerning Russian-speaking mentally retarded (MR) and developmentally backward (DB) children, delay in the development of psycholinguistic abilities (an insufficient command of grammar especially in written speech) was described by Petrova (1965), Triger (1972), and others.

The first part of the research, which is described below, was directed especially at the evaluation of abilities to use grammatical rules in the production of utterances, according to the conditions of the task and the level of mental development.

In the first task, children were asked to tell a short story about a picture that they were shown. This situation is similar to spontaneous speech. In the second task, they had to compose a sentence using the four words given in the initial form, and in the third task they had to match the words presented with the corresponding picture. In the last two cases verbal production was restricted by the given verbal material, and the difference was in the presence (or absence) of a visual aid.

Thirty-nine normally developing first graders, 30 MR pupils of the first grade of normal school, and 151 DB children from the same grade took part in the experiment. The chronological age of all these children was between 7.6 and 8 years old. Another group of 32 MR pupils from a special school were one year older. The results of both groups of MR children were combined in data processing.

In the process of production of utterances on restricted verbal material, difficulties were found in the establishment of syntagmatic as well as paradigmatic connections. These were characteristic of children of all the groups.

The most numerous and strongly pronounced disturbances in grammatical structure observed in MR children were incomplete sentences, disturbances of word order, incorrect transformation of words, or their retention in their initial form when transformation was required, and failure to use all the words given. There were no disturbances in normal children in the first task and in the second and third tasks disturbances were less pronounced.

The number of wrong sentences in the second and third tasks for normal, MR and DB children are shown in Table 1.

All the differences between the groups were significant by χ^2 criterion in all the variants of the experiment at the 0.01 probability level. χ^2 for the normal group and DB in the second task was 12.799, and in the third task, 15.293.

It was especially difficult for children to compose sentences of word sets presupposing spatial relations or consecutive subordination or transformation of a noun into its adjectival form, e.g., wood into wooden, in English.

The facilitation of establishment of paradigmatic structure by means of a picture does not lead to complete regularity of syntagmatic connections, because some of them are not formed in children of that age.

Difficulties in the grammatical structuring of utterances correlate strongly with lack of comprehension of grammatical forms. This was found in a special series of experiments in which children were asked to compare phrases of different meaning (according to different word orders), and their ability to follow several verbal instructions was examined. It was found that the more advanced the level of intellectual development, the higher the children's scores in all the experiments.

The experimental results also furnished evidence that the formation of grammatical structures in normal children is not finished by 7—8 years of age, as was supposed previously (Gvosdev, 1961) but considerably later, as was also

Table 1. Percentage of incorrect sentences in normal, mentally retarded (MR) and developmentally backward (DB) children

| | Tasks | |
Groups	II	III
Normal	34.2	17.0
Mentally retarded (MR)	56.2	71.5
Developmentally backward (DB)	45.0	36.7

shown by the American researchers of speech development in English speaking children (Chomsky, 1969). The differences between our conclusions and earlier observations are likely to be accounted for by the fact that the latter were obtained on the basis of studying the children's spontaneous speech (diary techniques). In such forms of speech, the child makes use of verbal stereotypes and strongly formed grammatical generalizations, avoiding subconsciously the use of words which are not kept within the limits of those stereotypes and generalizations. When the child is asked to compose an expression restricted to certain given words, the use of these stereotypes and generalizations becomes difficult or even impossible because a conscious manipulation of the material is necessary and this ability is often not formed till much later in development.

To ascertain the relative roles of level of mental development together with development of speech, a comparative study of a number of psycholinguistic abilities in mentally retarded children, pupils of grade 4 of a special school and normal second graders (125 children in each group) was carried out. The MR children were older on the average by three years than the normal children, and the duration of their learning was longer by the same period, since they were taught for one year at the general school before they were transferred to the special one.

MR children differed most from normal children in indices of verbal hearing sensitivity as measured by precision of reproduction of complex phonetic structures ($\chi^2 = 42.6$; $p < 0.001$) and verbal memory, which was assessed by the efficiency of memorization of a short poem and unknown words ($\chi^2 = 78.3$, $p < 0.001$; and $\chi^2 = 30.5$, $p < 0.001$, respectively). However, differences were statistically insignificant in the level of command of the grammatical structures, as determined by construction of simple extended sentences from single words. Significant differences were absent not because the MR children coped well with this task. On the contrary, differences were absent because normal children also experienced great difficulties in application of structural variations to the transformation of the given verbal material (Puoshlene, 1974).

These findings justify the claim that among the factors determining the formation of grammatical structures, the effect of intellectual level may be exceeded within certain age limits by the factors of the duration of the period of speech command and the duration of learning.

REFERENCES

Chomsky, C. (1969) The Acquisition of Syntax in Children from 5 to 10. Cambridge, Massachusetts: M.I.T. Press.

Gvosdev, A. (1961) Problems of the Study of Children's Language. Moscow: AP Sci. Press (in Russian).

Kirk, S., and McCarthy, J. (1961) The Illinois test of psycholinguistic abilities: An approach to differential diagnosis. Amer. J. Ment. Defic. 66:399.

Petrova, V. G. (1965) Language of mentally retarded school children. *In* Peculiarities of Mental Development of Mentally Retarded School Children (Ed. Shif, Z.), p. 129. Moscow: Education Publishing House (in Russian).

Puoshlene, E.-P. (1974) Comparative study of psycholinguistic ability of normal and mentally retarded children. Defectology 2:9 (in Russian).

Triger, R. D. (1972) Reading mistakes in developmentally backward children. Defectology 5:35 (in Russian).

RESEARCH TO PRACTICE IN MENTAL RETARDATION
Education and Training, Volume II
Edited by Peter Mittler
Copyright 1977 I.A.S.S.M.D.

MATERNAL SPEECH IN NORMAL AND DOWN'S SYNDROME CHILDREN

J. A. Rondal
*Department of Psychoeducational Studies, Pattee Hall, University
of Minnesota, Minneapolis, Minnesota 55455, United States*

Interest has arisen recently in the nature of the linguistic environment within which children develop linguistic competence. Accordingly, many efforts have been directed toward analyzing parental speech, especially maternal speech, addressed to young children. In a parallel fashion, mothers' speech to their mentally retarded children has been of interest to several investigators. Kogan, Wimberger, and Bobbitt (1969), Marshall, Hegrenes, and Goldstein (1973), and Buium, Rynders, and Turnure (1974) compared maternal speech directed to normal and to retarded children matched for chronological age (CA). The children were between two and seven years old. They were addressed by their respective mothers in a play- or tutoring-like situation in a laboratory setting. The results were similar in the three studies. First, mothers of retarded children provided a generally less complex type of linguistic environment than mothers of normal children. Second, mothers of retarded children tended to use a more controlling type of speech (containing more requests and imperative sentences, for example) and to solicit leadership on the part of the child less often than mothers of normal children. The interpretation offered by the investigators was that the mothers of retarded children tended to provide a different type of verbal environment to their children. They also suggested that exposure to such a restricted type of linguistic environment may adversely affect the retarded children's language development.

The interpretation offered by Marshall et al., Buium et al., and Kogan et al.

This research was supported by a grant from the Belgian National Board for Scientific Research (F.N.R.S.) and by a grant from the Bureau of Education for the Handicapped, U.S. Office of Education, Department of Health, Education, and Welfare to the Center for Research, Development, and Demonstration in Education of Handicapped Children, Department of Psychoeducational Studies, University of Minnesota.

requires comment pertaining to the CA-matching used as a basis for their studies. It is known that at corresponding CA, retarded children, particularly moderately and severely retarded, do not talk in the same way as normal children. Therefore, when with their mothers, the retarded children are likely to interact verbally in a way different from that of the normal children of similar CAs. Because a verbal interaction is an interpersonal process by definition, it is reasonable to assume that such differences in children's speech are capable of affecting the speech of the adult interlocutor. In other words, because the three studies mentioned above have all matched normal and retarded children for CA and because at corresponding CAs normal and retarded children are at different levels of speech and language functioning, it is not clear whether the differences observed in maternal speech must be attributed to differences in the children addressed according to type of children (retarded versus normal), or according to level of speech and language development. The more controlling style of speech used by the mothers of retarded children can also be explained in a similar manner. It is possible that relatively less mature children, such as retarded children, in comparison with their CA-matched peers, proved less manageable, particularly in an unfamiliar situation like the laboratory setting, and, consequently, obliged their mothers to resort to more directive speech in order to keep the children under control and cooperative.

The CA-match that served as a basis for the studies of Marshall, Buium, and Kogan thus had the unfortunate consequence that it does not distinguish between the effects of type of children versus level of speech and language development (and levels of mental level in general) on maternal speech. The purpose of the research to be reported here was to avoid this confounding by comparing the maternal linguistic environments of normal and retarded children matched for level of language development as assessed by mean length of utterance (MLU).

The subjects of the study were 21 Down's syndrome (DS) children and their natural mothers and 21 normal children and their natural mothers. Seven normal children and seven DS children were matched at each of three MLU levels: 1.00–1.50, 1.75–2.25, and 2.50–3.00. MLU was computed in number of morphemes, using the criterion given in Brown (1973). The only exception to Brown's criterion was that the MLU count was based on the total speech sample rather than just the first 100 utterances, as suggested by Brown. Normal children ranged in CA from 20 to 32 months. DS children ranged in CA from three to 12 years. The mothers of normal and the mothers of DS children were matched on ethnic group (Caucasian), familial monolingualism, familial structure (both husband and wife living at home), maternal intelligence (not obviously outside the normal range), socioeconomic status (predominantly middle class), and maternal educational level (using Hollingshead's Educational Scale, after Hollingshead, 1957).

The verbal interaction between mother and child was tape recorded at home in a free-play situation. There were two recording sessions, lasting half an hour for each mother-child pair. The two recording sessions took place on two different days at approximately a one-week interval.

Maternal speech was analyzed for 20 measures related to its output-numerical, lexical, syntactical, semantic-structural, semantic-pragmatic, and language-teaching aspects. The 20 measures were: 1) total number of words produced, 2) type-token ratio (TTR, a measure of vocabulary diversity) 3) MLU, 4) proportions of utterances of specific lengths, 5) sentence complexity index, 6) mean preverb length, 7) proportions of utterances without verbs, 8) number of modifiers per utterance, 9) different types and subtypes of sentences (declaratives, imperatives, yes/no questions, raising intonation questions, wh-questions, tag questions) and grammatically incomplete sentences, 10) major and optional verb types (from a semantic-structural point of view and according to Chafe (1970), 11) proportions of different types of requests for action and proportions of adjuncts to request for action according to Garvey's analytical scheme for the study of requests for action (Garvey, 1975), 12) proportions of word in dysfluencies, 13) acoustical clarity of maternal speech, 14) explicit direct verbal approvals and disapprovals of children's utterances, 15) attentional utterances, 16) mothers' exact repetitions of their own utterances, 17) auxiliary development ratio, 18) proportions of expansions and corrections of children's speech, 19) proportions of prodding of children's speech, and 20) proportions of mothers' repetitions of children's utterances.

Eight measures of children's speech were computed as a means of testing the validity of the MLU-matching performed on the children as a basis for the study. The eight measures were: 1) total number of words produced, 2) TTR, 3) upper bounds, 4) proportions of utterances without verb, 5) number of modifiers per utterance, 6) different types and subtypes of sentences and proportions of utterances that were sentences (a sentence was defined as containing at least a noun and a verb in a subject-predicate relationship), 7) major and optional verb types, and 8) percentages of children's repetitions of mothers' utterances.

The reader is referred to Rondal (1976) for a definition of the above categories and for information on the statistical analyses made on the data.

Reliability, in terms of percent of agreement between two independent raters, was calculated separately for those measures that seemed to involve some subjective judgment on the rater's part. Agreement was high in all instances, varying between 84 and 98%.

The results were particularly clear-cut. None of the measures of children's speech computed, except TTR, revealed a significant difference between normal and DS children. TTR slightly but significantly favored DS children over normal children. Aside from this difference, the similarities in the speech of normal and DS children matched for MLU were often striking at each of the three language levels. As expected, there were numerous significant differences between the children in the different aspects of speech considered according to language level. The results of the analysis of children's speech thus validated the MLU-matching performed initially.

None of the comparisons of mothers' speech to normal and to DS children led to differences that were significant or close to significance for any of the children's three language levels. Similarly, there was no significant *type of children* X *children's language level* interaction effect on any of the comparisons made of mothers' speech to normal and to DS children. It appeared that the maternal linguistic environments of DS and normal children at corresponding MLU levels were similar in all respects. Additionally, it is interesting to note that, once the DS and the normal children were matched for MLU, there were no differences left in maternal speech for proportions of imperative sentences and proportions of different types of requests for action. This suggests that the differences observed by Kogan, Marshall, and Buium in the controlling aspects of mothers' speech may have been more reflective of differences in level of development in the children addressed than of differences in mothers' speech according to type of child (normal versus retarded).

In contrast to the absence of differences in maternal speech to normal and to DS children at corresponding MLU levels, there were numerous significant differences in mothers' speech according to the language level of the children. This confirms that the expressive language level of the children, as assessed by MLU, is a far more powerful factor in influencing maternal speech than whether these children are normal or have Down's syndrome.

Largely based on the data reported and the interpretations offered by Marshall (1973), Buium (1974), and Kogan (1969), a number of authors have begun referring more or less explicitly to the familial linguistic environment of mentally retarded children as deficient (e.g., Dolley, 1974; Mitchell, 1976; Seitz, 1975; Mahoney, 1975).

What the results of the present investigation indicate is that the maternal linguistic environment of DS children between MLU 1 and 3 is an appropriate one, if by appropriate it is meant the kind of linguistic environment that is generally the one of normal middle class children at corresponding MLU. The preceding sentence remains the only, even if circular, definition that is available today of a "good" linguistic environment for first language acquisition. According to the present investigation, and within its limitation, the connotation of deficit that has become associated with the familial linguistic environment of mentally retarded children in the last ten years should be seriously reconsidered, and note should be taken, once more, of the great difficulty involved in making an appropriate and rigorous investigation in matters related to normal and abnormal children. In summary, it may be that the major implication of the present research for language intervention is the possibility that the familial linguistic environment of language-learning DS children may be as appropriate for the language development of those children as the familial linguistic environment of normal children at corresponding levels of language development. It is an open question whether or not similar data can be obtained and similar conclusions can be made for other groups of mentally retarded children.

SUMMARY

Mothers' speech to 42 normal and Down's syndrome children at MLU levels 1.00 to 3.00 were recorded at home and were analyzed for measures related to syntactical, semantical, and language-teaching aspects of speech. No significant difference was found between mothers' speech to their normal children and mothers' speech to their Down's syndrome children.

ACKNOWLEDGMENT

This report is based on a doctoral dissertation completed by the author at the University of Minnesota with the considerable support of James E. Turnure, adviser and chairman of the Dissertation Committee.

REFERENCES

Brown, R. (1973) A First Language: The Early Stages. Cambridge, Mass.: Harvard University Press.
Buium, N., Rynders, J., and Turnure, J. (1974) Early maternal linguistic environment of normal and Down's syndrome language-learning children. Amer. J. Ment. Defic. 79:52.
Chafe, W. (1970) Meaning and the Structure of Language. Chicago: The University of Chicago Press.
Dolley, D. (1974) Mothers as Teachers: Instruction and Control Patterns Observed in Interaction of Middle-class Mothers with Trainable Mentally Retarded and Non-retarded Children (Report No. 7.32). Bloomington, Ind.: University of Indiana, School of Education, Center for Innovation in Teaching the Handicapped.
Garvey, C. (1975) Requests and responses in children's speech. J. Child Lang. 2:41.
Hollingshead, A. (1957) Two-factor Index of Social Position. Unpublished manuscript. (Available from A. Hollingshead, 1965 Yale Station, New Haven, Connecticut 06520)
Kogan, K., Wimberger, H., and Bobbitt, R. (1969) Analysis of mother child interaction in young mental retardates. Child Dev. 40:799.
Mahoney, G. (1975) An ethological approach to delayed language acquisition. Amer. J. Ment. Defic. 80:139.
Marshall, N., Hegrenes, J., and Goldstein, S. (1973) Verbal interactions: Mothers and their retarded children versus mothers and their non-retarded children. Amer. J. Ment. Defic. 77:415.
Mitchell, D. (1976) Parent-child interaction in mental handicap. In Language Communication in the Mentally Handicapped (Ed. Berry, P.) London: Arnold.
Rondal, J. (1976) Maternal Speech to Normal and to Down's Syndrome Children Matched for Mean Length of Utterance. (Doctoral Dissertation, University of Minnesota) Ann Arbor, Mich.: University Microfilms.
Seitz, S. (1975) Language intervention—Changing the language environment of the retarded child. In Down's Syndrome (Eds. Koch, R., and De la Cruz, F.) New York: Brunner/Mazel, p. 157.

RESEARCH TO PRACTICE IN MENTAL RETARDATION
Education and Training, Volume II
Edited by Peter Mittler
Copyright 1977 I.A.S.S.M.D.

DEMANDING LANGUAGE

P. Mittler[1] and P. Berry[2]
[1] *Hester Adrian Research Centre for the Study of
Learning Processes in the Mentally Handicapped,
University of Manchester, M13 9PL, England*
[2] *Schonell Educational Research Centre, University
of Queensland, Brisbane, Australia*

The theme of this chapter is the nature of the demands we make on mentally retarded people. Although we discuss this question largely in the context of language studies, many parallel illustrations could be provided from work in the fields of social education, rehabilitation studies, and vocational training.

We have now reached a situation where we can say with some confidence that severely retarded people are capable of learning far more than was previously expected of them, provided they are taught systematically. We know that application of certain principles of teaching and learning can produce excellent results, and, conversely, that failure to teach effectively is unlikely to result in the development of new skills and abilities.

But we know also that mentally retarded people frequently achieve less than might be expected of them, and that underfunctioning is particularly common in the sphere of language and communication skills. Although the reasons for this underfunctioning are not adequately documented or understood, we want to draw attention in this paper to just one of many possible sources of failure—the failure on the part of those working with retarded people to provide appropriate settings of demand, expectation, and opportunity for effective language performance. We are talking here about the use of ordinary situations of living and learning to help retarded people to make fuller use of existing abilities, as distinct from the task of helping them to acquire new skills.

This is not merely a problem for research or for professional staff, but for all who come into contact with retarded people, particularly parents. In fact, we see the task of setting, maintaining, and systematically extending an appropriate level of demand as one specific reflection of the conference theme of "Research to Practice." Research has already begun to demonstrate that language and communication skills can be taught to severely retarded people: our task now is

Some of the work reported in this chapter was supported by grants from the Social Science Research Council and the Schools Council, England.

to adapt and modify our research techniques in such a way that their relevance to the needs of every day living is obvious to practitioners from the outset. It is not then a question of "translation" from research to practice, but an incorporation of research findings and methods not only into training programmes delivered by paid staff but also into the ordinary social encounters that all of us have with retarded people (Mittler, 1975a).

We are arguing at a general level for some blurring of the distinction between our professional roles and our personal relationships with retarded people. Practitioners might, we suggest, become more sensitised to their own behaviour, as well as the behaviour of those with whom they work. They can learn to assess their own performance and become more skilled in self-analysis, in monitoring their own effectiveness not just as trainers or therapists, but as human beings.

Relating these general considerations to language development, we would like to distinguish two sources of demand: first, direct demands for language performance from the retarded person and, second, environmental arrangements that encourage and facilitate optimum language functioning.

Direct demands for language performance can take a variety of forms, but we know that they can be quite effective. For example, imitation training is a powerful means of eliciting speech and language responses from severely retarded people, given careful task analysis and systematic shaping and reinforcement. Our earlier work has also suggested that elicited imitation of adult speech and language models provides important clues to the child's understanding of linguistic rule systems: by progressively increasing the grammatical complexity of the material to be imitated, we can study the error patterns made by the child for clues about his understanding of the language (Berry, 1976a).

Although direct language demand can be a powerful means of teaching, our concern in the present paper is with more indirect demands, with ways in which we can make the most effective use of what is already available in ordinary everyday environments to encourage effective language and communication in retarded people. We are arguing for a wider social and environmental context to language facilitation, a context concerned with the world of people, objects, and relationships, a context that will help people to express wants and needs, rather than merely phonology, syntax, and semantics.

Before we consider studies of highly structured demand, we should briefly consider environmental demand in global terms, and note one arresting, almost paradoxical, finding. We refer here to the apparent absence of social class and socioeconomic differences in language performance within the severely retarded population, in contrast to the repeatedly demonstrated existence of such differences both in the nonhandicapped population and especially among mildly retarded subjects. It is remarkable that social class differences within the severely retarded (trainable) population have hardly been investigated by research workers, since it is well known that the incidence of severe mental retardation is fairly evenly distributed among all social classes, whereas mild retardation is disproportionately skewed towards the poorer and most disadvantaged sections of the population, at least in urban Western societies. Our attention was first drawn to this subject by the work of Janet Carr (1970) who failed to find any social class differences in a longitudinal study of some 60 Down's syndrome children living with their families. We later studied all the 1,400 mentally retarded children attending 19 special schools in N.W. England, and also failed to detect any evidence that children from "middle class" homes showed even the slightest tendency to achieve higher scores on a series of language measures than children from "working class" homes, as defined by reference to the Registrar General's classification of parental occupation (Swann and Mittler, 1976). (See Table 1.)

The apparent absence of social class differences in language performance of mentally retarded children needs further investigation, but may be related in part to difficulties in incidental learning reported by some research workers (e.g., Denny, 1964). It is possible that the kind of "enriched environment" that seems to favour learning in normal children may by itself be inappropriate for severely mentally retarded children.

A more familiar example of global environmental demand can be taken from the many studies suggesting that hospitalized retarded children show inferior levels of language performance. This inferiority might be partly related to the fact that hospitalized children tend to be more severely impaired in the first place, but is usually attributed in part to lower standards of care in general, and inappropriate levels of language stimulation in particular. Insofar as there is any validity in the second explanation, it suggests that retarded children are certainly vulnerable to environments characterized by low levels of stimulation and demand. Nevertheless, we are still far from understanding the processes and mechanisms associated with reduced levels of language performance in institutions, though it seems likely that lack of demand for language performance is one important factor (Rutter and Mittler, 1972; Mittler, 1974).

Table 1. Averages and standard deviations for children in social classes I–V on language production and reception scales and on English picture vocabulary test[a]

Social class	Production scale			Reception scale			E.P.V.T. raw score		
	average	S.D.	N	average	S.D.	N	average	S.D.	N
I	8.6	3.6	37	6.4	3.0	37	18.2	11.7	27
II	8.4	3.6	87	6.6	3.4	87	20.0	11.9	55
III	8.4	4.1	250	6.7	3.6	250	20.7	11.9	177
IV	8.5	4.0	71	6.2	3.4	70	18.0	12.9	44
V	8.5	3.2	27	6.0	3.0	27	19.6	12.1	19

[a]Leeming et al., 1977. S.D. = standard deviation from the mean.

But we also know that inferior language development is not an inevitable consequence of institutionalization (Tizard and Tizard, 1974), nor are the effects irreversible; moreover, we have recently established, during the course of the Schools Council Language Survey, that children living in residential hostels may be indistinguishable in respect to language skills from those living with their own families (Swann and Mittler, 1976) (Table 2). This suggests that it is not separation or residential care as such that is associated with language retardation: instead we should look more closely at the fine grain aspects of interaction between mentally handicapped people and their caregivers, whether these are parents, nurses or residential care staff.

We would like to illustrate examples of language demand by referring first to a small single case study carried out by our colleague Dorothy Jeffree (1971); it demonstrates how variations in the content and context of demands made on a child can elicit systematic variations in the language forms used. After a baseline period that took the form of a fairly typical play and conversational interchange, five different styles or strategies of teaching were introduced, each of which resulted in the use of different language forms, including increases in phrase length, in the ratio of verbs to nouns, and in the type token ratio. The child was not being taught to produce new structures but to make more effective use of language that she already possessed.

This study demonstrated that planned variations in the nature of demand can result in marked changes in language performance. We want to suggest that this can be done by everyone who comes into contact with retarded people, provided they acquire a certain amount of insight into ways in which their own language and social skills can help a retarded person to make better use of abilities he already possesses but does not fully use.

These considerations have led us toward an interest in what teachers say to children in the course of ordinary classroom activities and also in more struc-

Table 2. Average and standard deviations for children living at home, in hospital, in hostels, and in other forms of care on the production and reception scales and E.P.V.T. (Leeming et al., 1977)

Type of care	Production scale			Reception scale			E.P.V.T. raw score		
	average[a]	S.D.	N	average[a]	S.D.	N	average[b]	S.D.	N
At home	8.5	3.9	1050	6.6	3.4	1031	18.4	12.7	755
In hospitals	5.9	4.0	142	3.9	2.9	142	13.5	13.0	50
In hostels	8.4	4.0	54	6.7	3.3	55	20.9	11.0	37
Other forms	8.1	4.0	47	6.5	3.6	47	15.9	10.0	30

[a] $p = 0.001$
[b] $p = 0.05$
S.D. = standard deviation from the mean.

tured teaching situations. In a study of the language used by a small number of teachers in both structured and unstructured situations, only a small proportion of the teachers' utterances were questions requiring anything other than a yes or no answer; about half the text took the form of declarative statements and about a third was in the form of imperatives.

Although questions constitute a demand for an answer, some questions are more demanding than others. Adults wishing to elicit language from a retarded child frequently make use of the "what's that?" strategy. If the child is going to respond at all, he is likely to do so by means of a one word response, probably in noun form. This adult tendency to reinforce one-word labelling responses may be partly responsible for the delay in reaching the two-word, or pivot-open stage of language development (Jeffree, Wheldall, and Mittler, 1973).

A number of alternative strategies are open to the adult who wants to avoid the usual barren interchange that follows the "what's this called?" type of questioning; for example, even the child who is unable to produce more than single-word responses can be asked to respond with action verbs as well as with nouns, or be given binary questions requiring choice and decision-making: questions such as "would you like tea or coffee?" "shall we go out now or later?" or even, in a story-telling situation, "do you think he was happy or sad?" Various classification systems have been suggested for questioning (Cazden, 1972; Mitchell, 1976); the point we wish to emphasize here is that professionals and parents alike could be much more sensitive in monitoring their questioning in such a way as to help the retarded person to extend his use of language — perhaps by increasing the verb:noun ratio, by using longer phrases or subject-verb-object sentence types (see Mittler, 1976 for further discussion of this point).

We can return to consider the all too familiar situation of a child who is given a picture showing a number of different people and activities, and asked "Tell me all about the picture." He then proceeds to list each separate part of the picture, often earning applause and reinforcement for these single word noun labels, when in fact he might be helped to indicate what the characters on the picture were doing, or how the various activities depicted were related to one another.

A group of teachers working on the Schools Council curriculum project (Leeming et al., 1976) tackled this problem in the following way. After the child was shown the usual kind of complex picture and had duly listed the individual elements, he was shown a series of single pictures, each of which depicted only one of the subsidiary characters engaged in a particular activity. The teacher largely refrained from direct teaching or modelling of longer responses, but simply repeated her demand "Tell me about the picture" until the child produced a longer response. By indicating that she was not satisfied with a simple label, the teacher elicited longer utterances from the child. Thus, instead of simply labelling a picture as "That's a girl," the child spontaneously produced a longer subject-verb-object sentence, such as "The girl's picking flowers." Once the children learned that single-word responses were not satisfactory and that longer answers resulted in strong social reinforcement, they spontaneously produced longer responses when they were once again shown the larger picture.

This is only an isolated example of a teaching style emphasising demand characteristics; in general, we see an important need for educationalists to develop situations, games, pictures, and materials that can be used flexibly and naturally to develop a fuller use of language, as opposed to sterile naming exercises. We can also be more resourceful in modifying the environment in such a way as to give people opportunities for decision-making and for expressing choice and preference between alternatives—for example, in choice of food, clothing, toys, or activities.

CONCLUSIONS

Many more examples of language demand could be given from our own experience and not just from the literature. We now have a considerable volume of research showing that severely retarded people can be helped by means of a systematic teaching technology to become much more proficient in the acquisition and use of language, and we know much more than we did even at the time of our last Congress three years ago about learning and teaching a first language. But we also have to admit that much of the research has concentrated on specific skills such as noun-labelling and teaching the elements of syntax or the rules of morphology. Only in recent years has there been any serious interest in meaning and content or in the social and interpersonal uses of language (Mittler, 1975b; Berry, 1976b).

Although systematic and structured language teaching has much to offer, we should not neglect the innumerable opportunities for furthering language development that are present in ordinary everyday situations. Parents, professionals, care staff, and all who come into contact with retarded people can become more skilled in using casual social encounters to help them respond to situations of greater demand and higher expectation, and to seek help and guidance if the demands we make really do exceed their ability to respond.

We can all become more skilled not merely in making demands, but also in dealing with those many situations where a demand apparently produces no obvious result. We should not be satisfied with failure to respond but learn to vary the nature or context of the demand and to be much more resourceful in providing alternative opportunities for responses.

We believe that retarded people may be handicapped as much by the underexpectation of those who live and work with them as by their primary disabilities. Research and experience suggest that people—whether retarded or not—respond to the challenge of demand and expectation. Many of us would probably admit that we have in the past tended to underestimate the abilities of retarded people, and that the trend in recent years has been to look more closely at our own limitations to teach than at the limitations of retarded people to learn. Of course, there must be limits to what can be achieved, but we do not know at all precisely what those limits are. We have only just begun to make higher demands, but we still have a long way to go and a lot to learn.

SUMMARY

This chapter illustrates the thesis that language functioning of retarded people could be increased if professionals, parents, and caregivers learned to make more appropriate demands for language performance not only in the course of structured teaching situations but also during ordinary social encounters.

REFERENCES

Berry, P. (1976a) Imitation of language by mentally handicapped children: A language assessment technique. *In* Language and Communication in the Mentally Handicapped (Ed. Berry, P.) London: Arnold.

Berry, P. (Ed.) (1976b) Language and Communication in the Mentally Handicapped. London: Arnold.

Carr, J. (1970) Mental and motor development in young mongol children. J. Ment. Defic. Res. 14:205.

Cazden, C. (1972) Child Language and Education. New York: Holt, Rinehart & Winston.

Jeffree, D. (1971) A language teaching programme for a mongol child. Spec. Educ. Forward Trends 15:33.

Jeffree, D., Wheldall, K., and Mittler, P. (1973) The facilitation of two-word utterances in two Down's syndrome boys. Amer. J. Ment. Defic. 78:117.

Leeming, K., Coupe, J., Swann, W., and Mittler, P. (1977) Teaching Language and Communication to the Mentally Handicapped. London: Schools Council (in press).

Mitchell, D. (1976) Mentally Handicapped Children in Structured Dyadic Interaction with their Parents. Unpublished Ph.D. Thesis, University of Manchester.

Mittler, P. (1974) Language and communication. *In* Mental Deficiency: The Changing Outlook, 3rd edition. (Eds. Clarke, A. M. and Clarke, A. D. B.) London: Methuen; New York: Free Press.

Mittler, P. (1975a) Research to Practice in the Field of Handicap. London: Institute for Research in Mental and Multiple Handicap.

Mittler, P. (1975b) Language facilitation. Procs. 3rd Congr. IASSMD, The Hague, 1:562. R.S.N.H., Larbert, Scotland: IASSMD.

Mittler, P. (1976) Assessment for language learning. *In* Language and Communication in the Mentally Handicapped (Ed. Berry, P.) London: Arnold.

Rutter, M., and Mittler, P. (1972) Environmental influences on language development. *In* The Child with Delayed Speech (Eds. Rutter, M., and Martin, J. A. M.) London: Heinemann; Philadelphia: Lippincott.

Swann, W., and Mittler, P. (1976) Language abilities of ESN(S) pupils. Spec. Educ. Forward Trends. 3:24.

Tizard, J., and Tizard, B. (1974) The institution as an environment for development. *In* The Integration of a Child into a Social World. (Ed. Richards, M. P.) Cambridge: Cambridge University Press.

RESEARCH TO PRACTICE IN MENTAL RETARDATION
Education and Training, Volume II
Edited by Peter Mittler
Copyright 1977 I.A.S.S.M.D.

LANGUAGE AND EMERGENT BEHAVIOR

J. E. Spradlin
Bureau of Child Research Laboratories, The University of
Kansas, Lawrence, Kansas 66045, United States

People often act appropriately in situations they have never encountered previously; that is, somehow behavior that is novel, yet appropriate or functional, emerges without direct training in novel situations. What are the precursors of such behavior? Can novel, yet appropriate, behavior be predicted? Two terms frequently occur when an appropriate response to a new situation is being discussed. These two terms are concepts and stimulus classes. But what defines membership in a stimulus class or concept?

A first obvious attempt to characterize the members of a concept or stimulus class is that they are objects or events that have some common characteristic or characteristics. It is these common characteristics that distinguish the members of one class from the other classes. Such an analysis, in general, seems quite appropriate when one speaks of classes such as cups, hats, books, triangles, and literally hundreds of other collections of objects or events. However, one runs into trouble when such classes as letters, numbers, fruits, vegetables, tools, or toys are introduced. Clearly there is no common physical characteristic that will allow one to distinguish the members of the letter class from the members of the number class. If it is not common characteristics that tie the members of such classes together, what does tie them together? The research to be reported in this chapter bears on the development of classes that do not have common physical characteristics.

In 1971, Sidman published an interesting case report. Sidman had selected a 17-year-old, microcephalic male, who could name common objects and who could select pictures of common objects in response to their names. The young man could not name printed words, select printed words in response to their names, or match printed words with the objects represented by those words. Sidman trained the young man to select the appropriate printed words in response to their spoken names. The subject was then able to name the words, and match the pictures with the words. These basic findings were later replicated by Sidman and Cresson (1973) with two more severely retarded young men.

Stimulated by Sidman's 1971 report, Spradlin, Cotter, and Baxley (1973) investigated the possibility that if subjects were taught to make a common response to two initially unrelated stimuli and then a new response was conditioned to one stimulus, the remaining stimulus would also control that response even though this S—R relationship was never trained or reinforced.

Spradlin et al. chose to test this notion within a match-to-sample task (Figure 1). They conceptualized the samples as stimuli and the response to the choice stimuli as responses. Initially they took a striped circle and a closed circle and conditioned them to control responding to a star and infinity-like figures, respectively. Then they substituted a horizontal bar for the striped circle and a vertical bar for the closed circle and conditioned these two new stimuli to control responding to the star and infinity-like figures. In essence, two stimuli have now been conditioned to control a single response. A third set of training trails used the striped circle and closed circle as samples but substitute a

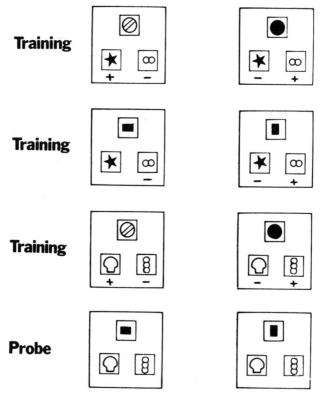

Figure 1. One-half of the training and probe slides used in Experiment II in Spradlin, Cotter, and Baxley (1973). Not shown are the eight slides in which the choice stimuli were reversed, so that the correct choices were on the right-hand position.

mushroom-like figure for the star and a vertical chain-like figure for the figure infinity sign. Finally, probe trails were introduced in which the horizontal and vertical bars were substituted as samples for the striped and closed circles and choices were the mushroom and chain-like figures.

The results were compelling. Three moderately retarded adolescents showed a high level of responding to the appropriate choice stimuli even though those choice stimuli have never been directly associated with the sample stimuli nor were the probes differentially reinforced (Figure 2). Now these results clearly are in line with the notion that if two stimuli control a common response, and through conditioning one is brought to control a second response, the remaining stimulus will also control that response. However, the research by Sidman and his colleagues indicate that while a common response may be sufficient to establish two stimuli as equivalent it is not necessary.

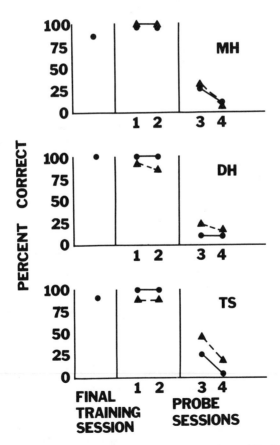

Figure 2. The results of Experiment II in the Spradlin, Cotter, and Baxley (1973) study.

While Spradlin et al. tested only one relationship among stimuli, namely the controlling properties of the samples over the choices, there are numerous other stimulus relationships they might have tested. For example, do the samples that have never been directly associated have control over each other when one is used as a sample and the other as a choice stimulus? Do the choice stimuli exhibit control over each other when one is used as a sample and the other as a choice? Finally, are the choices and samples reversible? Wetherby, Karlan, and Spradlin replicated the Spradlin, Cotter, and Baxley study with normal five-year-old children and then ran probes to answer the three above-mentioned questions. All were answered in the affirmative. Figure 3 shows the possible relations to be tested and the results with a typical subject when these results were tested. These results strongly suggest that a common response conception of generaliza-

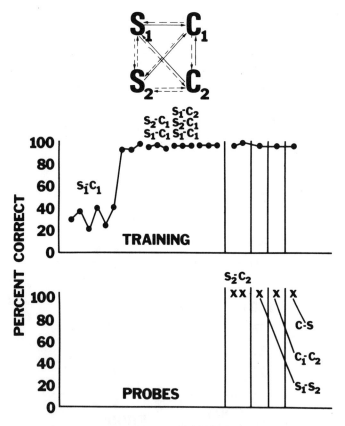

Figure 3. The possible tests for associations in the Spradlin, Cotter, and Baxley (1973) type study and the results obtained by Spradlin, Karlan, and Wetherby for a typical subject when these tests were made. The solid lines of the diagram represent trained associations. The broken lines represent possible associations.

tion is far too restrictive. What is suggested is that if stimuli are substitutable within one context, they may be treated as substitutable in other contexts.

The research of Spradlin, Cotter, and Baxley demonstrated that a stimulus class could be established if two stimuli were given the same function in a match-to-sample task. But, Spradlin et al. went on to speculate that stimulus classes might be an extremely important notion in explaining how it was that people acquired such rapid and appropriate use of vocabulary words. Taking a cue from certain psycholinguistic theorists, they suggested that if people had a concept or exhibited stimulus classes and some members of stimulus class were given a label, that label might be generalized to all of the members of the stimulus class. Dixon and Spradlin (1976) designed experiments to test this notion. They gave six moderately to mildly retarded adolescents training in which two classes of four visual stimuli within each class were established. They used the same basic type of two-choice match-to-sample task as has been described above. Each stimulus within a given class was used as both a sample stimulus and as a choice stimulus for every other stimulus within the class. After the subjects learned to select the choice from the same class, regardless of which samples or choices were presented, they were taught to select one member of each class in response to a spoken name. The trials in which the subject was given the receptive name training were intermixed into trials in which visual match-to-sample training was continued. After the subject has learned to select the correct two visual choices in response to their spoken names, trials were interspersed to determine if the subject would generalize the receptive names to the remaining three members of the classes. Three of the six subjects showed nearly complete generalization. That is, they used the name to apply to all members of a class after they had been trained to apply it to one member of the class. Two of the remaining three subjects showed generalization after thev had been given labeling training with one additional visual stimulus within each class. One subject showed generalization to the final member of the class after she had been given labeling training on three members within each class. All six subjects demonstrated the emergence of behavior that had never been directly taught. That is, they applied the label to all members of the class even though training had been given on only some members of the class.

Emergence of new behavior also occurred in the earlier studies by Sidman (1971) and Spradlin, Cotter, and Baxley (1973). What do these studies have in common? All involve the development of stimulus classes. In Sidman's research, a word and a picture are given equivalent functions by giving each the same receptive name. After establishing the word and picture as members of the same class in that task, they were then equivalent in two other tasks. Spradlin, Cotter, and Baxley established two visual stimuli as equivalent by using them as sample stimuli for the same choice. When one of them was given a new function, the other stimulus acquired that new function without direct training. Now, what kind of general statement could be made that would describe the results of these three studies? In all three studies, the stimuli were established as members of the same class through substitution; that is, each stimulus within a class could be substituted for the other stimulus or stimuli within the class without a change in the feedback reinforcement contingencies, or outcomes. In summary, one can say a concept or stimulus class consists of objects or events that are substitutable for each other within a given context. If two or more stimuli are established as functionally equivalent through training in one condition, there is an increased probability that they will be functionally equivalent in a second condition without all of the stimuli being used in direct training in that situation.

IMPLICATIONS

The research on procedures for establishing stimulus classes by equivalence training is relatively scarce and its application to nonlaboratory situations has been largely unexplored. However, the concept of stimulus class may be useful in understanding language phenomena. No one can observe the language development of children without being awed by the rapidity with which children learn their native language. This rapidity and ease has, of course, led to the postulation of innate mechanisms specifically tuned to language acquisition. However, the research that has just been presented suggests that rapid and easy development of new specific conditional discriminations can be acquired provided that one had established stimulus classes previously.

Lexical Acquisition

The research indicates that if several initially unrelated objects or events are given common nonverbal functions and then some of those stimuli are given a name, that name may be applied to other objects or events with that function without direct training. A hypothetical example will illustrate how this might occur in the child's natural environment. Consider the class of objects called toys. There will be certain responses allowed or required with every item in that class. Children will be allowed to hold toys, to play with them on the rug, or to place them in their toy boxes. Moreover, there may be a set of not-allowed behaviors with toys. Perhaps they are not to be placed on the stairs, in the kitchen cabinet, or on the dining room table. Suppose on some occasions the parent says, "Pick up your toys," and a child is reinforced for this activity. Now it is unlikely that the total set of toys will be out on the occasion when such a command is given. Yet that command, on later occasions, is likely to result in the child picking up toys that were present on earlier "pick up" training sessions as well as those that were not. In other words, the nonverbal function of playing with, and holding, may establish the toys as a class, so that when some toys are given the label "toy," that label is extended to other members of the class. Moreover, the child will learn a class of nontoys that includes radios, pipes, wristwatches, glasses, etc. These are items that the child is not allowed to take down on the floor and hold, and hence the label "toy" is unlikely to generalize to these items. Suppose father brings home two new items, a "thingamabob" and a "gismo." He gives the child the thingamabob and demonstrates how it works and then allows the child to play with it. He puts the gismo on the table and does not allow the child to play with it. Later he says, "It's time to pick up your toys." The child picks up the thingamabob with the toys and leaves the gismo. The thingamabob has been established as a toy through a nonverbal function equivalence to other toys. At another time the father might establish that an object could be held, played with on the floor, and picked up with the rest of the toys by simply labeling it as a "toy."

Werner and Kaplan (1963) demonstrated that if a nonsense word was used in a series of sentences that ordinarily were appropriate to a specific word people would soon recognize that nonsense word as meaning the same as the specific word. For example, the sentences "A corplum may be used for support," "Corplums may be used to close off space," "Wet corplums do not burn," and "The painter used a corplum to mix his paint," may lead a listener to say "A corplum is a stick." The listener may also then generate additional sentences such as "Children shouldn't play with sharp corplums," or "Corplums and stones may break my bones but words will never harm me." In this example the word "corplum" has been *substituted* into a series of verbal contexts in which the word stick occurs. Once "corplum" has occurred in a number of such contexts, it is established in a class with the word "stick," then new and appropriate uses of the word "corplum" emerge.

Phonemic Substitutions

When one considers substitutability as the key factor in the establishment of a stimulus class it becomes rather apparent why people show skill in decoding at a phenomenic level. Take the example of a child who substitutes $/\phi/$ for $/s/$ in his or her speech. The listener will have little problem understanding the speech as soon as the child says a few sentences, such as, "My thoes and thockings are wet," or "My coat is thoaking wet," or "The thun is awfully bright today." The listener will quickly expect the child to say things like "The horthes had thilver thaddles." The $/o/$ for this child is functionally equivalent to $/s/$, and in this context it will soon be established as equivalent to $/s/$ for the listener.

SUMMARY

In summary:

1. People often behave appropriately in novel situations.
2. The terms concept and stimulus class are often introduced in discussions of novel, yet appropriate behavior.
3. Laboratory studies demonstrate that classes can be established by giving initially unrelated stimuli common functions through substitution.

4. Such classes, based on substitution or equivalence, may be a powerful concept for explaining novel, yet appropriate behavior, which occurs in natural situations.

REFERENCES

Dixon, M. H., and Spradlin, J. E. (1976) Establishing stimulus equivalence among retarded adolescents. J. Exp. Child Psychol. 21:144.

Sidman, M. (1971) Reading and auditory-visual equivalences. J. Speech Hear. Res. 14:5.

Sidman, M., and Cresson, O. (1973) Reading and crossmodal transfer of stimulus equivalences in severe retardation. Amer. J. Ment. Defic. 77:515.

Spradlin, J. E., Cotter, V. W., and Baxley, M. (1973) Establishing a conditional discrimination without direct training: A study of transfer with retarded adolescents. Amer. J. Ment. Defic. 77:556.

Werner, H., and Kaplan, B. (1963) Symbol Formation. New York: Wiley & Sons.

RESEARCH TO PRACTICE IN MENTAL RETARDATION
Education and Training, Volume II
Edited by Peter Mittler
Copyright 1977 I.A.S.S.M.D.

LINGUISTIC AND EXTRALINGUISTIC INFORMATION IN LANGUAGE TRAINING OF MENTALLY HANDICAPPED CHILDREN

R. Grieve[1] and W. I. Fraser[2]
[1] *University of St. Andrews, Scotland*
[2] *Lynebank Hospital and Edinburgh University, Scotland*

In previous studies of language dysfunction in mentally handicapped children (e.g., Fraser and Grieve, 1975), we have found that the retarded child's auditory attention to language is lower than his visual attention to the extralinguistic situation with which the language is concerned. This suggests a need to enhance the retarded child's attention to language in language remediation. However, the retarded child's auditory attention to language cannot readily be enhanced in a direct way—for example, by increasing the strength of the linguistic signal compared to the background environmental noise (Fraser and Grieve, 1975). Therefore, we have recently been pursuing a further observation, that the retarded child's auditory attention to language is highly correlated with his visual attention to the attendant extralinguistic situation (Grieve and Williamson, 1977). In this chapter, we wish to consider some of the problems that face the child in processing linguistic and extralinguistic information, to summarise some of our preliminary findings in recent experiments, and to indicate directions in which further inquiry might proceed.

Those who study language development in normal children appreciate that the child's acquisition of language is an immense achievement, one that results from the complex functioning of intricate mechanisms, and this view will be supported by those experienced in working with mentally handicapped children who suffer linguistic difficulties. And yet, however much we argue that this is the case, or however hard we try to appreciate that this is the case, it is still exceptionally difficult for adult language users like ourselves to begin to understand the extent of the child's problem in acquiring language. Let us attempt to illustrate (after Clark, 1975). First consider some linguistic information:

Tha am fear a tha am meadhon na deilbh seo air a chòmhdach mar an t-Easbuig MacUalraig a Cill-Rìmhinn, fear de na feadhainn a stéidhich an Oil-thaigh. Thogadh an dealbh seo ann an Eaglais Collaisd an t-Slànuighear, collaisd a thog an t-Easbuig mu mheadhon na còigeamh linne deug. Air an laimh dheis chi sibh a'chùbaid anns an do shearmonaich Iain Knox, a reir aithris. Tha uaigh an Easbuig MacUalraig air an laimh chearr, faisg air far a bheil an duine 'na sheasamh ach tha i ro fhada thall, agus chan fhaicear i.

Now consider that the extralinguistic situation, to which this linguistic informa-tion refers, is a picture of a man, dressed as a bishop, photographed inside a church. Now reconsider the linguistic information, this time knowing what extralinguistic situation is being referred to. What happens? The answer, of course, is "nothing." *Because we do not know the language.* And of course this is the problem that faces the child when he is trying to acquire language. That is, he must learn to map (spoken) linguistic information, from a language he does not know, on to extralinguistic situations to which the linguistic information refers.

A translation of the linguistic information serves to remind us that this is in fact only part of the child's problem, for of course language serves a diverse set of ends and does not simply consist of words that refer to objects:

The man in the middle of this picture is dressed as Bishop James Kennedy of St. Andrews, one of the early founders of the University. The picture was taken in St. Salvators College Kirk, which Bishop Kennedy founded in the middle of the fifteenth century. On the right of the picture is a pulpit from which John Knox is reputed to have preached. Bishop Kennedy's tomb lies to the left of where the man is standing, but it cannot be seen in the picture.

Note how the linguistic information refers to objects that can be seen in the picture (the man, the pulpit), but also to objects that are not apparent (the tomb). The language refers to present events (the man standing in the middle of the picture), but also to events in the past (the founding of the kirk in the fifteenth century). Of course the language may serve the function of directing attention to an object (e.g., the pulpit on the right), but note how easy it is to forget that this function of language is heavily dependent on knowledge of meaning: unless we know the meaning of pulpit, we can make an error about what our attention is being drawn to. While our present illustration is clearly intended for an adult audience, we have presented evidence elsewhere that similar problems face the child in understanding and producing language during the early stages of acquisition (e.g., Grieve and Hoogenraad, 1976).

In a sense all this is obvious, but perhaps it is so obvious that it lets us forget the high-level, complex skills that are involved in language processing and language acquisition. The child has not yet developed such skills when he is first faced with acquiring language, and while we cannot begin to consider here the range of phonological, syntactic, semantic, and pragmatic skills involved in language development, we can at least begin to consider the part of the problem we have tried to illustrate—that is, the child's mapping of linguistic information on to extralinguistic situations. While some preliminary study has been conducted on this topic with normal adults (e.g., Clark, Carpenter, and Just, 1973; Trabasso 1973), and with normal children (e.g., Donaldson and Lloyd, 1972; McGarrigle and Donaldson, 1975; Clark, 1975; Hoogenraad, Grieve, and Campbell, 1976), here we mostly concentrate attention on mentally handicapped children.

In considering the integration of linguistic and extralinguistic information, three topics immediately arise. These concern the effects of order of presentation of the two types of information; the types of linguistic information presented; and the implications for remedial training techniques. Thus, in recent studies we have asked if, compared with normal children, mentally handicapped children find it easier to integrate linguistic and extralinguistic information when these are presented simultaneously, or in succession: either sentence before picture, or picture before sentence. Also, we have asked whether mentally handicapped children experience differential difficulty in processing different types of linguistic information, such as instructions principally involved with different parts of speech, for example, nouns, adjectives, prepositions, and verbs. We have done this by presenting normal and mentally handicapped children with (spoken) sentences and pictures of varying sorts, as indicated in Table 1.

Such information has been presented in three ways—picture before sentence, sentence before picture, and sentence simultaneously with picture. (Mode of presentation has also been varied, so far without effect. That is, we have not detected differences, at least using error as a response measure, between presentations of extralinguistic material on cards, slides, and video tape.) These studies

Table 1. Sentences and pictures

Sentence	Picture
Show me the *apple*(noun)	apple, orange, knife, fork
Show me the *white* dog(adj)	white dog
	black dog(1)
	white cow(2)
	black cow(3)
Show me the bottle *under* the shelf (prepn)	bottle under shelf
	bottle on shelf(1)
	book under shelf(2)
	book on shelf(3)
Show me the man *pushing* the barrow (verb)	man pushing barrow
	man pulling barrow(1)
	boy pushing barrow(2)
	boy pulling barrow(3)

are described elsewhere (Grieve and Knowles, in preparation), and here we are not concerned with their detail, but rather with their more general implications.

First, using error as a response measure, we have found that the order in which linguistic and extralinguistic information is presented has no significant effect on performance. This is broadly in accord with a result obtained at the Hester Adrian Research Centre in Manchester by Mittler and Wheldall, who also found little effect on error rate as a function of whether linguistic information was presented before, after, or simultaneous with extralinguistic information (Mittler, 1973; Wheldall and Mittler, 1977). However, this is not to say that there are no effects, for both in our studies and in those of Mittler, error has been used as an index of performance. And, of course, accurate or inaccurate responses merely reflect the end result of the process of integration of the two types of information, rather than illuminate directly the ongoing process itself. If language has a directive function (Luria, 1959), there should be certain effects of order of presentation of linguistic and extralinguistic information. We presume that such effects occur, but are not being detected by a gross response measure such as error rate, which fails to reflect immediately the ongoing process. Therefore, in future study of this topic, finer-grained response measures will be required.

With respect to our second topic—linguistic information concerning different parts of speech—we have observed that young normal children, and both high and low grade mentally handicapped children, experience comparatively little difficulty with nouns, rather more difficulty with adjectives, and most difficulty with prepositions and verbs. These results of course must be treated with caution. For example, increasing difficulty arises not only with increasingly complex instructions for the different parts of speech (Sentences, Table 1), the extralinguistic situations referred to also increase in complexity (Pictures, Table 1). However, that the results arise from the increasing difficulty of mapping one type of information on to another, not simply from the increasing complexity of either taken separately, is suggested, for example, by differences in verbs. Intransitive verbs (e.g., Show me the man standing) are easier than transitives (e.g., Show me the boy throwing the ball), which cautions us against assuming that it is parts of speech by themselves that lead to differential difficulty; rather, it is their role in the linguistic information, and how that linguistic information interacts with the extralinguistic environment. Also, our studies are preliminary and they may as yet suffer from a frequent difficulty with language research discussed by Clark (1973): that is, because we have found a certain pattern of results with particular nouns, adjectives, prepositions, and verbs, this does not imply that the pattern holds for nouns, adjectives, prepositions, and verbs in general. Further sampling of the language is required.

With respect to our remaining topic, what implications might this work have for remedial techniques concerned with language training of mentally handicapped children? We would argue that there are several. For example, it might be supposed that mentally handicapped children will find it more difficult to process two types of information simultaneously than to process the two types taken one at a time, in succession. However, with auditory information from sentences, and visual information from pictures to which the auditory information refers, this is not the case. This reminds us that part of the problem of language is concerned not with linguistic information by itself, nor with extralinguistic information by itself, but rather how one maps on to the other. That is, we need to consider how linguistic and extralinguistic information are *integrated* in language processing.

Also, while it may be observed, say, that mentally handicapped children find verbs more difficult than nouns (e.g., Jeffree, 1972), indicating a need for training on verbs, our studies serve to remind us that when the notion of "parts of speech" is unpacked, it in fact concerns how such parts of speech function in the language, and how this relates to extralinguistic information. Once we have some idea of how such processes operate, then we will have some idea of *what* requires remediation. (How to remedy most effectively what requires remediation is of course a distinct issue, but knowledge of what requires remediation is clearly primary.)

Further, by distinguishing different kinds of error that arise in our results, some more detailed information on what requires remediation is indicated. Three types of error can be distinguished, concerning the alternative pictures presented for inspection. For adjectives, prepositions, and verbs (this analysis is not appropriate for nouns), Type 1 errors involve pointing to Alternative Picture (1), Type 2 errors involve Alternative (2), and Type 3 errors involve Alternative (3) (Table 1). Thus, in Type 1 errors the subject of the sentence is correct but the part of speech being examined is wrong; in Type 2 errors the subject of the sentence is wrong but the part of speech is correct; and in Type 3 errors the subject and part of speech are both wrong. What we have found in our studies to date is that there tends to be a preponderance of Type 1 errors over the other two types. That is, the initial subject nominal in an instruction tends to be processed correctly. What might be happening here is that the child tends to pay greater attention to initial rather than later segments of the sentences presented. However, this by itself will not do, for the preponderance of Type 1 errors is especially marked for adjectives in both high and low grade retarded children: if results arose simply from higher attention to initial sentential position, this would not be expected with adjectives.

Again, we do not pursue detail here, concerning either data or explanations. However, the general implication seems clear. If study of the integration of linguistic and extralinguistic information can identify the nature of the errors the mentally handicapped child makes, this begins to indicate the experiments that will specify what requires remediation.

REFERENCES

Clark, E. V. (1975) Knowledge, context and strategy in the acquisition of meaning. *In* Developmental Psycholinguistics: Theory and Applications (Ed. Dato, D. P.). Georgetown University Round Table on Languages and Linguistics, p. 77.

Clark, H. H. (1973) The language-as-fixed-effect fallacy: a critique of language statistics in psychological research. J. Verbal Learn. Behav. 12:335.

Clark, H. H., Carpenter, P. A., and Just, M. A. (1973) On the meeting of semantics and perception. *In* Visual Information Processing (Ed. Chase, W. G.). New York: Academic Press, p. 311.

Donaldson, M., and Lloyd, P. (1972) Sentences and situations: Children's judgements of match and mismatch. *In* Problèmes Actuels en Psycholinguistique (Ed. Bresson, F.). Paris: CNRS, p. 73.

Fraser, W. I., and Grieve, R. (1975) Recent studies of communication problems in the mentally handicapped. Health Bull. 33:341.

Grieve, R., and Hoogenraad, R. (1976) Using language if you don't have much. *In* New Approaches to Language Mechanisms (Eds. Walker, E. C. T., and Wales, R. J.). Amsterdam: North Holland.

Grieve, R., and Knowles, E. Studies of sentence-picture processing in normal and mentally handicapped children (in preparation).

Grieve, R., and Williamson, K. (1977) Aspects of auditory and visual attention to narrative material in normal and mentally handicapped children. J. Child. Psychol. Psychiat. (in press).

Hoogenraad, R., Grieve, R., and Campbell, R. (1976) Comprehension as an interactive process. Paper presented at International Conference on the Psychology of Language, University of Stirling, June, 1976.

Jeffree, D. (1972) Assessment and remediation of language comprehension and production in severely subnormal children. SSRC (London) Grant HR 840, Third Progress Report. University of Manchester: Hester Adrian Research Centre.

Luria, A. R. (1959) The Role of Speech in the Regulation of Normal and Abnormal Behavior. Oxford: Pergamon Press.

McGarrigle, J., and Donaldson, M. (1975) Conservation accidents. Cognition 3:341.

Mittler, P. J. (1973) Assessment and remediation of language comprehension and production in severely subnormal children. SSRC (London) Grant HR 840, Final Report. University of Manchester: Hester Adrian Research Centre.

Trabasso, T. (1973) Language and cognition. *In* Visual Information Processing (Ed. Chase, W. G.). New York: Academic Press, p. 439.

Wheldall, K., and Mittler, P. J. (1977) On presenting pictures and sentences: the effect of presentation order on sentence comprehension in normal and ESN children. Brit. J. Educ. Psychol. (in press).

RESEARCH TO PRACTICE IN MENTAL RETARDATION
Education and Training, Volume II
Edited by Peter Mittler
Copyright 1977 I.A.S.S.M.D.

LANGUAGE PATTERNS OF ADOLESCENT AUTISTICS
A Comparison Between English and German

C. Baltaxe and J. Q. Simmons III
*The Neuropsychiatric Institute, University of California,
Los Angeles, 760 Westwood Plaza, Los Angeles, California
90024, United States*

Recently numerous studies have focused on language in the understanding of childhood psychosis (Rutter, 1971a, 1971b; Churchill, 1972). Speech and language abnormalities are early characteristics in the development of the disorder and include lack or delay of development, echolalia, problems in language comprehension, lack of spontaneity, and peculiarities of pitch, intonation, and rhythm (Kanner, 1943; Asperger, 1944; Rutter, 1966; Baltaxe and Simmons, 1975).

Some of the specific studies of these deficits described abnormalities of voice, phonation, rhythm, articulation, and language (Goldfarb et al., 1956, 1972) and correlated the number of words and average length of utterances with the clinical assessment of the severity of the disease (Wolff and Chess, 1965). Others reported that exact repetitions in echolalia indicated poorer language development and that a greater degree of mitigation indicated a higher level of linguistic ability (Shapiro, Roberts, and Fish, 1970). Studies comparing autistic and aphasic language showed that the differences between the two were less than previously thought, and that a specific profile utilizing the parameters studied could not be used as a diagnostic tool (Bartak, Rutter, and Cox, 1975; Baker, Cantwell, Rutter, and Bartak, 1976). In contrast, a study of speech and language in adolescent autistics by Simmons and Baltaxe (1975) suggests that a specific clustering of linguistic deficits may be unique to autism. These investigators found that such deficits relate to the prosodic features of language and at the same time involve violations of syntactic, semantic, and situational constraints.

Detailed linguistic studies have only been carried out for English-speaking autistics, although some references to similar speech and language abnormalities have been made in the German literature (Asperger, 1944; Bosch, 1962; Nissen, 1963). The question arises whether the abnormalities found are universal in nature or whether there are aspects of the linguistic deficit that are language dependent. Because there are differences in the structure of English and German, it would be of interest to investigate this question by comparing the language deficits found earlier in English-speaking autistic adolescents (Simmons and Baltaxe, 1975) with those found in a similar group of German-speaking autistic adolescents.

SUBJECTS

The subjects were four English-speaking and four German-speaking male autistic adolescents, matched as closely as possible for age, IQ, social class, and basic disorder (Table 1).

Table 1. Patient characteristics

Background	English speaking ($N = 4$)	German speaking ($N = 4$)
Age range	14–21 years	12–18 years
Age at onset	6 months–2 years	1–2 years
IQ	86–120	72–113
Early language abnormality	yes	yes

METHODS

Language samples were obtained in an informal situation by means of an interview designed for this study. The interviews were tape recorded and transcribed by a trained linguist using gross phonemic transcription.

The speech samples were analyzed by the two investigators using Goldfarb's criteria relating to abnormalities of volume, pitch, voice quality, rate of speech, phrasing, fluency, stress, intonation, and inflection. The data were then further analyzed following contemporary linguistic theory (Chomsky, 1957; 1965). English and German samples were compared, and those features that were common to both languages were separated from those features that only occurred in one language.

RESULTS

Common Deficits

Analysis Utilizing Goldfarb's (1972) Criteria   In the earlier study of English-speaking autistic adolescents, all of the subjects showed abnormalities in point-in-time vocal activity and in temporal sequencing. Similar deficits were observed for all of the German subjects. These included abnormalities in volume (too low, fading, whispering, with insufficient force for stress, too loud, with excessive force for stress). All of the English and three of the German subjects showed abnormalities of pitch level (too high, too low, showing excessive variation). All evidenced faults relating to speech rate (too slow, with insufficient variation, or staccato) as well as incorrect phrasing, and faults related to fluency (hesitations, repetitions, and prolongations). All of the subjects showed faults of stress (incorrect word stress) and intonation (insufficient pitch rise, excessive pitch rise, excessive inflection, contraindicated inflection, and stereotyped intonation).

Linguistic Analysis In the earlier study of the English-speaking autistic adolescents, the most general characteristic of all language deficient subjects had been a dysfluency feature. Linguistic patterning was disrupted on various levels of structure. Phonological patterning was disrupted due to the repetition of word initial sounds and syllables, or the repetition of entire words. Morphological patterning was disrupted because of a change in tense or person marker. Syntactic patterning was disrupted because of an apparent change in the intended meaning of an utterance. Dysfluency also was seen in perseveration on topic and the telescoping of ideas.

A similar dysfluency feature could also be observed in the German subjects.

Examples

a. Phonological patterning: darf ich—darf ich mal dahin
 (may I—may I go there)
b. Morphological patterning: ich hab—ich bin . . .
 (I have—I am)
c. Syntactic patterning: Nein das können die net—das machen die—das—die haben keine Zeit immer—das machen die net (no they can't do that—they do—they—that—they never have any time—they can't do that)

In the earlier study of English-speaking adolescent autistics, those subjects who showed deficits in the prosodic features of language (Goldfarb's list) also showed deficits in three other areas of language. These deficits were characterized in terms of violations of syntactic, semantic, and sociolinguistic co-occurrence constraints. Such violations were not systematic, because in some instances the rules governing the constraints were adhered to. Consequently, they had to be viewed as a "slipping-up" on a particular rule rather than its total absence. The same clustering was observed for the German subjects. However, as opposed to the English subjects, a considerable range of linguistic ability existed as measured by mean utterance length. The subject with the lowest mean utterance length (three words) also showed the highest frequency of the various types of violations. The following examples will illustrate some of these violations seen in German, with English examples, where comparable, listed under b.

Syntactic Constraints

1. Violations involving prepositions
   a. Ja, es ist mein Geburtstag. Ich hab nämlich grad *eine Woche* Geburtstag gehabt. (Target: ... *vor einer Woche* Geburtstag....) (Translation: Yes, it's my birthday. I had my birthday *for a week.* Target: ... my birthday was *a week ago*)
   b. He (the bird) was driven *from extinction* (Target: ... *to extinction*)
2. Violations involving adverbials
   a. *Jetzt warens* in der Steinzeit und jetzt sinds in der Zukunft. (Target: erst warens in der Steinzeit....) (Translation: *Now they were* in the stone age and now they are in the future. Target: *first they were* in the stone age...)
   b. Last Wednesday nights now *I watch* ... (Target: *Last Wednesday* night *I watched* or *Wednesday nights* I watch...)
3. Violations involving subject/verb agreement
   a. Heisst Erbsen Schote auf Englisch? (Target: *Heissen Erbsen* Schote auf Englisch?) (Translation: Is peas called pods in English? Target: Are peas called pods in English?)
   b. A few lambs *gets missing.* (Target: A few *lambs get* lost.)
4. Deletions
   a. Der Ball—wenn man also einen Ball durch ein Tor geworfen hat, dann darf man noch einmal... (Translation: The ball—therefore if one has thrown a ball through a gate, then one may again...)
   b. Then mankind foolishly cut down trees—not replacing—

Semantic Constraints

1. Inappropriate antecedent reference
   a. *Q* Wo hast du *die* (ref.she/her) denn getroffen? (Translation: Where did you meet *her?*)
   A Also *die waren* ziemlich in der Nähe. (Target: ...*die war*...) (Translation: They were rather close by. Target: ...*she was*...)
   b. Mankind is considering—*he is* considering—. (Target: mankind is considering—*it is* considering—)
2. Opposite reference from that of intended meaning
   a. Die Musik gefällt mir aber, aber ich *hör sie nicht* gern. (Target: ... *denn ich hör sie* so gern.) (Translation: Music pleases me—but I don't like to hear it. Target: ... I like to listen to it).
   b. He is getting rarer and rarer because *so many* of them are left. (Target: ... *so few* of them are left.)

3. Inappropriate word use where the word had some, but not all of the syntactic and semantic features of the target word
   a. *Vorher* zeichne ich mit dem Bleistift, *nachher* mit den Farben. (Target: ... *erst*... *dann*...) (Translation: *Previously* I draw with the pencil, *subsequently* with the crayons. Target: *first*... *then*...).
   b. *Q* Why do you think he did it?
      A *Questions me.*
      (Target: that's what I would like to know/ I am asking myself.)
4. Telescoping of ideas where both syntactic and semantic constraints are broken
   a. *Q* Was zeichnest du denn am liebsten? (Translation: What do you like to draw best?)
      A Sehr oft auf dem Schiff auf den Meeren und Westernstadt und Ferien und viel Sonnenblumen und Weltraum und Baum und 'ne Stadt und. .
      (Translation: Very often on the ship on the seas and Westernstadt? and vacation and many sunflowers, and space and a tree and a city and...)
   b. Sometimes the foreman is—gets—and that's when—what gets the foreman angry—sometimes he asks stuff and that he couldn't get any answer out of such and such.
5. Meaningless additions and insertions
   a. Wie viele Stunden hast du denn schon *oft* gebraucht? (Translation: How many hours have you already *often* needed?)
   b. Ads for different products *more or less.*
6. Vagueness of referent
   a. *Q* Was ist denn deine Lieblingsfarbe?
      A Weis.
      Q Warum?
      A Na ja, jeder hat seine Meinung.
      (Translation: *Q* What is your favorite color?
      A white.
      Q Why?
      A Well, everyone has his opinion.)
   b. *Q* What are you planning to do?
      A Just looking ahead in the future for all I care.
7. Inconsistency of response
   a. *Q* Was gefällt dir am besten in der Schule?
      A Englisch und deutsch.
      Q Sprichst du englisch?
      A Wir haben noch net englisch gelernt.
      (Translation: *Q* What do you like best in school?
      A English and German.

Q Do you speak English?
A We haven't learned English yet)

Instances of echolalia could be observed in the German samples. Echolalia occurred with the highest frequency in the subject poorest in linguistic ability as measured by utterance length. Both English and German subjects evidenced instances of direct quotes that may perhaps be considered a residue of earlier echolalia.

Situational Constraints

The most prevalent violation of situational constraints for the English subjects had been an apparent inability to switch from a formal to an informal style of speaking, giving their conversation a sense of formality and literariness. The same was true for the German subjects.

Examples

a. Ich bin sehr stolz, dass ich versetzt worden bin. Ich freue mich.
(Translation: I am very proud that I was promoted, I am happy.)
b. *Q* Do you have a girlfriend?
A No, I haven't met such a nice lovely young lady as yet.

In addition to this formal or literary way of expression usually associated with the written language, the subjects frequently used linguistic expressions more appropriate for an adult speaker, giving their conversation a sense of precocity.

Examples

a. Ich will so ein Schloss haben. *Das macht mich wahnsinnig* wenn ich das nicht hab. (Translation: I want such a lock. It *drives me crazy* if I can't have it.)
b. Where in the heck is the *goddamned blonde?*

In other instances sociolinguistic norms governing discourse between younger and older speakers were not observed, demonstrating a general lack of social sensitivity and an absence of a sense of humor.

Examples

a. *Q* Gibt es Blumen in der Blumenschule?
A *No so ein Quatsch.*
(Translation: *Q* Are there flowers in the Flower School?
A *What nonsense.*
b. *Q* I'm listening, but I'm curious, what's fun for you?
A I refuse to tell you, *you interrupted.* Now I'm not going to tell you.

A lack of linguistic self-restraint and poor social judgment was also evidenced in expressions such as the following:

Example

a. *Q* Und wer ist hier den du gerne hast?
    A ... den Thomas net, *der ärgert mich, den will ich tot haben.*
    (Translation: *Q* And who do you like best here?
    A Not Thomas, he angers me, I'd like him dead.)
b. *Q* What do you do when you get angry?
    A Sometimes, when I get *angry I rip things off the wall and that's what I'd like to do with that unit.*

All of the above examples show a lack of mastery of the sociolinguistic norms and constraints that are acquired in the course of normal language development and that appear, at the very least, incomplete in the autistic subjects.

This lack also became apparent in the confusion of the polite and familiar forms of address 'Sie' and 'du' that is made in German but not in English. The German subjects used these forms almost interchangeably in the same verbal exchange. In addition a third form consisting of 'ihr' and 'euch' (2nd pers., plur., fam., personal pronoun) also occurred.

Examples

a. Wann fahren *Sie* nach Amerika wieder?
    (Translation: When are *you* going back to America? (formal))
    Da fahrst *du* dahin?
    (Translation: *You're* going there? (familiar))
    Weil *Sie* doch amerikanisch reden. *Red halt* deutsch.
    (Translation: Well, because *you* speak American (formal) Go ahead speak German. (familiar))
b. Auch die Türschlingen gebraucht *ihr* garnicht.
    (Translation: Also the doorhandles *you* don't use at all.)
    ... und wenn ich *euch* vermiss
    (Translation: ... and if I miss *you*).

Deficits Specific to German

In addition to confusions in polite and informal address, the German sample showed several other deficits not shared by their English counterparts. At least in part, those deficits must be considered language dependent. The most prevalent of these deficits consisted of omissions, particularly of prepositions, definite and indefinite articles, and third person singular personal pronouns. Frequently these omissions entailed incorrect morphological markers in the associated noun phrase.

Examples of Omissions and Prepositions

a. Meistens *schimpft er die Kinder.* (Target: *. . . mit den Kindern.*) *Mir schimpft* er selten. (Target: *mit mir* schimpft er selten.)
   (Translation: Mostly he *scolds the kids.* He doesn't scold me much. German requires preposition *'mit'* and inflection for dative.)
b. *Letzte Zeit* kommt er wieder. (Target: *. . . in letzter Zeit. . .*
   (Translation: Recently he came again. German requires preposition "in" and inflection for dative.)

Examples of Omissions of Articles

a. *in Stadt* fahren. (Target: *in die* Stadt fahren)
   (Translation: Go *into city.* Target: go *to the* city)
b. Am 5. Stock kann man doch *Treppe laufen.* (Target: . . . kann man doch *die Treppe hoch*laufen.)
   (Translation: One can walk up stairway *to 5th floor.* (Target: One can walk up *the* stairway to *the* 5th floor)

At times the noun phrase was also marked incorrectly for case despite the presence of a preposition and in cases where prepositions were not obligatory.

Examples

a. . . . mit den Thomas net. (Target: . . . mit *dem* Thomas net—)
   (Translation: . . . not with Thomas. Target: German requires inflection for dative.)
b. . . . mit *diese Dinger* da. (Target: . . . mit *diesen Dingern* da.)
   (Translation . . . with these things there. Target: German requires inflection for dative.)

Omissions of pronouns, especially third person singular pronouns, occurred with some frequency.

Examples

a. *Kann* doch von der Tür abmachen. (Target: kannst es doch von der Tür abmachen.)
   (Translation: *Get* off the door. Target: *You* can get *it* off the door.)
b. *ist* ein Fernsehprogram. (Target: *Es ist* ein Fernsehprogram.)
   (Translation: *is* a television program. Target: *It is* a television program.)

The first person singular personal pronoun was also often omitted in initial position.

Examples

a. mag Autobus. (Target: *ich* mag den Autobus.)
(Translation: like bus. Target: *I* like the bus)

Verbs were also marked incorrectly for tense and person.

Examples

a. Meine Mama he*isse* Gudrun. (Target: . . . he*isst* Gudrun.)
(Translation: My mommy's name *be* Gudrun. Target: . . . *is* Gudrun.)
b. *Kann* doch von der Tür abmachen. (Target: *kannst es* doch. . .)
(Translation: can get off the door. Target: you can get it off. . .)

Additional problems that may be language-specific related to both grammatical and natural gender confusion. German distinguishes three grammatical genders, which need to be acquired for each noun and which are reflected by differences in articles (definite article: der, die, das; indefinite article: ein, einer, eines) and in inflectional endings in the noun phrase.

Examples of Grammatical Gender Confusion

a. *ein* Schachtel Pralinen. (Target: *eine* Schachtel Pralinen.)
(Translation: a box (masc.) of candy. Target: . . . a box (fem.) of candy.)
b. *Q* Was spielst du?
A Trommel, mit dem, mit dem Xylophon und mit *der* Glockenkranz
(Target: . . . mit *dem* Glockenkranz.)
Translation: *Q* What do you play?
A Drum, with the, with the xylophone and *with the* Glocken-
kranz. (Target: German noun is masculine)

This apparent difficulty also extended to the category of natural gender.

Examples

a. Ich hab keinen Doktor hier—*die Grosstanten*—eine heisst Frau Bretzig, eine heisst Martha, *eine* heisst auch Michael, so'n grosser Mann.
(Translation: I don't have a doctor here—*the great aunts*—one is named Mrs. Bretzig, one is named Martha, and *one* is also called Michael, such a big man.)
b. *Q* Has du einen guten Freund? Wie heisst er?
A Claudia.

Translation: *Q*   Do you have a good friend (masc.); What is his name?
              A   Claudia (fem.).

DISCUSSION

This comparative study shows that both the English and German subjects exhibit a cluster of linguistic deficits that appear to be universal to the disorder. These apparently universal features include deficits in the prosody of language, a general dysfluency characteristic, and violations of syntactic, semantic, and situational constraints. As did the English autistics, the German group also showed perseveration on topic and residues of echolalia.

In both languages these violations can be characterized as slipping up on rules. While the inappropriate use of prepositions was more prevalent in English, omissions of prepositions and articles were particularly frequent for the German samples. There are no further consequences to the inappropriate use of prepositions in English. On the other hand, omissions of prepositions in German frequently entailed an incorrect morphological marking in the associated noun phrase as well. There seems no obvious way to account for such omissions in German although they seem to represent a language-dependent deficit. Inspection of less mature autistic German language samples provided further evidence that these deficits were not incidental to the adolescent samples, but that they represented a persistence of earlier abnormalities. It may perhaps be hypothesized that morphological complexity associated with prepositional use in German acts as a deterrent to the use of prepositions. The resultant errors are compounded by the use of noun phrases in their unmarked form. Similarly, German requires grammatical gender for each noun. Although there are a few select suffixes that specify grammatical gender, no specific rules exist for the majority of nouns, and grammatical gender has to be learned separately for each noun. This adds complexity to the specification of each noun. The German subjects evidenced difficulties in this area by their confusion of gender markers. Therefore, they may, with some degree of awareness, opt to omit articles altogether, as is seen in the data. The seeming difficulties in natural gender distinction in the German subjects may be related. This distinction is marked with greater frequency for German than for English nouns (e.g., German = Freund-Freundin; English = friend). The confusion in natural gender by the autistic subjects may be compounded ·by a frequently reported lack of recognition of persons. This could be a cognitive deficit more difficult to identify in English because the language is not as highly marked for natural gender distinction.

German also evidenced a language-dependent violation of situational constraints related to the use of the familiar/polite form of address. This distinction is not made in the English language. The language-dependent deficit can be characterized as a specific instance of the general lack of social sensitivity displayed by the autistic subjects.

The above study provides evidence for the hypothesis that linguistic abnormalities associated with the autistic disorder, while forming a common core, show some variation depending on the language studied. The comparison of the samples of English and German subjects appears to indicate that such variation may be dependent on more complex aspects of linguistic structure. Such added complexity may well bring to light specific cognitive deficits. Other comparative studies, especially those involving nonIndoEuropean and tone languages would be useful in separating those deficits that may be universal to autism from those that are language-dependent.

SUMMARY

Language disabilities in autism have been found to persist into adolescence. Analysis of these disabilities reveals specific areas of linguistic deficit. The present study compares the language patterns of eight adolescent autistics, four English-speaking, and four German-speaking. It focuses on those features of language that may be the result of the basic disorder in contrast to those that can be attributed to differences in the structures of the two languages.

REFERENCES

Asperger, H. (1944) Die 'Autistischen Psychopathen' im Kindesalter. Arch. Psychiat. NervKrankh. 117 1:76.

Baker, L., Cantwell, D., Rutter, M., and Bartak, L. (1976) Language and autism. In Autism, Diagnosis, Current Research and Management (Ed. Ritvo, E. R.). New York: Spectrum Publications.

Baltaxe, C., and Simmons, J. Q. (1975) Language in childhood psychosis: A Review. J. Speech Hear. Dis. 40:439.

Bartak, L., Rutter, M., and Cox, A. (1975) A comparative study of infantile autism and specific development receptive language disorder. 1. The children. Brit. J. Psychiat. 126:127.

Bosch, G. (1962) Der Frükindliche Autismus. Monogr. Gesamtgeb. Neurol. Psychiat. 96:1–121.

Chomsky, N. (1957) Syntactic Structures. The Hague: Mouton, E. Co.

Chomsky, N. (1965) Aspects of the Theory of Syntax. Cambridge, Massachusetts: MIT Press.

Churchill, D. (1972) The relation of infantile autism and early childhood schizophrenia to developmental language disorders of childhood. J. Autism Child. Schizo. 2:182.

Goldfarb, W., Braunstein, P., and Lorge, I. (1956) A study of speech patterns in a group of schizophrenic children. Amer. J. Orthopsychiat. 26:544.

Goldfarb, W., Goldfarb, N., Braunstein, P., and Scholl, H. (1972) Speech and language faults of schizophrenic children. J. Autism Child. Schizo. 2:219.

Kanner, L. (1943) Autistic disturbances of affective contact. Nerv. Child. 2:217.

Nissen, G. (1963) Zum frükindlichen Autismus. Archiv. Psychiat. Z. Ges Neurol. 204:6:531.

Rutter, M. (1966) Prognosis: Psychotic children in adolescence and early adult life. *In* Early Childhood Autism: Clinical, Educational and Social Aspects. London: Pergamon.

Rutter, M. (1971a) The description and classification of infantile autism. *In* Infantile Autism: Proceedings of the Indiana University Colloquium (Eds. Churchill, D., Alpern, G., and DeMeyer, M.). Springfield, Illinois: Charles C Thomas.

Rutter, M., Bartak, L., and Newman, S. (1971b) Autism: A central disorder of cognition and language. *In* Infantile Autism: Concepts, Characteristics and Treatment (Ed. Rutter, M.). Edinburgh: Churchill Livingston.

Shapiro, T., Roberts, A., and Fish, B. (1970) Imitation and echoing in young schizophrenic children. J. Amer. Child Psychiat. 9:548.

Simmons, J. Q., and Baltaxe, C. (1975) Language patterns of autistic children who have reached adolescence. J. Autism Child. Schizo. 5:333.

Wolff, S., and Chess, S. (1965) An analysis of the language of fourteen schizophrenic children. J. Child Psychol. Psychiat. 6:29.

RESEARCH TO PRACTICE IN MENTAL RETARDATION
Education and Training, Volume II
Edited by Peter Mittler
Copyright 1977 I.A.S.S.M.D.

DEVELOPING EFFECTIVE MODES FOR RESPONSE AND EXPRESSION IN NONVOCAL SEVERELY HANDICAPPED CHILDREN

G. C. Vanderheiden and D. Harris-Vanderheiden
*Cerebral Palsy Communication Group, University of Wisconsin,
1500 Johnson Drive, Madison, Wisconsin 53706, United States*

Developing effective educational and habilitation programs for the child who has both physical and cognitive handicaps is a difficult task and one that depends upon the development of an effective mode of communication. If an accurate, consistent and reliable means of communication cannot be established with the child, the success of any intervention program will be in doubt. Without effective communication, the overall potential for development for the individual will also be seriously reduced.

For these reasons, the development of communication early in the child's life is essential. Yet severe physical and cognitive impairments can preclude or hamper the development of any functional vocal communication. For these individuals, augmentative modes of communication should be considered.

An augmentative mode of communication is one that serves as a supplement to whatever oral communication the child may have or develop. Thus, augmentative modes or techniques may be appropriately used both with the child who is not expected to develop functional speech and also with the child who may develop functional speech at some point in the future, but who has only limited intelligible speech at present.

A frequent concern related to the use of augmentative modes of communication, such as communication boards, has been that they may impede the development of speech. Clinical research programs have shown, however, that vocalizations have not decreased when augmentative techniques were intro-

---

The Blissymbols illustrated herein are in accordance with the Blissymbolics Communication Foundation approved symbols. © C. K. Bliss and Exclusive Licensee, Blissymbolics Communication Foundation.

duced, and that, in many cases, oral communication intelligibility has improved once the individual was provided with such a technique or aid (McDonald, 1973; McNaughton, 1974; Vicker, 1974; Harris-Vanderheiden, 1976). Improvement in oral communication for these children has been attributed to a decrease in pressure on the child that resulted once the child found that accurate interpretation of his message did not entirely depend upon the intelligibility of his vocalizations, which were difficult for him to produce and hard for others to understand. Increased motivation on the part of the child as a result of successful communication experiences has also been cited as a factor in the improvement of oral skills.

A COMMUNICATION SYSTEM—NOT A COMMUNICATION MODE

Augmentative modes should therefore not be seen as alternatives to speech but rather supplementary modes of communication. An individual's communication system should also not be thought of as a single mode, such as only speech or only a communication board, but as a system that may include several specific modes of communication, which are used at different times or in different situations. The most common example of this is the use of both partially intelligible speech and a communication board, where the mode used at any given time is dependent on the situation, the familiarity of the topic under discussion, and the listening skill of the message receiver.

This concept of a multi-modal system, however, can and should be extended to include the use of more than one nonvocal technique as well. For instance, a child who for speed and convenience is using a signing communication system in his ward or classroom may need a folding portable communication board for communication outside of his ward or classroom, with parents, and with others not familiar with his signing system. A second example would be a child who has a large and fairly complete laptray communication board that allows for relatively fast and flexible communication in the classroom but who may need a small, slower but more portable board of technique that he can always keep with him, in the car, at the park, at the pool, etc.

DEVELOPING COMMUNICATION MODES
FOR THE NONVOCAL PHYSICALLY HANDICAPPED CHILD OR ADULT

The problem then is one of finding appropriate communication modes that, taken together, can provide the individual with an effective communication system. When trying to identify or develop such modes it is useful to review the basic components of an expressive communication mode or channel. A basic three-component model for an expressive communication channel is shown in Table 1. The three components are:

A *physical mechanism* or means of indicating or transmitting the elements of a message to a receiver

Table 1. A simple model of expressive communication components for normal and nonvocal motor impaired children

Component	Function	Component as represented in the normal speaking child	Component as represented in a child using a communication board
Physical mechanism	To provide the child with a means of specifying or transmitting the elements of his message to a receiver	Oral speech mechanism	Pointing board
Symbol system and vocabulary	To provide the child with a set of symbols which he can use to represent things or ideas for communication	Spoken words	Pictures, printed words, other symbols
Rules for combining and presenting symbols	To provide the rules and procedures for presenting the ideo-symbols so that the message will be most easily understood by the receiver	Syntax, grammar, etc.	Syntax, grammar, etc.

A *symbol system and vocabulary* to provide the child with a set of symbols that can be used to represent things and ideas for communication to a receiver

Rules and procedures for combining and presenting the symbols so that they will be most easily interpretable by the receiver

In the normal vocal child, the first advanced mode of communication to develop is speech (Table 1). The physical mechanism by which the child presents his symbols to the message receiver is his oral speech mechanism. His symbols would be the sound patterns (words) for his language. If the sound symbols (words) are used in multiples, these symbols must be presented in some order to indicate relationships between them (e.g., Tom hit Mary).

For the child who cannot speak, or for the child whose speech is only partially functional, these mechanisms are not sufficient, and alternate mechanisms to provide these basic components must be developed for them. An example of what these alternate components might look like is also shown in Table 1. The physical mechanism might take the form of a communication board where the individual would indicate his message by pointing to the symbols displayed. The symbol system could be pictures, drawings, printed words or other symbols. Guidelines for combining symbols would be essentially the same as for early spoken English.

The process of developing augmentative communication through the use of a nonvocal means then would consist of:

1. providing the child with an effective and efficient means to indicate
2. providing the child with a symbol system with which to express his thoughts; a symbol system that meets all of his communication needs and that is compatible with his current cognitive and linguistic level.

PROVIDING THE CHILD WITH A MEANS TO INDICATE

Since a symbol system would be of little use if the child had no means to use it, the first step is to provide him with a means to indicate. Many different aids and techniques have been developed for this purpose by educators and clinicians working with severely physically handicapped children. Most of these aids or techniques are variations or adaptations of three basic approaches: direct selection, scanning, or encoding.

Direct Selection

The most straightforward and familiar approach is direct selection. In this approach the handicapped child directly indicates the elements of his message. Pointing communication boards (Figure 1) are familiar examples of this technique. When a child is unable to point with his hand, headsticks (Figure 2), feet, or other parts of the body have been used.

The Scanning Approach

Many children, however, are not able to point effectively with any part of their body. For these children, a different approach, called scanning, is often used. With this approach, a second person does the pointing for the child with the child signaling when the correct item is indicated. To do this, the second person scans over a communication board, pointing to the items one at a time while watching the child for a signal (Figure 3). When the desired symbol is reached, the child can signal by looking up, raising his arm, smiling, or any other previously agreed upon and recognizable movement. Since the particular movement for a child can be any reliable movement over which the child has voluntary control, this approach is very powerful and can be used by almost any child no matter how severe his physical disability.

The disadvantage of this type of scanning approach is its speed. Stepping over the elements on the board one at a time while allowing time for the child to respond at each one can be very time consuming. To offset this, several other scanning techniques have been developed. Two of them are row-column scanning and directed scanning.

In row-column scanning, the second person, or message receiver, points to the rows one at a time while asking the child if the desired element is in that

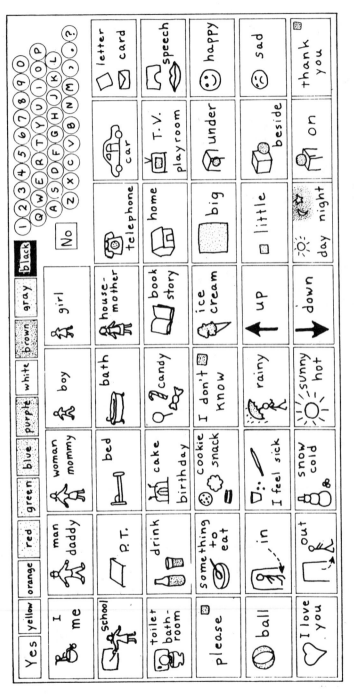

Figure 1. Picture/Word Communication Board—a direct selection technique.

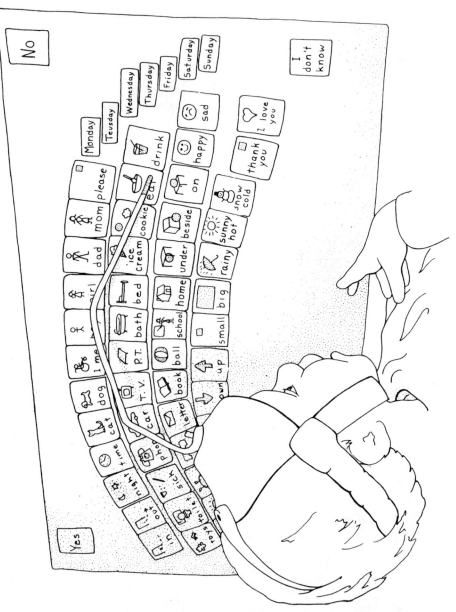

Figure 2.   Direct selection using a headstick.

Figure 3. Simple scanning technique.

row. Once the correct row is established, only that row need be scanned in order to locate the desired element.

The directed scanning technique operates by having the child indicate the direction he wishes the second person to scan (up, down, left, right) by pointing to directional arrows or by indicating the direction with his eyes.

The Encoding Approach

When first starting out with a child, one of the above two approaches is usually used. As the child's communication system develops, however, a child using a direct selection or scanning technique may develop a vocabulary that is large enough that he is no longer able to point to it and that would require an inordinate amount of time to scan. For these individuals, encoding techniques have been developed. With these techniques several movements are used to specify the desired element.

One simple technique is shown in Figure 4. Here a color and a number are used to indicate the elements on the display. No numbers concepts are needed for this technique, because the child needs only to point to the numeral in his pointing display that matches the numeral next to the desired element. If desired, other shapes or figures could be used instead of the numerals.

Combination Techniques

Often two of the approaches can be combined in order to capitalize on the advantages of each and to meet more efficiently the communication needs and abilities of the individual. One example of such a combination technique is the

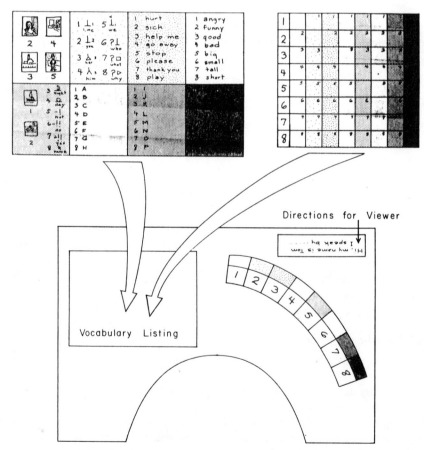

Figure 4. Two movement encoding technique using color.

"indicated area scanning" technique or "area scanning" technique. In this technique, an individual with limited pointing capabilities can greatly reduce the slowness of scanning over large numbers of vocabulary elements. To use this technique, the handicapped individual simply points to the general area on the chart where the desired element is (Figure 5). The message receiver then scans over just the area near where the child pointed. Two advantages of this technique are: 1) the message receiver can often use context to narrow down further the items to be scanned, thus reducing the communication time even more, and 2) this technique provides motivation and practice necessary for the development of better pointing skills and faster communication potential.

Other Techniques

Many other variations and combinations of the approaches have been documented, each with advantages and disadvantages (Vanderheiden 1976; Vanderheiden and Harris-Vanderheiden, 1976). The appropriate technique for a given child will depend upon his specific abilities and will change as he grows and develops new skills (Vanderheiden and Luster, 1976).

PROVIDING THE CHILD WITH A SYMBOL SYSTEM

Once the child has been provided with an initial means to indicate, his initial symbol system must be selected. Since this is only his initial and not his final

Figure 5. Indicated area scanning—a combination technique.

system, it should be chosen to match his present abilities and to provide him with a communication system that will be functional immediately. Long-range communication, academic, and language goals should be worked on only after the child has a functional system for communication and interaction.

Many different symbol systems have been used with nonvocal children, including three-dimensional objects, simple photographs, drawings, Blissymbols, Rebuses, and orthographic systems (Lloyd, 1976).

One of these systems that has been particularly successful with nonvocal physically handicapped children is the Blissymbol system. Blissymbols have been applied widely both with children of near-normal and normal intelligence and with severely mentally retarded children (Harris-Vanderheiden et al., 1976). Some of the features of this system that make it particularly applicable with nonvocal physically handicapped, mentally retarded children are the following: 1) It is not a phonetically based system—the symbols are constructed and based upon meaning units rather than sound units. 2) Blissymbols are pictographic and ideographic, making the symbols easy to learn (Figure 6). 3) The symbols are simple in form and therefore easy to draw. Accordingly, the second person can write the symbols down easily as the child points to them, thus allowing the child to see the sentence he is constructing. This type of feedback is important for the further development of communication skills. 4) There are approximately 50 symbols, which can be combined to form most of the other symbols in the system. Because of this and the concept basis of the system, it is easy for the children to combine symbols on their communication boards to express new concepts (Figure 7).

Blissymbols are but one system that has been used with severely mentally retarded children. They can, however, serve to demonstrate that there are symbol systems that can and have been successfully used with even severely mentally and physically handicapped children.

SUMMARY

Through this chapter we have attempted to examine the problem of developing communication in the nonvocal mentally retarded child. In our discussions we

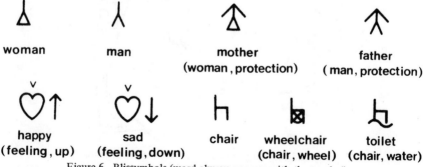

Figure 6. Blissymbols (word always appears with the symbol).

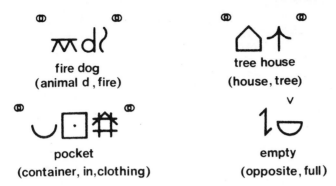

fire dog
(animal d, fire)

tree house
(house, tree)

pocket
(container, in, clothing)

empty
(opposite, full)

Figure 7. Combining Blissymbols to express new ideas.

have directed our comments toward aids and techniques for the physically handicapped child. However, the same principles may be applied to other populations and to adolescents and adults as well. Our primary aim has been to demonstrate that there are techniques for developing communication systems for even the severely physically handicapped, severely mentally retarded child. Although only a brief introduction to the basic techniques has been presented here, it is hoped that the fact that solutions for these children exist has been demonstrated, and that a framework has been provided for the development of practical programs utilizing augmentative communication techniques.

REFERENCES

Harris-Vanderheiden, D. (1976) Field evaluation of the Autocom. *In* Nonvocal Communication Techniques and Aids for the Severely Physically Handicapped (Eds. Vanderheiden, G. C., and Grilley, K). Baltimore: University Park Press.

Lloyd, L. (Ed.) (1976) Communication Assessment and Intervention Strategies. Baltimore: University Park Press.

McDonald, E. T., and Schultz, A. R. (1973) Communication boards for cerebral palsied children. J. Speech Hear. Dis. 38:73.

McNaughton, S., and Kates, B. (1974) Visual symbols: Communication system for the pre-reading physically handicapped child. Paper presented at the American Association on Mental Deficiency Annual Meeting, June, Toronto.

Vanderheiden, G. (1976) Providing the child with a means to indicate. *In* Nonvocal Communication Techniques and Aids for the Severely Physically Handicapped (Eds. Vanderheiden, G. C., and Grilley, K.). Baltimore: University Park Press.

Vanderheiden, G., and Harris-Vanderheiden, D. (1976) Communication techniques and aids for the nonvocal severely handicapped. *In* Communication Assessment and Intervention Strategies (Ed. Lloyd, L.). Baltimore: University Park Press.

Vanderheiden, G. C., and Luster, M. J. (1975) Nonvocal communication techniques and aids as aids to the education of the severely physically handicapped: A state of the art review. Trace Center, University of Wisconsin-Madison.

Vicker, B. (1974) Non-oral communication system project. Campus Stores, University of Iowa, Iowa City, Iowa.

EDUCATIONAL
AND BEHAVIORAL
INTERVENTION

RESEARCH TO PRACTICE IN MENTAL RETARDATION
Education and Training, Volume II
Edited by Peter Mittler
Copyright 1977 I.A.S.S.M.D.

THE CONTRIBUTIONS OF RESEARCH IN COGNITION TO THE FUTURE OF SPECIAL EDUCATION PRACTICES WITH THE MENTALLY RETARDED

L. S. Blackman
Teachers College, Columbia University, New York,
N.Y. 10027, United States

A number of psychologists are currently working in the field of mental retardation whose research is designed to provide the kinds of data that can be translated into changes, either immediately or ultimately, in special education practices.

One group, best described as cognitively oriented educational psychologists, is committed to generating "high educational impact" data, particularly as they relate to aiding higher functioning mentally retarded individuals to acquire the more complex skills involved in reading. A recent paper (Heintz and Blackman, 1977) has identified three major data sources that have contributed to the development of special education curriculum and methods for the mentally retarded. One of these data sources is subject matter itself. This data source is expressed in terms of our ability to analyze the knowledge structure hierarchy inherent in subject matter and to sequence curriculum objectives in a way that reflects the interaction between developmental factors and the structural hierarchy of that knowledge (Bruner, 1960).

The second data source, which reflects primarily on the statement of curriculum objectives for special education, is society. This data source has to do with analyzing society's expectations for the mentally retarded. At different levels of retardation, society expects varying levels of vocational competence, social interaction with family and peers, and assumption of citizenship responsibilities.

293

The third data source, and the one that has offered cognitive psychologists entry to the pedagogical process, is the mentally retarded learner himself. Understanding the pattern of perceptual, learning, and cognitive abilities and disabilities in a particular mentally retarded learner, as a basis for prescribing instructional strategies that may be uniquely suitable to that learner, represents the area of operation for those whose special education approach emphasizes this data source. Bateman (1967) contributed to the clarification of the category of "learner as data souce" when she stated that this approach:

> ... redirects our attention to question-asking as the foundation of teaching and curriculum planning, to specific factors affecting and determining learning processes, to individual appraisal of patterns of cognitive abilities, to a re-examination of a philosophy of teaching through strengths or to weaknesses, and to the need for direct teaching of the processes of thinking rather than the products of someone else's thinking (p. 25).

To emphasize the "learner as data source" orientation to special education practices, Blackman (1967) maintained that the effective modification of the classroom behavior of mentally retarded children depends on the development of a "school-relevant taxonomy of their psychoeducational characteristics." By psychoeducational characteristics is meant: "An analysis of the retarded child's profile of abilities and deficits in a wide range of psychological processes such as perception, learning, retention, transfer, attention, discrimination, and language among others" (p. 8). The proposed taxonomic approach also maintains that knowledge of a retarded learner's disabilities has ". . . little educational utility independent of its relevancy to school; that is, a comparable understanding of the psychoeducational prerequisites for acquiring specific school tasks" (p. 8). The stress on understanding the nature of school tasks as the second anchor point in the taxonomy reflects the relevance of the learner's psychological assets and disabilities to the subject matter being acquired. Subject matter, therefore, must be understood not only in terms of its own logical structure but also in terms of the demands that it places on the perceptual, learning, and cognitive abilities of the learner for whom the didactic material is targeted. The final component of this taxonomic system deals with the design of instructional systems predicated on the known parameters of learner and task characteristics.

There is a line of research implied in calling for the improved design of instructional delivery systems for the mentally retarded based on a better understanding of the learner's perceptual and cognitive characteristics, as well as the cognitive demands placed on learners by specific school tasks. We must first do the research that will identify the cognitive prerequisites for the acquisition of school-related skills. Next, if these cognitive prerequisites are found to be deficient in mentally retarded learners, we must evaluate their amenability to remediation. Finally, if these cognitive processes are remediable, we must determine the extent to which the learning of the more complex skills related to successful school performance may be accelerated. In line with that research strategy, I would like to describe briefly a sequence of research studies completed at the Research and Demonstration Center for the Handicapped at Teachers College, Columbia University. This work has been concerned primarily with the identification of cognitive strategies predictive of reading performance in educable mentally retarded adolescents, and the remediation of those strategies.

An initial step in this direction was a study by Blackman and Burger (1972) that investigated the role of a variety of psychological factors, primarily those in the perceptual domain, in the acquisition of early reading skills by young, educable mentally retarded and normal children. The variables in this factor analytic study, in addition to the reading criterion variable, included measures of: 1) visual and auditory discrimination, analysis, and synthesis; 2) intersensory integration; and 3) visual and auditory memory. The results of this study suggested strongly that memory processes were associated more saliently with the acquisition of reading skills in both retarded and normal groups than with a large selection of intra- and intermodality perceptual variables.

The finding that a cognitive variable such as memory overshadowed the traditional array of perceptual variables in predicting early reading performance suggested that other cognitive variables also might be of prime importance in predicting the reading achievement of mentally retarded adolescents. A second study (Blackman et al., 1976) was undertaken, therefore, to investigate the interrelationships among a variety of cognitive skills and to determine their relationship to the performance of educable mentally retarded adolescents in standardized measures of reading achievement.

The cognitive variables used in this study ranged across tasks that involved short- and long-term memory, abstraction, sorting, multiple classification, class inclusion skills, and problem-solving. The reading scores were obtained from the Wide Range Achievement Test (WRAT). In confirmation of the first study in this series, memory variables were preeminently related to reading. While recognizing the importance of the memory variables in predicting early reading achievement skills in the educable mentally retarded, it would be premature to exclude from consideration the other cognitive predictor variables used in this study. These variables may well be important cognitive prerequisites for the more advanced levels of reading skill acquisition involved in the comprehension of materials read.

Having replicated the finding that memory variables were powerfully related to reading scores, two training studies were undertaken to determine if the performance of mentally retarded on memory tasks could be significantly improved. The first training study (Burger and Blackman, 1975) involved an attempt to improve the digit recall performance of educable mentally retarded children by developing a grouping schema as the appropriate strategic behavior for that task. Those educable mentally retarded children who received this training program appeared to have interiorized and used the grouping schema in that they improved their recall performance by at least two digits over their baseline measures. Control subjects who were not trained to use a grouping schema but who did receive continuing practice in the recall of random digits did not improve their digit recall scores.

In a second investigation (Burger and Blackman, 1976), the ability of educable mentally retarded children to acquire and retain a mediational strategy for paired associate learning was increased dramatically by a training procedure which included several components that had been found to be effective in isolation in previous studies. These components included separating training sessions by one-week intervals, overt verbalization, verbal context mediation, and imagery mediation.

In addition to these studies, other findings have demonstrated the efficacy of training programs designed to teach educable mentally retarded children and adolescents to employ conceptual strategies. McIvor (1972) improved the verbal abstraction ability of mentally retarded adolescents by teaching them strategies for finding the similarity between sets of nouns in an abstraction task. Bilsky and Gilbert (1975) found relatively durable improvement in the class inclusion performance of adolescent EMRs after brief correctional training.

The impact of these studies for special education practitioners is to consider cognitive strategy training an important component of the special class curriculum. Although the potential for improvement in the use of several cognitive strategies has been documented, more research is needed to link more definitively the utilization of these strategies to the more efficient acquisition of specific content areas. As Mann (1971) has contended, however, until there is empirical validation of this linkage, the assumption that laboratory oriented "cognitive therapy" will lead inevitably to improved classroom performance is a form of unjustifiable theoretical hubris.

There are still a number of important issues, however, that remain to be resolved. There is, first, the issue of permanence. That is, can strategic behavior acquired in a particular setting become a permanent component of an individual's cognitive repertoire for that setting? Second, there is the issue of transfer or how far afield strategic behaviors will roam after being taught in a particular context. Finally, there is the issue of the versatility and fluency of strategic behavior (Butterfield, Wambold, and Belmont, 1973). That is, in addition to having a cognitive strategy permanently available for acquiring information in particular and related tasks, can a mentally retarded individual, when facing a relatively novel task, scan the variety of strategies available to him and select the one most appropriate for resolving that new problem? It is this matter of strategic fluency that probably defines the essence of cognitive normalcy. To raise the possibility that whatever mechanisms mediate this fluency are identifiable and, more improbably, amenable to training, may be an indulgence in fantasy. The more conservative position at this juncture in scientific development is that cognitive fluency is an inherently available control system that can be characterized as a predictable feature of the higher quality central nervous system.

The definitive research leading to the scientific resolution of this question is probably many years away. Before the millenium descends upon us, psychologists and special educators of the mentally retarded must use the tools at hand to achieve desired outcomes. What is being suggested in this chapter is that making special education for the mentally retarded genuinely special will require the identification of those cognitive strategies that are deemed, either through empirical or intuitive task analysis procedures, to be prerequisite to the acquisition of academic skills. Systematic training programs should be designed to upgrade the functioning of these cognitive strategies in the mentally retarded wherever possible.

Lest it be misunderstood, there is no suggestion here that, in the future, mentally retarded children will receive their cognitive strategy training from psychologists in laboratory settings while subject matter content dependent upon those strategies will be taught in the classrooms. It is far more reasonable that retarded children should receive both cognitive training and content instruction in "real-life" classroom settings. Both logic and intuition suggest that the "country cousin" strategic behaviors required in laboratory-type simple digit span, paired-associate learning, verbal free recall, and class inclusion tasks are likely to differ in important ways from those "city cousin" strategic behaviors that would be prerequisite to the more complex forms of learning required in classrooms, e.g., letter sound correspondence, word recognition, and comprehension of meaningful word sequences.

If we are able to continue to expand the number and types of cognitive strategies that can be taught to mildly retarded children and be retained by them over relatively long periods of time, and if we can extend the range of stimulus settings to which these strategies will transfer, and if we can make new inroads into the problem of cognitive fluency or the retarded individual's self-selection of strategies appropriate to learning, remembering, and problem-solving, and if we can demonstrate reliably the contribution of those strategies and their control mechanisms to upgrading performance on traditional school learning tasks, then we may yet see a significant transformation in the way in which mentally retarded, and perhaps all children, will be educated.

The central feature of this transformation can be understood best in terms of changing teacher roles and expectations. Curriculum objectives and the methods that serve as their vehicles will have dual emphases. As always, teachers will be concerned with transmitting content or, to recall Bateman's words, the products of other people's thinking. Perhaps more importantly, teachers will also be concerned with the development in their retarded children of thinking itself. Regardless of whether one feels optimistic or pessimistic about that possibility, there is sufficient data currently available to support a serious effort in this direction. Clearly, such an effort also would be in the best traditions of the teaching profession.

SUMMARY

Improved special education practices with the mentally retarded will be based on a better understanding of the contribution of particular strategies to the acquisition of specific school tasks. Research in the identification and remediation of educationally relevant cognitive strategies in the mentally retarded is summarized and interpreted.

REFERENCES

Bateman, B. (1967) Implications of a learning disability approach for teaching educable retardates. Ment. Retard. 5:23.

Bilsky, L. H., and Gilbert, L. (1975) The Effects of Correction Training on the Performances of a Class Inclusion Task by Mildly Retarded Adolescents. Continuation Progress Reports, Input Structure and Retardate Performance, 1975, HDO7329-03, Appendix III-F, 273-295.

Blackman, L. S. (1967) The dimensions of a science of special education. Ment. Retard. 5:7.

Blackman, L. S., and Burger, A. L. (1972) Psychological factors related to early reading behaviors of EMR and nonretarded children. Amer. J. Ment. Defic. 77:212.

Blackman, L. S., Bilsky, L. H., Burger, A. L., and Mar, H. (1976) Cognitive processes and academic achievement in educable mentally retarded adolescents. Amer. J. Ment. Defic. 81:125.

Bruner, J. S. (1960) The Process of Education. New York: Vantage.

Burger, A. L., and Blackman, L. S. (1975) Acquisition and retention of a mediational strategy for PA learning in EMR Children. Amer. J. Ment. Defic. 80:529.

Burger, A. L., and Blackman, L. S. (1976) Visual memory training of digit recall in educable mentally retarded children. Educ. Train. Ment. Retard. 11:5.

Butterfield, E. C., Wambold, C., and Belmont, J. M. (1973) On the theory and practice of improving short-term memory. Amer. J. Ment. Defic. 77:654.

Heintz, P., and Blackman, L. S. (1977) Psychoeducational considerations with the mentally retarded child. In The Psychology of Mental Retardation: Issues and Approaches (Eds. Bialer, I., and Sternlicht, M.) New York: Psychological Dimensions Inc.

Mann, L. (1971) Psychometric phrenology and the new faculty psychology: The case against ability assessment and training. J. Spec. Educ. 5:3.

McIvor, W. B. (1972) Evaluation of a strategy-oriented training program on the verbal abstraction performance of EMRs. Amer. J. Ment. Defic. 76:160.

RESEARCH TO PRACTICE IN MENTAL RETARDATION
Education and Training, Volume II
Edited by Peter Mittler
Copyright 1977 I.A.S.S.M.D.

SCIENCE AND PLANNING IN EDUCATION
A Dynamic Relationship— A Summary

I. Liljeroth and L. Wessman
*Lärarhögskolan i Mölndal, Fack, S-431 20 Mölndal,
Sweden*

In Sweden since 1968 we have tried to find a model that can accommodate the demands made by both the scientist and persons representing the field. The year 1968 was a crucial point because a special Act came into force. It stated that all mentally retarded had the right to educational activities including training for those formerly considered noneducable. This meant that we had to form programmes for those usually regarded as noneducable.

Our experience with training was positive but limited. The programmes could not contain many elements that one finds in the conventional school for the mentally retarded. Many questions, especially about programmes and methods, were raised. The National Swedish Board of Education initiated and financed two research projects, one regarding primary ADL-training (1968–70) and one regarding the development of personality (1970–75). The leader of these studies was one of the authors (Liljeroth).

The job of the scientist was to analyse the problem, formulate the design, and make decisions about theoretical aspects and the shape of the report. The method of ADL-training was based on a behavior modification technique. We achieved good results. Training resulted in new skills for the mentally retarded, an easier care situation for the mentally retarded and the staff, and a new consciousness of the importance of breaking down a skill into small items and giving praise when the pupil really had performed or tried to perform something.

During the two years between 1968 and 1970 the principles of normalisation and integration also had been formulated and developed.

The concept of training became crucial. It was expected that everyone should contribute to training. The programmes in school and the programmes for living, especially in institutions, tended to be looked upon as very similar.

The pedagogical atmosphere always surrounded the child. We even talked about 24-hour training.

This was a time of optimism. We believed that we had found a model according to which we could develop services for retarded persons. However, there were new problems manifested in the ADL-project. In summary, the difficulty for the pupil was not in the learning but in the using of his new skills. This led us to the conclusion that we had to analyse the development of personality and the living-situation of the mentally retarded person. We needed deeper knowledge of the retarded person as an individual.

In the development of cooperation between the planning authority and the scientist, one of the questions that we have met deals with how the problem ought to be defined. The ADL-project was defined in a dialogue between persons representing practice, science, or planning. The results led, however, to new problems. New questions were now raised by the scientist. A dialogue between the different parties gives possibilities of formulating problems that are of interest to everybody.

This seems simple but it is controversial. There is a gulf between theory and practice, science and reality. Often, we plan services on ideological principles and experience and only in a limited sense on scientific results.

The controversial issue is that there are contradictory demands and expectations from universities and practitioners. The academic tradition and the scientific methods often are not adapted to those in need of solving practical problems. Because one of the scientist's motives is to make a career for himself, he yields to demands from the university. The scientist chooses his own problem without connecting it to experience in practice.

We are not intending to censure existing research but to emphasize that we need new research methods that can be used to answer new kinds of problems and to satisfy new expectations. The basic concepts of experience, analysis of experience, ideology, and science/theory can be seen as four angles in a tetrahedron. There must be a natural and direct communication between the different parties. At different periods, different angles are of importance. Sometimes the angle of experience is up and sometimes that of ideology (Figure 1).

There are many problems that the scientist will meet if these expectations are to be satisfied. In the field of mental retardation the scientist has often laid stress on the differences between the retarded and the nonretarded. Retarded persons are then seen as a group in which all the members are expected to show common reactions as a result of the intellectual handicap. Instead, the retarded person must be seen in the same perspective as others where we point to his possibilities to develop. He is a member of society and therefore in a social relationship in the same way as others. He has a role in society through attitudes from other persons including his family, persons working in institutions, in special schools, etc., and those who are responsible for planning and for political decisions. These facts are difficult to take into consideration in a scientific job.

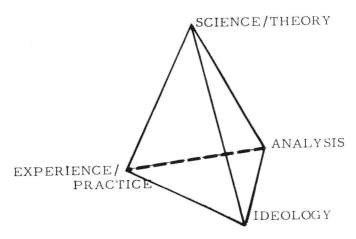

Figure 1. A cooperative model.

The problems are many. One of the existing scientific ideals is that science must be objective in the sense of being free from values. Often, it is not permitted to talk about subjective experiences, feelings, ideals, and values, either of the scientist or of the objects of his experiments. But psychology and education are subjects that cannot be isolated from values.

Another problem concerns goal and methods. An acceptance of the usually used methods can lead to a displacement of the goals. The role of the scientist therefore must be changed. It is not possible only to observe and to analyse; the scientist must participate and evaluate. Research in Anglo-Saxon countries has been influenced strongly by the ideals of the natural sciences. This has led to methods that are characterized by possibilities of registering data schematically and quantifying them. The scientist is an observer, not a participant. These methods are of course sometimes usable. The serious problem in this connection, however, is that most scientists of psychology believe that they have to be used in all kinds of studies. They also are looked upon as superior.

Every psychological theory has a perspective on man. When we choose to work from a special theoretical basis we also choose a view of man, mostly unconsciously. It is possible to keep to an unconscious perspective if the scientist assumes the role of the observer. But when one wants to collect data through participation, it is not possible. One is then confronted with demands not only of explanation but also of understanding. However, this is not enough. We also need to be critical. This is a controversial area. Being critical of methods of analysis, interpreting results, etc., is permitted, but being critical in the sense of analysing contradictions and conflicts at the territory and choosing a clear position based on values is not.

In the tetrahedron (Figure 1) this discussion of values is illustrated in the angle of ideology. Ideology is found on a practical basis and is not bound to science. The scientist is a member of society in the same way as mentally retarded persons, parents, nurses, or teachers are, and he also must take an ideological position.

This scientific discussion led us to some practical insights. The basic fault was that we had given the mentally retarded person the possibility of learning, but not of living in a way in which it was useful or desirable to apply his knowledge.

This affects the choice of theory. In Sweden, like many other countries, during the last few years there has been a trend toward an antitheoretical psychology. This is disastrous. It is also a manifestation of the triumph of the ideals of objectivity through denial of values. It is, of course, difficult to choose. Often, some accidental circumstance influences the choice. Instead the choice ought to be done with more consciousness than it often is. In the ADL-project, we based the job on behavior modification, a simply theory. When we developed the theory of development of personality, such a theory was not satisfying. Other demands had to be fulfilled. The system of concepts had to include needs, motives, intentions, actions, language, etc. Moreover, it had to be possible to generate a number of hypotheses because human expression, development, and experience are very complicated and individual. The choice was psychoanalytic theory. Other theories answer other problems.

The consequence, if we continue the traditional research methods and develop more and more refined techniques, will be that the knowledge we obtain will be alienated from reality. Another consequence of the traditional trends in psychological science is that it is difficult to inform people who could be interested in the results. If there is cooperation between people who represent theory and practice, the development of scientific work can be adjusted to the situation and the results can be put into a meaningful context. Then the information will not be a problem but will meet the needs of people in practice.

If we have cooperation between planning people and practitioners it will also be possible to use results during the working period. We need not just wait. At the same time, the scientist has the opportunity of testing his new knowledge and seeing if it is usable in practice. For example, different scientific groups have contributed to the development of the curricula of the different streams of schools for the mentally retarded.

Many scientists are afraid of how this will influence their jobs. For many, it is not a criterion of good science that results can be used in practice. They also are afraid of being manipulated and of not being objective. There are risks, of course. But the scientist can cope with the situation if the goals are clear, the values analysed, and the theory comprehensive enough to cover the problems studied.

We also need a discussion of what it is to be objective. The objectivity is not that the empirical material is disconnected from the scientist as a subject. Objectivity is that the scientist can do a theoretical analysis of material collected in a participation. In the objective analysis the scientist himself is part of the material. The theory upon which the scientist bases his work is an important factor in the objectivity.

An example of a scientific method usable with the ideals of science presented here is action research. What is fundamental in this method is the dialectical interaction between theory and practice, the constant restructuring of research work and theory, and the continuously developing testing procedure. The analysis of competing contradictions opens possibilities of a new insight and actions.

This means that it is impossible to structure the whole scientific procedure. Many scientists are trained to design everything in detail before the empirical work begins. Consequently, we limit our possibilities of getting different kinds of data. But if we want to work in a way that also gives persons in practice opportunities to influence the work, we have to be open. We need not inventory schemes but dialogue, not statistical methods but meaningful contexts.

Following are a few examples of the meaning of our discussion. We have used results from Liljeroth's research project regarding the development of personality of the mentally retarded. First, the relationship between understanding and explanation is illustrated. Stig, a boy of 20, has a great interest in paper. Stig is diagnosed by some people as "fixated on paper" or as having a "mania for collecting paper." This is an explanation but it does not lead to understanding. If we want to understand Stig, we must see the interest in paper as an expression that means something to him. We must then use psychological, not neurological, terms. Our hypothesis (which was confirmed) was that Stig wanted to ask us to love him, to care for him and therefore give him something. If we understand this, we also can develop an interaction with Stig in which we use other means to satisfy these needs. The natural consequence is a reduced interest in paper.

The results of the studies of the development of personality or identity of the mentally retarded persons show that they risk receiving a particularly weak first feeling of identity, imperfect relations with important persons, and impaired development of the self-concepts. This is because they often have a special life situation as a result of crises in their families, institutionalization, etc. This leads to an interaction that gives the child experiences which are limited and different from those he would need. The special life situation also causes a development of weak control functions and means that the retarded person is readily drawn further and further away from a feeling of identity based upon social reality. If, however, he gets interaction and an environment that is like those of others, he follows the same pattern of development, although does not reach the same developmental level. The importance of the handicap is relative. Integration of identity is more influenced by emotional experience than by cognitive level of development.

The results of the development of the individual can be generalized and conclusions can be drawn about the importance of different environments. The meaning of an environment and of the persons in it is based on needs satisfied by the environment. The scheme outlined in Table 1 identifies the differences between the various types of environments.

Homes should be characterized by an expressive contact, i.e., an emotional dependence that forms the basis of the satisfaction of primary needs, identification, and separation. Contributing to the personality development is a development of emotional and motivational structures and control functions. School represents an instrumental contact that can encourage achievement of defined goals in the form of new knowledge, experience, and interest. The contribution to personality development is on the ego-level. Leisure time should provide a community of interests based upon personal relations and activities and its value deepens with the development of functions and abilities.

These results are usable on a planning level. The ideological background is the same and the theoretical knowledge is based on an analysis of data collected in practice. The consequence will be that we have to arrange a normal life situation for all mentally retarded, where it is natural and desirable to behave normally and to apply the knowledge achieved in school. For children and young people, it means living in a family or a family-like situation with warm contact,, leisure time activities, etc., but very little (if any) formal training. But it also means a school to attend where the child is trained. For adults it means living environments as much like ordinary adult homes as possible. It also means work, or some kind of occupation, and an adequate adult education.

Services for mentally retarded children and youth can be defined in three main functions—namely housing, education, and medical care.

These functions have different tasks and therefore need different conditions. The models for these activities are totally different as regards aim, planning,

Table 1. Goals of activities in home, in school, and during leisure time

Goal	Home	School	Leisure time
Relation	Expressive relation: emotional dependence by primary needs; Successive separation; Identification	Instrumental relation: understanding contact by need to learn; The teacher as intermediary	Common interests based on activities and/or personal relations
Worth of personality	Development of emotions and motivation; Experience of oneself; Development of control	Development of the ego: concepts, knowledge, experiences of society, expressions, Development of ability to participate and take responsibility	Development of different areas

contents, organisation, etc. Normalisation means that housing, education, and medical care for the nonhandicapped should serve as a model for the handicapped. We then have the greatest chance of reaching our goal.

An institution can be defined in many ways. Here, we define an institution as an organisation for two or more of the three main functions: housing, education, and medical care. Some total institutions have all three functions. Because of the confusion of different functions and goals, it seems to be impossible to normalise life at an institution. Efforts to separate the different functions within the institution can diminish but not eliminate the conflicts of the functions. A total separation of the three functions leads to abolition of the institution.

Housing facilities for the handicapped must be separated from facilities for daily activities and medical care and be made similar to normal dwellings in size, design, and location. The handicapped should not live together in larger groups than we normally do. In the same way, the normal school serves as a model for schools for the handicapped. This does not mean that all pupils should do the same things. Medical care for the handicapped should be based on the usual health service organisation and its resources. A mentally retarded sick child should be treated at home as long as possible as other children are, and be sent to hospital only if special medical treatment is necessary.

The important principle is that the three main functions of housing, education, and medical care can develop separately with the normal functions serving as models for the non-handicapped. One of the functions is not to be ruled by the other.

Certainly the different functions are dependent on each other. There is a necessary relation between school and home, expressed in the dialogue between the parents or foster parents and the teacher, a cooperation where every person knows his role. But also to this and other dialogues the normalisation principle can be applied. The principle of normalisation, of finding models that exist in society in general, is always functioning, not because it is right but because it does not remove the mentally retarded from society.

SUMMARY

In Sweden there is close cooperation between those who are responsible for planning of education and those who are working with pedagogical and psychological research. Problems arising when working on a traditional research basis are analysed, problems of control and influence of ideological principles and different attitudes are discussed and examples of useful results are presented.

RESEARCH TO PRACTICE IN MENTAL RETARDATION
Education and Training, Volume II
Edited by Peter Mittler
Copyright 1977 I.A.S.S.M.D.

THE MENTALLY RETARDED CHILD IN THE MAINSTREAM OF THE PUBLIC SCHOOL

His Relation to the School Administration, His Teachers, and His Age-mates

M. Budoff
Research Institute for Educational Problems,
29 Ware Street,
Cambridge, Massachusetts 02138, United States

Special education is now undergoing a quiet but thorough rethinking of many premises on which it previously operated. For the past seven decades, and at accelerating rates, special education services have largely been delivered in substantially separate arrangements away from the activities of nonhandicapped students in the school. This approach paralleled the isolated location of the institutions in which handicapped children were housed when they were sent for residential treatment. There has been an increasing awareness that children, even when diagnosed as being in a common category, often need distinctive services. Thus, a comment frequently heard is that mentally retarded children mainly share one common element, their IQ score. Their specific service needs have come to be recognized as of considerably more significance than the information provided by the IQ score.

A further and more radical development in recent years is that the range of children with handicapping conditions that schools must serve has been broadened considerably. The principle of every child's right to a free, appropriate public education was most dramatically enunciated in *PARC vs. the Common-*

This work was made possible by grant RO1 HD 08439 from the National Institute of Child Health and Human Development, National Institutes of Health.

wealth of Pennsylvania. This consent decree required that all mentally retarded children, regardless of the degree of their retardation, must be served by schools that had previously excluded them. Public Law 94-142, passed in 1975 by the U.S. Congress, broadly applies the principle to all children in need of special education.

While the language of court decisions, legislation, or regulations has emphasized the principle that a mentally retarded child be placed in the least restrictive programs, the educational community has interpreted this to mean maximizing mainstreaming, i.e., placement within the regular school program for maximal portions of the school day, often without clear understanding of the gains and potential losses which may be suffered by the child so placed. In large part, this is attributable to the origins of the concept in recent history.

Dunn's rhetoric (1968) and the major early focus through anti-poverty programs and court decisions on the overrepresentation of poor and/or minority status children in special classes for the mildly mentally retarded structured the argument around the inappropriateness of these classes for these children. The obvious response was that such placement was caused by misclassification, and resulted in undereducation, pejorative labels, and a sense of stigma experienced by the child. This highly focused thrust caused a ground swell of activity to be directed toward dismantling these substantially separate special classes, and mainstreaming these children, converting the special class teachers and their classrooms to "resource" rooms; it subsequently became generalized, in too many minds, to refer to all substantially separate programs. The principle of least restrictive alternative, the language of the new federal special education law, P.L. 94-142, which becomes effective in October 1977, does not mandate mainstreaming per se, although the philosophical thrust is embodied within the language and the intent is expressed by the U.S. Congress.

While academic progress is a critical criterion for judging the adequacy of the mainstreaming thrust, the new programmatic philosophy was generated out of a concern for the "quality of life" of handicapped children and their personal and social development. Critical to this "quality of life" concern is the degree of acceptance or rejection the handicapped child faces in the "normalized" environment. Consequently, there has been a growing interest in the study of attitudes and behaviors toward handicapped children exhibited by normal children, teachers, and other school personnel, particularly those responsible for facilitating the child's acceptance within the normalized environment of the school.

The net thrust of these changes is that handicapped children are assigned increasingly to school placements within the regular grades. In personal terms for the handicapped child, this means free access and association with nonhandicapped children that allows for a considerable increase in contacts and the development of friendships. The assumption is that such opportunities will lead to normalized contacts with children of the same sex and age, and will result in such salutary effects for the handicapped child as a more positive sense of self and in competencies in the social and interpersonal spheres more typical of children of their chronological age. The emphasis is on maximizing these children's potential strengths in the social and interpersonal areas, especially for those whose primary difficulties are academically related and for whom real and continuing academic limitations are probable. Further, there is a widespread assumption shared by advocates of delabeling and mainstreaming that children who feel stigmatized by placement in a special class, will feel more positively toward school and will perform more successfully in academic areas. These assumptions of social, interpersonal, and academic benefits from increased contacts available within the mainstream have not been largely substantiated empirically because almost no research on the effects of mainstreaming has been completed, and more important, the operational meaning of mainstreaming programs varies considerably.

Kaufman et al. (1975) have defined mainstreaming as, "the temporal, instructional, and social integration of exceptional children with their normal peers. Integration is based on an ongoing, individually determined educational planning and programming process. Mainstreaming requires clarification of the responsibilities of regular and special education administrative, instructional and supportive personnel."

Most discussions focus on the temporal dimension of mainstreaming, that is, *where* the child spends his time in school, rather than *what* the child is taught, and *how* one can design the positive treatments and supports that will assure the mentally retarded child's successful reintegration, or maintenance, within the regular class. The advocates of mainstreaming propose quite diverse goals ranging from deinstitutionalization of severely and profoundly retarded persons to placement within the regular class of children heretofore educated within self-contained classes.

The discussions about mainstreaming mainly describe administrative arrangements with no necessary indication as to *what* is to be taught or how. We are best at addressing *who* will do the teaching under what arrangements. Second, the models described relate especially to the means by which mildly handicapped children may be maintained within the regular school programs. The extent to which the model describes a primary reliance on the regular class teacher, the less handicapped the child client can be, unless there are ancillary helping personnel providing direct services to the child. A most powerful combination might be a resource consultant teamed with paraprofessional aides working in close collaboration with the regular classroom teacher. With the mildly retarded, working with the child in his regular classroom might be most effective, although, if the social standing of children is partially determined by one's need for help, it is likely that staying in or leaving the classroom may produce similar effects. Clearly a major research question, among many others, is to view how special help is perceived by children of different ages, what kinds of help may be positively or negatively perceived and in what types of contexts, and how these variables influence the handicapped child's social standing. We need to know considerably more about variables that influence social standing or acceptability of children more generally, but this more basic research information must be considered within the context of singling out children for special, additional help. Third, one should note the close working relationships special and regular educators must develop if the child is to be maintained for significant portions of the week in the regular grades. This represents a new and important thrust because it requires the closing of a major chasm, which has continued to exist for many years. This chasm is partly of our own making because we have been persistent in insisting that children in special education have different needs and require special treatment from specialists, and because we have made this point particularly strongly by maintaining the children in a separate system within the regular school. Of course, this was partly a function of history. The mentally retarded and other handicapped children were cast out by the regular educational system and have been historically viewed as different. To some extent, we have made the best of a bargain that was not of our choosing. The recent trend toward mainstreaming has permitted these administrative acceptance issues to once again surface constructively with the concern for the child, not the program, uppermost.

However, there are difficulties with the manner in which we must address the needs of these children, especially when they have visible impairments that are moderate to severe and, most particularly, when the goals and objectives for the children deviate markedly from the conceptual manner in which teachers view their roles with children. This becomes most apparent when we discuss the role of the regular class teacher with the moderately or severely mentally retarded. These children have limited prognoses, at best, for attaining any degree of academic proficiencies, yet those are the behaviors and goals with which regular education teachers are most clearly identified. When the objectives for a child require training in self-help skills, such as dressing or tying shoe laces, minimal communication competencies, or preacademic types of behavioral or literacy training, one can readily visualize the difficulties and dissonances experienced by the regular class teacher in viewing her relationship, as a teacher, to the time the child may spend in her class. In short, it is doubtful that moderately or severely retarded children can spend any portion of their time in the regular grades unless one can be certain that the time spent can be socially useful to the child. To achieve this goal, especially for the moderately and severely mentally retarded child, but even for those who are mildly retarded, one must engage in considerable in-service training and reeducation of regular classroom teachers.

The regular class placement for the borderline or marginally retarded child is not merely for his social and emotional growth, but also must serve as the primary educational vehicle. The special education services provide the special help required to build and develop the child's deficient skills, but the remainder of the school day also must serve to support the child's efforts to use and apply these skills. To attain this goal, the child's regular class teacher and the special educator must learn to communicate on a continuing basis.

The other major set of factors within the school setting that may influence even more critically the handicapped child's response to spending some major or minor portion of his school day in the regular class relates to the responses of the other children toward him. There is considerable evidence that the mentally retarded child perceives a lack of acceptance, whether in the special class (Folman and Budoff, 1972) or mainstreamed (White and Budoff, 1976). The dilemma is further complicated by evidence that after some period of reintegration, the retarded child's behavior in the classroom does not differ from that of his age-mates (Gampel, Gottlieb, and Harrison, 1974; Gampel, Harrison, and Budoff, 1972), and, in some wishful manner, the recently integrated ex-special class child feels that others do perceive him more positively (Budoff and Gottlieb, 1976).

During the past year we have been seeking ways to ascertain how the special education children experience their time in the regular class as opposed to the time they spend in the special education setting. To address this question, we have talked with the special education students in two elementary schools. All these children spend a majority of their school day in the regular grades, but attend the learning center, a resource room, for some portion of each day, varying in length depending on the child's need for special help. In one of the schools, all of the children are mildly handicapped, many of them falling in the learning disability category under a customary diagnosis. The second school, which had previously housed the special classes for the EMR, had a broader range of children, including children with mild to moderate emotional disturbances and learning disabilities.

When asked questions related to how they would prefer to spend their time during the coming school year, the children who preferred the learning center special education placement to the regular class had somewhat lower IQs, behaved better in the learning center than the regular class, spent less time voluntarily with their regular class teacher, looked visibly different from other children of their age, and were considered by an observer of their behavior in the regular class to be less well adjusted socially and to exude a sense of less comfort and relaxation there. The older children who functioned more appropriately in their regular classroom preferred the regular class and disliked having to go to the special education setting.

We also observed the behaviors of these children in the regular class for at least six and up to 12 half-hour sessions, evenly split between structured and unstructured classroom settings, and compared their behaviors with a control sample of nonhandicapped children from their regular classrooms. We were concerned with knowing whether or not the handicapped children's lack of social acceptance was attributable to exhibiting behaviors markedly different from those of their same-aged peers. In essence, is it the label of handicapped as evidenced by the fact that these children leave the classroom for special help in the learning center that is related to this nonacceptance, as some have argued in promoting a noncategorical system of special education service delivery, or, do these children act differently and/or more unpredictably than children of the same age?

When one examines the children's interpersonal behaviors with peers, one finds that the handicapped children had fewer conversations and that, of these, a disproportionate number of them were with other handicapped children. The handicapped children tended to be found at the periphery of the group activities in their vicinity while the normal controls tended to be in more central relationships to the group's activities. While as a group, the handicapped children exhibited twice as many negative responses toward other children, there was considerable variability. Some of them emitted much higher frequencies than others. Again, while as a group, the handicapped children drew four times as many negative responses from other children than the controls, there were some handicapped children who drew very high frequencies, others, few or none. Within the control sample, those who attracted negative responses from others had a high frequency of making strange sounds and noises, spent more time wandering aimlessly around the room, initiated more conversations with the teacher, and initiated more negative responses.

When observed, the handicapped sample emitted three times as many sounds and noises when working alone, but seemed more able to inhibit them when working with other children. They also made more strange movements and gestures, although these were also observed in the normal children. Interestingly, younger handicapped children make more sounds and noises than older ones, while the older children appear to inhibit the strange sounds and noises, maintaining a higher level of irrelevant movements and gestures.

In sum, it would seem that the handicapped children do appear to act differently than the normal controls, and it may be that, among a sample of mildly handicapped students, these differences, not the label that is ascribed to them, may induce the nonacceptance that characterizes the normal students' responses to these children. If this is indeed the case, then we must work very hard to learn more about the manner in which the handicapped child can become sensitive to his behaviors, and the negative manner in which other children respond to them. In the past, our efforts have been centered on seeking greater acceptance for the handicapped by treatments that try to help the nonhandicapped change their negative attitudes toward the mentally retarded.

More fruitful avenues would appear to be those which make the handicapped more sensitive to his social stimulus value to other children whom he might wish to befriend, and programs and support to help him change the behaviors which offend those children. It is a skill and sensitivity that we more naturally tend to develop, and that some handicapped children also possess. We expect to study the behaviors of handicapped chidren who are more accepted by their peers to discern whether, and to what extent, these children's behavior deviates from their peers' norms.

REFERENCES

Budoff, M., and Gottlieb, J. (1976) Special class EMR children mainstreamed: A study of an aptitude (learning potential) X treatment interaction. Amer. J. Ment. Defic. 81:1.

Dunn, L. M. (1968) Special education for the mildly retarded—Is much of it justifiable? Except. Child. Sept., p. 5.

Folman, R., and Budoff, M. (1972) Attitudes toward school of special and regular class adolescents. RIEP-Print No. 32. Cambridge, Mass.: Research Institute for Educational Problems (ED 085 971; EC 060 959).

Gampel, D. H., Gottlieb, J., and Harrison, R. H. (1974) A comparison of the classroom behaviors of special class EMR, integrated EMR, low IQ, and nonretarded children. Amer. J. Ment. Defic. 79:16.

Gampel, D. H., Harrison, R. H., and Budoff, M. (1972) An observational study of segregated and integrated EMR children and their nonretarded peers: Can we tell the difference by looking? RIEP-Print No. 27. Cambridge, Mass.: Research Institute for Educational Problems (ED 062 747).

Kaufman, M. J., Gottlieb, J., Agard, J. A., and Kukic, M. B. (1975) Mainstreaming: Toward an explication of the construct. In Alternatives for Teaching Exceptional Children (Eds. Meyen, E. L., Vergason, G. A., and Whelan, R. J.) Denver: Love.

Parc vs. The Commonwealth of Pennsylvania (1971) Pennsylvania Association for Retarded Children vs. Pennsylvania, 334.F Supp. 1257 E.D. Pa.

Public Law 94-142 (1975) Education for all handicapped children act of 1975. Washington: U. S. Congress.

White, B. N., and Budoff, M. (1976) 766 children's feelings toward being mainstreamed. Internal memorandum. Cambridge, Mass.: Research Institute for Educational Problems.

RESEARCH TO PRACTICE IN MENTAL RETARDATION
Education and Training, Volume II
Edited by Peter Mittler
Copyright 1977 I.A.S.S.M.D.

INCORPORATING THE FAMILY AS PART OF THE EDUCATIONAL STRATEGY FOR MENTALLY RETARDED STUDENTS

A. Armfield
Department of Special Education, University of Nebraska at Omaha, United States

How often have you heard a teacher or someone working with children say, "If only the parents wouldn't undo everything I try to teach," or "If only I could get the child's parents to care about what happens to the child in school," or "I'm really dreading tomorrow; we have parents coming to visit"? All of these statements reflect an alienation between the professional educator and a student's family. The professional does not believe that parents are truly interested in what is best for their child. They feel a sincere hostility toward parents who would infringe upon the sanctity of the professional's territory. Further, professionals develop the self-righteous attitude that they, alone, hold a concern for the future welfare of the child.

It can be assumed safely that many of the people who find themselves the parents of a handicapped child were not quite prepared to be adequate parents of any child, not to mention a child that is different from other children. We also must concede that there are many people in the world who had unpleasant experiences at school and have very negative or hostile attitudes toward teachers and education in general. In short, the chances are good that there are a fair number of parents of handicapped children who do not trust professionals for one reason or another, long before they send their child to an educational program.

Many parents never have an opportunity to learn to trust and enjoy professionals. Often the only communication parents have with the school is when their child has caused a calamity. Other parents observe that every time they visit the program, the teacher is observing their behavior for an explanation of the child's handicap. Some programs have a policy that only an "administrator" is to have contact with parents. This policy helps to remind the teacher that parents are, indeed, to be feared, and that they are incompetent to relate to such an unusual set of people. Imagine, if you will, that you are never allowed to discuss your child's educational progress with the teacher without an administrator being present. Your self-image as a potential "troublemaker" may well be enhanced a great deal by such careful arrangements.

Is it possible for professionals who work with handicapped children and parents of children who are handicapped to relate positively with each other? We think so. Further, we feel that a majority of parents can and want to be part of their child's educational program. For many years, a large number of professionals did not feel comfortable with their own efforts to work with the handicapped—not to mention involving other people in their efforts. The field of special education has matured to the stage where many professionals have a great deal to offer their students and the student's family.

Let us explore at least one plan for involving parents in the educational program. That plan is to establish a class for parents of children enrolled in special services. The class would be taught by professionals in the program with the cooperation of the administrative personnel.

We recommend the following steps:

ESTABLISH A PARENTS ADVISORY GROUP

A parents advisory group can help determine the topics to be covered in the class series, the length and format of the classes, and the date and site of the classes. A group that has helped determine all of the conditions of the class will be more than committed to the success of the program.

The membership of the parents advisory group should be carefully considered. We recommend the selection of the most notoriously vocal parents in the community. Choose those parents about whom rumors circulate that they are the most critical parents in the area. When we organized such a group two years ago, we included the organizers of a public hearing by a legislative committee investigating the practices of the public school special education program. These people were not the least bit shy about discussing their points of view. They were most unhappy! Also, include some people considered to be "level headed" and dependable. The point is to include those people who have distinguished themselves as being concerned, who think independently, and who will add some excitement to the adventure.

Organize the first meeting so that the newly invited group has something to consider immediately. Inform them in the invitation that they will help develop the class topics, format, times, and place. Have prepared a set of alternatives for each one of these considerations. Format, times, and place obviously depend upon facilities available. Some topics they may be asked to consider are: 1) legal rights of students and parents; 2) how students are screened, placed, and evaluated; 3) how to identify the developmental stages of your child; 4) planning an estate to protect your child's future; 5) helping your child develop in the areas of visual-motor coordination, auditory discrimination, and language skills; and 6) how to discuss your child's learning program with a teacher, a psychologist, an educational administrator, or a medical specialist. Be sure to have a rather long list of possible topics.

The professional may not feel qualified to conduct classes in all of the areas that parents would like to discuss. It has been our observation that when a professional such as a psychiatrist or a government official is approached to talk directly to a group of concerned parents, they are more than willing to cooperate. They are often overwhelmed by the thought that an educational program would be interested in working directly with parents. But don't ask them yourself, let one of the parents ask them to come to the class to cover a topic. Very often a parent can convey the invitation much more graciously and with a more direct description of purpose. Before discounting a plan that involves parents in selecting topics for a class and then inviting the speakers, remember that we're talking about a group selected primarily on the basis of being aggressive.

It should be possible to set meeting dates, time, style of format, and the first several lesson topics at the first meeting of the advisory group. At least one more meeting should be scheduled of the advisory group to establish the rest of the lesson topics. Perhaps a short meeting could be held before or after one of the lessons.

ADVERTISE THE CLASSES

Ask the advisory group to share the information about the classes with the organizations of which they are members. Other teachers can also spread the word by notifying the parents of their students. If the class is organized to cover a large system, contact the news media with information about the class.

CONDUCT THE CLASSES

If the express wishes of the parents advisory group have been used as agreed, the classes will begin with a lively group of parents motivated to learn about how to help with the education of their child. Professionals will begin to learn a great deal about the effect of a handicapped child upon the life of a family and what a handicap really means to a child.

Although the parents in the advisory group can best judge the appropriate length of time for classes and other scheduling considerations, it is appropriate to begin planning for a one-hour session plus at least one half hour for a completely open question-and-answer period. Frequency of classes will depend entirely upon the group, but some groups may become so enthusiastic that the professional may have to insist on protecting his own personal time.

Plan plenty of time during the first class session for parents to tell about themselves and their children. Almost everyone, including parents of the handicapped, appreciate an opportunity to discuss their problems with a sincerely appreciative audience. Many professionals disregard the catharsis as an unnecessary waste of their time, or they are too embarrassed to hear people discussing their personal problems. This is an opportunity to become well acquainted with parents. This can also be an opportunity for professionals to unburden some of their most private fears about not being able to teach adequately certain skills or types of students. The first meeting can establish a feeling of rapport, openness, and mutual respect that will prevail during the rest of the classes. Attempt to provide the most open forum possible. Try to establish a feeling that allows people to discuss their fears, hostilities, disappointments, and aspirations without fear of reprisal or of rejection on the part of the group. The best way to do this is for the professional to set an example by being very open, nonjudgmental, and not easily shocked or insulted.

Make sure that some of the classes revolve around the curriculum that is currently being taught in the child's classroom. Prepare some suggestions for parents who want to know what they can do with their child at home to improve his school performance. For those parents whose child is at a very basic developmental stage, the professional may wish to prepare a list of activities such as the one prepared by Mrs. Sandra Howard, a graduate student in Special Education at the University of Nebraska at Omaha:

1. *Visual Perception:* A child must be able to differentiate between written letters and words. This skill can be developed through the following activities.
   a. Find details in a picture.
   b. See how many objects a child can remember after looking at a picture for a minute.
   c. Make two sets of cards with various shapes or letters. Have your child match identical cards.
   d. Have your child close his eyes and describe his clothing.
   e. Arrange a bead pattern on a string. Show it to the child. Remove the beads and have him rebuild the pattern. Gradually increase the length of the pattern.
   f. Have your child match identical words written on cards.
2. *Visual-motor Coordination:* Eye-hand coordination affects both reading and writing skills.
   a. Put blocks or clothespins into smaller and smaller containers.

b. String spools or beads.

c. Trace large, simple figures.

d. Fill containers with rice up to a level marked with a rubber band.

e. Button and zip clothing.

f. Reproduce figures like triangles, squares, and rectangles that someone draws for him as models.

g. Give your child a box and a long piece of ribbon to practice tying bows.

h. Bounce a large ball back and forth, play catch, and bounce the ball off the wall.

i. Cut out pictures and shapes and paste them.

3. *Auditory Discrimination and Memory:* In order to analyze words phonetically, a child must be able to differentiate between sounds.

a. Listen to recordings of rhymes.

b. With the eyes shut, try to identify certain sounds, such as tearing papers, a pencil being sharpened, or a window being opened.

c. Have your child match pictures or words beginning with the same sounds.

d. Have your child repeat increasingly long sentences.

e. Give him a series of directions such as, "turn around, jump, clap your hands three times, and walk to the door."

4. *Classification:* Classification aids a child to generalize, an important facet of reading comprehension.

a. Cut out magazine pictures of different kinds of boats, animals, houses, etc. Group the pictures and assemble a scrapbook.

b. Label objects.

c. Sort buttons according to size, shape, number of holes, and colors.

d. Float objects. Take various objects and find out which ones float.

e. Sort playing cards according to number, color, or suit.

f. Help sort clothes and organize them in dresser drawers.

5. *Listening Skills:* A child must be able to listen attentively and follow directions.

a. Have your child identify various sounds.

b. Listen to the child and he will listen to you. Set a proper example.

c. Have your child deliver messages to other members of the family.

6. *Language:* Language and vocabulary development affect a child's ability to comprehend written thought.

a. Cooking—following a recipe, measuring, pouring, sifting, being in the kitchen together—also provides natural atmosphere for language development, word games, riddles, listening skills, etc.

b. Family trips to the zoo, farm, woods, park, or lakes offer a variety of learning experiences.

c. Encourage the use of full sentences.

d. Encourage the use of proper names for objects.
e. Give individual attention when listening to a child describe his experiences.

Please note that the activities described do not suggest certain academic class titles, but they are natural activities that can happen in the home without a child necessarily associating them with "school work." A modification of the activities can be used at a rather advanced developmental level. Ask parents to report to the school which activities have seemed successful.

Another suggestion is to borrow actual classroom material, set up a mock class using the parents at students, and conduct a class just as it is done during the day. Ask the parents to do the very same assignments that children are asked to do. Do not spend more than 15 or 20 minutes for each class setting. Try to "mock up" at least two classrooms so parents can get an idea of different classroom situations. Remember that adults have long since forgotten classroom routine so they may require more direction than students. Keep the whole experience on a rather light and somewhat humorous level so that the parents do not become anxious or embarrassed if asked to do something that requires a forgotten skill. Such a realistic exercise can help parents understand what is going on at school and can give them an opportunity to empathize with their child.

EVALUATE EACH CLASS

Develop a short questionnaire that parents can fill out following each class. This may be a three-sentence questionnaire asking: 1) What did you like about the class? 2) What didn't you like about the class? 3) What ideas did you get from the class that should be used as topics for future classes? It can be more elaborate if desired. Do not pass up an opportunity to allow each parent to evaluate each class. It not only provides an opportunity to improve future classes, it gives parents perhaps their first opportunity to say what they think about something in education and have someone actually respond positively to their suggestions. Please consider the ramifications of such a practice. It may be possible for parents to feel that they can actually be a part of their child's educational destiny—a revolutionary thought for this century. It is advisable to report a summary of the evaluations on a systematic basis.

In summary, we have suggested that the family can be incorporated into the educational program of their child. While a number of plans can be employed, one suggestion is to develop a class for parents of children enrolled in special classes using the following principles:

1. Involve parents, including parents who have been critical of the program, in the planning and implementation of the class.

2. Provide an atmosphere where parents can learn, complain, and plan with candor and openness.
3. Provide parents with some suggestions for activities that they can accomplish successfully at home that will contribute to their child's educational development.
4. Allow the parents an insight into the classroom experiences of their child.
5. Provide an opportunity for evaluation of the classes, and attempt to incorporate that evaluation into the classes as they are conducted.
6. Adopt the belief that parents can and should be a vital part of developing a child's educational program.

RESEARCH TO PRACTICE IN MENTAL RETARDATION
Education and Training, Volume II
Edited by Peter Mittler
Copyright 1977 I.A.S.S.M.D.

HELPING TEACHERS AND PARENTS TO MODIFY BEHAVIOR OF THEIR RETARDED AND BEHAVIOR-DISORDERED CHILDREN

R. V. Hall and M. Broden
*Juniper Gardens Children's Project,
2021 North Third Street, Kansas City,
Kansas 66101, United States*

The Juniper Gardens Children's Project is a community research project sponsored by the University of Kansas. Located in the inner-city area of Kansas City, Kansas, it is primarily devoted to investigating procedures for remediating and preventing developmental retardation in children from depriving environments.

Among the research emphases at Juniper Gardens has been a program of research designed to improve both social and academic behaviors of developmentally retarded learners in the public schools. Early studies were carried out which focused on decreasing disruptive behaviors and increasing attending behaviors of these pupils (e.g., Hall, Lund, and Jackson, 1968; Broden, Hall, Dunlap, and Clark, 1970; Copeland, Brown, and Hall, 1972). Other studies focused directly on increasing academic behavior of developmentally retarded learners (e.g., Wolf, Clark, and Lachowicz, 1968; Wolf, Giles, and Hall, 1968; Brown, Copeland, and Hall, 1972; Brown, Copeland, and Hall, 1976).

Concurrent with these classroom investigations, other studies were implemented which focused on the pupil in the home. Numerous studies showed that systematic consequences could be used by parents to modify home behaviors (e.g., Hall, 1971; Hall, Axelrod, et al., 1972; Hall, Copeland, and Clark, 1976). Other studies such as those by McKenzie, Clark, et al. (1968) and Copeland,

This research was carried out at the Juniper Gardens Children's Project and was supported by grant HD 03144 from the National Institute of Child Health and Human Development, Bureau of Child Research, Department of Human Development and Family Life and School of Education, University of Kansas.

Brown, Axelrod, and Hall (1972) indicated school performance could be affected by procedures involving parents.

Most of the school and home studies carried out at Juniper Gardens, as well as the majority of those reported elsewhere involving behavior modification or applied behavior analysis approaches, have focused on the systematic manipulation of consequences to bring about behavior change. While successful, many such procedures have required a high response cost on the parts of teachers and parents, and, in some cases, it has been found that providing more reinforcement in and of itself is insufficient to bring about the desired changes in performance (Hall and Harris, 1973).

The classroom study reported here is one of a series carried out in junior high school classrooms which were designed to increase the amount and quality of verbal responding in pupils, frequently an area of deficit and educational concern in retarded learners from depriving environments.

The home study describes a parent-implemented tutoring procedure which increased the in-school spelling performance of an inner-city student. This study indicated that inner-city parents can be taught to carry out specific procedures that require relatively little time but that can positively affect classroom performance.

EXPERIMENT I

Subjects and Setting

The subjects of the first experiment were 30 students enrolled in a seventh-grade junior high school unified studies class. The teacher was concerned because very few of her pupils participated in the daily discussion sessions which were a part of their history and English lessons. Classroom observations revealed there were no significant disruptive problems in the class but that few students responded to questions asked by the teacher during discussions.

Observation and Measurement

Daily observations were made by an observer who recorded data on a three-column form. One column was for writing down teacher questions, one was for recording the number of pupils who raised their hands to answer the questions, and the third was to record the student answers. In order to be counted as a hand raise, the elbow of the raised hand had to be above the surface of the pupil's desk and the wrist of the raised hand had to be at least chin high when the teacher called on someone to answer the question. Reliability checks were made by having a second observer record hand raises during each phase of the study. Comparisons of the observer records resulted in agreement ranging from 89–100%.

Latency of asking for a response was defined as the elapsed time between the end of the teacher's question and the point at which she called on a student to respond. Tape recordings were made of classroom discussion periods beginning with the ninth session of the study. Two observers independently listened to all discussion tapes to record latency in seconds. The agreement in their records ranged from 85–100%.

Experimental Conditions and Results

Baseline$_1$:   A 16-day baseline phase revealed that an average of only 2.7 students in the class of 30 raised their hands following a teacher question. As is shown in the lower graph in Figure 1, the mean latency from the end of a question until the teacher called on a pupil to answer was 4.9 sec.

Increased Latency$_1$:   On the seventeenth day the teacher was asked to pause for a longer time after she asked a question before calling on a pupil who had raised his hand. In this phase latency increased to a mean of 13.7 sec per question and the number of hands raised more than doubled to 5.7 per question.

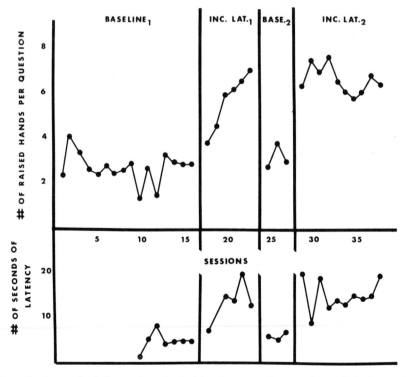

Figure 1. A record of the number of raised hands per teacher question and the latency in seconds between asking a question and calling on a student to respond.

Baseline$_2$:   When the teacher decreased the latency to 3.7 sec in the second baseline phase the number of pupils raising hands decreased to 3.2 per question.

Increased Latency$_2$:   When the teacher again increased the latency before calling in on a pupil to respond to a mean of 15.6 sec, the number of students raising hands increased to 6.6 per question.

EXPERIMENT II

Subjects and Setting

The subject of this study was Dirk, a ten-year-old boy enrolled in an inner-city classroom. He had been retained in the second grade the previous year because of poor academic performance. He consistently received D and F grades in all subjects. He lived with his mother and two brothers. His mother volunteered for the study because of her concern for her son's failure.

Observations in School

Dirk's teacher knew a spelling study was being conducted in her class but did not know which student was the subject nor that it involved home tutoring. An observer was present in her class during spelling-test periods. The teacher gave a pretest on Tuesday of each week. During the week the pupils studied their spelling words and were retested on Friday.

After each test the teacher collected the spelling papers and gave them to the observer. The observer left the room and graded them by comparing them to the words in the spelling book. At least once in each phase of the study the student papers were photocopied prior to grading and a second person graded the copies. Agreement in the grading of papers was always above 94%.

Observations in the Home

The mother recorded aspects of Dirk's behavior during home tutoring sessions. Recording sheets were provided which had four columns. In the first column she wrote the spelling words to be learned. The other three columns were used to record whether or not Dirk spelled the words correctly.

Each tutoring session was tape recorded. The tapes were analyzed to determine whether or not the mother had followed the designated tutoring procedures and had made accurate records to check the length of the tutoring sessions, etc. Agreement among independent observers for the various behaviors recorded ranged from 92–97%.

Experimental Conditions and Results

Baseline$_1$:   During the six-week baseline phase no home tutoring was implemented. As can be seen in Figure 2, Dirk's Friday test scores were always below

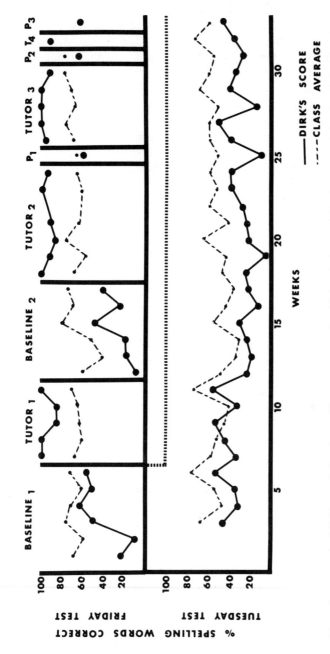

Figure 2. A record of Friday and Tuesday spelling test scores of a third-grade boy and his classmates during Baseline and various home tutoring conditions.

the mean scores of his classmates. During Baseline$_1$ his mean Friday test score was 41% while that of the class was 67%.

Tutor$_1$: During the Tutor$_1$ phase Dirk's mother tutored him on Tuesday, Wednesday, and Thursday evenings. On Tuesday night she presented the week's list of words three times. Each time through the list she pronounced each word. Dirk repeated it and spelled it orally. If his spelling was correct she said "Good" and pronounced the next word. If he misspelled the word, his mother spelled it aloud and asked him to spell it again until he had spelled it correctly three times without further prompting.

On Wednesday night the same procedure was followed the first two times through the list. The third time through, however, Dirk wrote the words on a piece of paper. His mother then checked them and had him write any misspelled words five times.

On Thursday night Dirk spelled the words orally the first time through the list but wrote them the second and third times his mother pronounced them.

As can be seen in Figure 2, when he was tutored his spelling scores on Friday tests increased to 94% correct while the class mean remained essentially unchanged at 65%.

Baseline$_2$: When Dirk's mother discontinued tutoring during Baseline$_2$ Dirk's Friday scores decreased to below Baseline$_1$ levels. Those of his class remained unchanged.

Tutor$_2$: During the Tutor$_2$ phase the mother tutored Dirk once again. Figure 2 shows his scores increased to 93%. Those of the class remained stable.

Probe$_1$: When the mother discontinued tutoring for one week during Probe$_1$ Dirk's scores decreased to below the class mean.

Tutor$_3$: In the Tutor$_3$ phase Dirk's mother tutored him on Tuesday and Wednesday nights only. Thursday sessions were discontinued. Dirk's spelling scores again increased above the level of his classmates.

Probe$_2$: As in Probe$_1$ Dirk's mother discontinued tutoring and his spelling scores decreased.

Tutor$_4$: During the week Tutor$_4$ condition Dirk's mother tutored him on Tuesday evening only and again his Friday scores increased.

Probe$_3$: Again his score declined when the mother stopped tutoring.

Tuesday Spelling Scores

The lower part of Figure 2 presents Tuesday spelling scores for Dirk and his class. In these tests given prior to tutoring each week, Dirk consistently scored below the class mean, providing further evidence that the improvement on Friday tests was attributable to tutoring.

Other Results

Observations of Dirk's classroom attending behavior showed an increase from 53% during Baseline$_1$ to approximately 90% during the latter phases of the experiment even though no direct attempt was made to manipulate attending.

An analysis of the tape recordings of the home tutoring sessions showed that Dirk learned to spell words more rapidly as the study progressed. The time spent on each word decreased from 2 min and 30 sec per word to approximately 20 sec per word by the end of the study, yet spelling scores remained high.

DISCUSSION

These two studies present procedures that teachers and parents of students from depriving environments can implement to improve school performance. Furthermore, they present evidence that providing an environment that promotes increased opportunity for such children to respond may be a critical factor in increasing academic performance of these children.

The students in the first experiment had been largely nonverbal and were reluctant to volunteer to answer teacher questions. Yet the simple expedient of having the teacher wait a few seconds longer before calling on them to answer an question more than doubled the number of those who participated in answering questions during discussion period. Other procedures carried out in this and another classroom of developmentally retarded learners, and reported in Broden, Beasley, and Hall (1977), indicated that providing instructions and consequences, and asking questions requiring more than one-word answers were also effective ways to increase the amount and complexity of verbal behavior in these children.

The home tutoring procedure described here provided an opportunity for a third-grade boy to practice making correct spelling responses that positively affected his performance in class. When his mother began tutoring his younger brother using a similar procedure, comparable results were obtained. Furthermore, the improved spelling performance in the younger sibling continued during reversal phases, indicating he had learned to spell independently of the tutoring procedures.

These studies provide some evidence supporting other research such as that carried out by Harris and Hall (1972) and Brown, Copeland, and Hall (1976) which indicates that the critical dimension for helping developmentally retarded learners to make academic progress may not lie in providing more reinforcement for what they are currently doing, but rather in providing more opportunity for them to practice making verbal and academic responses. If simple effective procedures for teachers and parents of these children can be developed, perhaps the high incidence of developmental retardation among this population can be decreased.

SUMMARY

Several studies are presented describing research carried out at the Juniper Gardens Children's Project in which behavior modification procedures were used in the public schools and in homes to increase appropriate social behaviors and academic performance of developmentally retarded and behavior-disordered children.

REFERENCES

Broden, M., Hall, R. V., Dunlap, A., and Clark, R. (1970) Effects of teacher attention and a token reinforcement system on study behavior in a junior high school special education classroom. Except. Child. 36:341.

Broden, M., Beasley, A., and Hall, R. V. (1977) Effects of parent home tutoring on in-class spelling performance. Behav. Mod. (in press).

Brown, R., Copeland, R., and Hall, R. V. (1972) The school principal as a behavior modifier. J. Educ. Res. 4:175.

Brown, R., Copeland, R., and Hall, R. V. (1976) Effects of an elementary school principal systematically reinforcing students for learning multiplication facts. Presentation at the Midwestern Association for Behavior Analysis, Chicago, Illinois.

Copeland, R., Brown, R., Axelrod, S., and Hall, R. V. (1972) Effects of a school principal praising parents for student attendance. Educ. Technol. 12:56.

Hall, R. V. (1971) Behavior Management Series. Part I. The Measurement of Behavior, Part II. Basic Principles, Part III. Applications in School and Home. H. & H Enterprises, Post Office Box 3342, Lawrence, Kansas.

Hall, R. V., Axelrod, S., Tyler, L., Grief., Jones, F. C., and Robertson, R. (1972) Modification of behavior problems in the home with a parent as observer and experimenter. J. Appl. Behav. Anal. 5:53.

Hall, R. V., Copeland, R., and Clark, M. (1976) Management strategies for teachers and parents: Responsive teaching. In Teaching Special Children (Haring, N. and Schiefelbusch, R. L.) New York: McGraw-Hill, p. 157.

Hall, R. V., and Harris, J. W. (1973) Effects of systematic reinforcement procedures on performance of underachieving high school pupils. Educational Technology Research, No. 51, New Jersey.

Hall, R. V., Lund, D., and Jackson, D. (1968) Effects of teacher attention on study behavior. J. Appl. Behav. Anal. 1:1.

Harris, J. W., Stillwell, C., and Hall, R. V. (1972) Effects of provision for individual differences and teacher attention upon study behavior and assignments completed. Child Study J. 2:75.

Harris, J. W., and Hall, R. V. (1972) The effect of a token system on out-of-seat behavior. Research in Education, ERIC Publication.

McKenzie, H., Clark, M., Wolf, M. M., Kothera, R., and Benson, C. (1968) Behavior modification of children with learning disabilities using grades as tokens and allowances as back-up reinforcers. Except. Child. 34:745.

Wolf, M. M., Clark, M., and Lachowicz, J. (1968) A pilot basic education program for school drop-outs incorporating a token reinforcement system. Behav. Res. Ther. 6:183.

Wolf, M. M., Giles, D., and Hall, R. V. (1968) Experiments with token reinforcement in a remedial classroom. Behav. Res. Ther. 6:55.

RESEARCH TO PRACTICE IN MENTAL RETARDATION
Education and Training, Volume II
Edited by Peter Mittler
Copyright 1977 I.A.S.S.M.D.

DISCRIMINATING A GENERALIZATION TECHNOLOGY
Recommendations for Research in Mental Retardation

D. M. Baer and T. F. Stokes
The University of Kansas, Lawrence, Kansas 66044, United States

The discipline of applied behavior analysis has begun to develop a technology of behavior change. When that technology is applied to retarded children, three major problems emerge: 1) teaching and maintaining the necessary behaviors of the people who apply behavioral systems to the children: parents, institutional staff, classroom teachers, aides, etc.; 2) analysis of what responses are most critical for inclusion in the systems' curricula; 3) development of a technology of generalization of behavior change.

Behavior change is a fairly well understood process today. The literature of the field shows that any of the behavior changes implied in the first two problems can be accomplished readily enough (e.g., Ayllon and Azrin, 1968; Panyon, Boozer, and Morris, 1970; Parsonson, Baer, and Baer, 1974). Those behavior changes have been made mainly in specialized training settings; yet, the children's new skills are meant to be practiced *outside* the training setting. A common observation is that they are not. An obvious solution to this problem is to set up behavior change processes in the normalized settings in which the new behavior is to be practiced (e.g., Tharp and Wetzel, 1969; Walker and Buckley, 1972). However, the specially trained personnel capable of developing new behaviors in retarded children are few in number and found primarily in centers dedicated to that purpose. This problem could be solved by developing reliable training programs for the parents, teachers, and other nonprofessionals who are to live and work with the children in their normalized settings. But that represents a problem in the process of being solved, rather than a solution in hand. Therefore, the present alternative is to develop a technology of generalization, such that children may be taught new skills by trained personnel in relatively few centers, but nevertheless will also display these new behaviors and related ones in other settings in which they live or are to live in the future.

Such a technology of generalization is almost a reality, despite the fact that, until recently, it has hardly been recognized as a problem in its own right. A technology for discrimination has long existed; generalization was often thought to result simply from failure to use discrimination technology well. In practice, however, generalization is a concept equally as important as discrimination, and in consequence there has appeared a budding area of "generalization-promotion" techniques. A review of some 250 studies relevant to the problem of generalization has been made by Stokes and Baer (1976a, in press). A central core of that literature is summarized here.

In general, techniques designed to promote generalization can be categorized on a continuum of directness of their application to the problem, according to at least seven general headings:

INTRODUCTION TO NATURAL MAINTAINING CONTINGENCIES

Perhaps the most dependable of all generalization mechanisms is one that hardly deserves the name: the transfer of behavioral control from the teacher-experimenter to stable, natural contingencies that can be trusted to operate in the environment to which the child will return, or that he already occupies. To a considerable extent, this goal is accomplished by choosing behaviors to teach that will normally meet maintaining reinforcement after the teaching. The reinforcement initially required for the first teaching of those skills then will become irrelevant; the natural community of reinforcement contingencies not only should maintain the new skills, but also may refine them and add new ones as well. However, especially in the case of retarded or institutionalized children whose dependency has become a stable fact in the lives of their caregivers, rearrangement of the natural environment may sometimes be necessary. A meaningful example was provided by Horner (1971), who taught an institutionalized, nonambulatory retardate to walk on crutches in an experimental setting. However, to generalize walking by the child, who previously had been taken everywhere in a wheelchair by solicitous caregivers, it was necessary to convince those caregivers to refrain from giving this help. The child then walked on crutches in all activities and settings.

An even more significant example was provided by Seymour and Stokes (1976). In their study, institutionalized delinquent girls were taught to solicit reinforcement from their natural community—the staff of their residential institution—who rarely offered reinforcement. The girls learned that when their work was objectively good, and when staff persons were nearby, calling these adults' attention to their good work would result in fairly consistent reinforcement. Thus, they learned to recruit the available but dormant natural community.

TRAINING SUFFICIENT EXEMPLARS

If the result of teaching one exemplar of a generalizable lesson is merely the mastery of the exemplar taught, with no generalization beyond it, then we must teach another exemplar of the same generalizable lesson, and then another, etc., until generalization occurs sufficiently to solve the problem. Stokes, Baer, and Jackson (1974) provided an example of the training of sufficient *stimulus* exemplars by having one experimenter teach institutionalized retarded children a social greeting response, and, upon discovering a lack of stable generalization of this greeting to all other members of the staff, having a second experimenter teach the same response. All children stably generalized the response to everyone after (at most) two successive teachings. Similar demonstrations of response generalization have been shown with motor imitations, articulation, grammar and syntax, question-asking, and compliance with instructions. A survey of these studies shows that the number of exemplars "sufficient" for desirable generalization varies widely; nevertheless, it is optimistic to note how frequently a sufficient number of exemplars is small; often no more than two are needed. In particular, the standard use of two trainers in the systematic education of a retarded child often may yield excellent generalization.

TRAINING LOOSELY

One relatively simple technique can be conceptualized as merely the negation of discrimination technique. That is, teaching is conducted with relatively little control over the stimuli presented and the correct responses allowed, to maximize sampling of relevant dimensions for transfer to other situations and other forms of the behavior. A formal example of this (most often informal) technique was provided by Schroeder and Baer (1972), who taught vocal imitation skills to retarded children in both of two ways, one emphasizing tight restriction of the vocal skills being learned at the moment, the other allowing greater range of these stimuli within the current problem. The latter method was characterized repeatedly by greater generalization to as-yet-untaught vocal imitation problems, thus affirming "loose" teaching techniques as a contributor to wider generalization.

INDISCRIMINABLE CONTINGENCIES

Intermittent schedules of reinforcement have been shown repeatedly to be particularly durable—generalized—in their effects, relative to fixed or continuous schedules. The essential feature of intermittent schedules may be the impossibility of discriminating reinforcement occasions from nonreinforcement occasions, until after the fact. This hypothesis may be extended to the case of generalization. In generalization, behavior occurs in settings in which it will not be reinforced, just as it does in settings in which it will be reinforced. Then the analogue to an intermittent schedule is a condition in which the organism cannot discriminate in which settings a response will be reinforced or not reinforced. A potential approximation to such a condition was presented in a study by Schwarz and Hawkins (1970). In that experiment, a school child with a posture problem was videotaped during several classes. After each school day had ended, the child was shown the tapes and awarded reinforcers according to how often good posture was displayed in those tapes. In fact, reinforcers were awarded only on the basis of good posture in one class during the school day, but posture improvements were observed in another class as well. The delayed reinforcement may have made it difficult to discriminate in which class posture was critical for earning reinforcement.

In general, it may be suspected that delayed reinforcement often will have the advantage of making the times and places in which a contingency actually operates indiscriminable to the subject. However, this is an advantage primarily for the goal of generalization. Otherwise, delayed reinforcement often would be considered an inefficient technique, most especially so for retarded children. However, its potential for fostering generalization suggests strongly that further research should evaluate its use *after* immediate reinforcement has accomplished the initial development of a new skill.

COMMON STIMULI

If generalization will occur when there are sufficient stimulus components occurring in both the training and generalization settings, then a pragmatic technique is to guarantee that common and salient stimuli will be present in both. One predictor of the salience of a stimulus for this role is its already established function for other important behaviors of the subject. In this respect, children's peers may represent peculiarly suitable candidates. An example has been provided by Stokes and Baer (1976b, in press). Two children with serious learning disabilities were recruited to learn several word-recognition skills. One child was taught these skills and concurrently shown how to teach them to the other child, acting as a peer-tutor. It was found that both children learned the skills to a high degree of reliability, but that neither generalized them reliably or stably to somewhat different settings in which the other child usually was absent. However, when the other child was brought into those settings, then each child showed greatly increased and stabilized generalization. Similar demonstrations have been provided by Johnston and Johnston (1972) for the skill of speech articulation.

MEDIATED GENERALIZATION

Mediated generalization is well known as a theoretical mechanism explaining generalization of highly symbolic learnings. In essence, it requires establishing a response as part of the new learning that can be utilized in other problems as well, and that will constitute sufficient commonality between the original learning and the new problem to result in generalization. The most commonly used mediator is language. However, a deliberate use of language to accomplish generalization is rare and little is known about what aspects of a language response make for best mediation. An example was provided by Risley and Hart (1968), who taught disadvantaged children to report at the end of play on their play-material choices. Mention of a given choice was reinforced, which produced increased mentioning of that choice, but no change in the children's actual use of that play material. When reinforcement was restricted to *true* reports of play-material choices, however, the children then changed their play behavior (the next day) so that when queried about that play, they could truthfully report on their use of the specified play material, and thus earn reinforcement. The lesson generalized, such that after several sequential experiences with these procedures, the children then used reports about play as mediators, even without reinforcement being restricted to only true reports. This technique has been extended subsequently to the case of social skills, specifically sharing and praising between young children (Rogers-Warren and Baer, 1976, in press).

In the case of retarded children, it might be particularly true that the ability to use verbal responses as mediators would lag behind that of normal children. Nevertheless, the potential power of the technique for generalization is so great that the research required for an appreciation of its applicability to retarded children's development deserves the effort.

TRAINING "TO GENERALIZE"

If generalization is considered as a response itself, then a reinforcement contingency may be placed on it. Informally, teachers often do this when they urge a student who has been taught one example of a general principle to "see" another example as "the same thing." Indeed, there exists the possibility of programming reinforcement specifically, perhaps *only*, for movement along the generalization gradient desired.

Very few studies exemplify this logic. Parsonson, Baer, and Baer (1974) for example, taught two teachers of retarded children to give appropriate social reinforcement to their students' behaviors, but taught the teachers from the outset to judge *all* child behavior as appropriate or inappropriate according to general criteria, rather than to attack only a few specified child responses. Apparently generalized changes were produced. Then it is worth hypothesizing that "to generalize" may be treated as if it were an operant response, and reinforced as such, simply to see what useful results occur.

Thus, within behavioral technology, there are little-appreciated principles and procedures that produce generalization when it does not occur "naturally." The refinement and elaboration of these procedures into a technology is an important piece of unfinished business for applied research.

SUMMARY

Behavior analysts often must teach retarded children in settings other than the normalized ones in which the new behavior has most value. Thus, a technology of generalization is necessary for normalization. That technology is almost available. Seven categories of generalization-promoting techniques are cited for application and intensive development through applied research.

REFERENCES

Ayllon, T., and Azrin, N. H. (1968) The Token Economy: A Motivational System for Therapy and Rehabilitation. New York: Appleton-Century-Crofts.

Horner, R. D. (1971) Establishing use of crutches by a mentally retarded spina bifida child. J. Appl. Behav. Anal. 4:183.

Johnston, J. M., and Johnston, G. T. (1972) Modification of consonant speech-sound articulation in young children. J. Appl. Behav. Anal. 5:233.

Panyan, M., Boozer, H., and Morris, N. (1970) Feedback to attendants as a reinforcer for applying operant techniques. J. Appl. Behav. Anal. 3:1.

Parsonson, B. S., Baer, A. M., and Baer, D. M. (1974) The application of generalized correct social contingencies: An evaluation of a training program. J. Appl. Behav. Anal. 7:427.

Risley, T. R., and Hart, B. (1968) Developing correspondence between the nonverbal and verbal behavior of preschool children. J. Appl. Behav. Anal. 1:267.

Rogers-Warren, A., and Baer, D. M. (1976) Saying and doing: The verbal mediation of social behaviors. J. Appl. Behav. Anal. 9:335.

Schroeder, G. L., and Baer, D. M. (1972) Effects of concurrent and serial training on generalized vocal imitation in retarded children. Develop. Psychol. 6:293.

Schwarz, M. L., and Hawkins, R. P. (1970) Application of delayed reinforcement procedures to the behaviors of an elementary school child. J. Appl. Behav. Anal. 3:85.

Seymour, F. W., and Stokes, T. F. (1976) Self-recording in training girls to increase work and evoke staff praise in an institution for offenders. J. Appl. Behav. Anal. 9:41.

Stokes, T. F., and Baer, D. M. (1976a) An implicit technology of generalization. J. Appl. Behav. Anal. (in press).

Stokes, T. F., and Baer, D. M. (1976b) Preschool peers as mutual generalization-facilitating agents. Behav. Ther. (in press).

Stokes, T. F., Baer, D. M., and Jackson, R. L. (1974) Programming the generalization of a greeting response in four retarded children. J. Appl. Behav. Anal. 7:599.

Tharp, R. G., and Wetzel, R. J. (1969) Behavior Modification in the Natural Environment. New York: Academic Press.

Walker, H. M., and Buckley, N. K. (1972) Programming generalization and maintenance effects across time and across settings. J. Appl. Behav. Anal. 5:209.

RESEARCH TO PRACTICE IN MENTAL RETARDATION
Education and Training, Volume II
Edited by Peter Mittler
Copyright 1977 I.A.S.S.M.D.

THE DEVELOPMENT OF A MOTOR CURRICULUM FOR THE SEVERELY HANDICAPPED

D. Grove, H. D. Fredericks, V. Baldwin, and W. Moore
Teaching Research Infant and Child Center, Monmouth, Oregon 97361, United States

This is a report on the development of a motor curriculum for severely handicapped children. The genesis of this curriculum was in two lines of basic research conducted by the staff of the Teaching Research Infant and Child Center, Monmouth, Oregon. These research endeavors eventually merged to form a task-analyzed curriculum which could be utilized by the classroom teacher, the parent, or the institutional worker.

A curriculum for the severely handicapped, because of the nature of the heterogeneous population which it serves, must be comprehensive. It must deal with basic motor movements of head-holding, prone movement such as crawling and creeping, sitting, independent weight-bearing, walking, and movement up and down steps or inclines. The curriculum must also include the entire range of fine motor skills such as upper extremity fine motor skills (e.g., the manipulation of pegs into holes) and lower extremity skills such as standing on tiptoe. It must therefore be sensitive to students with a wide range of physical and sensory handicaps.

EXPERIMENTAL BASIS FOR THE CURRICULUM

Dr. David Grove (1972) conducted a research project at Fairview Hospital and Training Center, Salem, Oregon, in conjunction with that institution's physical therapy department in which various methods of task analysis and progress measurement of basic motor movements like head-holding, independent weight-bearing, walking, and prone movement were examined. He also probed the effects of medication upon these motor movements and explored methods for inhibiting reflexes that fail to diminish with maturity. An example is the tonic neck reflex that persists in some handicapped children and that needs to be extinguished in order for the child to develop more appropriate motor movements. Two examples may suffice to indicate the methodology and techniques he utilized.

Case 1 was a patient whose objective was to establish head-extension. The baseline data indicated that he held his head in extension approximately 20% of the time. Electrical switches were designed, constructed, and mounted on a collar. When the collar was fitted around the neck of the child, any movement of the head away from the erect or the extended position was recorded. The switches were connected to a transistor radio so that each time the child brought his head into the designated position, the radio automatically turned on, delivering contingent music. This resulted in the head being held in extension about 85% of the time for each 20-minute session. When all reinforcement was withdrawn, i.e., reversal, the percent of time in which the head was held in extension dropped to 10%. Treatment was then reestablished with the child being reinforced continuously for keeping his head in extension. As the program progressed, he was reinforced only if his head maintained extension for two minutes, and during the last condition he was reinforced for head extension for a five-minute period. Consequently, the number of reinforcers were reduced, i.e., faded, but the percent of time the head was held in extension remained high. This process was continued—demanding more behavior for less reinforcement—until the child was capable of holding his head in extension without reinforcement. Eventually this behavior was maintained in the natural environment without specific reinforcement for that behavior.

This particular study demonstrated: 1) the role of consequences in modifying persistent maladaptive motor behavior, and 2) the necessity for building into a curriculum the fading process by requiring more performance before reinforcement is delivered.

Case 2 demonstrates a dramatic change in the motor behavior of a mentally retarded child who was engaged in a weight-bearing program in which the initial task was for the child to hold on to the therapist's arm with his hand while both knees were extended and his feet were on the floor. This was a part of a sequence in the weight-bearing program. While holding on to the therapist's arm the child stood for an average of one minute. However, when a different cue, a wooden bar, was substituted for the therapist's arm, the child's response rate immediately increased until he reached criteria on Steps 8 and 9. Subsequent attempts to transfer him back to the therapist's arm resulted in a return to his previously low levels. By returning him to the wooden bar, he continued to progress through the steps. It was decided not to transfer him back but rather to fade the wooden bar by allowing him to hold with only one hand and then no hands.

The steps devised by Grove through which the patient moved demonstrated the utilization of a task-analyzed curriculum for the development of basic motor skills in combination with behavior modification techniques.

Another member of the Teaching Research Infant and Child Center followed a line of research examining the utilization of behavior modification and reverse chaining on the effects of fine motor coordination, both upper and lower extremity. In a research study which compared Down's syndrome children on two treatment methodologies, (behavior modification, Doman-Delacato and one control group), Fredericks (1969) found that in four daily five-minute sessions with a 15-minute rest between each five-minute session,and utilizing only social reinforcement, which included verbal approval and physical contacts, the children made significant gains in motor activities. The activities were winding string around pegs, placing pegs in holes, placing discs in slots, cutting, jumping, board walking, doing pencil mazes, pencil coordination. Each of the activities was, as in Grove's research, broken down into a series of steps. Children were taught these steps in reverse sequence and were reinforced on a continuous schedule only at the conclusion of the final steps. With measures being taken on the Lincoln-Oseretsky Motor Development Scale, the behavior modification group scored significantly higher than the other treatment group and the control group. Follow-up using the same scales was administered three months after the conclusion of the post-test to all children. No significant differences were noted between the follow-up test scores and the post-test scores obtained three months earlier. The same pattern of significant difference obtained during post-testing maintained for the follow-up scores, strongly supporting the argument for the stability of the gains made during the treatment period.

Thus, the results of these two independent lines of research, one looking at basic motor movements with a severely handicapped population in an institutional setting, and the other looking at fine motor coordination at both upper and lower extremities, but with a less handicapped institutional population, indicated that a curriculum in the hands of a trained teacher could form the basis of a program to change the motor behaviors of children. The staff at Teaching Research undertook the development of that curriculum during the summer of 1972, when both areas of research described above were either completed or drawing to completion.

At about that same time the Teaching Research Infant and Child Center was engaged in consulting with a number of teachers throughout the State of Oregon and elsewhere. An informal consortium of those teachers was formed to write individual prescriptive programs for children in the area of motor skills. And, in the summer of 1972, the Teaching Research Infant and Child Center attempted to assemble in a curriculum not only the sequences that were written by the consortium of teachers but also those that had been developed through the research of Grove and Fredericks. It was determined that the curriculum was to be a series of behavioral objectives that would be task-analyzed for the young moderately or severely handicapped child. In early fall of 1972, the first version of that curriculum was developed, and, during the ensuing year, it was applied at the Teaching Research Infant and Child Center Preschool, by the Preschool for Handicapped Children in Corvallis, Oregon, by the Coeur d'Alene National Model Center for Early Childhood Education for the Handicapped in Idaho, and by approximately 25 other classrooms throughout Oregon, Washington, and

Idaho. A process of continuous feedback by teachers utilizing the curriculum was initiated. Revisions were made based on the feedback and a consensus of the teachers involved.

The motor curriculum, revised in the spring of 1973 together with curriculum sequences in self-help, language and cognitive skills, became the official curriculum in the Northwest Region for Deaf/Blind. During the summer of 1973, all teachers of the deaf/blind in the Northwest were trained in the utilization of the curriculum; 90% of those trained employed the curriculum in their classrooms during the school year 1973–74. Feedback was systematically obtained from all of these teachers and from others who were using the curriculum, which resulted in its present format for publication, *The Teaching Research Curriculum for Moderately and Severely Handicapped* (Fredericks et al., 1976). The curriculum in its present form has sequences in the motor areas as shown in Table 1.

Table 2 shows a breakdown of one of the motor development sequences, that of weight-bearing, where the child has a grasping reflex. The entire

Table 1. The motor sequences of the teaching research curriculum for the moderately and severely handicapped

---

Tone normalization activities
  A. Head-righting with ball
  B. Trunk-righting reaction
  C. Weight-bearing with ball
Gross motor skills—basic
  A. Independent movement-prone
  B. Rolling-supine to prone
  C. Head-holding—sitting position
  D. Sitting-child's chair
  E. Sitting-adult chair
Gross motor skills—lower extremity
  A. Weight-bearing—Grasping reflex
  B. Weight-bearing—Nongrasping reflex
  C. Standing
  D. Walking—independent movement grasping reflex
  E. Walking—independent movement nongrasping reflex
  F. Running
Gross motor skills—upper extremity
  A. Reaching for object
  B. Grasps objects with hand
Body orientation
  A. Stepping over obstacle at knee height
  B. Ducking under bar
  C. Stepping sideways
  D. Touching nose
  E. Opening and closing hands
  F. Opening and closing doors
  G. Imitating arm movements

---

continued

Table 1. *continued*

Fine motor skills—lower extremity
- A. Walking up inclined surface
- B. Walking down inclined surface
- C. Walking up stairs
- D. Walking down stairs
- E. Walking heel to toe
- F. Walking forward on a line
- G. Walking backward on a line
- H. Standing on tiptoe with eyes open
- I. Crouching on toes
- J. Standing on tiptoe with eyes closed
- K. Standing on one foot with eyes open
- L. Standing on one foot with eyes closed
- M. Jumping on toes
- N. Jumping over knee-high bar

Fine motor skills—upper extremity
- A. Picking up objects
- B. Multiple shape box
- C. Rings on a peg
- D. String beads
- E. Shapes on a board
- F. Graduated cylinders
- G. Pegboard
- H. Picture puzzle
- I. Pasting
- J. Holding pencil or crayon
- K. Colors within a circle
- L. Cutting with scissors
- M. Touching fingers in succession with thumb

Strength skills
- A. Pushing-pulling objects
- B. Lifting objects
- C. Carrying objects
- D. Waist bending
- E. Leg lifts
- F. Curl-ups
- G. Jumping jacks
- H. Modified push-ups
- I. Squat thrusts
- J. Chin-ups

Recreation skills
- A. Ball skills—rolling and throwing
- B. Ball skills—bouncing and catching
- C. Ball skills—catching
- D. Swimming—entering water
- E. Swimming—submerging
- F. Swimming—floating
- G. Swimming—moving
- H. Swimming—jumping off diving board
- I. Swimming—diving

Table 2. A detailed weight-bearing sequence from the teaching research curriculum for the moderately and severely handicapped

---

Weight-bearing—Grasping reflex
Terminal behavior: Child bears
weight without grasping objects

Phase I   Child must be held and bear little or no weight with his feet on the floor.
(The following times apply to Phase I.)

Steps   1–12 at 10 sec intervals = 120 sec

Phase II   Child bears weight and grasps solid object with two hands. He may or may not need mechanical support braces.
(The following times apply to Phase II.)

Steps   1–5   at   2 sec intervals =   10 sec
6–9   at   5 sec intervals =   20 sec
10–12 at 10 sec intervals =   30 sec
13–20 at 30 sec intervals = 240 sec
300 sec

Phase III   Child bears weight and grasps flexible hose with two hands.
(The following times apply to Phase III.)

Steps 1–4   at 5 sec intervals   =   20 sec
5–8   at 10 sec intervals =   40 sec
9–16   at 30 sec intervals = 240 sec
300 sec

Phase IV   Child bears weight and grasps flexible hose with either (a) right or (b) left hand three inches from therapist's hand.

Phase V   Child bears weight and grasps flexible hose with either (a) right or (b) left hand six inches from therapist's hand.

Phase VI   Child bears weight and grasps flexible hose with either (a) right or (b) left hand nine inches from therapist's hand.

Phase VII   Child bears weight and grasps flexible hose with either (a) right or (b) left hand 12 inches from therapist's hand.

Phase VIII   Child bears weight and grasps flexible hose with either (a) right or (b) left hand 16 inches from therapist's hand.

Phase IX   Child bears weight and grasps flexible hose with either (a) right or (b) left hand 20 inches from therapist's hand.

Phase X   Child bears weight and grasps flexible hose with either (a) right or (b) left hand 24 inches from therapist's hand.

Phase XI   Child bears weight and grasps flexible hose with either (a) right or (b) left hand 30 inches from therapist's hand.

Phase XII   Child bears weight and grasps flexible hose with either (a) right or (b) left hand 36 inches from therapist's hands.

---

continued

Table 2.*continued*

The following times apply to Phase IV through XII.

Steps	1		15 sec
	2		5 sec
	3–6	at 10 second intervals =	40 sec
	7–11	at 30 second intervals =	150 sec
	12		60 sec
	13		30 sec
			300 sec

---

curriculum is divided into specific skills and subskills and then into phases and steps. A detailed discussion of the recommended utilization of the curriculum is contained in Fredericks et al. (1975) and Fredericks et al. (1976).

The curriculum has been utilized in over 200 classrooms throughout the Northwest and is being adopted in over 100 other classrooms by teachers trained at the Teaching Research Infant and Child Center. In addition, an unknown number of classrooms are utilizing the curriculum in part or in whole.

The beneficial results of utilizing the curriculum can best be illustrated by a comparison of the results achieved at the Teaching Research Infant and Child Center with five other preschools that were not utilizing the curriculum. Such a comparison was possible because Oregon is in the unique position of being the only state that conducts a statewide evaluation of all school programs for the moderately and severely handicapped. Each child in every program is administered a pre- and post-test in the 13 curriculum areas of the *Student Progress Record* (Mental Health Division, Salem, Oregon, 1974). "Motor skills" and "physical fitness" comprise the motor sections of the instrument. This statewide testing constitutes, in essence, a third-party evaluation of each classroom and program in the state. For comparative purposes, six preschool classes were found which had the following two characteristics: 1) the teacher in each classroom was the same for a period of two years, 2) no more than 25% of the children moved out of the classroom during the two-year period. The Teaching Research class was one of these programs. The results achieved by these six preschool programs in the areas of motor skills and physical fitness are shown in Table 3. The Teaching Research model, utilizing the curriculum described herein, as compared with the other five preschools, had pupils who made a higher total mean gain than pupils in each of the other preschools. This gain was significant at the 0.05 level, utilizing a t-test.

SUMMARY

The development of the motor portions of the Teaching Research Infant and Child Center Curriculum for the Moderately and Severely Handicapped was the

Table 3. Mean gains in motor area of students in preschool classes for a two year period

Preschool classes	Motor skills	Physical fitness
Teaching research	13.3	9.8
1	6.9	7.9
2	.9	7.8
3	10.4	5.7
4	9.6	.2
5	.2	2.1

result of basic research conducted in an institutional setting, the thrust of which was examining the utilization of behavior modification in conjunction with physical therapy principles and a task analysis of each of the motor behaviors to be taught. The curriculum has been demonstrated to be applicable to children with a wide variety of handicapping conditions. Test results indicate that those classrooms utilizing the curriculum have pupils achieving higher mean gains that pupils in classrooms not utilizing the curriculum.

REFERENCES

Fredericks, H. D. (1969) A Comparison of the Doman-Delacato Method and Behavior Modification Method upon the Coordination of Mongoloids. Project No. RD-275-3-P-68, January.

Fredericks, H. D., et al. (1975) A Data Based Classroom for the Moderately and Severely Handicapped. Instructional Development Corporation, P.O. Box 361, Mommouth, Oregon.

Fredericks, H. D., et al. (1976) The Teaching Research Curriculum for Moderately and Severely Handicapped. Springfield, Illinois: Charles C Thomas.

Grove, D. N. (1972) Behavior Modification and Physical Therapy. Final Report for Grant Number 5 RO1 NS09747-02 EXP.

Grove, D. N., Dalke, B. A., Fredericks, H. D., and Crowley, R. F. (1975) Establishing appropriate head positioning with mentally and physically handicapped. Behav. Engin. 3, No. 2.

Student Progress Record (1974) Salem, Oregon: Mental Health Division.

RESEARCH TO PRACTICE IN MENTAL RETARDATION
Education and Training, Volume II
Edited by Peter Mittler
Copyright 1977 I.A.S.S.M.D.

REASONING ABILITIES OF MILDLY RETARDED CHILDREN

H. Goldstein
Ferkauf Graduate School of Humanities, Yeshiva University,
55 Fifth Avenue, New York, N.Y. 10003, United States

From the earliest days of education's involvement with the retarded, there has been the expectation that it would somehow play a role in mitigating or ameliorating the problems in social adaptation that have always been associated with mental retardation, particularly among the mildly retarded. The underlying hypotheses in the work of Itard, Seguin, Howe, and their successors dealt with effecting some kind of change in the retarded that would manifest itself in the form of behaviors and skills more in harmony with norms for assimilation in society.

In contrast, the research that attempts to uncover the basis for the maladaptive behavior of the retarded is a-educational in its conclusions, if not in the style in which it is reported. The two major directions of research and contemplation suggest that the source of maladaptive behavior is either in the personality structure or in the cognitive processes of the retarded. The first has a more extensive message for mental health treatment than it does for education. The second more often than not is reported in such ways that it has more meaning for the laboratory than for the school.

While the literature is increasing in both the personality and cognitive positions and confirms their rationality, teachers, more often than not, come to other kinds of conclusions empirically. They will agree that some of their students have personality disorders but that these do not necessarily get in the way of social adaptation. Others, they will point out, develop personality disorders as an outcome of maladaptive behaviors, and they would say that ameliorating the personality disorder would not necessarily affect the basis of the problem. They could point to some children who do not seem to have cognitive problems because they seem to know the rules and can describe appropriate behaviors. The problems begin, they often report, after the evidence of cognitive abilities has been established; they begin at the point where actions take the place of words. Experience suggests that this occurs more often in problem-solving in sociopersonal situations than it does in academic pursuits.

This suggests that something other than, or along with, personality and cognitive factors is at work or, more accurately, is not at work. Given that such a notable proportion of the mildly retarded exhibit discrepancies between their verbal and acting behavior, it seems probable that they lack a systematic way for organizing what they know into a sequence that is logical in the stimulus situation; the situation that calls for action. This empirically derived assumption opens an additional avenue to educational intervention along with whatever efforts are being made to modify undesirable personality characteristics and/or cognitive deficits.

Two approaches are available for the purpose of building into retarded students a knowledge/action mediator in the form of a logic-based problem-solving strategy; one that is relevant to situations that call for a systematic ordering of concepts and facts. One way would be to teach directly for the acquisition of the strategy. This approach is indicated when the individual exhibits a satisfactory knowledge base. The objective in this case would be to augment knowledge with a problem-solving strategy that would hopefully lead to appropriate behaviors. Another educational tactic would be to combine knowledge and strategy acquisition in the same process. This tactic is more appropriate for young retardates who are mainly in a knowledge-acquisition stage. The tactic in this case would be to organize the learning of concepts and facts so that learning would be an outcome of problem-solving that consistently incorporated a logical problem-solving strategy. Thus, students would have both intensive and extensive experiences with both information and actions based on information.

The Social Learning Curriculum (SLC) is based on the foregoing premise. The information consists of a developmentally sequenced array of concepts and facts relevant to social adaptation. The information is organized into problem-solving activities that follow a system of inductive logical reasoning. Thus, having been confronted with a sociopersonal problem, the students are guided by the teacher into identifying the elements of the problem (labeling), identifying the nature or characteristics of the elements (detailing), evolving one or more possible solutions to the problem (inferring), reviewing the possibilities and evolving a single most probable solution (predicting), and testing or observing the outcomes of this probability statement (verifying). When indicated by the situation or the readiness of the student to do so, the student is encouraged to evolve a rule or principle that will be helpful in solving similar problems (generalization). The objectives of this tactic are to promote in mildly retarded students the linked abilities to think critically and act independently.

The fact remains, however, that there is little direct evidence that the assumptions underlying the inductive teaching method described above are meritorious. Goldstein, Moss, and Jordan (1958) found that retarded children who were taught inductively were significantly superior to their counterparts in more methodologically eclectic settings in problem-solving that required reasoning. Tisdall (1962) in studying the same children, found the inductively taught group was significantly more creative as ascertained by a test that measured divergent thinking abilities. Edmonson et al. (1974) have demonstrated that retarded students can learn to make inferences in social situations. Greenberg and Smith (1974) tested the assumption underlying the incorporation of the inductive method in the SLC, namely, that the five basic steps of labeling, detailing, inferring, predicting, verifying, and generalizing are hierarchical. They found this to be the case.

Given the foregoing, there are still many questions to be answered. Not the least of these is concerned with the extent to which retarded children can reason along inductive lines. Greenberg (1976) has addressed this issue in a study that had as its objective the development and validation of a procedure to assess the inductive problem-solving behavior—the reasoning ability—of mildly retarded students. The test used in this study, the Test of the Hierarchy of Inductive Knowledge (THINK), was developed at the Curriculum Research and Development Center in Mental Retardation under the leadership of Smith and Greenberg.

The THINK is an individually administered test designed to measure inductive problem-solving ability. The materials and the procedures employed in testing were designed with reference to the inductive teaching methodology as described by Goldstein (1974). To attain more precise measures in each step, some steps were divided into behavioral elements. Thus, performance at the inference step was segmented into an assessment of performance level, the statement of the problem level, and solutions and qualifications level. The THINK includes materials that pictorially depict: 1) problem situations relating to social learning concepts, and 2) alternate resolutions to the problem situations. The testing and scoring procedures provide for the examination of the subject's ability to perform on nine levels of inductive problem-solving, namely, labeling, detailing, visual inferences, statement of problem, solutions and qualifications, best solution, predictions and verifications, learning statement, and generalization. THINK consists of three sets of pictures, each set related to one of four themes. The first picture in each set portrays the problem situation. Subsequent pictures represented verifications of possible solutions. Subjects are presented with the stimulus pictures and asked to report everything seen in each picture. The questioning follows the inductive sequence to the point that the subject is asked to state the problem portrayed and then to state possible solutions. This requires that he proceed beyond the details of the picture. Responses at this stage are subject to verification in subsequent pictures. After predicting and verifying the solution to the problem, the subject is directed to the stimulus picture and asked to state what he has learned from the experience. Then all three stimulus pictures in a given theme are presented at the same time for the purpose of evolving a rule or generalization that applies to all three.

The scoring of THINK is based on responses to the structured questions used in the interview. The questions are designed to elicit performance on the elements of the inductive problem-solving process. In turn, the scoring system uses a combination of techniques to assess performance on the separate elements of the process. Thus, subjects are scored on the quantity of productions or the quality of productions as appropriate for the level.

SUBJECTS

The subjects consisted of 120 EMH primary and intermediate level students ($\overline{X}_{IQ}$ = 68.9, SD_{IQ} = 6.8; $\overline{X}_{MA}$ = 8.2, SD_{MA} = 1.4). Twenty subjects were tested at each age level between nine and 14 years, inclusive. The population was drawn from 26 EMH classrooms located in mixed urban and rural areas in southeastern Pennsylvania where the population is predominantly white, working class. Although the subjects were located in a total of 12 separate school districts, entry into these classrooms was controlled by a single centralized agency ensuring uniform placement procedures.

In order to minimize possible confounding classroom membership effects, an attempt was made to test no more than five subjects per classroom. These individuals were randomly chosen from the total membership of each class excluding only those students who were completely nonverbal.

Procedure for Testing

The administration of the THINK required approximately 50 to 65 minutes per subject. Each subject was brought individually into a room, seated at a table at a right angle to the experimenter, and after a brief warm-up period was presented with the THINK. The warm-up included an explanation of the task. The subject was also shown a sample card similar to the stimulus material used in the THINK. The word *rule* was reviewed and defined as a statement about how to do something or a way to act. Additionally, subjects were asked to provide examples of classroom, street crossing, and hallway behavior rules. The only modifications in the procedure were occasional simplifications or repetitions of the instructions to ensure that the subjects understood the task.

Immediately following the warm-up period, the subject was handed the stimulus card from the first stimulus set in Theme I and was told to hold it in an upright position on a desk directly in front of him. The accompanying resolution cards in the stimulus set were placed face down to the subject's left. As the subject examined the stimulus card, the experimenter began the standard interview used during assessment. This procedure, apart from the warm-up period was followed through the four themes. The full range of the nine expanded steps of the inductive problem-solving method was covered with each subject.

Scoring procedures had been established for each of the nine levels within each theme. The protocol for each subject was then scored by an independent rater who was trained by the experimenter. Ten randomly selected protocols were rated by both the experimenter and the rater. Interrater reliability for each of the nine steps across 12 stimulus pictures (three in each of the four themes) was over 0.80 in all but three cells that had reliability of 0.70, 0.65, and 0.49.

The criterion estimate for the subjects academic and social competency (TRS), was a seven item bipolar rating scale on which teachers rated each of their students in this study. The items were designed as global indications of functioning and emerged from logical consideration of the relationship between problem-solving ability and competency. Teachers were asked to read each pair of items that reflected positive and negative aspects of functioning and place an X on the line between the items to indicate the student's behavior on the dimension being considered. The ratings related to social competency required judgments of the subject's adaptability, social appropriateness, socialization skills and ability to act responsibly. The ratings related to academic competency focused on attitudes toward school work, involvement in group activities, and willingness to persist in efforts to attain goals.

Scoring of the TRS

The score assigned for each item was a numerical value corresponding to the teacher's judgment of the student's behavior. A minimum score of 0.5 indicated negative aspects of functioning on a dimension while a maximum score of 6.5 indicated positive aspects of functioning. Additionally, a total score was calculated for each subject by summating the seven individual item ratings.

The use of a scale such as the TRS allowed for comparison of criterion estimates of functioning among subjects within a given classroom. However, differences among teachers reflected by their response biases partially limited the usefulness of the scale. That is, subjects in different classrooms who demonstrated similar behaviors could be rated differently by their respective teachers. To compensate for the inherent limitations of this type of rating scale, a second measure of competency was developed.

The RS was an on-site judgment made by the teachers regarding the subject's *overall* academic and social competencies. The experimenter listed the names of the subjects and then requested that the teacher rank-order them from most academically and socially competent to least academically and socially competent. The rank-order judgments were made by each teacher at the conclusion of the testing of the subjects in the class and before the experimenter and teacher discussed the subjects' performances.

Scoring of the RS

The score assigned to each subject to reflect his rank-order position relative to the other tested members of the class was a percentage score ranging from 0% to 100%. Thus, a score of 50% was assigned to any subject who was ranked in the median position of the class for overall academic and social competencies. Likewise, scores of 100% and 0% were assigned to the subjects ranked highest and lowest in each class, respectively.

The RS was designed as an alternate means of assessing the behaviors considered by the TRS. The use of a rank-order scaling procedure had the advantage of permitting the comparison of similarly ranked subjects across classrooms and of avoiding the response biases of specific teachers. Additionally, by converting the ranked positions into percentage scores, the effect of testing differing numbers of subjects in various classrooms was obviated. The limitation of a rank-order scaling system was that subjects in different classrooms who demonstrated different levels of overall competency might receive the same percentage score.

RESULTS

Three hypotheses were stated in this study as follows.

1. There is a linear and developmental relationship between age and performance on the expanded levels of the inductive problem-solving strategy.
2. The relationship among the levels of the inductive problem-solving sequence form a causal chain. That is, the ability to label affects detailing which, in turn, affects the ability to make visual inferences and so on, up to and including generalization.
3. Performance, or the levels of the inductive problem-solving sequence, will be related to criterion estimates of student behavior in school-related and social situations as measured by teacher ratings.

Trend analysis was employed to test hypothesis 1. The data relevant to hypothesis 2 were subjected to path analysis, while multivariate regression analysis was used in reference to hypothesis 3.

There is not space enough for an elaborate discussion of the results of this study. Nevertheless, it is important to keep in mind that the central objective of this study was to examine the underlying process of social behavior, namely, a logical reasoning process whereby available knowledge is capitalized upon in a specific problem-solving style, which, in its utilization, fosters the development of social content knowledge in the form of generalizations. This is in contradistinction to the currently conventional use of rating scales and observation schedules that, while valuable in describing the current status of the individual, offer little in the form of prediction.

Stated briefly, all three hypothesis were supported by the data. The fact that the five steps in inductive reasoning are hierarchical and age-related offers a basis for assessing the conditions of learning in the classroom and elsewhere. For example, the younger children were mostly limited to the first two steps of labeling and detailing, while older children were able to proceed through all five. Thus, the function of experience in providing the content of social adaptation is evident. Similarly, the function of content along with the application of the process of inductive reasoning is revealed at the prediction, verification, and generalization steps. For teachers and others concerned with intervention, then, guidelines are available based on both the age and the knowledge of the learner. For example, threshold ages for each of the inductive steps can be established with the content basic to the solution of any given problem held constant.

The nature of the learner's performance at each level—a picture of how the learner processes information toward the end of social problem resolution—is very much related to his performance at each level, and therefore revealing of the mechanisms of social competency. To put it another way, being able to ascertain the learner's competency at each level of the process reduces the speculations stimulated by the more or less nonverbal child. The performance of such children in the guided experiences with the problem-solving process at each level is a more revealing estimate of his ability to act on his information independently than is the more global observation typical of behavior rating scales.

The fact that there was a significant correlation between teachers' ratings of academic and social competence suggests that the THINK fulfills the expectations for its use as a predictor of social competence. To put it another way, the measured abilities of the retarded to apply the process of inductive problem-solving, given evidence of the knowledge of concepts and facts related to social adaptation, appears to be a predictor of success in coping with the problems inherent in social adaptation. Thus, an individual who cannot process information beyond the labeling and detailing could not be expected to perform independently within the norms of society.

The acceptance of the hypotheses suggests a predictive quality to the THINK. While this suggestion must be approached cautiously, it does suggest that there is merit to rigorous exploration along the lines established by this study to further refine the predictive capabilities of this instrument.

SUMMARY

This paper describes the development of a procedure for assessing the reasoning ability of mildly retarded children. The rationale for this assessment approach is based on an inductive teaching methodology built into a large-scale curriculum for use with retarded children, namely, the Social Learning Curriculum.

REFERENCES

Edmonson, B. deJung, J., Leland, H., and Leach, E. (1970) Manual: A Test of Social Inference. Eugene: University of Oregon.
Goldstein, H. (1974) The Social Learning Curriculum. Columbus, Ohio: Charles E. Merrill.
Goldstein, H., Jordan, L., and Moss, J. (1958) Early School Development of

Low IQ Children: A study of Special Class Placement. (US Office of Education Cooperative Research Program, Project SAE 8204, Interim Report) Urbana, Illinois: University of Illinois, Institute for Research of Exceptional Children.

Greenberg, S. (1976) The Assessment of Inductive Problem-Solving in the EMH. Doctoral dissertation in preparation, Yeshiva University.

Greenberg, S., and Smith, I. L. (1974) Structural validation of a behavior hierarchy underlying an inductive teaching methodology. Research Report 3, Yeshiva University, Curriculum Research and Development Center in Mental Retardation.

Tisdall, W. (1962) Productive thinking in retarded children. Except. Child., 36.

RESEARCH TO PRACTICE IN MENTAL RETARDATION
Education and Training, Volume II
Edited by Peter Mittler
Copyright 1977 I.A.S.S.M.D.

TEACHING SOME BASIC PREREQUISITES FOR READING

M. Sidman
Eunice Kennedy Shriver Center and Psychology Department
Northeastern University, 360 Huntington Avenue,
Boston, Massachusetts 02115, United States

At sophisticated levels of analysis we tend to overlook some of the behavioral processes that are necessary for the development of reading, and we often take for granted the large number of basic skills a successful reader must bring to the task. When we study reading in retarded people, however, we are forced to ask questions that do not arise with normal readers who have already developed the basic skills through exposure to natural contingencies. Our interest here, therefore, is not in the level of complexity at which you and I operate when we read, but rather in skills and processes which by themselves may not be considered reading but which are prerequisite if the retarded student is to take advantage of an existing capacity.

Here is a laboratory version of a simple reading comprehension task. Figure 1 shows a student in front of a display panel of nine windows onto which stimuli can be projected from the rear. A three letter word is first projected on the center window; this is the sample. The student responds to the sample by touching it (Figure 2) and pictures then appear on the outer windows; the pictures are the comparison stimuli. The student's task then is to touch the comparison picture which corresponds to the sample word (Figure 3). If he selects the correct picture a reinforcer is delivered into the tray at the right, and a new trial begins with another sample word. If he has selected the wrong picture, there is no reinforcer.

When a student can match each of a set of pictures to its appropriate printed name, we have reason to suspect that he is reading the names with comprehension. But can we be sure? Pigeons and monkeys have been taught matching tasks that are just as arbitrary as picture-to-word matching, but we are somehow skeptical about classifying their performance as reading. How can we tell

---

Preparation of this chapter was supported by grants HD 05124 and HD 04147 from the National Institute of Child Health and Human Development.

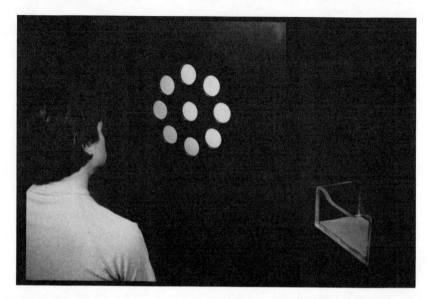

Figure 1. A student seated at the nine-window matching-to-sample apparatus. Visual sample stimuli will appear in the center window; dictated samples are presented via a loudspeaker. Comparison stimuli will appear in the eight outer windows. Reinforcers will be delivered into the tray at the right.

Figure 2. Student touching the sample word.

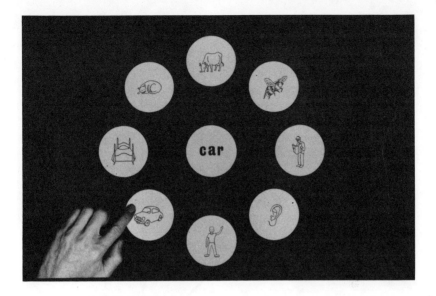

Figure 3. Student touching the comparison picture which corresponds to the sample.

whether matching-to-sample is a linguistic performance or whether it represents an arbitrary stimulus-response chain that has no linguistic relevance?

The feature of matching-to-sample that is critical to its status as a linguistic process is the development of stimulus classes. In a well learned matching-to-sample performance, each comparison stimulus and the sample to which it is matched become a pair of equivalent stimuli. They become substitutable for each other, as is implied by the term "matching."

This distinction between the human and the lower-animal matching-to-sample performance, although real, does not show up in the performance itself. To determine whether or not stimulus classes have become established requires something more. We can set up an independent test of stimulus equivalance in the following way, as is diagrammed in Figure 4. We begin by teaching the student to match each of a set of pictures not to its printed name but rather to its dictated name (B–A in Figure 4). For example, the student hears the word "boy" and is then to pick out the picture of a boy from several choices; when the word "car" is dictated, the student must pick out the picture of a car, etc.

Next, we teach the student to match each of a set of printed words to the same dictated names to which he has learned to match the pictures (C–A in Figure 4). Now, for example, the sample word "boy" is dictated, and the student must select the printed word *boy* out of several available choices.

Suppose the matching-to-sample tasks have indeed caused each comparison to become equivalent to its corresponding sample. Equivalent stimuli are by

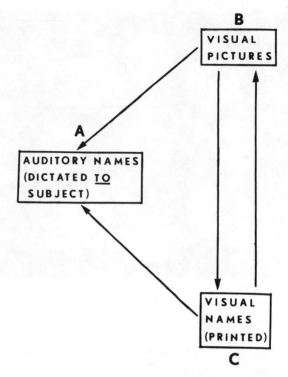

Figure 4. The matching-to-sample tasks. Arrows point from comparison to sample stimuli.

definition substitutable for each other. It should be possible then to substitute the printed word *boy* (C) for the dictated word "boy" (A), and the student should now be able to match pictures to appropriate printed words (C–B in Figure 4) *even though he has never learned explicitly to do this.* Similarly, we should be able to substitute the picture of a boy (B) for the dictated sample word "boy" (A), and the student should be able to match the printed word to its picture sample (B–C in Figure 4).

We found that some retarded students, who had only the indirect training described above, were indeed able to match picture comparisons to printed-word samples, and printed-word comparisons to picture samples (Sidman, 1971; Sidman and Cresson, 1973; Sidman, Cresson, and Willson-Morris, 1974). The emergence of these two performances confirmed the formation of stimulus classes in the original matching tasks, and provided us with a legitimate basis for regarding the two emergent tasks as reading comprehension. The teaching sequence provides a test for the formation of stimulus classes, a process that is fundamental to linguistic competence because it makes it possible for words to mediate the emergence of new behavior that has never been directly taught.

Furthermore, the test is itself a vehicle for teaching. We have taught this elementary form of reading comprehension to retarded youths whose formal IQs were 30 or less and who had been given up as hopeless prospects for any type of preacademic training. The students emerged with a reading comprehension vocabulary of 20 words, a substantial starting point for a teacher who would otherwise be at a loss as to how even to begin to teach such students to read. It should also be noted that the use of dictated words spoken *to* the students, rather than the usual method of requiring students to name the pictures and words themselves, permits the teaching to be accomplished via teaching machines. In view of the general shortage of teachers who are skilled in working with severely retarded students, teaching-machine techniques make it possible to introduce a larger number of such students to reading than would otherwise be feasible.

However, such children cannot simply be exposed to the test with the expectation that their scores will reveal their actual capabilities. Students functioning at this retarded level usually do not possess the behavioral prerequisites that are necessary to render the test valid. Although many of these prerequisites are nonverbal, they are necessary for a meaningful evaluation of the student's linguistic competence. Where does one start with a severely retarded student who has none of the required skills?

A major problem is to motivate the student to work at the learning tasks. Students who have no history of successful learning cannot be expected to be motivated by learning for its own sake. Normal children discover early that learning is useful; it increases their options. Everything they learn helps open up new worlds of exploration, environmental manipulation, and social interaction. Severely retarded students, especially those residing in institutions, have not yet made this discovery, and their learning must at first be motivated from sources extrinsic to the learning tasks themselves. It is necessary to make it worthwhile for such students to sit, attend, and learn effectively for reasonable periods of time. To this end, one may take advantage of reinforcers discovered through careful observation and test—food, candy—or one may go to the effort, time consuming at first but more efficient in the long run, of establishing a generalized reinforcer such as tokens or points. The establishment of generalized reinforcers is not usually regarded as a necessary teaching skill, because normal children come to the classroom with such reinforcers already available. The teacher of severely retarded students, however, must know how to establish and use generalized reinforcers if advanced teaching is to succeed.

Given an effective reinforcer, it is still not possible simply to expose the student to the matching-to-sample tasks. The student must learn the procedures; they require specific behavior, e.g., touching the relevant stimuli, waiting for stimuli to appear, scanning the display and searching for relevant stimuli, and discriminating the stimuli from each other. First, therefore, we teach the student some skills that do not involve matching-to-sample but that are prerequisites for the matching-to-sample performance. We start by teaching something easy, and then build upon that, step by step. We teach the student simply to touch whichever window of the stimulus display is lighted—reinforcing each correct response along the way. Then, by shifting the bright stimulus from position to position on different learning trials, we teach the student to scan the display in order to locate the relevant stimulus.

Next, we teach the student not simply to touch a bright window, but rather to touch only the bright window which also has a form on it. We superimpose a circle on the bright window, and dimly illuminate the other windows without superimposing a form on them. By gradually increasing the brightness level of the incorrect windows from trial to trial, it is possible to teach the student, often errorlessly, to select only the bright window that has the circle on it and never to choose any of the blank bright windows. We now have a more advanced discrimination—form vs. no form.

Next, we want to teach the student to select only a particular form and to reject other forms; we gradually fade a flat ellipse onto the incorrect windows. At the end of this teaching phase, which the gradual fading often causes to be errorless, the student selects the window that has a circle on it and never chooses any window that contains an ellipse. We now have a simple form discrimination—circle vs. ellipse (Sidman and Stoddard, 1966; 1967).

We can then change the circle and the ellipse into other forms, and, by making these changes extremely gradual, we can teach the student to discriminate other forms from each other. For example, the circle may be collapsed into a vertical line, and the ellipse to a horizontal line, and the student will end up, often without any errors, always selecting the vertical and rejecting the horizontal line. Many such transformations can be made, and in this way the student can be taught to tell the letters of the alphabet from each other, stimuli that are critical for the learning tasks we are eventually to set for him. This may be a long process, even with a teaching machine, but it is necessary if the severely retarded student is to be given a fair chance to demonstrate his true capacities.

Only now can we begin to teach matching-to-sample. By programming the steps carefully, and reinforcing each correct response, we can instruct the student even if we are unable to communicate verbally. We must first teach the student that two responses are now required for reinforcement; touch the sample (to tell us he has observed it) and then touch a comparison stimulus. To teach this double response, we first present a sample alone, so that it looks bright. When the student touches the sample, a single comparison window is illuminated with the same stimulus that is on the sample window. When the comparison appears, however, the seemingly bright sample is seen to be relatively dim. Therefore, instead of continuing to touch the sample, the student shifts to the brighter comparison window. We then gradually increase the sample brightness until it is exactly the same as the comparison, and at the end of this stage we have established the two-response chain—touch the sample and then the comparison.

Adapting a technique that was first reported by Moore and Goldiamond (1964), we next teach the student to refrain from touching any comparison window unless it contains the same stimulus as the sample. Along with the matching stimulus, we also present a nonmatching stimulus on one of the other comparison windows. But the nonmatching stimulus at first is not nearly as bright as the matching stimulus, so the student continues to select the bright matching comparison. From trial to trial we gradually increase the brightness of the incorrect stimulus. By the time the incorrect and correct comparisons are equally bright, the student will have learned to choose only the one that matches the sample. Then, we gradually introduce additional nonmatching stimuli on the other windows.

The student is now doing identity-matching, and we are ready to teach arbitrary matching tasks. The first to be taught is matching pictures to their dictated names (B–A in Figure 4), and we use a variation of the delayed-cue technique (Touchette, 1971; 1972). Again, we build upon what has already been learned, making use of identity-matching to instruct the student how to respond to the unfamiliar dictated picture names. At first, the dictated samples are accompanied by picture samples; even though the student does not yet know how to respond to the dictated names, he can use the picture samples as instructions. Later, the presentation of the picture samples is delayed for progressively longer periods. So long as the student has not yet learned which comparison picture goes with a dictated name, he can still respond correctly by waiting for the sample picture. But once the student has learned which comparison picture is appropriate to a dictated name, he can select the correct picture without waiting for the visual instruction. By eventually anticipating the delayed instruction, the student indicates that he has learned to match a picture to its dictated name, and we can go on to teach new dictated names and pictures in the same manner.

The same method is then used to teach the student to match printed to dictated words (C–A in Figure 4). The instruction stimuli now are the identical printed words, and as long as the student is unable to match printed to dictated words he can wait for the instruction and make a correct choice on the basis of the identity match. When he has learned the correspondence between printed and dictated words he will no longer need the instruction, and will inform us of his new skill by anticipating its appearance.

The delayed-cue technique permits the student to apply previously acquired knowledge to the solution of new problems. Lengthy and discouraging trial-and-error learning is circumvented by teaching the student instead to use instructions that he already understands.

Having learned the two crossmodal matching tasks (B–A and C–A), the student is now ready for the critical test: Can he now match the pictures to their printed names (B–C and C–B)? If the student proves capable of these reading comprehension tasks, he is a likely candidate for additional language teaching. If the test shows the student incapable of reading comprehension, there is reason to doubt his basic linguistic capability. In any event, such a failure cannot be attributed to inadequate preparation.

This description of a test for an elementary but fundamental form of linguistic competence, and of methods for preparing severely retarded students for the test, exposes the tragedy inherent in the usual assumption that such students are not amenable to language teaching. Changing their behavior is no easy task, but it can be accomplished if we as teachers will learn first to change our own behavior.

SUMMARY

This paper describes a linguistic paradigm for evaluating a child's ability to learn a simple form of reading comprehension. Methods are presented for teaching prerequisite skills for this performance even to children who are so severely retarded that they are usually considered incapable of learning to read.

REFERENCES

Moore, R., and Goldiamond, I. (1964) Errorless establishment of visual discrimination using fading procedures. J. Exp. Anal. Behav. 7:269.

Sidman, M. (1971) Reading and auditory-visual equivalences. J. Speech Hear. Res. 14:5.

Sidman, M., and Cresson, O. (1973) Reading and crossmodal transfer of stimulus equivalences in severe retardation. Amer. J. Ment. Defic. 77:515.

Sidman, M., Cresson, O., and Willson-Morris, M. (1974) Acquisition of matching to sample via mediated transfer. J. Exp. Anal. Behav. 22:261.

Sidman, M., and Stoddard, L. T. (1966) Programming perception and learning for retarded children. In International Review of Research in Mental Retardation, Vol. 2. (Ed. Ellis, N. R.) New York: Academic Press, p. 151.

Sidman, M., and Stoddard, L. T. (1967) The effectiveness of fading in programming a simultaneous form discrimination for retarded children. J. Exp. Anal. Behav. 10:3.

Touchette, P. E. (1971) Transfer of stimulus control: Measuring the moment of transfer. J. Exp. Anal. Behav. 15:347.

Touchette, P. E. (1972) Teaching listening. Paper delivered at the Gatlinburg Conference on Research and Theory in Mental Retardation.

RESEARCH TO PRACTICE IN MENTAL RETARDATION
Education and Training, Volume II
Edited by Peter Mittler
Copyright 1977 I.A.S.S.M.D.

THE IDENTIFICATION OF COMPETENCIES IN TEACHERS OF THE SEVERELY HANDICAPPED

H. D. Fredericks, R. Anderson, and V. Baldwin
Teaching Research Infant and Child Center,
Monmouth, Oregon 97361, United States

OBJECTIVES

Shores, Gegelka, and Nelson in an article entitled "Competency Based Special Education Teacher Training," (1973) state that the available literature about teacher competencies indicates that specific competencies tend to be derived from "expert" opinion rather than the direct observations of teacher behavior.

The study reported herein was an attempt to derive teacher competencies from the direct observation of teacher behavior and not from expert opinion.

The basic orientation of this study was to identify those competencies possessed by teachers whose severely handicapped students made the greatest gains and were not observable in those teachers whose students did not show comparable gains. The strategy to accomplish that objective was as follows:

1. Identify a wide range of potential competencies—training, experience, and practices that might be characteristic of good teachers. These would be the independent variables of the study.
2. Choose an instrument that would measure student gain. This would be the dependent variable of the study.
3. Choose a pool of teachers to observe.
4. Develop a methodology for observing and collecting information about the training, experience, and practices of the teachers.
5. Analyze the information collected to determine which training, experiences, and practices of the teacher were associated with maximum gain by severely handicapped students.

METHODS

The first step of the study was to identify potential independent variables—the training, practices, and characteristics of teachers that might help them influence children's performance. A panel of 86 teachers was assembled to identify these variables.

In addition to the panel of teachers, the work of others was referred to in developing the list of variables. Altman and Meyen (1974) developed a pool of competencies by sending questionnaires to 587 public school personnel. Reid et al. (1972) demonstrated that immediate and intensive contact with a variety of exceptional children was both a beneficial and a desirable practice that should be incorporated into teacher-training programs. Bullock, Dykes, and Kelly (1974) elicited responses from trained teachers and supervisors of teachers of behaviorally disordered children and youth regarding 123 competency goal statements. Courtnage et al. (1975) describe a noncategorized competency-based teacher-training model based upon the experiences of a university staff. Rosenshire (1974) provides an excellent summary of work done to date in this area.

Once the independent variables, the potential list of competencies, had been selected, the dependent variable had to be determined.

A measure was necessary that would allow the examination of student gain. The state of Oregon had developed an instrument suitable for this purpose. The Oregon State Mental Health Division required that all moderately and severely handicapped children be tested, pre and post, each year. This test, the *Student Progress Record,* is a skills checklist which covers 13 areas of learning: receptive language, expressive language, motor skills, social skills, reading, writing, number concepts, money, time, eating, dressing, personal hygiene, and physical fitness.

The scores achieved on this test served as the dependent variable in the study. Only seven subtests covering those skill areas most often taught to the severely handicapped child—social skills, receptive language, expressive language, eating, dressing, motor skills, and personal hygiene—were chosen for purposes of this study. Although it was recognized that some severely handicapped children are taught the other skill areas—reading, writing, number concepts, money, time and physical fitness—they are not part of *every* severely handicapped child's curriculum, and consequently were omitted from the analysis.

The next step was to select teachers who were to be observed and interviewed. On the assumption that teachers' performances are consistent from year to year, and that teachers whose students made large gains during 1973–74 would have students making large gains in 1974–75, student gains for the academic year 1973–74 were examined and teachers were selected. Likewise, teachers were selected whose students made small gains.

Initially, 40 teachers, 20 whose students made large gains and 20 whose students made small gains, were selected. However, because of transfer, retirement, or other circumstances, observations and interviews could only be conducted in 27 classrooms.

After the determination of the independent and dependent variables and the selection of the teachers to be studied, it was necessary to develop a method for observing or collecting information about the independent variables, the practices, characteristics, and training of teachers. An instrument for collecting this information was formulated, field-tested in the classrooms that would not be part of the study, modified, and finally adopted. The instrument collected information through a combination of observation and interviews. Observations included data on consequence delivery in the classroom (teacher, aide, and volunteer), how the teacher managed the classroom, and whether children were taught in group or by individual instruction.

Before observations were conducted in any of the classrooms under study, the reliability of the observation procedure was checked in classrooms that were not part of the study. One investigator was designated as the principal observer for the study. A second investigator was used to check the reliability of the observations of the principal observer. The two investigators correlated their observations and succeeded in reliability coefficients of 0.85 or above on each of the observation instruments.

After the actual classroom observations began, interrater reliability checks were conducted approximately every 10 days to ensure the maintenance of consistent observations over time. While the principal observer conducted observations in the teacher's classroom, the second observer also observed the same individual but in such a manner that each observer's scoring was kept confidential. Interrater reliability with this procedure consistently exceeded 0.80.

To gather data for analysis in the study, two days spaced 90 days apart in each classroom were devoted to observations and interviews. The observer spent all day in the classroom. Data from repeated observations of the same phenomenon, e.g., volunteer interaction with children, were averaged, and mean scores were used.

RESULTS

After observations and interviews were completed on all teachers, weighted gain scores were computed and ranked from those teachers with the best class gain scores down to those whose pupils achieved the poorest gains through the year. The top seven teachers (26%) and the bottom seven (26%) were then compared using each of the 86 competency variables.

The Mann Whitney U Test was used to determine whether or not the difference in each variable between the two groups was statistically significant. As a result of this analysis, 13 variables were isolated that showed a level of significance of at least 0.05. In order to determine the relative strength of each of these variables, a step-wise regression was conducted which ordered the variables as shown in Table 1. The results of the step-wise regression indicated that the first four variables accounted for 90% of the variance.

Table 1. Order of variables as determined by step-wise regression

Order	Number	Variable
1.	11	Length of instruction day
2.	72	Percentage of programs task analyzed
3.	31	Positive consequence delivery of volunteer
4.	33	Consequence delivery of teacher and aide
5.	82	Cue and consequence delivery—teacher, aide, and volunteer
6.	36	Consequence delivery of teacher, aide, and volunteer
7.	79	Cue and consequence delivery of teacher
8.	24	Consequence delivery of teacher
9.	60	Appropriate consequence delivery/min—teacher and volunteer
10.	85	Daily number of volunteers in class
11.	56	Appropriate consequence delivery/min—teacher/aide
12.	44	Appropriate consequence delivery/min—teacher
13.	6	Training in content area for aide

Thus, we find four variables that account for the main difference between teachers whose students make good gains and teachers whose students do not make good gains. Those four variables are:

1. length of instruction day.
2. percentage of programs task-analyzed
3. positive consequence delivery by volunteer
4. consequence delivery by teacher and aide.

DISCUSSION

One of the purposes of this study was to isolate those variables essential for successful teachers of the severely handicapped. Successful teachers are being defined as those whose students are making large gains. The main implication of the study is that the variables identified must then be an essential part of teacher training. A discussion of each of these identified variables follows:

Length of Instruction Day

The results of this study indicate that three major areas of teacher training should be emphasized. The first of these is what Prehm (1975) calls the orchestration of the classroom. This in essence refers to the organization of the classroom to maximize the instruction time of the child. The teacher and the aide must provide instruction for the child for as many minutes as possible during the day and thus must utilize a system of volunteers, scheduling, and materials arrangement so as to maximize instructional time. Little attention has been paid to this variable in the average teacher-training institution. Moreover, little research is available regarding this subject.

Special education publications have not focused on this area. Although behavioristic writings do talk about classroom management in the sense of managing reinforcers and contingencies, they do not delve into the utilization of personnel and scheduling, and combining these with volunteers and materials. Recently Fredericks et al. (1975), in *A Data Based Classroom for the Moderately and Severely Handicapped,* provided a model that orchestrates all of these various components to maximize the length of instructional time of the child. The results of their research indicate that in a comparative study with other preschool environments, a preschool established under this system demonstrated significantly better gains for the children than did preschools operating under other systems.

A Task-Analyzed Curriculum

The second variable that stands out as a result of this study is the utilization of a curriculum that is task-analyzed. The degree of task analysis was not ascertained although it was found that most of the teachers in this study whose children achieved superior results were utilizing a curriculum modified after the curriculum developed by Fredericks et al., *The Teaching Research Curriculum for the Moderately and Severely Handicapped* (1976a), which has been widely accepted as a detailed task-analyzed curriculum for the severely handicapped. Of 49 possible curriculum areas (seven teachers with seven curriculum areas each), in both the high and low group, 26 (63.06%) of the curriculum areas in the high group had task-analyzed curricula. In the low group, only five curriculum areas of the 49 (10.20%) had task-analyzed curricula.

The necessity for modifying the task-analysis, contingent upon the performance of the child, usually is associated with this ability to task-analyze an instructional sequence. This modifying process is referred to as branching. Although not statistically significant, 57% of the teachers in the successful group branched task-analyzed progress when necessary, whereas 28% of the unsuccessful teachers branched programs.

Delivery of Consequences

A final variable that is pinpointed by this study is the necessary delivery of appropriate consequences to the child who is being taught. This area is certainly nothing new to the behavioristic philosophy which has long emphasized the necessity for appropriate feedback. Study after study could be cited demonstrating the importance of feedback and consequences in all learning environments. One need only refer to the wealth of literature about the severely and profoundly handicapped and the teaching of specific skills to this population to comprehend the importance of consequence delivery to these children in the learning situation.

Encouragement of research in this area is essentially unnecessary since behaviorists seem to continue their research in this area at a prolific pace, although there are certain questions raised as a result of certain variables being found significant and others not significant. What exactly constitutes a proper consequence? Is the ratio of positive consequences to negative feedback important and what is the optimal ratio? What about the rate of feedback in a learning situation? Admittedly this implies some schedule of reinforcement but again it may not. It may simply talk about numbers of consequences delivered per minute. All of these questions are variables that were not answered by this study. Because of the difference in results achieved, one must design studies specifically to answer these questions.

SUMMARY

This project has isolated three major sets of variables—increase in instructional time, task-analyzed curriculum, and appropriate consequences to the learner—as important to achieve change in students. The study indicates that these variables are skills that a teacher needs to be successful. The study implies that a teacher must be a master of classroom management. She must be able to "orchestrate" the learning environment so as to maximize the amount of instructional time for the severely handicapped child. This study implies that what is taught to the handicapped child must be task-analyzed and finally that the quality of feedback to the child must be such that the child's learning environment will be maximized. These are all highly technical skills. They are skills to which teacher-training institutions will have to attend. A complete report of this study is found in Fredericks et al. (1976b).

REFERENCES

Altman, R., and Meyen, E. L. (1974) Some observations on competency based instruction. Except. Child. 40:260.

Bullock, L. M., Dykes, K. M., and Kelly, T. J. (1974) Competency based teacher preparation in behavioral disorders. Except. Child. 41:192.

Courtnage, L., Brody, R., Suraski, A., and Schmid, R. (1975) Preparing competent teachers: A concategorized competency based teacher training model for special education. Focus on Except. Child. 7:6.

Fredericks, H. D., Baldwin, V. L., Grove, D. N., Riggs, C., Furey, V., Moore, W., Jordan, E., Gage, M. A., Levak, L., Alrick, G., and Wadlow, M. (1975) A Data Based Classroom for the Moderately and Severely Handicapped. Monmouth: Instructional Development Corporation.

Fredericks, H. D., Riggs, C., Furey, T., Grove, D., Moore, W., McDonnell, J. J., Jordan, E., Hansen, W., Baldwin, V. L., and Wadlow, M. (1976a) The Teaching Research Curriculum for the Moderately and Severely Handicapped. Springfield: Charles C Thomas.

Fredericks, H. D., Anderson, R. B., Baldwin, V. L., Baird, J. H., Moore, W. G., and Grove, D. N. (1976b) The Identification of Competencies in Teachers of the Severely Handicapped. Monmouth: Teaching Research Publications.

Prehm, J. (1975) Personal communication.

Reid, W. R., Reid, B. A., Whorton, J. E., and Reichard, C. L. (1972) An experimental special education program for college freshmen. J. Spec. Educ. 6:127.

Rosenshire, B. (1974) Teacher competency research. *In* Competency Assessment: Research and Evaluation. Report of a National Conference, Houston, March.

Shores, R. E., Gegelka, P. T., and Nelson, C. M. (1973) Competency based special education teacher training. Except. Child. 40:192.

VOCATIONAL REHABILITATION

RESEARCH TO PRACTICE IN MENTAL RETARDATION
Education and Training, Volume II
Edited by Peter Mittler
Copyright 1977   I.A.S.S.M.D.

THE PRIDE OF WORK, THE PRIDE OF BEING

B. Posner
The President's Committee on Employment of the
Handicapped, Washington, D.C. 20210, United States

The setting: an occupational training center in an Eastern city. I am there as a "client," to see for myself what goes on when mentally retarded people are trained for work. The only person who knows my identity is the center's director.

I am assigned to a corner room for behavior modification. Nine of us are seated around a table. A hawk-eyed young psychologist observes us. When we perform our duties properly, we receive poker chips; when we do not, we don't. We are sealing envelopes for the National Institute of Health.

The young man seated next to me, my "instructor," is twenty-four, mentally retarded. Meticulously, he shows me how much water to put on my sponge so the envelopes stay glued. At first, he inspects each envelope I seal. He is critical but honest. He shows me air bubbles and unglued corners and explains how to eliminate them. I find myself growing a little tense; I want his approval. He is proud of his work; his pride is contagious. [*Some days later, I happen to be introduced to his counselor. "Poor Jerry," the counselor says. "Envelope sealing is about all he can do. Not much, is it?" Not much? It is Jerry's life.*]

Another city, in the North. Another training center. This one has an arts and crafts program funded by a local agency on the other side of town. Trainees love it. One day, because of budget shortages, the program comes to an abrupt end. No warning; the doors don't open. The trainees are aroused. On their own, they call a protest meeting. They dictate, to one young lady who knows how to write, a strong statement, demanding resumption of the program.

They elect a second young lady as messenger—short, plucky, mongoloid features. She is to deliver the written statement to the agency. She takes the bus across town; thank goodness for her mobility training. She enters the agency building. If she had not been retarded, she would have done what you and I would have done: find the office of the director; politely ask to see him; if he is busy, leave the statement with his secretary. But she is retarded. And she is direct. Unannounced she brushes past the secretary right into the office of the director. She hands him the statement. What's more, she delivers a scathing speech of her own. He listens, open-mouthed. She leaves, puffed with pride at a mission well done. [*He picks up the telephone, calls the workshop. "Well, which one of you put her up to coming here? And who told her what to say?" He couldn't give her credit for having the courage and the ingenuity to act on her own.*]

Rap session in suburbia. I join a dozen young retarded men and women in a circle. They compare notes about work and life—and about being retarded. After a while, I take a deep breath and ask my question. "This is pretty rough and you don't have to answer. Do the people you work with ever think about you as being . . . uh . . . different? (I can't bring myself to say the words "mentally retarded.") Silence. Then answers cascade. "I'm not retarded," proudly proclaims a young man, "I'm brain injured." Admits another: "I never tell people I have a rehabilitation counselor; then they'll know I'm retarded. I just tell them I have a counselor, and they think I'm a prisoner out on parole." A quiet female voice: "Retardation. That means rejection, doesn't it?" [*Are these truly their voices, I wonder? Or are these the reflected voices of their parents and teachers and counselors and all the rest who have instilled in them shame about their retardation?*]

I wonder about these people and so many others like them. And I wonder about us. Do we really accept them as people? Do we really look beneath their retardation at their essential manhood and womanhood?

Do we? By we, I mean all who educate and habilitate and evaluate and employ and write about and talk about mentally retarded persons. I also include all parents who worry about them. They are just as entitled as anybody else to pride, to dignity, to the right to be listened to. Yes, regardless of IQ number.

Obviously, there are many factors that lead to pride, dignity and the right to be listened to. Let's pick three: *work*—doing whatever you do best and doing it well, and *self-acceptance*—being comfortable with yourself no matter who you are, and *self-organization*—speaking in concert with others so your voice will not be lost. Irving Howe, in *World of Our Fathers*, tells us that when the immigrants poured into the United States from the Old Country, the first three things they did were: to find work so they could eat, to reestablish their institutions (synagogues and schools) so they could feel comfortable with themselves in their new land, and to create organizations so they could be heard. Immigrants needed these two-thirds of a century ago; mentally retarded people need them today.

WORK

What about work? I get the feeling that sometimes we encourage placement of retarded people not in jobs that fit them the best, but in jobs that fit our own predilections the best. On the one hand, there are those of us who insist that mentally retarded people can do far more than we give them credit for. As one special educator wrote, "It is possible that the service occupations have received too much emphasis." And he proposed more emphasis on higher-level jobs that might almost be considered semi-professional.

So some mentally retarded people are placed—squeezed would be a better word—in jobs above their capacities. Some meet the challenge; some do not. All because some counselors impose their own value scales on work—skills rank high, nonskills rank low. On the other hand, there are those who take the line of least resistance and place all retarded clients in the easiest-to-fill jobs: busboy, busgirl, dishwasher, janitor's helper, and the like. Their reasoning goes like this: "Retardates can tolerate boring jobs better than the rest of us."

So some retarded people are placed in jobs beneath their capacities. They could do better if they had a chance. Some quit in boredom. We never quite forgive them, because they upset our myths about boredom. Retarded people *do* get bored, and we are disappointed.

Those in both camps—the overplacers and the underplacers—have one characteristic in common. They have a difficult time seeing retarded people as individual people, with their infinite richness of differences. They try to force human beings into molds. Where is our basic respect for retarded people as people?

SELF-ACCEPTANCE

Now, what about self-acceptance? Perhaps we worry too much about eliminating labels and IQ numbers. We try so hard to erase labels that I get the feeling we are a group of Lady Macbeths, forever washing our hands and muttering, "Out, out, damned spot." But the spot doesn't go away. We can change names or eliminate names. We can de-label. But we still have people, no matter what we call them, with special problems of learning and working and living.

We de-label on the grounds that by doing so we will reduce the stigma with which society regards retarded people. I wonder how retarded people feel about it. They don't have to be overly sensitive to recognize that much of our stigma is directed not at the label but at the person bearing the label. It's almost as though there is something wrong about being retarded and something right about being not retarded. As Erwin Goffman puts it in *Stigma,* we expect people to behave and to think like we do. When someone fails to live up to this image of ourselves—someone who can't match us in mental agility—we "discount" him. We consider him inferior. We don't verbalize it, but we think it.

We tend to "discount" retarded people, and to counteract the discount process, we try to remove the label. But the melody lingers on. Somehow, these unlabeled people still are "discounted" in our minds. As a result, retarded people become ashamed of their retardation. They try to cover it up, to deny it. Sometimes they are successful; sometimes their efforts are pitiful—the young man who pretends to be a prisoner on parole rather than a retardate.

I do not contend that retarded people should be proud of their retardation. But neither should they be ashamed of it. They should be able to live with it—as one of the facts of their existence. Jean Paul Sartre put it this way: people, retarded people included, must be made aware of what they are and must accept what they are; their honest self-awareness sets them free. Perhaps self-acceptance comes with age. Edgerton, in the follow-up to his book, *The Cloak of Competence,* interviewed nearly three-dozen retarded people a quarter of a century after they left an instition and found that most of them were no longer concerned about matters of stigma. They used to be concerned when they were younger; but no more. Labels didn't bother them now.

THE RIGHT TO ORGANIZE

Finally, what about the right to organize and to be heard? We are just beginning to detect the voices of retarded people, speaking for themselves. I don't think it matters what they say. What does matter is that they are starting to speak for themselves. Their voices are reminding us of their presence in society. For years, their parents have spoken out for them, and they still do. But there is nothing so effective as groups advocating their own cause, directly, with no intermediaries.

Wherever I travel, I try to sit in on meetings of retarded adults. When they are left alone, I am impressed with their common sense. But sometimes they are not left alone, and in these meetings I hear the overwhelming voices of their parents and professionals who tend to take over. When that happens, the retarded people grow quiet; they submit to other voices. All of which reminds me of these words by Jerome Nitzberg, assistant director of a training center and workshops in New York City:

> Retarded people by and large are made to order for authoritarians. Some do stand up for their rights, although few do so effectively. While some do protest and demand, most do not beyond a murmur. Generally, retarded adults yield to authority, plod along grumbling, irritably resigned.

Despite his words, despite the take-over voices of parents and professionals, there is growing evidence that retarded people are starting to organize for themselves and speak for themselves—without our help. One prerequisite, of course, is self-acceptance. You really cannot start an organization of retarded people if you try to hide what you are.

In Wisconsin, retarded people publish their own newspaper. It may not win any prizes, but that isn't the point. They are speaking their own words and thoughts—well worth reading. In Maryland, a state conference of retarded people took place, with delegates grumbling about the same things we do—too many panels, too many speeches, too high a registration fee. In Oregon, a state-wide organization of retarded people held its second annual convention, presenting demands for dignity of being and quality of services. I wanted to print portions of Judy Cuneo's keynote address in a newsletter I publish. I read it and was let down; it didn't exactly have the eloquence of Thomas Paine. But why was I measuring this by my own standards? Why didn't I respect it by its own standards? I read it again . . . not bad. Here are a couple of sentences:

> I don't want to separate the mentally retarded from the rest of the world because the Bible says all men are equal. If a person wants to try to do something, he should be given a chance. He will never know what he is capable of doing if he doesn't try.

I rest my case with these words of Judy Cuneo, keynote speaker. "A person will never know what he is capable of doing if he doesn't try."

This means working at whatever he or she does best—and it doesn't matter how "lowly" the job might seem by our standards. This means self-acceptance— so people can build upon the solid base of what they are. This means self-organization into a "consumers" movement—a first step to gaining the respect and the attention of the world at large.

Pride, dignity, the right to be heard. Minimum objectives in life for all people, retarded included. Judy Cuneo has pointed the way: "If a person wants to try to do something, he should be given a chance."

Let's memorize her words.

SUMMARY

This paper contends that there can be pride in all forms of work, even that which we consider "low-level jobs." Mentally retarded people can fill these jobs with pride, if the rest of the world (parents and rehabilitation courselors included) let them. The problem is that all too often we look with disdain on such jobs; our attitudes carry over to the retarded; their pride can vanish . . . along with their self-confidence and sense of self-worth.

RESEARCH TO PRACTICE IN MENTAL RETARDATION
Education and Training, Volume II
Edited by Peter Mittler
Copyright 1977 I.A.S.S.M.D.

BASIC WORK-SKILLS TRAINING AND VOCATIONAL COUNSELLING OF THE MENTALLY HANDICAPPED

E. Whelan
*Hester Adrian Research Centre, The
University, Manchester, M13, 9PL England*

The main community-based service for the rehabilitation of mentally handicapped adults in Britain is provided by the Adult Training Centre (ATC). Some 32,000 trainees attend on a daily basis; the majority live at home with their families and some have accommodation in hostels or flats. The ATCs cater mainly to moderately and severely mentally handicapped adults, although a small number of mildly mentally handicapped adults can also be found in every ATC. A recent national survey of ATCs (Whelan and Speake, 1977) has shown that their general aim is to develop the trainees' work habits, work skills, and social competence, and wherever possible to direct them to sheltered or open employment. The major emphasis in training in the area of "work skills" may be understood in terms of the historical development of ATCs, under the influence of a number of factors including: the official guidelines provided, the background from which many staff are selected, and the general values of society itself, reflected through the views of service providers, parents, and of mentally handicapped individuals themselves. Nevertheless, actual employment success is very low indeed (less than 5%), despite reliable staff estimates that over 11% of trainees could succeed in open employment and a further 25% in sheltered employment if places were available.

There are obviously many factors that influence the outcome of a training programme when it is measured in terms of employment success. Many of these factors (e.g., the local level of unemployment) are largely independent of the training centre, even though its staff may be collaborating closely with placement officers. For this reason, ATC staff agree that they should concentrate initially on improving their training programmes. In addition to a growing awareness that the ATC should become more "educational," using that term in its broadest sense, staff are keen to become more effective instructors and to apply more systematic methods in their everyday work. It is important that research should be shown to be relevant by focusing first on areas that are of immediate concern to staff. For this reason our team has mainly concentrated on work-skills training so far.

Of those trainees who *are* successfully employed, only about one in three enter a job that is similar to anything they have experienced during training. The Survey also revealed that little was known about the job interests of trainees. A study of the skills and the equipment available within the ATC, and the way in which its daily schedule is organised, suggests that it is best fitted to provide a general prevocational form of training rather than preparation for specific jobs. Included in this should be such basic work skills as recognition and use of basic tools, manual dexterity and coordination, ability to follow instructions, attention to safety, development of good work habits, together with other (social) skills specifically related to the work situation (e.g., cooperation, teamwork, and appropriate response to supervision). The latter should be dealt with by the planned programmes of social education—I wish to focus here on the work skills themselves. In a previous review of this topic (Whelan, 1973), the types of training situation that may be made available were listed as follows: 1) in-placement training on a specific job, 2) within-the-unit job experience, 3) simulated job training, 4) synthetic jobs, and (5) perceptual motor training devices.

The range of work available within any training centre is necessarily restricted. When, in over 89%, of cases this consists of subcontract work for local industry, the result is an inadequate, unstable, and unstandardized form of training known as the "work-sample" approach. A major failing of this approach is the lack of attention to *content* and hence skill requirements, especially in view of the many studies of transfer of training.

WORK SKILLS TRAINING KIT

Attempts to develop a comprehensive scheme of basic perceptual-motor training, a "Work Skills Training Kit," commenced in 1970. The results of applying the first version of this have been very encouraging and recent collaboration with an industrial designer has resulted in the new "Work Skills Training Kit," the prototype of which has just been built.

The aim was to design a mobile piece of equipment that would enable all components of the kit to be presented in turn and stored when not in use, with space for further items to be added later where necessary. It should be attractive in appearance, suitable for use in workshop or even classroom settings, and include a certain degree of automated recording of performance (Figures 1 and 2).

The various components of the kit have been determined as a result of an intensive review of the elemental operations that can be found, in various combinations, in any job. Important influences in this analysis have been the various predetermined motion time systems that are widely used in industry, the

Figure 1. The Work Skills Training Kit: A mobile cabinet which provides both storage space for materials and work stations for instructor and trainee.

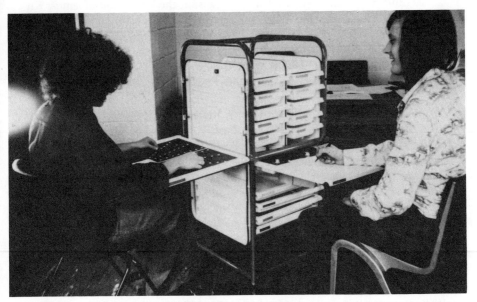

Figure 2. The Work Skills Training Kit in use. The trainee's performance is scored and timed at the end of each training session (simulation shown).

concensus concerning items included in many scales for assessing work skill, and the particular areas of performance that research has shown to present difficulties for many retarded individuals (Grant, 1971; Grant et al., 1973, 1975; Whelan, 1971, 1973, 1974.) The theoretical basis of the approach is supported by many studies of transfer of training which have shown that transfer most readily occurs when the initial learning task and the transfer task are quite similar (Drew and Espeseth, 1968). The Work Skills Training Kit should be used by practitioners to supplement the "work-sample approach."

It should be noticed that the emphasis is on *training,* though it is clear that the distinction between assessment and training is no longer clear-cut in practice. The kit will provide a valuable profile of perceptual-motor skills together with measures of other relevant skills (such as decision-making, memory for sequences, and specific discriminatory ability). It provides both an indication of present abilities and of further training needs, and should not be used to make predictive inferences about an individual's ability to respond to training.

The performance norms, soon to be developed from a representative sample of trainees in Adult Training Centres, will make us of the shape of an individual's performance curves for each task presented on several occasions. The absolute value of their performance, in relation to acceptable industrial standards, will be readily afforded by reference to the standard time for each task, defined by a Methods-Time Measurement (MTM) Analysis. This standard time will appear as a horizontal line on the scoring sheet provided for each task.

In order to obtain some measure of transfer, the Work Skills Training Kit will include two composite tasks, for each of which a pictorial programmed manual is provided. The trainee is taken through the first manual by the instructor who shows him how to perform the task, using the various components and carrying out the necessary operations in the order and manner illustrated in the manual. Once the trainee has learned to use the manual in this way, the instructor replaces it with a second manual, together with a new set of components, and monitors the trainee's attempt to complete this novel task solely by reference to the pictorial manual. If trainees are able to acquire this self-instructional strategy, then the implications for the design of new manuals, both for use in the workshop and in the social education area, are considerable. Once we are sure that each trainee is capable of performing the basic operations that are the building bricks of any task, surely an important function of prevocational training, then we are able to present him with tasks that make successively greater demands on his skills, allowing progress to be reflected by his movement through the various Departments in the Unit—from the induction workroom to the most advanced workroom where more specialised job training is available prior to placement in his employment. Successful techniques of training on real tasks have been described by a number of workers (Crosson, 1969; Screven, 1971; Gold, 1968, 1969, 1972, 1974; Tomlinson, 1976).

THE ILLUSTRATED VOCATIONAL INVENTORY

The Survey of Adult Training Centres showed a need for staff to learn more about the job knowledge and job interests of trainees. When staff do enter into conversation, it is usually in a group setting, and, although it plays an important part in establishing friendly relationships, "chatting" is no substitute for purposeful and systematic attempts to involve the individual, listening to his ideas and encouraging him to express them where difficulties are found. Staff concerned with the vocational planning, training, or job placement of individuals need to obtain systematic information about their interest patterns in the many unskilled and semiskilled jobs that are, or could be made, available to them.

Although a large number of sophisticated tests of vocational interest are available for use with nonhandicapped individuals, these usually require a high level of reading ability and comprehension. A small number of tests of vocational interest are available for use with mentally handicapped individuals, including the Vocational Interest and Sophistication Assessment Test (Parnicky, Kahn, and Burdett, 1971) and the Reading-Free Vocational Interest Inventory (Becker, 1973). However, all the known tests were designed for use with borderline or mildly mentally handicapped adults. Attempts to apply these to more severely handicapped adults resulted in the conclusion that a new instrument is required when working with this group. In addition, it was found that the use of line drawings introduced some ambiguity, and the provision of fewer occupational categories for females than for males provided unnecessary limitations in some tests.

It was for these reasons that the Illustrated Vocational Inventory (IVI) was designed. It is a reading-free instrument which provides a framework for staff to explore the vocational knowledge and interests of moderately and severely mentally handicapped individuals. The IVI is based on 11 areas of work, a common list of occupations to be used with both males and females: 1) domestic work, 2) simple factory work, 3) industrial laundry work, 4) food service—catering, 5) horticultural/agricultural work, 6) animal care, 7) local services, 8) patient care, 9) garage work, 10) office and shop work, 11) building and allied trades.

Several considerations led to the choice of the above list of occupational areas. A survey of research and reports concerning jobs held by mentally handicapped persons, for example that carried out by Collmann and Newlyn (1956), indicated a wide range of possible occupations. The National Survey of Adult Training Centres also provided information concerning the range of jobs successfully held by ex-ATC trainees in open employment.

During pilot studies (Reiter, 1976), it was found that photographs are more effective in stimulating verbal responses from trainees than are line drawings. The IVI, therefore, is based on a large number of monochrome photographs.

Large numbers of photographs were taken of people in the course of their normal work and finally 11 representative photographs were selected as representing each occupational category. One photograph from each category is used in the occupational knowledge inquiry and ten from each in the interest inquiry.

The occupational knowledge inquiry consists of 11 large photographs, one for each of the work areas listed, with an extra photograph at the beginning to serve as a practice example and for subsequent reference. Six basic questions concerning general aspects of the work are asked about each picture in turn.

The occupational interest inquiry consisting of 110 photographs (10 representing each work area) involves a forced-choice procedure. Every occupational area is matched with every other one, resulting in 55 paired photographs each on a separate page, as illustrated in Figure 3.

Figure 3. An example of a stimulus pair presented during the occupational interest inquiry of the Illustrated Vocational Inventory.

The individual is asked to indicate which of the two tasks depicted by the photographs he would prefer. In five of the ten cases the picture representing a particular occupation appears at the top and in five cases at the bottom, of the pair, to overcome any possible response bias.

The IVI has now been administered to over 400 trainees and raw scores have been converted into percentile distributions for males and females separately on the two inquiries (Figures 4–7). Measures of validity and reliability have been

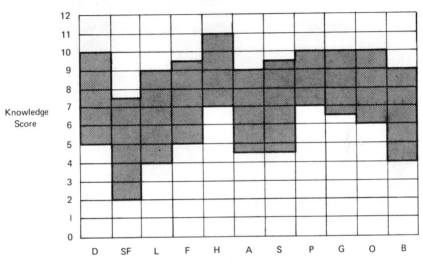

Figure 4. IVI Occupational knowledge, male.

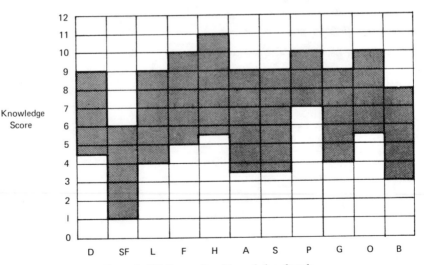

Figure 5. IVI Occupational knowledge, female.

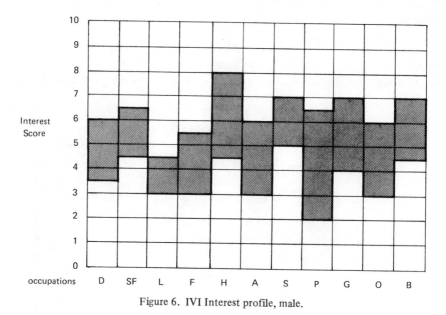

Figure 6. IVI Interest profile, male.

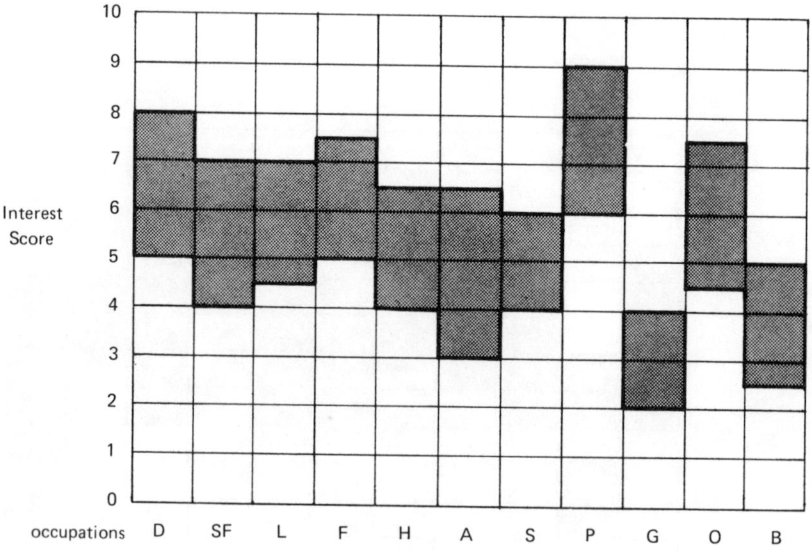

Figure 7. IVI Interest profile, female.

carried out on the IVI, a handbook has been prepared, and the new instrument is now in process of publication.

When applied to children in their final year at special school, it was found that the IVI knowledge inquiry would need to be supplemented by more detailed questions if it is to become applicable to mildly handicapped school-leavers. This inquiry was found, however, to be suitable for the severely mentally handicapped school children, most of whom will proceed to the ATC at the age of 16 years. The occupational interest profile of both groups of children fell within the average range obtained by ATC trainees.

Both of the techniques that have been described in this paper are intended for use by practitioners. One of the aims of the research team has been to enhance the professionalism of ATC and associated staff by giving them a share in the skills that often have been regarded as the monopoly of more highly trained professionals, such as psychologists. We believe that staff who have been taught how to use a new technique will be more likely to incorporate that area of training within their daily programme and to experience an increase in job satisfaction which will ultimately benefit those whose futures depend upon their professional skills and standards of practice.

SUMMARY

Two new techniques have been presented for use in the prevocational training of moderately and severely mentally handicapped individuals. The Work Skills Training Kit allows intensive practice of those basic operations required in combination in any task. The Illustrated Vocational Inventory is a reading-free test of vocational knowledge and interests.

ACKNOWLEDGMENTS

The author acknowledges the contributions made by Mr. T. Lloyd of the Department of Industrial Design, Manchester Polytechnic, and by Dr. Shunit Reiter, co-author in the production of the Illustrated Vocational Inventory.

REFERENCES

Becker, R. L. (1973) The Reading-Free Vocational Interest Inventory. Ment. Retard. 11:11.

Collmann, R. D., and Newlyn, D. (1956) Employment success of educationally subnormal pupils in England. Amer. J. Ment. Defic. 60:733.

Crosson, J. E. (1969) A technique for programming sheltered workshop environments for training severely retarded workers. Amer. J. Ment. Defic. 73:814.

Drew, C. J., and Espeseth, V. K. (1968) Transfer of training in the mentally retarded: A review. Except. Child. 35:129.

Gold, M. (1968) Preworkshop skills for the trainable: a sequential technique. Educ. Train. Ment. Retard. 3:31.

Gold, M. (1969) The acquisition of a complex assembly task by retarded adolescents. Final Report, Project No. 8-8060. Champaign, Urbana: University of Illinois.

Gold, M. (1972) Stimulus factors in skill training of the retarded on a complex assembly task: Acquisition, transfer and retention. Amer. J. Ment. Defic. 76:517.

Gold, M. (1974) Redundant cue removal in skill training for the mildly and moderately retarded. Education and Training of the Mentally Retarded. Champaign, Urbana: University of Illinois, Childrens Research Centre.

Grant, G. W. B. (1971) Some management problems of providing work for the mentally disordered with particular reference to mental handicap. Unpublished M.Sc. thesis, University of Manchester.

Grant, G. W. B., Whelan, E., and Moores, B. (1973) Assessing the work needs and work performance of mentally handicapped adults. Brit. J. Ment. Subnorm. 19:71.

Grant, G. W. B., Moores, B., and Whelan, E. (1975) The application of Methods-Time Measurement in training centres for mentally handicapped adults. M.T.M. Journal 2.

Parnicky, J. J., Kahn, H., and Burdett, A. (1971) Standardisation of the (VISA) vocational interest and sophistication assessment technique. Amer. J. Ment. Defic. 75:442.

Reiter, S. (1976) Vocational counselling of mentally handicapped adults. Unpublished Ph.D. thesis, University of Manchester.

Screven, C. G. (1971) Applied behavioural technology in a vocational rehabilitation setting. In Behaviour Modification in Mental Retardation (Ed. Gardner, W. I.) Chicago: Aldine Atherton.

Tomlinson, E. (1976) Evaluating the relative effectiveness of different methods of developing the work skills of retarded adults. Unpublished Ph.D. thesis, University of Manchester.

Whelan, E. (1971) Assessment and development of industrial skills of retarded adults. Proceedings of International Research Seminar on the Vocational Rehabilitation of the Mentally Retarded (held in the USA June 5–26, 1971) Washington, D.C.: AAMD.

Whelan, E. (1973) Developing work skills: a systematic approach. In Assessment for Learning in the Mentally Handicapped (Ed. Mittler, P. J.) Edinburgh: Churchill Livingstone; Baltimore: Williams & Wilkins.

Whelan, E. (1974) The 'scientific approach' in the practical workshop situation. In Experiments in the Rehabilitation of the Mentally Handicapped (Ed. Gunzburg, H. C.) London: Butterworth.

Whelan, E., and Speake, B. R. (1977) The National Survey of Adult Training Centres in England and Wales. Hester Adrian Research Centre, University of Manchester.

RESEARCH TO PRACTICE IN MENTAL RETARDATION
Education and Training, Volume II
Edited by Peter Mittler
Copyright 1977 I.A.S.S.M.D.

AN INTEGRATED PROGRAM FOR THE MENTALLY HANDICAPPED

R. I. Brown
The Vocational & Rehabilitation Research Institute,
University of Calgary, Alberta, Canada

RESEARCH TO PRACTICE

There is a considerable amount of knowledge that should be applied in the field of mental handicap, but a survey of training centres makes it obvious that this information is not applied to any large or consistent degree. Research and demonstration have been done but application often results from waves of optimism that enable specific units to function for brief periods of time, followed by collapse and disintegration. When demonstration does take place, it usually involves application of particular and specific findings rather than integration and evaluation of a broad range of findings. This chapter argues for an integrated program approach.

There are dangers of overgeneralizing results from laboratory experiments, and special interest projects do not necessarily produce the same results when applied over a range of practical situations, but this is the very reason that attempts to generalize findings should be carried out.

BASELINE BEHAVIOR AND ASSESSMENT

Research indicates that vocational training and transfer of knowledge or skills to new situations is possible for severely handicapped persons. Failure occurs when individuals do not commence training at their baseline of performance or when the training steps are too large and too rapid. This failure is not so frequent in vocational training as in the less structured areas of social, home-living, and leisure time.

Research shows little evidence that success or failure can be predicted from traditional assessment procedures (Cobb, 1972). Assessment raises three major problems:

1. Do the programs of the agency cover the baseline functioning of the individual?

2. What are the individual's specific difficulties? (This includes lack of opportunities to attempt particular activities.)
3. Can we modify our training environment to meet the individual's baseline needs?

This places the emphasis on program and trainee match; to succeed at this, the content of assessment changes from formal tests to practical measures of behavioural functioning. Furthermore, assessment is a continuous function which modifies the training procedures throughout the rehabilitation process.

SOME ASPECTS OF PROGRAM INTEGRATION

Since incidental learning is poor in the retarded and structure is a necessary component of training (Clarke and Clarke, 1973), failure will occur frequently unless wide-ranging, long-term and highly organized programs integrating training, placement, and follow-up are developed. The effects of the unfamiliar on the handicapped are well known (Brown, 1976) and this is exacerbated by lack of structure.

Three aspects of integration seem important. One is longitudinal integration, that is, the possibility of providing steps that are clearly defined, from very basic prevocational training, through vocational units, to group or independent employment (see Figure 1). Outlines are of value for staff and parents so the overall program is clear. However, many vocational programs are still concerned with simply exposing the individual to occupation rather than using occupation as a tool for teaching concepts and applying the training techniques that are now well known in terms of strategy for habilitation. For example, we should ask what type of work skills does it teach the individual in relation to visual discrimination, motor manipulation, group interaction, working with different supervisors, working different time shifts, etc.

Even though staff may have training principles at their fingertips, it does not follow that these skills are applied. Keeping programs at a level that provides adequate training means enabling staff to assess their own application of these techniques in the training situation. In our own work units we have employed two major approaches:

1. A liaison officer system provides for a member of the professional staff to work closely with shop supervisors, providing a sounding board and a practical hand wherever necessary but also helping to integrate the program. Each liaison worker and shop supervisor is associated with a team, all of whom have professional training and experience in different areas of rehabilitation. In this way we have come to grips with the "we" and "they" which often occurs between professional and front line personnel, and we have made available to the training area an integrated multidisciplinary team of staff that also serves to diminish interdisciplinary rivalries.

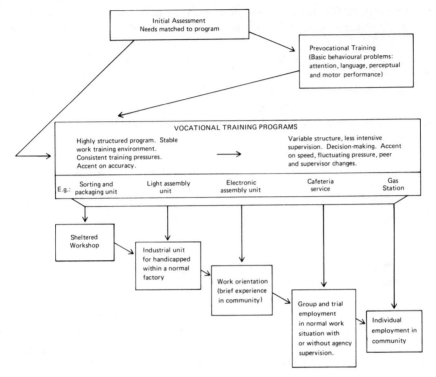

Figure 1. Schematic outline of vocational training and employment units. (Service provisions should be detailed for each unit.)

2. Workshop supervisors are assisted in assessing daily standards of program training. These include problems such as shop layout, tool availability and maintenance, work flow, and suitability of training stations. The group involved in assessment visits each work station and notes in writing points associated with the above. Staff discussions follow the tour, plans are adopted for change, and the effects of this are evaluated on subsequent visits. This approach has a number of effects. The mere fact of someone standing, observing, and writing down what they see seems to upgrade perception. Supervisors often say, "I didn't notice this before," although the supervisor may have received considerable training plus experience on the job.

In this way, new supervisors receive extensive training in the aims and techniques of the unit, and staff can note gaps in training and begin to provide better and individualized programs.

An integrated program also involves vocational, social, recreational, and home-living training, and placement and follow-up. Many see these areas discreetly, with staff from one area referring to the others as "back-up" services, but each of these areas is equally important and should be part of the total package. Only when we recognize this can adequate integration of programs and transfer to new situations be provided. For example, social education is part of the home-living, vocational, and leisure time activities. Moreover, staff cannot afford to have trainees come to them for purely specialized treatment. A hearing-aid provided through the audiology unit is not likely to be of maximal use unless the social and behavioural implications of its use are recognized and training applied in other units. Placement in the community involves careful preplacement training in which placement needs of the individual are precisely dealt with in the training units. The steps within placement must provide opportunities for structured support (e.g., a factory involving teams of moderately handicapped or severely handicapped workers earning on a piece-work basis or supervisors going with trainees to a work situation, and modelling the tasks).

The third aspect of integration concerns the difficulty that trainees have in transferring their skills to a variety of situations. We often hear, "I train him in this situation but he cannot do it in that situation;" "He can use this particular tool but not a similar one." Many agency staff argue that the mentally handicapped cannot easily transfer their skills, but research evidence (Clarke and Clarke, 1975) shows that given certain situations this is not the case. What has happened to create an apparent difference between research and practice? Trainees are poor as incidental learners and perhaps we expose trainees to a situation not structured as in the research condition. In other words, we do not provide transfer training programs. Strategy must include clearly defining the social situation in which people show the behaviour, analyzing the components of behaviour, and breaking the task down so that it becomes a more readily learnable program. Two examples follow. The first concerns mealtime behaviour of severely handicapped persons (Eaton and Brown, 1974). Eating behaviours were observed in social situations, rated by staff, dissected into their specific components, and the inappropriate activities dealt with by a combination of video-taping, modelling, and reward techniques. Table 1 shows the very rapid change in behaviour when the individual skills were dealt with separately.

The second example is a bus training program (Hughson and Brown, 1975) in which we had to deal with the initial behaviour of the trainee in the community by applying the following:

1. observation of trainee behaviour (we let them make mistakes if someone was there to save serious problems)
2. careful route analysis (we picked the simplest route though not always the shortest)
3. one-to-one training with modelling, followed by trainee-initiated behaviour with visual or auditory feedback (often supervisors prevent spontaneous behaviour because they find it is easier to lead, demonstrate or take over).

Table 1. Effects of training on specific aspects of mealtime behaviour

	Pretraining		Posttraining			
	$\overline{X}$		$\overline{X}$		Score in	No.
Behaviour	A	IA	A^a	IA^b	number of:	of Ss
Feet on floor while sitting at table eating. (5 training sessions)	0	610	598	2	seconds	5
Cutlery to mouth, not moving mouth to cutlery. (8 training sessions)	1	26	19	2	incidents	4
Food to mouth after swallowing previous mouthful. (10 training sessions)	4	19	16	6	incidents	4
Eating with mouth closed. (8 training sessions)	<1	16	1	8	incidents	3

^{a}A = appropriate behaviour
^{b}IA = inappropriate behaviour

This program demonstrated the need for individual training. Trainees' transit routes vary so one-to-one training program planning is essential; yet, few agencies do much training of this type. The training must also take place within the outside community. To learn something in an agency and then expect it to work outside is naive unless we have built "transfer bridges" to the community.

Much of the one-to-one training that structuring of programs demands can be carried out by volunteers under supervision, plus a volunteer coordinator. For example, just over 4,000 hours of volunteer help per year can supply ten minutes of individual training per day for 100 trainees per year (based on 250 days per year). The implications of mobilizing this manpower are considerable.

STRUCTURE AND TRAINING

These situations all imply structure, by which is meant:

1. the rigorous application of training techniques, such as breakdown of tasks into suitable units, use of discrimination training and use of goal setting techniques
2. timetabling, including the precise time that an individual is taught what and by whom. (In early learning the program must be spelled out very clearly, but later, opportunities for variation, and the unexpected should be built into the program.)
3. use of instructions, visual, verbal, or both.

   We often muddle the type of instructions most effective for a particular individual because we confuse one aspect of the program with another. If we wish to teach a new motor or visual task we have to depend on previous visual or motor learning and/or make use of verbal concepts that are very familiar to the individual. Many will say this is obvious, but I very much doubt whether most instructors analyze the type of language they use in training the handicapped. In a recent study (McLeod and Brown, 1976), it was shown that even skilled counsellors talk too much, and use too complex concepts when working with the handicapped.

Structure can also relate to physical environments which can be modified to enhance learning. The work of Gunzburg and Gunzburg (1973) is well known in this context. Specialized environments are needed for early learning. Not only is one-to-one training required, but individual cubicles can reduce extraneous stimulation. Although this has been recommended for a number of years, it is still not consistently applied as a device to enhance initial learning.

Initial learning is fatiguing, so we do not subject the individual to it for long periods, but we can apply it with effect several times a day. A number of people can receive individual instruction during the day, and we can arrange the times so that initial learning for one individual is coupled with periods of later learning for other trainees, e.g., improving speed on tasks for which early learning has been completed. Computer Assisted Instruction also can be used to structure and individualize training in early learning. For example, in a food recognition program for physically and mentally handicapped persons (Holtz and Brown, 1978), it was demonstrated that the problems of recognizing food packages in a store could be resolved on a computer program using POSSUM adapted terminals. Transfer learning of the skills to local stores was very high.

DECISION-MAKING AND TRAINING

Because we live in a highly variable environment, structured training must merge into programs that provide for flexible decision-making by the handicapped. A successful trainee is often defined as one who learns what we want him to do. This reveals a lack of concern with how the individual sees himself and a lack of attention to the quality of life within the current habilitation models. It is of minimal value to enable individuals to enter society and keep their jobs if they still perceive themselves as incompetent and segregated from the rest of society.

Recently, Ryba and Brown (1977) examined trainees in terms of their self-concepts and reaction to real-life problems when social pressure was applied (e.g., signing documents, following through a commitment under adverse pressure). From the results it was apparent that most trainees could not resist even mild social pressure, although they showed competence in many vocational and social skill areas. A training program, moving from structured demonstration and modelling to informal decision-making, was carried out and considerable improvement obtained, although transfer to other situations was inadequate.

CONCLUSIONS

Unless we are prepared to apply research to practice, chance our arm in closing the research-practice gap, and develop practical demonstrations, little development is likely to occur in the field of rehabilitation, despite the fervour of private and public agencies or the research ardour of their academic counterparts.

SUMMARY

The program presented demonstrates the principles of coordinated training and research in vocational, social and home-living skills; integration of assessment and training; determination of program levels by baseline performance; structuring of program into variable training steps leading to group and individual placement in vocational and residential areas; and a continuous placement and follow-up service.

REFERENCES

Brown, R. I. (1976) Psychology and Education of Slow Learners. London: Routledge & Kegan Paul.

Clarke, A. M., and Clarke, A. D. B. (1973) What are the problems? An evaluation of recent research relating to theory and practice. In Mental Retardation and Behavioural Research (Eds. Clarke, A. D. B., and Clarke, A. M.) Edinburgh & London: Churchill Livingstone.

Clarke, A. M., and Clarke, A. D. B. (1975) Experimental studies: An overview. In Mental Deficiency: The Changing Outlook, 3rd edition (Eds. Clarke, A. M., and Clarke, A. D. B.) New York: The Free Press.

Cobb, H. V. (1972) The Forecast of Fulfillment. New York: Teachers' College Press.

Eaton, P., and Brown, R. I. (1974) The training of mealtime behaviour in the subnormal. Brit. J. Ment. Subnorm. 20:78.

Gunzburg, H. C., and Gunzburg, A. (1973) Mental Handicap and Physical Environment. London: Baillière & Tindall.

Holtz, E., and Brown, R. I. (1978) The application of computer assisted instruction in training the physically and mentally handicapped in a social task. Journal of Practical Approaches to Developmental Handicap. In press.

Hughson, E. A., and Brown, R. I. (1975) A bus training program for the severely handicapped. Brit. J. Ment. Subnorm. 21:79.

McLeod, M., and Brown, R. I. (1976) Verbal communication and the developmentally handicapped. Brit. J. Ment. Subnorm. 22:1, 42, 26–34.

Ryba, K., and Brown, R. I. (1977) Encouraging decision making in the mentally handicapped. Journal of Practical Approaches to Developmental Handicap. In press.

RESEARCH TO PRACTICE IN MENTAL RETARDATION
Education and Training, Volume II
Edited by Peter Mittler
Copyright 1977 I.A.S.S.M.D.

TESTING SOCIAL AND PREVOCATIONAL AWARENESS OF RETARDED ADOLESCENTS AND ADULTS

A. S. Halpern
*Rehabilitation Research and Training Center
in Mental Retardation,
University of Oregon,
Eugene, Oregon 97403, United States*

INTRODUCTION

Research and common sense have similarly concluded that vocational adjustment of mentally retarded adolescents and adults is most likely to occur when accompanied by concomitant personal and social adjustment. In spite of this fairly common understanding, vocationally oriented services for retarded adolescents and adults have frequently neglected the personal and social domains.

One important exception to this trend can be found in the cooperative work-study programs that have served mildly retarded adolescents in the United States during the past 15 years. Frequently involving an interface between special education and vocational rehabilitation, these programs typically address many of the components of adult adjustment. More recently, broad spectrum programs for moderately retarded adolescents and adults have also emerged in school classrooms, community residential facilities, and community activity centers.

Even though service providers have become more and more interested in addressing the social and personal aspects of adult adjustment, success has not come easily in these endeavors, attributable in part to the fact that several basic issues remain largely unresolved. Which aspects of personal and social adjustment should be the focus of adolescent and adult training programs? What methods of training are most likely to produce good results? How can the specific needs of retarded adolescents and adults be identified, and how can the impact of our attempts to remediate these needs be measured?

During the past five years, the Rehabilitation Research and Training Center in Mental Retardation at the University of Oregon has conducted a major research effort at the measurement end of this continuum of related issues and problems. The major product of this effort thus far has been the articulation of a measurement strategy and the creation of a standardized series of tests known as the Social and Prevocational Information Battery (SPIB). The SPIB was originally developed for use with mildly retarded people (Halpern et al., 1975a; Irvin and Halpern, 1976), and has been available in published form since September 1975 (Halpern et al., 1975b). A major revision of the SPIB for use with moderately retarded people has recently been completed, and should be available within six months to a year.

DOMAINS MEASURED BY THE SPIB

The domains measured by the SPIB relate to five broad areas of adult community adjustment: employability, economic self-sufficiency, family living, personal habits, and communication. Within these five broad areas, nine separate tests have been developed, measuring the examinee's knowledge of job-search skills, job-related behavior, banking, budgeting, purchasing, home management, health care, hygiene and grooming, and functional signs (survival reading).

TEST FORMAT AND ADMINISTRATION

The SPIB consists of 277 items, either true/false or picture selection in format, that are administered orally to examinees in order to neutralize the impact of differential reading ability. Each of the nine tests contains approximately 30 items that can be administered separately, requiring 10 to 15 minutes for completion.

Items were selected in accordance with a domain sampling model, whereby each domain or area to be tested was further specified hierarchically in terms of content areas and subcontent areas. This process resulted in the identification of 54 content areas and 180 subcontent areas across the nine SPIB domains. The subcontent areas then served as a blueprint for generating test items for possible inclusion in the battery. Extensive field testing and item analyses eventually produced the 277 items that are included in the battery.

The revision of the SPIB for use with moderately retarded people, known as SPIB-T, contains the following modifications of the original battery: 1) approximately one-third of the items were revised or replaced, simplifying the language of the items but retaining the concepts to be tested; 2) response format was changed from true/false to yes/no; 3) a pretest was developed to screen out those people not able to respond to the test format; and 4) the test administration manual was simplified in order to increase the types of people who might serve as test administrators.

RESEARCH AND STANDARDIZATION SAMPLES

Many samples of retarded people have been involved in the development of the SPIB. Approximately 1,100 mildly retarded students from special education classrooms in Oregon participated in the initial development of test items. An additional 900 students, half in junior high school and half in senior high school, provided data for final standardization of the SPIB. Three additional samples of retarded adolescents and young adults have provided confirmation of the statistical properties of the SPIB, and two samples of vocational rehabilitation clients have provided evidence of SPIB validity.

Two more samples have participated in the development of SPIB-T: 1) residents of community facilities in five western states, and 2) moderately retarded students in special education classes in Pennsylvania. The first of these samples also participated in a validity study of SPIB-T.

The mean age of these several samples ranged from a low of 15 years to a high of 27 years. Most of the subjects were 21 years of age or younger. The mean IQ of the mildly retarded samples was around 68, whereas the mean IQ for the moderately retarded samples was around 55.

DIFFICULTY OF THE SPIB

One of the criteria for including items in the final form of the SPIB was item difficulty level. In an ideal situation, the difficulty level of each test would exhibit several characteristics. Tests should be neither too easy nor too hard, in order to permit the measurement of growth, but not at the expense of discouraging most examinees with a large number of difficult items. Furthermore, the tests should reflect the level of examinee intelligence and maturity, so that older and brighter people would receive generally higher scores. Finally, the test scores should be variable enough to reflect genuine and relevant individual differences within each domain. Both SPIB and SPIB-T possess these desirable characteristics. For the moderately retarded samples, the average test difficulty ranged from 51–66% correct. The average performance of mildly retarded samples on the SPIB ranged from 59–83% correct. When the age of the subjects was considered, test data revealed that older people tended to produce higher scores on the SPIB than younger people.

RELIABILITY OF THE SPIB

A second major criterion for retaining items in the final form of the SPIB was the internal consistency of the set of items within each test. Following standard procedures of test development, item sets were sought with average interitem correlations of approximately 0.1, and point biserial correlations in the range of

0.2 to 0.5. This produced satisfactory reliability coefficients for both SPIB and SPIB-T, using Cronbach's coefficient alpha as the index of reliability. The reliability indices across all samples for all tests ranged from 0.58 to 0.86, with a median value of 0.75. Only four of the 72 reliabilities calculated were 0.65 or less.

GUESSING THE RIGHT ANSWER

A frequently expressed concern about test items utilizing a selection response format is the extent to which examinees can guess the right answer without actually knowing the right answer. This problem can be especially severe in tests which utilize a two-choice format. Since random guessing, when it occurs, will always lower the reliability of a test, a highly reliable test can be construed as evidence for the minimal influence of random guessing. Systematic guessing, however, can be more deceptive, in some cases, actually increasing artificially the reliability of a test. In order to prevent this from occurring, any tendency toward systematic guessing must be both understood and controlled.

In order to investigate the possibility of systematic response biases within the SPIB, each test was scored as two subtests, one consisting of all the true items within the test and the other consisting of all the false items. The difficulty levels of each subtest were then examined, showing clearly that the false subtests were harder than the true subtests. This implies that there will be a greater tendency to guess on false items than on true items. These findings are found in Table 1.

The next step in the analysis involved calculating the reliability and average interitem correlation for each true and false subtest. In every case, the false subtests are more reliable than the true ones, both internally and across time. These results are shown in Table 2.

When taken together, the information that false subtests are more difficult and more reliable than true ones has one major implication: when mildly retarded examinees guess, they tend to guess true more often than false. Guessing behavior is systematic rather than random. As a result, false items are better discriminators than true ones.

If guessing behavior were more random in nature, a completely different picture would have emerged. Since the false subtests are more difficult and therefore present more opportunity for guessing to occur, a pattern of *random* guessing would have resulted in lower reliabilities for the false subtests than for the true subtests. Since the opposite of this occurred, we must conclude that guessing is for the most part systematic and in the direction of selecting true. The implication of this finding for future test construction procedures seems clear: when true/false items are used to test mildly retarded examinees, the majority of the items should be keyed false.

Table 1. Difficulty levels for SPIB true and false subtests

Score	M^a	S.D.^{b}	Number of items	Difficulty level
Purchasing				
True	8.1	2.0	11	0.74
False	13.2	4.4	20	0.66
Budgeting				
True	8.7	2.0	11	0.79
False	10.7	4.2	19	0.56
Banking				
True	8.8	2.3	13	0.68
False	10.2	3.7	18	0.57
Job-related behavior				
True	10.9	2.5	14	0.78
False	8.7	3.3	16	0.54
Job-search skills				
True	7.3	1.8	10	0.73
False	13.5	4.6	22	0.61
Home management				
True	6.2	1.5	8	0.78
False	10.6	3.9	18	0.59
Health care				
True	9.3	1.7	11	0.85
False	16.2	5.2	26	0.62
Hygiene and grooming				
True	10.4	2.2	13	0.80
False	9.8	3.6	15	0.65
Functional signs				
True	6.0	1.4	8	0.75
False	9.8	3.3	13	0.74

Note: Ns ranged from 396 to 412.
$^a M$ = mean.
^{b}S.D. = Standard deviation from the mean.

VALIDITY OF THE SPIB

A major concern pertaining to the validity of the SPIB is whether or not social and prevocational knowledge is related to the actual performance of social and prevocational skills. Unless such a relationship exists, one might reasonably question the relevance of measuring knowledge in a set of domains in which applied performance is usually the ultimate objective. Several arguments, both theoretical and practical, can be postulated for the relevance of knowledge. Theoretically, knowledge can be presumed to mediate and enhance the retention and generalizability of applied performance, if not the initial acquisition of specific applied behaviors. On the practical side, it is much easier to measure

Table 2. Reliability and average item intercorrelation estimates for the SPIB true and false subtests

Score	$R_I{}^a$	r^b	$R_T{}^a$	Number of Items
Purchasing				
True	0.56	0.10	0.52	11
False	0.82	0.18	0.72	20
Budgeting				
True	0.64	0.14	0.52	11
False	0.80	0.17	0.71	19
Banking				
True	0.54	0.08	0.47	13
False	0.76	0.15	0.71	18
Job-related behavior				
True	0.70	0.13	0.60	14
False	0.72	0.14	0.75	16
Job-search skills				
True	0.51	0.09	0.49	10
False	0.81	0.16	0.77	22
Home management				
True	0.43	0.08	0.41	8
False	0.77	0.18	0.76	18
Health care				
True	0.55	0.10	0.46	11
False	0.84	0.17	0.76	26
Hygiene and grooming				
True	0.64	0.12	0.51	13
False	0.82	0.23	0.74	15
Functional signs				
True	0.39	0.07	0.54	8
False	0.85	0.30	0.79	13

Note: Ns ranged from 346 to 412.

[a]"I" indicates coefficient alpha reliability; "T" indicates test-retest reliability.

[b]r indicates estimates of average item intercorrelation.

knowledge than applied performance in most of the domains that are measured by the SPIB.

Three studies have been conducted to examine the relationship between SPIB performance and applied performance. In order to estimate predictive validity, a sample of vocational rehabilitation clients was rated by rehabilitation counselors on 29 behaviors in the broad areas of community integration, economic self-sufficiency, family living, personal habits, and communication.

This same sample had been tested on the SPIB one year earlier, just before graduation from high school.

The concurrent validity of the SPIB also was estimated with a second sample of vocational rehabilitation clients. These clients were tested on the SPIB and rated by their counselors within a three-month period of time.

The concurrent validity of SPIB-T was estimated within the sample of residents from community facilities. The applied performance scale in this study consisted of 87 items that were constructed to parallel directly the content of the SPIB-T. Testing and ratings were both accomplished within a three-month period.

A variety of correlational analyses were performed within each of the three validity studies. Some of the most interesting results were provided by canonical correlations, using the nine SPIB tests on one side of the relationship and the major subscales of the criterion instrument on the other side. These analyses produced canonical correlations of 0.58 in the SPIB predictive validity study, 0.61 in the SPIB concurrent validity study, and 0.75 in the SPIB-T concurrent validity study. These results strongly suggest that knowledge and applied performance in the SPIB domains are moderately related to one another.

FUTURE RESEARCH NEEDS

As promising as these findings seem to be, they raise more questions than answers about the techniques for measuring vocational, social, and personal adjustment of mentally retarded adolescents and adults. To what extent should criterion-referenced tests be used as a substitute or embellishment for norm-referenced tests? Does knowledge really enhance the maintenance and generalizability of applied skills? What is the role of direct observational strategies in the measurement of SPIB-type domains? How can the results of assessment be utilized most effectively in the planning, implementation, and evaluation of remedial programs? Can other response formats, such as multiple choice, be used effectively with retarded people? Several researchers are currently addressing some of these questions, but a much larger effort will be required if we are to make significant gains in the development of a comprehensive measurement strategy.

SUMMARY

The Social and Prevocational Information Battery (SPIB) has been developed over the past five years to assess knowledge in the areas of job-search skills, job-related behavior, banking, budgeting, purchasing, home management, health care, hygiene, and survival reading. This paper presents the reliability and validity of the SPIB within multiple EMR and TMR samples.

REFERENCES

Halpern, A., Raffeld, P., Irvin, L., and Link, R. (1975a). Measuring social and prevocational awareness in mildly retarded adolescents. Amer. J. Ment. Defic., 80:81.

Halpern, A., Raffeld, P., Irvin, L., and Link, R. (1975b). The Social and Prevocational Information Battery. Monterey, California: CTB/McGraw-Hill.

Irvin, L., and Halpern, A. (1976). Reliability and validity of the social and prevocational information battery for mildly retarded individuals. Working Paper No. 101. Rehabilitation Research and Training Center in Mental Retardation, University of Oregon, Eugene, Oregon.

RESEARCH TO PRACTICE IN MENTAL RETARDATION
Education and Training, Volume II
Edited by Peter Mittler
Copyright 1977 I.A.S.S.M.D.

USE OF GROUP TECHNIQUES IN THE REHABILITATION OF THE RETARDED IN ISRAEL

E. Chigier
Israel Society for Rehabilitation of the Disabled,
10 Ibn Gvirol Street, Tel Aviv, Israel

All over the world, thousands of severely retarded adolescents and young adults can be found in institutions or in sheltered work environments. Usually they have little choice of changing their setting and going out into the open world of work. They are regarded as trainable, but not educable. They are regarded as requiring individual approaches because they have Intelligence Quotients of under 50, poor coordination, poor concentration, low levels of emotional stability, minimal motivation for work, a lack of responsibility and a low self-esteem. They are regarded as being capable only of doing routine, stereotyped, repetitive mechanical tasks, and, what is more, it is considered by those who know about the retarded that they are happy and satisfied to do this kind of work. If there are behavior problems that cause trouble, the solution is sought through liberal use of sedative or tranquilizing drugs and further administrative withdrawal from the general setting. Interpersonal reactions are generally regarded as being negative or dangerous when they occur. Although people the world over generally function best in small groups, a group approach to the retarded is not regarded as being desirable or worthwhile because of the verbal, cognitive, and behavioral limitations of those who are severely retarded.

Since 1965, as a result of the research projects in Israel sponsored by Social and Rehabilitation Services, United States Department of Health, Education and Welfare, I have had the opportunity of looking at the above-mentioned facts and have found that most of them are wrong. Those items that are true pertain just as much to the mode of treatment that the retarded receive as to the fact that a moderate to severe level of retardation is present.

Most rehabilitation workers working with groups of retarded people tend to make the same sort of mistake that the general public makes when reacting to the retarded. We tend to plan our management of the retarded according to the way they are, rather than to what they might be. We regard Intelligence Quotient as the upper limit of possible achievement, rather than see it as the floor—the present, functional ability of a person. And worst of all, we tend to treat the retarded in a way that we think is good for him, and good for society. We do not usually begin with the viewpoint as to what are the needs of the retarded person himself.

It is the theme of this chapter that one of the basic needs of a retarded person is the need to belong. A severely retarded person often has trouble belonging. In his own family, he is usually out of step. Often they are ashamed of him. In the street, he does not belong. He has no affiliation to a peer group. In the institution, residential or ambulatory, he often has difficulty developing a sense of belonging, of pride and identity with the institution, because of the size and nature of the institution, the attitude of the staff, and the social implications of requiring to go to an institution.

Because most of us satisfy our need to belong through membership in small groups, the object of my research over the past 10 years has been to evaluate the efficacy of the use of a group approach in rehabilitation of the moderately to severely retarded.

The first research project (1965–68) was carried out in Israel through Akim–Israel Society for Rehabilitation of the Mentally Handicapped, and dealt with retardates in a residential institution, sited in an agricultural area, about a 30-minute drive outside Tel Aviv.

In applying the principles of group dynamics to severely retarded persons, the project first established four peer groups, oriented toward becoming work groups and using a group milieu approach. Each consisted of approximately 10 members and had its own group instructor, experienced in working with youth. Chronological age of the retardates was 16–32 years, with an average of 20 years, mental age 3–8 years, with an average of five and a half years. About one-third had an associated handicap such as Down's syndrome, cerebral palsy, or epilepsy. Three groups lived in an institution that was set up at a work colony. The retardates in the fourth group lived at home with their parents in an urban area.

Each group functioned as a group eight hours a day for five and a half days a week. The first three months were devoted solely to consolidation of the group through games, walks, social activities, and an intensive program of physical education. The next stage was a group project, such as setting up a rose garden—a tangible project with a clearly defined goal. In the third phase, the group worked outside the institution in citrus groves on a voluntary basis. When the group had demonstrated its capabilities, work was obtained on a piecework basis, with payment based on the productivity of the group as a whole. Fifty percent of the pay went to the institution, 25% to the group fund, and 25% to the individual members. Because there is a labor shortage in Israel, the groups were able to find enough work in various fields to keep them employed throughout the year.

Thus, within a period of eight or nine months, the role of the institution became that of a "rural hostel." Trainees were able to walk as a group from it to orange groves two or three miles away, allocate the work among themselves, stop for lunch in the grove, and return to the institution after a day's work—all with only nominal supervision by the instructor. The same ability was demonstrated by all four groups.

FINDINGS AND IMPLICATIONS

The basic principles of a group approach to the mentally retarded are the establishment of a peer group, the opportunity of the group instructor to have maximal responsibility for his own group, and the creation of a group milieu covering a full work day.

Through the process of group dynamics, individuals working within a group experienced greater satisfaction, found effective means of coping with the crises and stresses of an open society, and exhibited more mature behavior—even though their cognitive abilities continued to be extremely limited.

Retardates, within the security of their own group, enjoyed the experience of working in the open labor market and were able to reach 30–40% of the productivity of regular agriculture workers.

Opportunities for employment of retardates were better when applicants were considered as a group, the employer thus being relieved of responsibility for the individual. Where groups of retardates had been working for a year, studies indicated that although the inhabitants retained their negative attitude toward the mentally retarded in general, two-thirds of them were willing to have a group of severely retarded males from the institution work in their area. They actually preferred retarded workers to the regular labor force because the retardates worked more slowly, and carefully and thus damaged less fruit—only 7% as opposed to 13%. Since agricultural work is paid for on a piecework basis, this represented a saving for the citrus farmer. He also benefited from their willingness to pick the oranges at the very top and the very bottom of the tree, which the regular pickers would not do because of the extra effort involved.

FOLLOW-UP

When the project ended, a group of about 17 trainees was set up to work in the orange groves while maintaining its headquarters at the institution. Nine years later the group members are still working, with no difficulties whatsoever. They have become an accepted part of the labor force in the village, and their productivity has increased with experience. Of particular interest is the fact that new members who did not participate in the research project have joined the group and have been successfully absorbed. Although further research needs to be done in this area, it appears that when a group of retardates is well established and working regularly and smoothly, the group as a whole, together with the instructor, can act as a therapeutic medium for the training and rehabilitation of new members. The established group members become "auxiliary therapists," and help modify the behavior and increase the work motivation of newcomers.

Five retardates from the urban group, who live at home, continue to work in the same park nursery where they were employed throughout the demonstration. The director of the nursery supervizes their work himself. They are paid on an individual basis by the city. All have shown improved behavior, and one has reached 80% of the productivity of a trained regular worker. A sixth member, after making outstanding progress with the group, was accepted as a worker in the parks of his home town.

GROUP WORK WITH THE RETARDED IN INDUSTRY

Since 1973, a second project sponsored by SRS is under way in Tel Aviv, carried out by the Israel Society for Rehabilitation of the Disabled, with the cooperation of the Tel Aviv branch of Akim (Project 19–P–58073–F–01). This research project is a study of the effect of a group approach on the behavior and productivity of mentally retarded adolescents and youth in a sheltered workshop.

The specific aims of the project are:

1. to ascertain the applicability of a group approach to retardates in sheltered workshops
2. to investigate the stages of group formation among severely mentally retarded adolescents and young adults
3. to measure the effect of a group technique on the productivity of trainees in a sheltered workshop
4. to ascertain the effect of a group technique on the behavior of trainees in a sheltered workshop
5. to derive conclusions and present practical recommendations on the use of a group technique for the rehabilitation of the mentally handicapped.

In the first phase of the project, 13 male trainees were selected for the experimental population, and 13 others, matched for age, IQ, and family background, were chosen for the control population. They were selected out of a population of 123 retardates working at the Achikam workshop in Tel Aviv. In both populations, average IQ was 50 (range 44–65), and average age was 20 years (range 16–28 years). Socioeconomic status in the experimental population was good in five cases, average in four, and poor in four. In the control population socioeconomic status was good in one, average in eight and poor in four. The average length of time working in the sheltered workshop was four years two months, and for the control population three years and two months.

All members of both groups were examined psychologically, and a home interview was carried out to get some basic findings with regard to intellectual level, family set-up, and behavior pattern as described by the mother and father on home interview. Only male trainees were used because they comprise the majority in the workshop. Cooperation was maximal, and no problems were encountered on psychological testing or at the home interview.

The work instructors were allocated their respective groups and were briefed with regard to scoring work output, work behavior, and general behavior during the baseline period. All the staff of the workshops were informed about the nature of the research project, including the two instructors, but in a carefully balanced manner, so that the possible advantages and disadvantages of using a group technique were given equal weight. Any bias toward positive belief in the value of the group approach was avoided as much as possible. During the baseline period of measurement and observation, neither of the two work instructors knew which group would be the experimental group and which the control group. The baseline period lasted for four weeks during the month of March 1974.

ESTABLISHMENT OF EXPERIMENTAL SITUATION

At the end of the baseline period, one instructor's group was designated to be the experimental group and the other the control group. Both instructors were informed that it was up to them to demonstrate which method would show better results in productivity, i.e., the individual or the group method. If anything, the instructor working with the control group and using the individual method was more enthusiastic about the individual approach than the instructor working with the experimental group was about the group approach. Measurements of productivity, work behavior and behavior pattern were continued as before. In order to stimulate greater productivity, the instructor working with the control group posted figures on individual output next to the work area of each of her trainees for each week.

The work with the experimental group was carried out in a "low profile" manner, as follows:

Trainees remained at their regular work areas within the workshop. They were informed that, from now on, they were to work together, on a collective basis, and that productivity would be scored for the group as a whole on a weekly basis. The instructor was under close supervision and in close contact with the research assistant. The group met as a group every day usually at the end of the work day, for a period of about 15 minutes to discuss the progress of the group. These meetings were eagerly anticipated, were very lively, and turned out to be a great success. A weekly chart showed the rating of the group on productivity for the work on a five-point range from excellent to poor. At the end of the month, trainees were paid almost equally with a slight difference in payment between "good" and "average" workers. The group tended to go together to the dining room for snacks and for lunch, sitting together in the dining room at the center. The experimental group was set up without any difficulty. Both populations functioned in their respective ways for a period of one year, and data was obtained from each population on work behavior, general behavior, and productivity of trainees in both populations.

At the end of the experimental period findings were as follows:

1. Trainees in the experimental population showed improved behavior in terms of less agression (active or passive aggression), less withdrawal, and greater prosocial behavior. The director of the Center, the group instructor, and other personnel who had contacts with the trainees were definitely impressed by the better behavior, greater alertness, and improved emotional attitude of the trainees in the experimental population as compared to the control population.

2. Despite time taken off for group meetings, and discussion during the working day, productivity of the experimental population was greater than that of the control population.

It was concluded that a group approach is feasible in a sheltered workshop, can be carried out without disruptions, and can provide a medium for better behavior, self-satisfaction, and productivity on the part of retardates working in a group setting.

In the second phase of the project, new groups are being set up. From the original experimental group, five retardates have been placed as a group in open industry since April 1975. They work making tubes in a plant that has 180 employees. After the first month, it was possible to withdraw the group instructor. They are now under direct supervision of the foreman in the factory. Part of the time they work together as a group, but more and more they are working individually or with other workers. Their sense of belonging is maintained through the loose, small group structure, while at the same time they are integrated into open industry and have numerous work and social contacts during the day with other workers—male and female. The work is of a satisfactory standard, they come on time, are generally conscientious, have had no accidents, and there have been no difficulties in relationships between them and others. This is because group placement was done carefully with adequate preparation of management and staff, the group instructor was present for the first month, and intensive follow-through contacts were maintained all the time. Productivity is satisfactory, two retardates almost reaching the productivity of a regular industrial worker. Payment is made in terms of productivity, and full social benefits have been provided. If the opportunity exists, the management is interested in increasing the number of retardates working in the plant, and is willing to recommend the same procedure to other employers. (One of the five has left the work in the plant because of personal difficulties.)

Subsequent to the placement of the first small group in open industry, two further groups are in the process of preparation, organization and consolidation:

1. a mixed group, mostly girls, who after adequate training will be placed as a group to work as nursing aides in a rehabilitation hospital for the physically disabled
2. a mixed group of retardates who have physical handicap(s) in addition to their mental handicap, e.g., cerebral palsy, epilepsy, and who are being trained to work together as an industrial unit. They will work together in assembly work, in a sheltered setting, but on a cooperative basis.

This project is almost completed. The findings up to now have reinforced the findings and conclusions from the previous research study in an agricultural setting. When retardates acquire a sense of belonging through the use of a *group milieu approach,* motivation for work is developed, a zest for living is apparent, behavior is improved and, despite the severe limitations, positive rehabilitation can be achieved. (Two movies, each dealing with the above mentioned projects, have been produced in English.)

ACKNOWLEDGMENTS

I wish to thank Dr. James F. Garrett and Dr. J. Fenton, Social and Rehabilitation Services, U.S. Department of Health, Education and Welfare, Washington, D.C., for their support of the project, and Mrs. B. Ben Amotz, Director Achikam Center, for the Retarded, Tel Aviv, for her help and cooperation.

RESEARCH TO PRACTICE IN MENTAL RETARDATION
Education and Training, Volume II
Edited by Peter Mittler
Copyright 1977 I.A.S.S.M.D.

DESIGNING FOR DEVELOPMENT
Adult Training Centres

S. Shipman
Scottish Development Department,
Argyle House
Edinburgh EH3 9SF Scotland

The case for an active and comprehensive normalisation programme for people with mental handicap has long been firmly established. It is also generally recognized that development of the individual requires a wide range of physical, emotional, and intellectual experience in as rich and varied an environment as can reasonably be achieved. To be valid, a normalisation programme must relate to this requirement, and it follows that a building provided for such a programme should be designed to help achieve its fulfillment.

For most mentally handicapped adults beyond the borderline category who are living in the community, the opportunity to gain much of this experience will be dependent upon their attendance at some kind of day centre. In Britain, this would usually be an Adult Training Centre (ATC).

These centres are mainly work-oriented, directed towards the development of work potential, with other potential being largely neglected. In the beginning, a centre may offer a more balanced programme, but, as the years pass with scarcely any throughput of trainees, impetus is lost, work becomes the dominant element, and social education assumes a minor role. It is held that the initial emphasis on work training is counterproductive in terms of achievement of social competence and may increase dependency factors instead of diminishing them. There are several reasons for this failure, not the least being that ATC buildings are seriously inhibiting in design. Over 85% of the training area is allocated to workshop space, leaving a very small balance for social education. In addition, the workshop areas are often designed arbitrarily for specific purposes such as woodwork and metalwork, allowing the staff very limited scope for innovation.

It was dissatisfaction with current design policy that led to the evolution in Scotland of the pilot project which came to be called the Kirkcaldy Centre. The

---

The views expressed are those of the author and are not necessarily those of the Scottish Office.

concept is of a dynamic centre providing individually tailored educational, vocational, and social training programmes for young mentally handicapped adults 16 years of age and older. It is not envisaged that profoundly handicapped people will attend, but people who are also physically handicapped may well do so. With emphasis being on assessment, training and evaluation of progress toward social competence, a trainee will attend only for as long as he continues to respond to his programme, and, when his potential has been realised as far as can be expected, he will then "graduate." Graduation of trainees, which, it must be stressed, is essential if the centre is to remain potent, will be to the work situation best suited to each one.

The Kirkcaldy Centre (see Figure 1), which is for 120 people, is equal in area to an ATC for the same number (Figure 2), but differs substantially in that space is available equally to each of the training elements. It is intended that all parts of the building shall be capable of flexibility of use, and although areas are designated Classroom, Work Area, Domestic Training etc., this should not be seen as a constraint on their use for other purposes. There is nothing novel in this idea of providing comprehensive facilities for training in self-help, socio-academic, and interpersonal skills, coupled with vocational training and recreation. The design of the Kirkcaldy Centre is different in that it does not allow one element to dominate, and actually encourages programme diversification by providing options in sizes and shapes of areas and changes in their scale and character. Another feature that distinguishes this centre from its predecessors is the introduction of Home Bays, which are soft areas in what has hitherto been a hard environment. Few day centres have comfortably furnished areas for relaxation and companionship. Indeed, there are few that even have space for recreation and social activities other than a canteen, which is seldom anything but austere. Apart from the loss of learning opportunity resulting from such omission, it is regrettable because many of the more seriously handicapped people have no other opportunity for social contact in convivial surroundings.

The home bays are to be used for meals and coffee breaks, as meeting places and withdrawal places, and for activities in conjunction with the adjoining Recreation Area. They are essentially personal places, designed to engender a sense of identity. Each home bay will belong to one group; each trainee will belong to and, hopefully, will identify with his own group and therefore with a particular home bay that he will use as his base within the centre.

Other accommodation, which is not exclusive to the Kirkcaldy design but which is infrequently found elsewhere, includes: a beauty salon for training in the use of cosmetics, hairdressing, deportment and other aspects of self-care; a conference room for multi-disciplinary case conferences which will be frequent and regular—this room will also be used for staff training, tutorials, seminars and the like; a coffee bar and shop to be run by the trainees themselves; and library and project rooms. The social core of the building will be available for after-hours use by trainees, their families and friends, use by handicapped people in

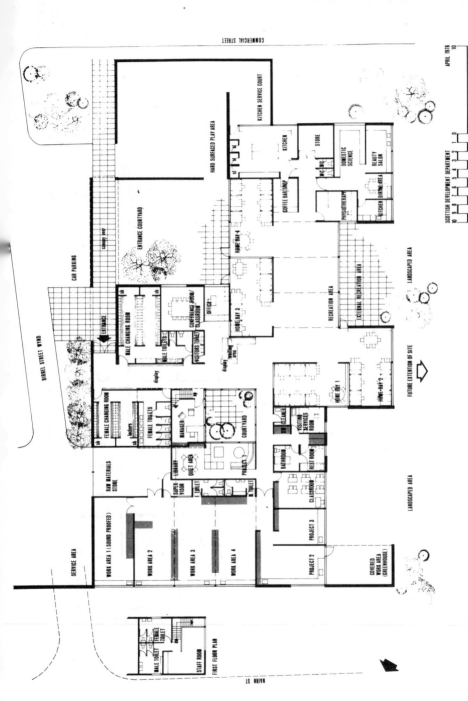

Figure 1. Kirkcaldy Senior Training Centre, Fife, Scotland.

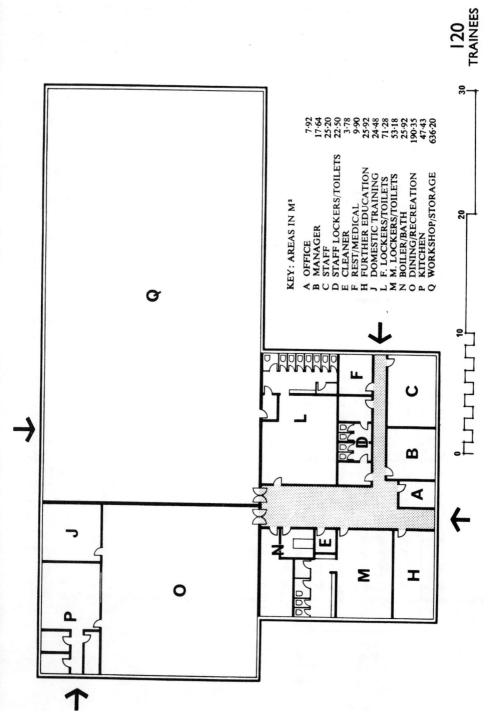

120 TRAINEES

KEY: AREAS IN M²

A	OFFICE	7·92
B	MANAGER	17·64
C	STAFF	25·20
D	STAFF LOCKERS/TOILETS	22·50
E	CLEANER	3·78
F	REST/MEDICAL	9·90
H	FURTHER EDUCATION	25·92
J	DOMESTIC TRAINING	24·48
L	F. LOCKERS/TOILETS	71·28
M	M. LOCKERS/TOILETS	53·18
N	BOILER/BATH	25·92
O	DINING/RECREATION	190·35
P	KITCHEN	47·43
Q	WORKSHOP/STORAGE	636·20

Figure 2. Plan of the equivalent Department of Health and Social Security Adult Training Centre.

the neighbourhood who have already graduated or who do not otherwise attend the centre, and for community use generally. Parts of the building may be closed off quite readily if necessary when it is being used for these extracurricular purposes.

To be viable, a centre of the Kirkcaldy type must serve a clutch of satellites to which its trainees will be directed on completion of their training programmes. The satellites will comprise work-oriented ATCs, sheltered workshops, small craft workshops, and enclaves in open employment. The centre and its satellites will operate on a reciprocal basis, each complementing the other—the satellites offering to trainees a choice of work according to their needs and abilities, and the centre providing sophisticated assessment and training facilities followed by the support and back-up of skilled staff. By this method, scarce professional and management resources can be concentrated to greatest effect. It should be appreciated that this development in no way negates any existing community services for the mentally handicapped. It is certainly not intended to supersede ATCs, nor is it suggested that ATCs should be converted to this concept. All work centres of whatever kind are potential satellites and could become part of a comprehensive system rather than remaining as separate units, often isolated, and with inadequate resources. ATCs may continue to offer programmes of vocational training combined with some social education, but the latter would be a topping-up process and no longer the total input.

Finally, a few points about size and location of centres. The Kirkcaldy Centre is for 120 and it will serve part of the highly populated central belt of Scotland. Less populated areas may not need a centre of this size, but the number to be accommodated should not fall much below 60 people. This is because the number and size of rooms within a centre can be reduced only to a certain level if the centre is to continue to offer a full range of facilities. On the other hand, some work centres in the satellite situation could be relatively small, perhaps for as few as 10 to 12 people, particularly in areas of sparse population, because it would no longer be necessary for them to be large enough to support their own specialist services. This would avoid the transportation problems that cause many of the present large centres to operate on what is, in effect, a four-hour day—a grossly uneconomical use of precious resources.

This is the profile of the Kirkcaldy Centre and its logical place in a range of community provision for mentally handicapped people. It arose out of the combined efforts of a multi-professional team within the Scottish Office who developed the brief, in cooperation with a Local Authority team in what is now Fife Region who undertook to build and operate the centre. The design is required to maximize the use of space, to create an environment that can be manipulated by the people using it, trainees as well as staff, and to produce a building that will be useful, stimulating, and relevant. That was the challenge and this is just one way of meeting it.

COMPUTER-ASSISTED INSTRUCTION

RESEARCH TO PRACTICE IN MENTAL RETARDATION
Education and Training, Volume II
Edited by Peter Mittler
Copyright 1977 I.A.S.S.M.D.

COMPUTER-ASSISTED INSTRUCTION FOR THE MENTALLY RETARDED

H. J. Hallworth
Faculty of Education Computer Applications Unit,
University of Calgary,
2920 24 Avenue, N. W., Calgary, T2N 1N4 Canada

The first question we are likely to hear when we speak of computer-assisted learning for the mentally retarded is, "Is it possible?" It is, indeed, difficult to believe that a mentally retarded child or adult can sit at a computer terminal, press appropriate keys, understand a response from the computer, and learn from the interaction.

Yet the answer to the question is, "Yes, it is possible. More than that, it has already been done, successfully, for several years."

The following chapter shows how computer-assisted learning (CAL) already has been used with the mentally retarded, and how it is likely to develop in the future. Sufficient work has been done now to indicate that CAL with the retarded can be very successful, and experience has been accumulated that will help chart future directions.

One important consideration is very simple: the computer terminal must be taken to the learner. To attempt to move the retarded adult or child to the computer and its terminals is to invite so many practical difficulties as to ensure the project's failure. Seven years ago, when CAL with the retarded was first attempted, communications problems made it necessary to move the learner to the computer. Such problems have since been overcome. It is now practicable to deliver CAL to the retarded in their schools or institutes, or even in their homes. The following chapter shows how this is being done.

Moreover, it can be done on a cost-effective basis. One procedure for measuring cost is to calculate the cost of instruction for one hour for one learner, first in a conventional learning situation, then for CAL. In Calgary, the cost per student/hour of conventional instruction already averages more than $1.20 in the public school system. For the mentally retarded it is considerably above this figure. At the Vocational and Rehabilitation Research Institute, it is anticipated that, by the end of 1976, the cost of education will be approximately $4.00 per student/hour. In contrast, CAL can be delivered at a cost of $1.50 per terminal hour, or less, assuming the computer is used for only 1,000 hours a year of school time, and both computer and terminals are amortised over a six-year period. Some would say the cost is now $1.00 per terminal hour. Much depends upon the kind of terminal used. However, there is no doubt that the cost of conventional instruction is rising, while the cost of CAL is coming down rapidly.

This cost relationship makes the computer terminal a reasonably priced tool for the teaching of the mentally retarded.

Many problems, of course, still exist. Although some of the mentally retarded can use a standard Teletype terminal, others learn more effectively when they are provided with simplified devices to input their answers. A terminal which shows pictures and diagrams is useful. A terminal which also replies with a recorded voice, or with synthetic speech, is desirable for all the mentally retarded and essential for many.

Other problems relate to the need for coordination of effort in the design of terminals, in the promulgation of a common computer language, and in the sharing of learning programs. In Canada, the National Research Council has taken an important lead in working toward a solution of each of these problems.

Meanwhile, a problem of increasing importance is the development of CAL programs designed specifically for the mentally retarded, with guidance from those workers who already have done so much research on learning among the retarded.

The following chapter is concerned primarily with this last problem. It is intended to draw to the attention of the reader the need for specialists in mental retardation to become aware of the implications of CAL. Recent technological developments, such as the introduction of microcomputers, suggest that within the near future a centre such as the Vocational and Rehabilitation Research Institute in Calgary will find it possible to use CAL as a tool for much of its instruction, and to do this using its own in-house computer.

The problem of research to practice is assuming yet another dimension. We wish to draw this to your attention.

RESEARCH TO PRACTICE IN MENTAL RETARDATION
Education and Training, Volume II
Edited by Peter Mittler
Copyright 1977   I.A.S.S.M.D.

COMPUTER-ASSISTED INSTRUCTION PROGRAMS AND TERMINALS FOR THE MENTALLY RETARDED

A. Brebner, H. J. Hallworth, and R. I. Brown
Faculty of Education Computer Applications Unit,
University of Calgary,
and
Vocational and Rehabilitation Research Institute,
Calgary, Canada

In a symposium at the Third Congress in 1973 (Hallworth, et al., 1973), it was mentioned that a project had recently been started to introduce computer-assisted instruction (CAI) into an institute for the mentally retarded. Since that time, the initial experiments have been extended to the point where CAI programs are now an established part of the education provided at the Vocational and Rehabilitation Research Institute in Calgary. Similar programs also are being used in a school for the retarded.

The trainees at the Institute are drawn from throughout Alberta and have, therefore, very different educational backgrounds and have acquired widely differing types of skills. Consequently, there is a crucial need for an individual program for each trainee that concentrates on those skills in which he is deficient. The philosophy of the Institute is to provide an integrated training program covering vocational, social, educational, home-living, and leisure time skills. Such skills are essential in order that, when the trainees leave the Institute, they can maintain themselves adequately within the community.

The major part of the CAI project has been carried out in the social education area where the basic skills are taught. At the present time, there are three terminals in use all day and some work is also carried out in the evenings. They are linked, through the ordinary telephone network, to a Digital Equipment TSS-8 computer system in the Faculty of Education Computer Applications Unit, in which the programs are stored.

Programs are being progressively developed to cover the entire curriculum taught at the Institute. The first programs introduced were drill and practice programs in simple arithmetic, which cover the areas of counting, addition, and subtraction. These have been followed by programs on coin recognition. They take the trainee from recognizing a cent and attaching a value to it, through instructional sequences with the other coins and with combinations of coins, until he is able to assign a value to any group of coins.

From this point, the trainee progresses to programs that introduce paper money, and then to a program on single-item purchases. Here he is trained in some of the skills required for the task of going shopping. He is taught to identify price tags on items, to determine whether or not a given amount of money is sufficient to buy the item and, finally, to calculate the amount of change he would receive (Strain, 1974).

After further programs on buying, the trainee uses a set of programs to help him develop budgeting skills, and to enable him to maintain a bank account (Sandals, 1973).

Throughout the development of this courseware, various teaching strategies have been investigated. Some of these have proved remarkably successful and are worth noting here. First, in some of the programs, the trainees follow the activities of a fictitious person, helping him to make decisions. This technique has worked well because the trainees seem to relate very easily to such a character. Second, the trainees need to associate concrete objects with abstract numbers; for example, addition and subtraction of decimals is taught only in connection with dollars and cents. Also, trainees are taught initially to type .01 for 1¢ and thus avoid what would be for them a difficult change of format when amounts become greater than one dollar. Third, programs that shape behaviour are very much more successful than programs that are didactic in their approach. One reason for this is that the latter invariably require the user to read and comprehend substantial amounts of material, an ability which the trainees do not possess (Brown and Hughson, 1972). Finally the trainees appear to need much more positive reinforcement than normal students. Such reinforcement is more effective when it follows a consistent format.

Another program concerned with teaching shopping skills is in use with the cerebral palsied trainees. The majority are in wheelchairs and a shopping trip for them is a major undertaking, requiring the provision of special transport. Hence, a program was developed that teaches them to recognize various food items, both individually and as the packages appear stacked on the shelves of the local supermarkets. When the trainees later go shopping, they are able to recognize and pick out items much more quickly.

Reading is an important area of the curriculum for which another series of programs has been developed. This series first teaches the recognition of the shapes of different letters, and, by small steps, brings the student to the point at which he can pick out identical words four letters in length (Eaton, 1975). The student next will proceed to a program that is, at present, under development. This is a computerized version of the Clifton Audio-Visual Reading Materials (Brown and Bookbinder, 1967), an individualized reading program specifically for the adolescent mentally retarded population.

For those who are not yet able to attempt formal reading, social sight vocabulary programs are available. These teach the student to recognize and react appropriately to a limited set of words that he will meet and need to understand in his everyday environment (Holz, 1976).

Other programs in regular use teach the trainees to use a calendar, tell time, apply for a job, and dress appropriately for the various activities in which they are likely to engage.

The terminal equipment has been developed gradually as the courseware has been written, and as needs for specific devices have become apparent. The objective has always been to reduce the barriers of communication between the trainee and the computer.

Initially, a single Teletype terminal was placed in the Institute to determine whether or not the trainees could handle the ordinary keyboard of a computer terminal. As it was found that many of them could do so, a mobile trailer owned by the Computer Applications Unit was moved to the Institute. The trailer contained four CAI stations, each of which consisted of a Teletype, a computer-controlled random access slide projector, and a rear view screen. Programs implemented on these CAI stations include the series on coin recognition, shopping, budgeting and banking, and the programs on calendars, job application, and appropriate dress. These all make extensive use of slides in the teaching sequences. The arithmetic programs use the Teletype part of the station only.

When an extension to the V.R.R.I. building was completed, the CAI stations were moved into the classroom area. This move proved to be significant; with the terminals more readily accessible, use of CAI grew rapidly and is now an important and integral part of the social education program.

There is, however, a large group of trainees who cannot use these terminals; for example, some cannot read, and others have physical handicaps which prevent them from manipulating an ordinary keyboard. For the former, terminals with computer-controlled audio devices are in experimental use; and for the latter, a variety of simplified input devices have been devised.

For both groups, experimental equipment developed by the Radio and Electrical Engineering Division of the National Research Council has proved to be very satisfactory. This consists of an interface that is connected to the computer by means of an acoustic coupler and a telephone line. To the interface are attached a cathode ray tube terminal, a tape recorder, a random access slide projector, and a touch sensitive display panel (Hlady, 1969). The latter allows the computer to determine where a finger is pointing, and makes a very effective input device, when used in conjunction with the slide projector. A large television monitor can be slaved to the cathode ray tube terminal to provide larger characters for those trainees with poor vision.

Among programs implemented on this terminal are those that teach how to tell time, in which the trainee is required to point at hours and minutes on a circular clock face, and the series on prereading, in which he points at two sets of identical letters.

Also in use is a commercial version of this apparatus. The audio is produced by a cassette player, and the touch sensitive display has the advantage of covering both the slide projector screen and the cathode ray tube. This proved very successful for the social sight vocabulary program in which the student is required to associate a situation depicted on a slide with a word chosen from a list displayed on the CRT. The Clifton Audio-Visual Reading program is also being implemented on this terminal.

For those with physical handicaps, a variety of input devices have been built. The first of these, a POSSUM indicator board, consists of a 9 X 9 matrix of characters, any one of which can be selected for input by moving a light horizontally and then vertically on the board. Controls for the board include a joystick, a dual rod control, a large hand switch, a foot switch, a head control, and a pneumatic control. Although rather complicated in appearance, in practice the POSSUM equipment has presented no problems for the cerebral palsied trainees. It is in constant operation for five hours daily for arithmetic and shopping programs, and is used in conjunction both with an ordinary CRT terminal and with the CAI stations. All trainees have chosen the large hand switch as the control device. The apparatus has proved to be an excellent tool, and there are now no trainees to whom the computer is inaccessible because of their physical handicaps.

Another input device is a POSSUM Expanded Keyboard. This has a full set of keys but they are large, recessed, and widely spaced. The user may therefore slide his hand over the keyboard before pressing down a key. A delay mechanism allows him to change his mind and press another key if he inadvertently presses the wrong one the first time. This keyboard is in regular use and can be attached to any terminal.

Recently developed and brought into operation is a simplified keyboard consisting only of the numbers and a few required control keys. Special features of this keyboard include differently shaped keys for control functions, a capability to switch off any of the numbers as required by the level at which the trainee is working, and a switchable hardware option that will automatically send a "return" code after each number entered. Initial trials with this keyboard indicate its potential usefulness, and some trainees previously using the POSSUM indicator board have been able to graduate to this higher level device.

In the design and development stage are two other keyboards. The first of these is for use in conjunction with money handling programs and consists of keys that are replicas of paper money and coins. It is hoped that the user will learn coin recognition and money handling more easily when he is able, for example, to press a dime instead of the number 1 followed by the number 0.

The second keyboard under construction simply consists of two keys YES and NO and will hopefully enable CAI programs to become available to the lowest level trainees in the Institute.

With the installation in the Computer Applications Unit of a much more powerful computer system, it is intended to expand the project in several ways. More terminals will be placed in the Institute and a management system will be developed. This will provide information for the staff about each trainee's progress. It also will guide the trainee through the continuum, by automatically routing him to the next program in the sequence when he has satisfactorily learned a particular skill.

In conclusion, it has been demonstrated that computer-assisted instruction is an effective way of teaching the educable mentally retarded population at the Vocational and Rehabilitation Research Institute in Calgary, provided programs are designed specifically for their needs, and special terminal equipment is developed. Not only is CAI viable, but it is also a cost-effective teaching procedure for trainees who have widely differing abilities and require individualized instruction. There appears every reason to believe that computer-assisted instruction for this and similar populations will develop rapidly in the future.

SUMMARY

Computer-assisted instruction has become an established procedure for training developmentally handicapped adults at the Vocational and Rehabilitation Research Institute in Calgary. Recent research in the areas of money handling, purchasing, social sight vocabulary, reading and pre-reading is reviewed, and special terminal equipment designed for the Institute's trainees is described.

REFERENCES

Brown, R. I., and Bookbinder, G. E. (1967) The Clifton Audio-Visual Reading Programme. Harlow, England: Educational Supply Association.
Brown, R. I., and Hughson, E. A. (1972) Verbal instruction in the performance of non-verbal tasks. Report to the Alberta Human Resources Research Council.
Eaton, P. (1975) Visual discrimination and computer-assisted learning. Unpublished Ph.D. thesis, University of Calgary.
Hallworth, H. J. et al. (1973) Computer-assisted instruction in the training of the mentally handicapped. Proc. 3rd Congr. IASSMD, p. 579.
Hlady, A. M. (1969) A touch sensitive X–Y position encoder for computer input. Proc. Joint Fall Computer Conf., Amer. Federation of Information Processing Societies.
Holz, E. (1976) A study of the use of computer-assisted instruction for teaching

a social sight vocabulary to mentally handicapped adolescents. Unpublished M.Sc. thesis, University of Calgary.

Sandals, L. H. (1973) Computer-assisted learning with the developmentally handicapped. Unpublished Ph.D. thesis, University of Calgary.

Strain, A. R. (1974) Computer-assisted instruction in social arithmetic for the retarded. Unpublished M.Sc. thesis, University of Calgary.

AUTHOR INDEX

SUBJECT INDEX